Between Christ and Caliph

DIVINATIONS: REREADING LATE ANCIENT RELIGION

SERIES EDITORS

Daniel Boyarin
Virginia Burrus
Derek Krueger

A complete list of books in the series is available from the publisher.

Between Christ and Caliph

LAW, MARRIAGE, AND CHRISTIAN COMMUNITY IN EARLY ISLAM

Lev E. Weitz

PENN

UNIVERSITY OF PENNSYLVANIA PRESS *Philadelphia*

the modern language initiative

THIS BOOK IS MADE POSSIBLE BY A COLLABORATIVE GRANT FROM THE ANDREW W. MELLON FOUNDATION.

Published by
University of Pennsylvania Press
Philadelphia, Pennsylvania 19104-4112
www.upenn.edu/pennpress

Printed in the United States of America
on acid-free paper

10 9 8 7 6 5 4 3 2 1

Cataloging-in-Publication Data is available from the Library of Congress

ISBN 978-0-8122-5027-5

CONTENTS

A NOTE ON TRANSLITERATION, TRANSLATIONS, AND DATES

In order to keep the text reasonably free of clutter, I have employed full diacritics in the transliteration of Arabic and Syriac only in quoted passages, first instances of technical terms, and the endnotes. I transliterate Arabic with the standard system modified from that of the *Encyclopedia of Islam*, 2nd edition (Leiden: Brill, 1954–2009). Syriac transliterations follow East Syriac orthography, thus noting the vowels *a*, *ā*, *e*, *ē*, *i*, *o*, and *u* but not, for example, distinguishing between *u* and *ū*. I transliterate according to the West Syriac vowel system only West Syrian proper names. I note gemination of consonants but not spirantization. I render the phonemes /x/ and /ʃ/ as *kh* and *sh*, respectively, in all transliterations of Arabic, Syriac, and very occasionally Middle Persian.

I have not been entirely consistent in rendering Syriac proper names into English. Generally, I render those of Greek derivation with an Anglicized form of the Greek (e.g., Kyriakos rather than Syriac Quryaqos). Syriac names of Semitic linguistic derivation I tend to transliterate according to the guidelines above (e.g., Ishoʿyahb), unless a different usage is standard in scholarship (e.g., Jacob, rather than Yaʿqub, of Edessa). I render Arabic names using standard transliteration, leaving aside diacritics in the body of the text. Following generally standard practice, I give the titles of Syriac texts in English but those of Arabic texts in transliteration.

All endnote citations of Arabic and Syriac text editions published with a translation into a modern language include the translation in the page ranges cited, or separate the text and translation pages with a forward slash. All translations into English given in this book, however, are my own unless otherwise noted. Biblical citations are either of the New Revised Standard Version or translated from the Syriac

Peshitta. I quote the Quran according to the translation of M. A. S. Abdel Haleem (Oxford: Oxford University Press, 2008).

Most of the individuals who appear in this book thought of the passage of time in terms of one or both of the Seleucid and Hijri calendars. In the interest of simplicity and intelligibility I have opted to use only Common Era dating.

Between Christ and Caliph

Introduction

What makes [the Christians] great in the hearts of the commoners and beloved to regular folk is that among them are scribes to sultans, attendants to kings, physicians to noblemen, pharmacists, and moneychangers; while you won't find a Jew other than a dyer, tanner, cupper, butcher, or repairman.

Despite the great number of monks and nuns, and the fact that most priests imitate their [celibacy] . . . and the fact that anyone among [the Christians] who does marry cannot exchange his wife, marry another in addition to her, or take concubines—despite all this, they have covered the earth, filled the horizons, and conquered the nations in number and progeny. This has compounded our calamities and magnified our tribulation.

—Abu ʿUthman al-Jahiz, *al-Radd ʿala l-nasara* (*The Refutation of the Christians*)

To hear Abu ʿUthman al-Jahiz (d. 868/69) tell it, one would think that the Muslims of the ninth-century Abbasid Caliphate were in trouble. Al-Jahiz was one of the medieval Islamic empire's great litterateurs and spent his life in the thriving cities of its Iraqi heartland. Yet everywhere he looked he claimed to see not the signs of a confident Islamic polity but its prominent, self-satisfied Christian subjects. Christians filled the halls of power, running the imperial bureaucracy and attending to caliphs, generals, and viziers, and received the adulation of the Muslim masses. Just as they did not shy away from taking good Muslim names like Husayn and ʿAbbas, they could get away with slandering the Prophet Muhammad's mother.[1] Despite their bizarre aversion to sex and infatuation with celibacy, the Christians had managed to become the most populous nation on God's green earth.

Such is the picture of the ninth-century caliphate that al-Jahiz paints in *The Refutation of the Christians*, one of the many incisive essays he composed over the course of a long and productive career. Although it is undoubtedly a caricature to a certain degree, embedded in al-Jahiz's literary stylings are two striking insights into medieval Middle Eastern society that serve as this book's departure points.

One is that al-Jahiz's Abbasid Caliphate, two centuries after the emergence of Islam and at a time when the Muslims' state was at the height of its powers, was not an "Islamic society" in any simple or straightforward way. Whether or not it was filled with Christians to the degree that al-Jahiz laments, his comments remind us that the caliphate was fundamentally an empire—a state governing an expansive territory and a population of great diversity, including Christians, Jews, Zoroastrians, Manichaeans, Mandaeans, Samaritans, and others alongside Muslims. What does the history of the medieval Middle East look like if we recognize non-Muslims to have been as integral to the landscape of the Islamic empire as al-Jahiz suggests that they were?

The second point of interest is al-Jahiz's focus on Christian sexuality. From the perspective of a ninth-century Iraqi Muslim, Christian distinctiveness rested not only in theological doctrines like the Trinity, rituals like baptism and the Eucharist, and institutions like churches and monasteries but also in social practices—particularly, marriage and the structures of the household. A reverence for celibacy, prohibitions of divorce, polygamy, and concubinage—to al-Jahiz, these principles were characteristic of Christians and decidedly different from the rhythms of Muslim conjugal life. What role did the household play in structuring the myriad religious communities that made up caliphal society in al-Jahiz's day?

This book examines the making of the multireligious social order of the medieval Middle East with these two questions as its framework. Focusing on the encounter between the Islamic caliphate and its numerous Syriac Christian subjects from the seventh to the tenth century, it argues that bishops in Syria, Iraq, and Iran responded to Islamic law and governance by creating a new Christian law of their own, one centered on marriage, inheritance, and the distinctive features of Christian family life. In essence, caliphal rule spurred Christian elites to root the integrity of their communities in a newly redefined social institution: the Christian household. Above all, this study maintains that processes of interreligious contact such as this are integral to the history of the medieval Middle East. Enormous socioreligious diversity was a definitive feature of the region, but scholarly narratives focused on the triumphant formation of classical Islam often obscure it. Too long neglected, encounters like the one in question—in which the caliphate's non-Muslim subjects transformed themselves in response to Islamic institutions and traditions—lie at the very heart of the story of the medieval Middle East's formation.

MUSLIMS AND NON-MUSLIMS IN THE HISTORIOGRAPHY OF THE MEDIEVAL MIDDLE EAST

Non-Muslims on the Margins of Islamic History

The notion that Christians and other non-Muslims might have a more central place in the history of the medieval Middle East than scholars typically accord them arises from a few simple premises in the study of empires. Because empires typically expand through the conquest of new territories, they necessarily bring different peoples under their rule. They are thus fundamentally heterogeneous, no matter how fraught the relationships among their constituent groups. More significantly, an imperial society is never an orderly creation imposed perfectly from above by the ruling elite after the initial phases of conquest. Rather, it is the product of an ongoing process in which the empire's subjects encounter its institutions and methods of rule. Through varying actions of adoption, adaptation, and resistance, they reproduce those institutions in some form while simultaneously transforming themselves.[2] This perspective has been extraordinarily productive in the study of many world empires. But in the historiography of the medieval Middle East, it remains underexplored in key respects that distort our understanding of the caliphate's "Islamic society." One way to recast that picture is to put at the center of the narrative the caliphate's interactions with its vast and variegated non-Muslim populations. What do we learn when we consider that their responses to Muslim rule were constitutive of the empire's institutions and social structures just as much as the activities of the Muslim elite?

From the mid-seventh century to the end of the ninth, adherents of a new religion, Islam, conquered territories from the Iberian Peninsula to the Indus Valley and incorporated them into a single polity, the Islamic caliphate. Especially after the Abbasid dynasty's assumption of power in 750, new governing institutions, patterns of social organization, and intellectual disciplines took shape that would characterize the caliphate's Middle Eastern heartlands for centuries. By the time the caliphate's political unity fragmented in the late ninth century, Muslim elites across the region were united by an emergent high culture rooted in Islamic religion and Arabic literacy, as well as certain military and administrative traditions. This, in a nutshell, is many a historiographical narrative of the Middle East from the seventh century into the tenth—the initial coherence of what became the "classical forms" of Islamic empire, Islamic society, and Islamic tradition.[3]

While the substance of this narrative is widely accepted and assuredly sound, it is also marked by significant absences and a distorting teleology. Telling the history of the early medieval Middle East as the formation of classical Islamic civilization assumes that certain long-term outcomes—Muslim demographic majorities and the transregional hegemony of Islamic traditions—were self-evident from the beginning. The result is a historiography in which the history of the caliphate is largely that of its Muslim elite and their activities. This picture crucially obscures the caliphate's populations of extraordinary linguistic, ethnic, and especially religious heterogeneity. Throughout centuries of rule by the Medinan, Umayyad, and Abbasid caliphs, Christian monks from Egypt to Iran cultivated their learned spiritual disciplines in Greek, Coptic, and Syriac. In the Abbasid crown lands of southern Iraq, Jewish, Christian, Zoroastrian, Manichaean, Mandaean, and pagan traditions were mixed up and mashed together by a dense population of Aramaic-, Arabic-, and Persian-speaking villagers and townspeople. Across the Iranian Plateau and into Central Asia, mountaineers and rural noblemen adhered to ancient Iranian religions and aristocratic cultures.

The gradual conversion and incorporation into the Muslim community of many of these peoples, as well as the cultural and religious materials they brought with them, is one of the most important storylines of Islamic history.[4] Yet anyone who browses a textbook on the subject might be forgiven for failing to discern that the majority of the population in much of the Middle East remained non-Muslim until well into the medieval period.[5] In such narratives, non-Muslims exist only in the background and rarely merit more than a chapter, and sometimes less than that, of their own.[6] The caliphate's tolerant governance leaves them to their own devices: as long as they stay obedient and pay their taxes, they are accorded "communal autonomy" to attend to their internal, insular affairs. At key moments, they participate in the historical mainstream by providing the stew of ideas from which Islam emerges, keeping the wheels of the caliphal bureaucracy turning, or translating classical texts into Arabic for interested Muslim patrons. But any sense of non-Muslims' own traditions and transformations is absent; within the standard historiographical framework of Islamic civilization, they are historical actors only insofar as they convert or make other contributions from the sidelines to the grand Islamic synthesis. The tacit implication is that, since most of their descendants would eventually be Muslims anyway, their history is ultimately inconsequential.

That implication runs counter to the tenets and practice of historiography, and it badly distorts the richness of Middle Eastern history. By the same token, making non-Muslims the singular subject of the story is no corrective. While Muslims were a demographic minority in most regions of their polity for a considerable amount of time, demography can also be a distorting prism through which to approach the history of the preindustrial world; sovereignty and the identities of states and societies were based not on popular demographic majorities but on military prowess and claims to divine favor.[7] Furthermore, it is easy enough to focus on the history of, say, Christians as the majority population of the early Muslim-ruled Fertile Crescent or Zoroastrians in Iran instead of on Muslims. But that does no more than reproduce from a different angle the problematic framework of discrete religious communities on parallel tracks of development and decline implied by the Islamic civilization model.

Non-Muslims in the Making of the Islamic Empire

How might one write a more integrated history of Muslims and non-Muslims in the highly diverse polities in which they lived? One way to begin is to consider critically some implications of the fact that the Islamic caliphate was an empire. That fact has not always been heeded in the study of the caliphate, and it offers some useful, integrative models with which to frame the interactions of Muslims and non-Muslims in the making of medieval Middle Eastern society.

A widely held historiographical perspective maintains that empires establish their hegemony not only through violent coercion but also by co-opting the peoples they rule. Empires exist tangibly through a range of local agents, intermediaries, and representatives, some with roots in the metropole but many from among subject populations themselves, who do the work of enacting imperial policies and building institutions in one form or another.[8] An imperial order thus simultaneously subjects and relies upon the peoples it rules. As a result, outside of conditions of overwhelming violence and in spite of considerable asymmetries of power, the representatives of subject peoples necessarily have some role in establishing the terms and practice of their subjection.[9] If those representatives are military elites, they may threaten to take over the imperial order as they are co-opted into it.[10] If they fill civilian roles of one kind or another—as administrators or religious leaders, for example—it is frequently their mediation of imperial dictates that constitutes the empire's institutions and reorders local societies accordingly. Indeed, some historians (particularly of the Spanish Americas) have made the subject or indigenous intermediary the locus of the story of empire itself.[11] At that nodal point, we see both the channels of imperial power in operation and a degree of agency among subjugated peoples. The practical reorganization of subject communities and traditions facilitated by subject intermediaries exemplifies the ongoing production of imperial systems in a way that official, schematic descriptions of those systems never can.

The goals and coercive powers of premodern Muslim rulers in the Middle East were a world away from those of later European empires, of course, but many of these insights remain analytically useful. Scholars of the medieval Middle East have put some to productive use while attending to others less assiduously. Provincial Muslim elites and their conflicts with the Umayyad caliphs in Damascus or the Abbasids in Baghdad, for example, are central to scholarly narratives of the caliphate's political development.[12] Scholars have also devoted much attention to the Iranians and Central Asians who were absorbed into the caliphate's military elite.[13] Regarding the empire's vast numbers of non-Muslim subjects, standard narratives acknowledge their importance to the caliphal administration.[14] But largely missing from these narratives is serious consideration that the activities of non-Muslim elites outside the sphere of government service might have transformed their own communities, much less that the transformations they set in motion were constitutive of a new imperial society itself.[15] The notion that non-Muslims enjoyed "communal autonomy" from state oversight, coupled with the fact that their histories predate Islam, has been taken too readily to imply that non-Muslims were organized into self-evident social groups that persisted unchanged, other than suffering increasing attrition due to conversion, under their new Muslim rulers.

This book contends, to the contrary, that caliphal rule fundamentally transformed even the most well-established non-Muslim communities. The response of their elites to the structures and imperatives of caliphal rule led to significant reforms to their communal institutions and traditions, and ultimately to the redefinition of their very character as religious communities.[16] Moreover, in light of the insights of the historiography of empire discussed above, the reforms undertaken by non-Muslim subject elites should be understood as the very process by which a new imperial society was taking shape. This perspective facilitates an integrative approach to the history of the medieval Middle East that takes into account both its considerable diversity and the central importance of Islam. Organizing historiographical narratives solely within the framework of Islamic civilization ahistorically relegates vast numbers of non-Muslims to the margins; focusing on their elites' responses to caliphal rule makes them historical actors and returns to historical time the early medieval caliphate's massively variegated societies. At the same time, this approach in no way empties Middle Eastern history of its "Islamicness." In fact, it shows us Islamization—in the sense of the rising influence of Islamic traditions, institutions, and norms of social organization—as a process rather than an inevitable fact. Non-Muslim subjects of the caliphate faced new symbols of power, techniques of governance, and intellectual discourses, all connected in one way or another to a new ruling religion. Their adaptive strategies in response show us the uneven but ongoing process by which those facets of Islamic empire became ever more hegemonic. The activities of non-Muslim elites, viewed in the context of the conditions established by caliphal rule, index the great transformations that Islam brought to the peoples and societies of the medieval Middle East.

LAW, THE HOUSEHOLD, AND CHRISTIAN COMMUNITY IN THE MEDIEVAL CALIPHATE

Among the most significant but understudied of those activities were the efforts of Christian bishops in early medieval Syria, Iraq, and Iran to redefine Christian marital practices and reshape Christian households. From the seventh to the tenth century, Syriac- and Arabic-speaking bishops responded to the establishment of the caliphate and the development of Islamic jurisprudence by elaborating new traditions of communal law for their respective churches. They translated legal works from Greek and Syriac into Arabic, compiled newly systematized collections of late antique canon law, convened synods that issued legislation for the faithful, and wrote innovative jurisprudential treatises in various areas of civil law; and they did all of this on a much wider scale than had their ecclesiastical predecessors of late antiquity. The most significant feature of these new traditions of Christian law was their focus on marriage, inheritance, and the structures of the household. While the disciplining of sexuality had long been central to Christian thought, the notion that Christian affiliation could be delineated in legal terms and inscribed in the material relationships of households and lineages took on a new import for the Christian communities of the caliphate.

Several factors recommend this subject as a basis on which to build an integrative narrative of medieval caliphal society. Christians of a variety of churches were the most numerous of the caliphate's subjects from the Iberian Peninsula to the foothills of the Zagros Mountains; their history is obviously germane to any consideration of the transformations set in motion by Muslim rule. Scholars have examined changes in Christian intellectual culture in this vein, such as the adoption of Arabo-Islamic theological idioms and participation in the Greco-Arabic translation movement.[17] But for the most part, the social history of medieval Middle Eastern Christians has yet to be written, much less integrated into that of the caliphate more widely. Strikingly, the considerable body of Christian legal literature of the period has gone virtually untapped by social historians.[18] This literature, produced mainly in Syriac but also in Arabic, consists of a wide array of episcopal letters to lower clerics and laypeople, records of regulations issued by assemblies of bishops, and treatises penned by individual ecclesiastical jurisprudents.[19] The traditions of Christian civil law embodied in these texts took shape largely in response to Islamic law and the caliphal judiciary; they claimed regulatory authority over lay social practice and thereby defined the requisites of communal affiliation for Christians in the caliphate. These characteristics make Christian law an ideal base of material from which to examine the making of caliphal society and its non-Muslim communities.

The family is a locus of investigation of even wider significance. Because the family, in whatever forms it takes, has usually been the foundational institution through which human societies reproduce themselves—"the social form through which the two deeply related processes of biological reproduction and the transmission of property are pursued"—it provides a crucial vantage point from which to view wider structures of social organization and the "construction of cultural or national identities."[20] Indeed, sexuality and the household proved centrally important to the reorganization of Middle Eastern societies in the centuries after the establishment of Muslim rule. In the overwhelmingly Christian western half of the caliphate from the Iberian Peninsula to northern Iraq, Islam brought new attitudes toward sexuality and family life. The Christian "sexual revolution" of late antiquity had upended ancient attitudes toward sex and reproduction by esteeming virginity and looking askance at human sexuality; Islamic thought and practice, by contrast, reenshrined a typically ancient valorization of sex and worldly family life.[21] In Iran and Central Asia, Muslim mores encountered and gradually supplanted very different marital and household reproductive practices, including close-kin marriage and polyandry, which were central to local forms of social organization.[22]

The establishment of the caliphate thus introduced new and different attitudes toward sexuality, strategies of social reproduction, and household forms to the diverse populations under its rule. Christian family law both reveals and exemplifies the social-institutional transformations that subject communities undertook in response. At times, lay Christians adopted the customs and mores of the new Muslim ruling classes; at others, bishops sought to retrench traditional Christian attitudes to household life in new legal idioms and thereby produced an idea of the Christian household distinct from that of the Muslims, Jews, and Zoroastrians among whom laypeople lived. All such activities were part of an ongoing process of defining the nature of the household and the wider religious community to which it was connected. That process offers us a window onto the encounter between the caliphate and its non-Muslim subjects, as well as the new imperial society that that encounter produced.

THE CHRISTIANS OF THE MEDIEVAL MIDDLE EAST: A SNAPSHOT

The inauguration of Muslim rule thus set in motion transformations to law, the family, the household, and other social institutions across the Middle East's religiocommunal spectrum. All religious communities, however, did not experience these in the same way. This was particularly true of the region's large and diverse Christian populations, which were divided among a number of distinct church communities. At the heart of our story will be the Church of the East, whose members are commonly referred to as East Syrians or Nestorians.[23]

The Church of the East traced its roots to the hierarchy of bishops and lay believers who lived in the Sasanian Empire, east of Roman territory, in late antiquity. Its adherents were concentrated in northern Mesopotamia, but it also claimed many members and jurisdictions throughout the Fertile Crescent, Iran, and at times Central Asia, India, and China. The chief East Syrian bishop, who took the title of Catholicos and Patriarch of the East, resided in the Sasanian capital of Seleucia-Ctesiphon and, after 775, in Baghdad. East Syrian ecclesiastical identity was defined by the use of Syriac as a literary and liturgical language; fidelity to the teachings of Theodore of Mopsuestia (d. 428), a late antique Christian thinker from Antioch in Syria; and diophysite Christological doctrines that stressed both the human and divine natures of Christ.

For reasons to be examined, the East Syrians developed the most extensive tradition of Christian law in the medieval caliphate and underwent some of the most marked communal-institutional changes. They will be central to our narrative, but other Christian communities will figure in important ways as well, especially the West Syrians and the Melkites. Like the East Syrians, the West Syrians—known also as Jacobites and today as the Syriac Orthodox—used Syriac as their chief literary and liturgical language.[24] The West Syrians, however, adhered to a miaphysite Christology that stressed the unity of Christ's nature and therefore considered East Syrian doctrines heretical. Their chief bishop took the title of Patriarch of Antioch. In the medieval period the West Syrians were concentrated in northern Syria and Mesopotamia and also had a significant presence in central Iraq.

The Melkites were Christians who lived under Muslim rule, adhered to the official orthodoxy of the Byzantine Empire, and quickly adopted Arabic as a literary language after the establishment of the caliphate.[25] Their Byzantine orthodoxy was closely associated with the Christological definitions of the Council of Chalcedon of 451 (diophysite but not identical to the East Syrians' Christology), so they are sometimes referred to as Chalcedonians. We will refer to them as Melkites beginning in the eighth century, when their Arabic literary production gave them an ecclesial identity distinct from the Byzantines even as they continued to share the same doctrinal commitments. The Melkites were concentrated in Syria and Palestine, with a substantial population in parts of Egypt.

While Muslims ruled over many other Christians outside the Fertile Crescent and Iran, transformations to Christian law, the household, and the religious community in the early medieval period took place especially in the core territories of the Umayyad and Abbasid caliphates. We will consider the history of other Christian groups, especially the Copts of Egypt, for comparative purposes at times, but they will remain largely outside the scope of this study.

From the sixth century to the tenth, the Christian communities of the Middle East underwent an array of transformations related to connections among the household, religious affiliation, and imperial rule. In the Islamic caliphate in the latter centuries of this period, increasingly intensive interactions between Christian elites and Islamic institutions spurred the former to reimagine the nature of Christian communities within caliphal society. Part 1 of this book traces the overall arc of these developments. Chapter 1 sets the backdrop by examining marriage and Christian canon law in the late antique Roman and Sasanian empires, arguing that in both realms ecclesiastical attempts to reform lay sexual practices ran up against enduring civil law traditions that defined marriage as a social institution. The seventh century and the early decades of the Umayyad Caliphate, by contrast, show evidence of the beginnings of a shift, which Chapter 2 explores. Regulating marriage became an increasingly prominent part of Christian bishops' efforts to define communal boundaries amid the fluid socio-religious and institutional conditions brought on by the fall of the old empires and the introduction of a new ruling religion. In response to apostasy to Islam and intermarriage with the conquerors, bishops asserted for the first time the exclusive authority of ecclesiastical law, rather than civil, tribal, or local custom, to govern marriages between Christians. These Umayyad-era transformations developed into the great elaboration of Christian communal law in the central lands of the Abbasid Caliphate from the late eighth century through the ninth, the fulcrum of the book's narrative and the subject of Chapter 3. In response to new caliphal institutions of governance and the emergence of robust traditions of Islamic law, ecclesiastics in the Abbasid heartlands made newly comprehensive efforts to define communal boundaries through confessional law. Above all else, they focused on regulating the full range of marital and inheritance practices that facilitated the social reproduction of households and lineages. Christian law thus reformulated the household as a Christian institution not only in theological terms but in its material and social constitution; and it established the link between ecclesiastical legal authority and lay households as the defining feature of Christians as social collectivities within the caliphate.

Prescribing rules, however, was always simpler than achieving their desired end, the reshaping of communal relations. In this vein, the book's second part focuses on the details of Christian family law in the Abbasid Caliphate to examine how lay practice, Christian confessional law, and Islamic institutions interacted to shape Christian social boundaries around the institution of marriage. It demonstrates further that putting Christian legal materials into conversation with Islamic ones expands our view of the region's intellectual culture. Bishops drew their basic legal doctrines and instruments, the subject of Chapter 4, from a mix of regional common law traditions, both ancient and Islamic. Christian family law exemplifies in this respect the high diversity of the Middle East's early medieval legal culture. Chapter 5 takes up ecclesiastical judges and their competition with Muslim courts to administer lay marriage contracts and regulate lay divorce, arguing that Christian social groups were shaped in practice by both communal and extracommunal institutions. Jurist-bishops also devoted considerable attention to the relationship between Christian teachings and certain contested marital practices that functioned as markers of difference between religious communities in the caliphate. Marriage between close relatives, particularly first cousins, was an ancient regional institution but one whose lawfulness became a point of debate for Abbasid-era bishops. The methods of legal reasoning they deployed in this dispute, explored in Chapter 6, push us to recast the standard historiographical account of the formation of Islamic law in a comparative, transreligious framework. Polygamy, the subject of Chapter 7, became a locus of contestation over the boundaries of Christian belonging between ecclesiastical and lay elites in Abbasid cities. Ecclesiastics sought to disinherit the children of polygamous laymen and thereby to sculpt Christian lineages in a form sharply distinct from Muslim ones. Jurist-bishops similarly condemned interreligious marriage, but in this case they shared much common ground with Muslim jurists. Both adopted a gendered approach to the subject, analyzed in Chapter 8, that allowed men to marry outside the religious community but prohibited women from doing so. Christian law thus promoted the same conception favored by Muslim jurists of a social structure built of segmented religious communities.

The processes of Christian communal reordering and interactions with Islamic institutions that began in the early medieval caliphate continued into the later medieval period as well. Part III follows these down to the early fourteenth century in order to argue for the continued historiographical significance of non-Muslims and their traditions even as the Middle East was becoming more straightforwardly Islamic. The later development of Syriac and Arabic Christian family law gauges for us the uneven progress of Islamization, which Chapter 9 charts. Across this period, Islamic legal norms and categories increasingly structured the form and content of much Christian law; but some Christian jurists continued to draw on a diversity of resources other than the dominant Islamic models. Ultimately, Christian family law facilitated both a degree of Christian communal integrity and Christians' accommodation to the Islamic caliphate and other Islamic polities. These developments call us to reconsider the place of non-Muslim traditions in shaping the societies of the medieval Middle East, the key problem to which the conclusion returns.

A productive historiographical approach to the societies of the medieval Islamic Middle East does justice to the multiple communities and traditions that inhabited and built those societies. This perspective might not have been so foreign to al-Jahiz, despite the very different value system from which it arises. Al-Jahiz's rhetorical goal in *The Refutation of the Christians* was to warn of Christian perfidy, but he simultaneously testified to the integral place of Christians and other non-Muslims in the early medieval caliphate. Tracing the formation of caliphal society through the reformulations of Christian law and the Christian household that Muslim rule spurred allows us to apprehend a sliver of the diversity and vitality that, even when he did not approve of it, characterized al-Jahiz's world.

PART I

Empire, Household, and Christian Community from Late Antiquity to the Abbasid Caliphate

CHAPTER 1

Marriage and the Family Between Religion and Empire in Late Antiquity

A man from Babta betrothed a woman to his son in the customary manner.
When the day of the wedding banquet approached, he went to the holy one
and convinced our Rabban to pray over them lovingly.
The blessed old man said to him, "Hear what I have to say to you.
See when you go to the Euphrates to bring the bride to your son
that no singers inviting destruction go with you on your way.
Instead, gather joyfully priests and chaste Levites.
Go and come in service to the church, and Christ shall be with you."
. . . .
When [the man] went [home], his brothers and family would not listen to him, saying,
"We won't spoil our pleasure, which will be celebrated according to our custom."
But when they arrived halfway on their way
a demonic vision appeared at once to the bride.

—*History of Rabban Bar ʿEdta* (d. c. 611)

In the mid-seventh century, an East Syrian monk composed a laudatory biography in Syriac of Rabban Bar ʿEdta, his spiritual master and a Christian holy man who spent his life in the Christian plains and hill country of Sasanian-ruled northern Mesopotamia.[1] Among Bar ʿEdta's many spiritual exploits was the episode recounted above, in which a man from the village of Babta sought the holy man's blessing for his son's impending marriage. Bar ʿEdta agreed, as long as the ceremony was to be conducted in an appropriately chaste and pious manner. Here, however, "custom" (*ʿyādā*) got in the way; the groom's uncles insisted on having whatever celebratory music the people of Babta were used to hearing at their parties, and no holy man was going to ruin this one. What did these "singers inviting destruction" (*zammārē mawbdānē*) sound like? Were the rhythms or lyrics of their songs too suggestive for the holy man's liking? The author gives us no details, but apparently the Babta singers made literal devil's music—their voices attracted a troop of evil demons (*plaggtā d-shēdē bishē*) that, among other things, caused the bride to strip off her clothes as she rode a donkey to the wedding. Only with some holy oil from Bar ʿEdta, and by replacing the singers with psalm-chanting priests and deacons, was the bride's procession able to fend off the demons, get back on track, and make it to the church on time.

This passage encapsulates tensions between the requisites of Christian belonging, on the one hand, and practices associated with the institution of marriage, on the other, in the empires of the late antique Middle East, tensions that it is this chapter's goal to explore. In the societies of late antiquity on both sides of the Roman-Sasanian frontier, marriage had long been understood as a foundation stone of social and political organization. It was the institution that legitimized sex so as to reproduce humans not only as a species but as social beings organized in specific household, lineal, and political forms. At the same time, the theological import of human sexuality to Christian tradition made marriage a locus of debate and reform in the eyes of bishops and other Christian thinkers. Christian thought and ecclesiastical regulation called for sweeping changes to its practice, enjoining monogamy, restricting divorce, and emphasizing chaste avoidance of sexual overindulgence (hence Rabban Bar ʿEdta's opposition to the singers of Babta). Yet older marital practices did not simply disappear. Imperial, civil, and local legal traditions continued to set the norms by which marriage as a legal relationship was enacted, governed, and dissolved, and these were often at odds with Christian prescriptions. Ecclesiastical law in both the Roman and Sasanian empires never usurped that constitutive authority; rather, it encouraged pious modifications to an ancient social institution, and many of the associated elements it condemned lingered on in practice. Thus could the people of Babta seek simultaneously a Christian holy man's blessing and transgressive entertainment at a wedding. These tensions at the nexus of marriage, law, and religious belonging in the late antique world form, in turn, the backdrop to developments in later centuries, when Christian bishops' encounter with Islamic empire spurred them to bring marriage and the household wholly under the authority of ecclesiastical law.

MARRIAGE AND SEXUALITY IN THE LATE ANTIQUE IMAGINATION AND CHRISTIAN THEOLOGY

Although demonic interference was no doubt a singular and unexpected event, when the bride and groom from Babta went down to the waters of the Euphrates to marry, they were partaking in a wholly ancient institution that had been enacted untold numbers of times in the thousands of years of the Middle East's recorded history. The challenges of various ascetic movements notwithstanding, an average observer of the societies of the late antique Roman and Sasanian empires could have taken marriage largely for granted as a common social institution—that is, as a collection of recognized "ways of doing things" that structured particular human actions and relationships, and which "provide[d] stability and meaning to social life."[2] Anthropologists maintain that while marriage is nearly ubiquitous in human societies, any universal, cross-cultural definition will be inadequate.[3] Essentially all late antique eastern Mediterranean and Middle Eastern societies, however, shared a general sense of what marriage was and what it did. It was the enduring crux of biological and social reproduction; it enabled the formation of the other institutions that were the building blocks of social and political organization, the family and the household.[4] Marriage rendered sex between a man and a woman licit and any resulting progeny legitimate (though some other institutions that were not marriage in strict terms could do the same). It established new ties between previously unrelated individuals and kin groups. By affiliating progeny to families and lineages, furthermore, marriage outlined the paths by which both material property and genealogical cultural capital—the status associated with ancestry—would devolve to new generations. Marriage, in other words, was the chief institution that facilitated the reproduction of both the human race biologically and the hierarchies of lived human societies, generation after generation.[5]

The peoples of the ancient Middle East were well aware of this fundamental connection between marriage and the broader associations to which humans belonged, and so they often assigned the institution particular cultural weight. Augustus, the first Roman emperor, enacted legislation promoting marriage and childbearing among Roman citizens for the good of the empire.[6] In Zoroastrian cosmology, marriage with particular kin relations was a pious act that modeled the "divine and mythical unions" of the good god

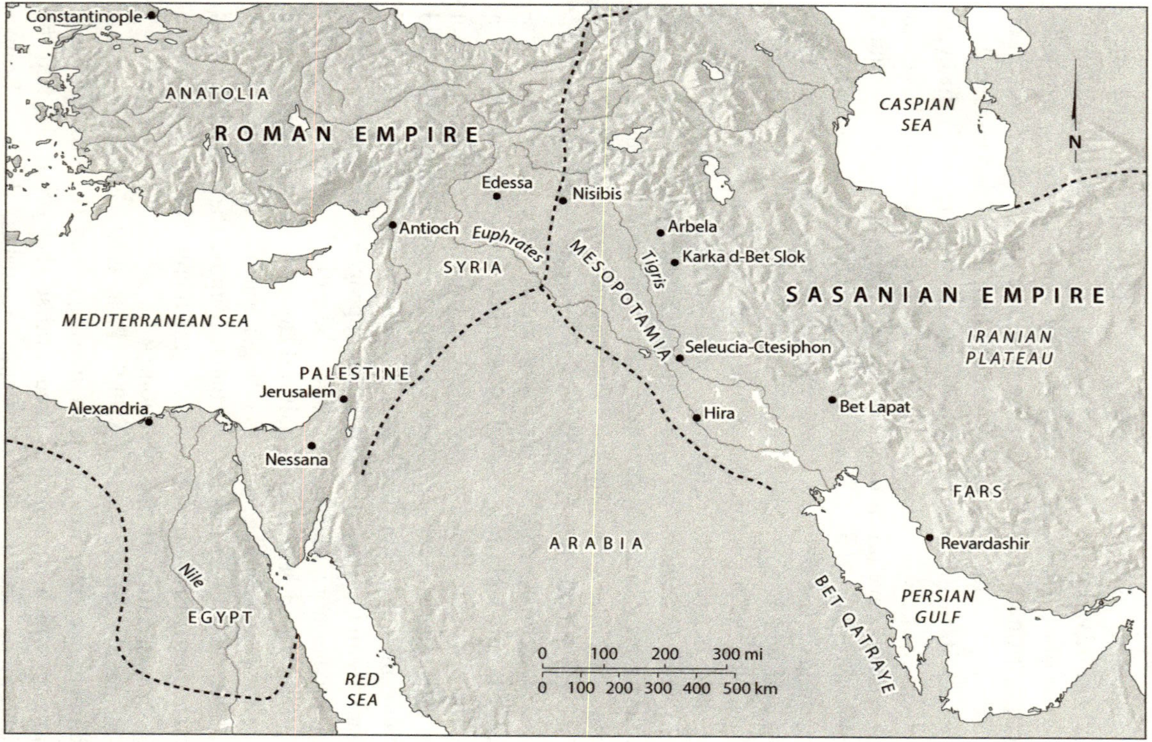

Map 1. The Middle East in Late Antiquity

Ohrmazd with his daughter and mother.[7] For early rabbinic Judaism, distinctive marital customs signaled the continuity of "one Israel" stretching deep into the biblical past.[8] In a similar vein, marriage, as the legitimate channel of human sexuality, became an important locus in the development of Christian thought, which from its earliest days recognized a fundamental connection between sexuality and humans' potential to achieve salvation. Characteristically Christian understandings of that connection, however, departed radically from most Greco-Roman, Zoroastrian, and Jewish traditions (not to mention later Islamic ones). Most ancient marital regimes and systems of sexual morality were organized around the reproductive imperative and placed great value on it. Essentially all Christian traditions, on the other hand, came to see abstention from sex as the highest, most pious mode of living in the material world in anticipation of perfection in the next one. The very utility of marriage and its reproductive purposes was uncertain at the least and wholly superfluous when this logic was followed to its extreme. A theology and ethics of sexuality rooted in the valorization of continence thus became an integral piece of Christian thought in the late antique and medieval Mediterranean world.[9] It persisted in marked tension, however, with the practice and regulation of marriage as a social institution in the imperial legal orders of late antiquity.

The notion that membership among the Christian faithful required chaste sexual practice was rooted ultimately in the teachings of Paul's epistles, most famously in 1 Corinthians 7. Paul's letter gives a "passing endorsement of continence as an optimal state," which, while not providing a systematic theology of sexual renunciation, set the parameters of later Christian thought on the subject.[10] Early Christian thinkers of later generations outlined a soteriological vision that valued virginity and continence—the eschewal of human sexuality altogether—as the most perfect way of life in an imperfect world and the surest path to salvation in the next. The institutions through which early Christians put these ideas into practice were highly varied and contested. More radical groups called Encratites by their opponents required celibacy of all the faithful; in northern Syria and Mesopotamia, lay celibates known as Sons and Daughters of the Covenant lived among their householder neighbors; cenobitic monasticism, celibates living in communities separate from lay believers, developed especially in Egypt before spreading elsewhere.[11] By the fifth century, a rough pattern had begun to emerge that increasingly cordoned off sexual renunciation as the proper vocation of monks and high ecclesiastics.[12] But virginity and continence retained their supreme rank on the scale of chaste sexual practice in the Christian imagination.

If sexual renunciation was of such value, however, where did that leave the vast majority of Christians—ordinary householders who had sex and had children, and without whom the church in society would no longer exist? Virginity and continence had theological weight; they were perfection in imitation of Christ and the angels, which sexually active lay marriage was not. Yet scripture carved out at least some place for the latter in Christian cosmology. Genesis 1:28 commanded humans to be fruitful and multiply. Ephesians 5:23 compared marriage to Christ's relationship with the faithful—"the husband is the head of the wife just as Christ is the head of the church." As Christianity grew from a marginal movement to the dominant religion of the Roman Empire and beyond, it became all the more imperative for Christian thinkers to expand on these teachings and articulate conceptions of sexual practice within marriage that, if not as perfect as continence, constituted at least an acceptable standard of chastity for everyday believers. In the late antique eastern Mediterranean, Christian teachings on chaste lay sexuality coalesced around three principles: the indissolubility of the marriage bond, the unlawfulness of sexual activity outside of monogamous marriage, and the procreative purpose of sex within marriage.[13] The Church Fathers built these principles out of a range of received teachings. Especially foundational was the biblical notion that a man and woman become "one flesh" through sexual intercourse (Genesis 2:24). Christian thinkers understood this as a divinely decreed, essentially indissoluble ontological status—hence Jesus' teaching against divorce, "what God has joined together, let no one separate" (Matthew 19:6, Mark 10:8–9). Equally significant was Paul's insight that, given the divine institution of the singleness of flesh, any sex outside of a monogamous marital union was fornication (*porneia*), inherently defiled and defiling (1 Corinthians 7).[14] Finally, strands of Stoic philosophy contributed to the early Christian imagination the conviction that if sex within marriage was lawful, it was so only for reproduction rather than for pleasure, wage labor, or any other purpose.[15]

These perspectives defined late antique Christianity's theology of conjugal, chaste sexuality. In the centuries before Christianity became the official religion of the Roman Empire, they were a radical departure from a Greco-Roman sexual culture in which divorce was relatively simple and extramarital sex with dishonorable bodies (slaves and prostitutes) had been perfectly acceptable for men. The circumscription of licit sexual activity to the single, indissoluble, procreative marital bond was thus a major innovation.[16] It was also a practical one, in the sense that it provided householders who could not achieve perfection in virginity or continence a means to ensure their worthiness of salvation. The Greek and Latin Church Fathers (John Chrysostom and Augustine are two major exemplars) constructed this message in a substantial body of theological literature, much of it admonitory and for lay consumption. Little has been written on the theology of lay marriage in the early Syriac traditions of the Christian east, our main area of interest. In general, early Syriac writers like Aphrahat (fl. fourth century) and Ephrem (d. 373) contemplated the virtues of virginity extensively while devoting less attention to worldly marriage,[17] although they invested great significance in an ecclesiology of marriage according to which the church looks forward to union with Christ the bridegroom in the world to come.[18] When late antique churchmen of the Syriac traditions did consider the theological dimensions of marriage, they offered a formulation of chaste, procreative sexuality likely deriving from the synthesis of biblical, Stoic, and Aristotelian perspectives found in the writings of Clement of Alexandria (d. 215).[19] In a nutshell, marriage for them was the divinely instituted, rational ordering of sexuality for procreative purposes that distinguished humans from non-rational animals. In Jacob of Serugh's (d. 521) homily *On Virginity, Fornication, and the Marriage of the Righteous*, for example, sexuality outside the framework of procreative marriage is associated with subhuman, non-rational animals:

> Anyone who remains in virginity is of the spiritual ones,
> and anyone who walks the path of the righteous [i.e., the married] is of the holy ones;
> but anyone who descends to fornication is of the animals. Of the one [human] race there are three classes of people.
> Among them are those who walk in virginity with the spiritual ones, in the path higher than worldly ways.
> Others take the path of the righteous with marriage, the path pure of blame and censure.
> Others descend to fornication, the wicked life, and resemble beasts and animals.[20]

Virginity is the highest degree of spiritual achievement to Jacob, but a rational sexuality within marriage, distinct from the random mating of animals, is still a mark of righteousness. The East Syrian patriarch Mar Aba (r. 540–52) gives a more definitive if less poetic expression of the same ideas. Mar Aba describes marriage as the institution "which God has established [*sāmēh*] for admirably administering the maintenance of our nature and the succession of our lineages [*yubbālā d-sharbātan*], not in the likeness of beast[s] lacking discernment [*law ba-dmut bʿirā d-lā purshānā*], but in an order that suits rational beings [*b-ṭaksā d-ʿāhen la-mlilē*]."[21] Here we find the core elements—marriage as the ordered facilitator of the procreation of rational humans, as opposed to non-rational animals—of a characteristically late antique Christian conception of licit sexuality within the confines of the marital relationship.

LAW, MARRIAGE, AND RELIGION IN THE LATE ANTIQUE EMPIRES

The Roman Empire

The connection between sexuality and salvation spurred Christian thinkers in the empires of late antiquity to define the elements of Christian marriage—monogamy, indissolubility, and the restrained practice of sex. These ideas departed in several key respects from accepted norms in the Roman world, especially in their dramatic narrowing of the horizons of licit sexual practice. But in fact, Christian theology was only one of several normative orders that claimed the authority to govern the ancient institution of marriage and the domestic and familial relationships associated with it. These orders overlapped and interlinked in significant ways, but they remained distinct and Christian perspectives on sex and marriage never achieved absolute predominance within them. As a result, the reception of those perspectives by lay populations across the Roman Empire, as well as in Sasanian territory, was halting, uneven, and incomplete throughout late antiquity and into the medieval period.[22]

The most significant of the normative orders with which Christian thought interacted in this respect were the imperial and local traditions of civil law that governed the formation, maintenance, and dissolution of marriage as a legal institution.[23] In the Roman Empire, this meant Roman law above all else, as well as its provincial iterations. An ancient and venerable imperial tradition, Roman law set the norms that governed relationships among persons, groups, and the state, in areas ranging from family law to property law to criminal law; it defined procedural rules for state organs; and it represented the will and authority of the emperor, his officials, and imperial institutions.[24] In the area of the family, Roman law regulated the contracting of marriage, the transmission of property connected to it, and the other points at which citizens' conjugal life intersected with the public arena.[25] Indeed, Roman emperors had a long track record of legislative intervention in the affairs of Roman families and households (which, as elsewhere in the premodern world, were not necessarily coterminous because households often included slaves and other dependents in addition to biologically related family members). These legislative programs aimed to tie the citizenry to the imperium's wider interests and ideological commitments. The trend began with Augustus at the turn of the millennium; it continued in Constantine's highly novel legislation in the fourth century and, especially, Justinian's massive legal codification project and Christian "moral activism" in the sixth.[26] Significantly, however, Christian perspectives on sexuality were incorporated into Roman civil law only very partially, even as late antique emperors and jurists came to frame that law as divinely inspired and founded on Christian authority.[27] Overall, Roman law continued to recognize as perfectly lawful many of the acts—chiefly divorce, remarriage, and men's extramarital affairs with low-status women—that constituted unchaste, defiled sexuality in the Christian vision. Divorce is a particularly telling case. Constantine restricted the classical doctrine, which had allowed unilateral repudiation by either spouse without cause. His successors variously eased and reimposed restrictions; but all of this may have been motivated more by the need to regulate marital property exchanges than by Christian morals. Justinian, on the other hand, took the unprecedented step of prohibiting consensual divorce for two spouses who simply did not want to remain married, which was certainly a Christianizing reform in the context of his broader project of imperial regeneration. Yet this reform was so far outside the bounds of centuries' worth of common practice that Justinian's successor quickly rescinded the prohibition.[28] Thus, across its tangled path of development and even in its partially restricted late antique form, the Roman legal doctrine of divorce never came close to the ecclesiastical ideal of indissolubility. From late antiquity into the medieval period, the Christian model of marriage continued to compete with old social mores encoded in or tacitly sanctioned by the civil legal structures of the Roman Empire.

Ecclesiastics had two principal tools to encourage laypeople to conform to their norms for conjugal conduct: "pastoral care and penitential discipline."[29] Persuasion and moral chastisement on the topic of sexuality became a central concern of late antique preaching for lay audiences, a trend perhaps best represented in the sermons of John Chrysostom (d. 407).[30] More germane to our interests, penitential punishments for sexual transgressions were incorporated prominently into ecclesiastical or canon law, the legal tradition developed by Christian bishops to regulate matters particular to the church. From a very early date, Christian communities had been preserving treatises, pseudo-apostolic teachings, patristic epistles, and proceedings of church councils written in Latin, Greek, and Syriac that set down regulations for church affairs. By the fifth century, this body of texts had come to constitute a coherent legal tradition distinct from the law of the state.[31] Representative works of ecclesiastical law range from early church orders like the *Didache*, a second-century text that regulated the duties of the ecclesiastical hierarchy and liturgical administration, to the proceedings of the Council of Nicaea and other ecumenical synods of the fourth and fifth centuries that defined orthodox dogma. While ecclesiastical law fundamentally concerned church affairs, it also included under its purview prescriptions of a broadly moral character directed to laypeople, particularly concerning sexuality. Lacking the same prerogatives of enforcement as imperial law, the ecclesiastical tradition usually sought to punish transgressors with exclusion from Christian rituals and communal participation. So, for example, the canonical letters of Basil of Caesarea (d. 378) prescribe exclusion from the Eucharist for fornication, among a number of other sexual offenses.[32]

Just as Christian moral teachings played a role in at least some of the later Roman emperors' legislation, secular Roman law influenced the ecclesiastical tradition in significant ways. Justinian's civil codification project was almost assuredly a major model of emulation for the ecclesiastical jurisprudents of the Greek east who began to produce newly systematized collections of canon law in the sixth century; in the late sixth or early seventh century, furthermore, canon lawyers incorporated pieces of Roman law relevant to church affairs into those collections, producing the joint ecclesiastical-civil legal compendia that scholars call nomocanons.[33] But however much late antique Roman and ecclesiastical law overlapped, they ultimately claimed parallel jurisdictions with respect to the Roman family. When ecclesiastical law addressed itself to sexuality and marital practices, it extended into a civil area traditionally under the authority of Roman law; but only the latter retained the constitutive power to render marriage valid as a legal relationship (not to mention other civil contracts and transactions). To take another example from Basil's canons, the Church Father could stipulate that the church would not recognize as marriage the union of a man and his third wife, but Roman law would still accord the relationship validity.[34] Basil could exclude fornicators at the church's door, but visiting prostitutes remained lawful in the eyes of the imperium.[35] To promote properly Christian sexuality, late antique ecclesiastical law sought to modify behavior within an ancient institution that continued to be governed by and partly understood in terms of civil traditions.

The degree to which ancient attitudes toward marriage and the family persisted into the Christian empire is most evident in local legal practices as represented in documentary evidence—marriage agreements, divorce settlements, and related documents preserved in a number of Rome's eastern provinces, especially Egypt. Marriage in ancient civil law traditions was always in some sense a contractual arrangement, in that it was a legal relationship created by an agreement between parties (usually the spouses and their families), but the law did not require the contract to be written in order for it to be valid.[36] Those inhabitants of the eastern Roman world who did record their marriages and related transactions in documents, however, have left us evidence of strong continuities in the legal practices attendant to marriage and the formation of households throughout the era of Christianization; they demonstrate the conservatism of the Roman institution of marriage, which in practical terms changed slowly in response to Christian perspectives and even to new civil legislation.[37] Divorce is perhaps the most emblematic civil practice of which orthodox Christianity disapproved but which clearly endures in the documentary record. Though they are not ubiquitous, a sizable number of deeds of divorce in Greek and Coptic, with provisions for the remarriage of the divorced spouses, are extant from Egypt from the sixth century into the eighth.[38] So, for example, a no-fault divorce deed of 569 from Upper Egypt between one Mathias and his wife, Kyra, blames their separation on "an evil demon."[39] A sixth-century Greek document from the Palestinian village of Nessana records a divorce in which one Stephan retains the dowry of his former wife, who had either separated from him without cause or committed some transgression and thus forfeited her property to him.[40] In a case that would have horrified any well-schooled bishop, an Egyptian fisherman named Shenetom divorced his wife, married another woman, and married his daughter to his new wife's son—all on a single scrap of papyrus.[41] Two other documents from Nessana evoke from a different angle the centrality of Roman civil tradition to marriage in the Christian empire. Both are marriage agreements, one dated 537 and the other 558, in which the groom acknowledges receipt of a dowry from the bride's family "according to Roman custom."[42] Nessana was "an outlying village" on the edge of the desert in the province of Palaestina Tertia.[43] Like elsewhere in the Roman world, Nessana's Christian institutions, including churches, a monastery, and their officials, were central to local life.[44] In a provincial setting like this in the heavily Christian later empire, the fact that these marriage contracts explicitly invoke the Roman example (whatever the actual content of their law) underscores how the legal-practical aspects of marriage and social reproduction remained intimately connected to notions of Roman citizenship, imperium, and law.

It is important to note that even though civil law retained constitutive authority over marriage as a legal relationship, ecclesiastics played important roles in its administration. It would take several centuries for the Latin and Greek churches to develop a systematic theology of marriage as a sacrament, but by the fifth century it was standard in the eastern empire for clerics to bless first marriages.[45] Furthermore, many of the scribes and judicial figures who administered civil law, including that of marriage, were themselves Christian clerics. Constantine had granted official recognition to ecclesiastical courts in 318, and a career in the church was a path to status in the later empire.[46] As such, the local notables who traditionally drew up deeds and contracts or witnessed documents might frequently hold clerical positions. To take one of numerous examples from the Egyptian papyri, a marriage contract of 610 from Panopolis (modern Akhmim) was witnessed by two priests, Moses and Yohannes.[47] But while they certainly played judicial roles in administering marriage law, we should not assume that all Christian clerics were invested in enforcing the high tradition's teachings on marriage and sexuality to the letter. In handling legal affairs they were carrying on a civil tradition that had always been a duty of prominent local men and officials; in the later empire Christianization had simply brought clerics to overlap with those categories. Indeed, the involvement of Christian figures in marriages did not necessarily imply the eschewal of practices lawful in civil terms but unchaste in ecclesiastical ones. Another Greek Nessana document, from the period of Umayyad rule but rooted in pre-Islamic Roman and local practices, is instructive here. The document, written in 689, records a divorce effected when Nonna, the wife, gives up her dowry and other marital property to John, her husband and a priest.[48] Three of the seven witnesses are clerics associated with the local monastery of Saints Sergius and Bacchus, and the scribe is the priest and future abbot Sergius son of George. Though it may appear incongruous to encounter so many clerics affixing their signatures to a document attesting to a marriage's dissolution (not to mention the crosses and invocations of God's grace with which they embellished it), it is not necessarily so. These individuals were churchmen, but they were also custodians of the enduring civil traditions, rooted in Nessana's recent Roman past, that governed the formation, maintenance, and dissolution of marriage.[49] Christian tradition taught a radically new sexual morality, the Church Fathers and other ecclesiastics promoted it among their flocks, and some Roman emperors took it seriously when they promulgated new laws; but these developments never completely reformulated the Roman institution of marriage in the terms of Christian morality. Old and durable civil frameworks for contracting marital bonds and reproducing household life remained central to the understanding and practice of marriage in the later Roman world. The effort to create Christian marriage largely meant preaching Christian morals as chaste modifications to an ancient civil institution.

The Sasanian Empire

If imperial traditions defined the legal framework of marriage in the Roman Empire, how did the East Syrian Christian subjects of the Sasanian Empire relate to and interact with the judicial structures of a Zoroastrian polity? Which legal traditions had constitutive authority to render marriages legitimate? What role did ecclesiastical law play in the lives of East Syrians? These questions are more difficult to investigate than those concerning the Roman world due to a nearly complete lack of documentary evidence from Sasanian Mesopotamia and Iran and the fragmentary character of the extant Sasanian legal sources. Nonetheless, we can essay an educated outline. The available evidence indicates that Sasanian Christians, much like their coreligionists in the Roman Empire, followed a mix of imperial and local civil traditions to contract marriages. They did so under the purview, to varying degrees, of the Sasanian judicial apparatus. The Church of the East's ecclesiastical law also did not differ greatly in its goals from canon law to the west: it encouraged suitably Christian forms of marriage, and ventured beyond the typical territory of Roman ecclesiastical law only in response to distinctively Iranian practices like close-kin marriage. Christian law did not have constitutive power over the formation of marriages; Sasanian Christians moved within a legal sphere defined by the empire's official traditions.

The judicial institutions of the Sasanian Empire included a hierarchical array of courts staffed by a range of officials, many of whom were Zoroastrian religious professionals.[50] The empire's avowed Zoroastrianism, however, did not preclude the access to its courts of subjects of other religions; Christians, Jews, and other non-Zoroastrians were ineligible only for specific services closely connected to Zoroastrian ritual and doctrine.[51] If Sasanian courts were open to Christians, however, did they actually make use of them? If nothing else, the question is worth asking because of the close connection between Zoroastrian doctrine and Sasanian judicial practice, and because we know East Syrian ecclesiastics to have maintained some form of their own communal judicial institutions, as did rabbinic Jews.[52] Several factors, however, militate against the possibility that these resources constituted a completely autonomous system of law that obviated any need for Christians to make use of the imperial judiciary.[53] Notably, Sasanian-era East Syrian bishops never claimed for themselves exclusive jurisdiction over the civil affairs of laypeople; they did so only for clerics. The bishops thus at least tacitly recognized the authority of Sasanian law and the imperial judiciary over all of the empire's subjects, again like the rabbis.[54] Christian judicial institutions, moreover, are likely to have been more informal audiences of ecclesiastics, monks, and lay notables rather than a centrally organized, hierarchical court system.[55] Furthermore, the East Syrians' ecclesiastical law never developed to cover the full range of civil affairs that would have been necessary had the bishops intended to fully insulate Christians from extracommunal law. Throughout the Sasanian period, East Syrian law was embodied in two main groups of texts: first, Syriac translations of foundational works of Roman ecclesiastical law—the canons of local and ecumenical synods, associated episcopal letters, and pseudo-apostolic writings—and second, the canons and proceedings of the Church of the East's own synods.[56] Like the received materials of Roman provenance, the East Syrians' early synodal legislation dealt mainly with the organization of the ecclesiastical hierarchy rather than the civil affairs of laypeople (with a few important exceptions, discussed below). According to one recent analysis, this material demonstrates that East Syrian bishops never claimed the coercive powers of the Sasanian judiciary even when their law concerned civil transactions; they offered only spiritual punishments (essentially, exclusion from the Eucharist) for transgression. East Syrian law's primary aim, rather than drawing laypeople into some discrete Christian legal sphere, was pastoral admonishment that not all the legal institutions available to Sasanian subjects were appropriate for true-believing Christians.[57] In this respect, East Syrian law under the Sasanians was not unlike ecclesiastical law in the Roman Empire. Rather than providing a comprehensive legal system for Sasanian Christians, East Syrian ecclesiastical elites conceived of their legal tradition and their jurisdiction as complementary to other legal orders in the Sasanian Empire. We can be sure that many Christians sought the services of communal figures of authority to settle disputes. As subjects of the Sasanian King of Kings, however, they also certainly made use of state judicial institutions for at least some purposes.

The question of whether and how often they would have done so when they sought to contract marriages is more problematic. Sasanian bishops never claimed exclusive jurisdiction over the administration of marriage among Christians, nor did East Syrian law set any rules for how marriage was constituted as a legal relationship.[58] The rabbinic tradition of the Mishnah and Talmud, by contrast, offered a thorough explanation of what made marriage marriage; in a rabbinic audience in the Sasanian Empire, a marriage was valid if it had been contracted according to rabbinic law.[59] East Syrian law of the Sasanian period gave no such direction. At the same time, the family law administered by the empire's courts was heavily structured by Zoroastrian cosmological principles—its "ideological foundation," in the words of one scholar.[60] A medieval Zoroastrian marriage contract that scholars believe to be based on Sasanian-era models, for example, is laden with Zoroastrian imagery and phraseology. It alludes to the liturgical recitation of "good utterances"; it calls marriage a "pious act" in the terms of Zoroastrian cosmology; and the bride states that she will not "deviate from . . . being an Iranian (*ērīh*) and (practising) the Good Religion (*weh-dēnīh*)" (i.e., Zoroastrianism).[61] This model marriage contract is thus very much a Zoroastrian one.

Did Zoroastrian scribes and judges only draw up marriage contracts like it? If they did, would Christians have made use of them?

One way or the other, it remains probable that Christians interacted with Sasanian judicial structures when dealing with legal business related to the family. The best reading of the evidence suggests that when the empire's Christian subjects sought to record their marriages in written contracts, they would have had them drawn up by local scribes according to the conventions of either Sasanian law or local civil traditions. Subsequently, they would have had those documents confirmed by the seals of state officials or local notables, including ecclesiastics, making them eligible for adjudication by Sasanian courts. In this manner, even if Christians did not contract marriages according to Sasanian law, they still acted within a legal arena defined by imperial judicial practice.

In heavily Zoroastrian, Middle Persian–speaking regions of the empire that also had Christian populations, such as Khuzistan and Fars, it is reasonable to think that some Christians would, in fact, have gone to Zoroastrian scribes and judges to have marriage contracts drawn up according to Sasanian law. The writings of the East Syrian patriarch Mar Aba are instructive here. In the mid-sixth century, Mar Aba wrote a treatise and issued canons prohibiting Christians from practicing close-kin marriages, such as unions between a man and his father's widow, his uncle's widow, or his aunts. These practices were lawful and in some cases encouraged by Zoroastrian ethics and Sasanian law, but to Mar Aba they were fundamentally un-Christian.[62] They were apparently common enough among Sasanian Christians, however, to warrant active condemnation. Notably, this indicates that the offenders (from Mar Aba's perspective) were directly familiar with the substance of Sasanian family law, or at least with the distinctive marital practices it recognized and regulated. That such Christians would have contracted marriages before Zoroastrian judges or through Zoroastrian scribes is not at all unlikely. Perhaps they simply left the most overtly Zoroastrian language out of their contracts (or perhaps they did not).

For Christians in other regions of the empire, it is likely that local civil law traditions—what we might call common law—held sway. In these areas, Sasanian Christians would have turned to Christian scribes and notables, who often had positions in the church and/or the state and who were versed in local legal practices, to draw up marriage contracts. Generally, we might expect this to have been the case more in the heavily Christian areas of Mesopotamia than in the Iranian provinces of the empire. As we will see in Chapter 4, law books written by East Syrian bishops in the early ninth century prescribe forms of betrothal and marriage very similar to those of other regional legal cultures and to ancient, pre-Sasanian ones. Without overstating direct connections, this implies the continuity of regional common law traditions in Sasanian Mesopotamia, likely transmitted through scribal practice rather than encoded in normative treatises.[63] When Sasanian Christians did not go to Zoroastrian judicial figures to contract marriages, we should imagine them doing so according to these regional legal traditions through the services of local Christian scribes.

Either way, Sasanian Christians would have been operating within the framework of Sasanian norms of judicial practice. The standard method of validating the content of a legal document in the Sasanian Empire was to attach to it a clay bulla impressed with the seals of office-holders and witnesses. If a document was sealed by a state official, a Sasanian court accepted it as fully valid. If a document carried only the seal impressions of private individuals as witnesses, it was up to the judge to determine its probative value.[64] Presumably, any marriage agreement drawn up by a Zoroastrian judge would have received an authenticating seal impression. But even if non-Zoroastrian contracts were sealed only by witnesses, the descriptions of Sasanian judicial procedure we have suggest that they still would have been admissible before Sasanian judges, just at a lower level of evidentiary value. In other words, they still functioned under the auspices of the Sasanian judicial system, not in a fully autonomous Christian legal sphere. Additionally, Christian formulas and iconography on recent seal findings indicate that some Christians held imperially recognized offices, as does the Sasanian dynasty's frequent interest in employing bishops in official capacities such as imperial embassies.[65] Such individuals' seals would presumably have granted marriage contracts full legitimacy, even if they did not conform to the Zoroastrian norms we see in the Middle Persian model contract. In these various ways, we should imagine Sasanian Christians operating under the purview of the Sasanian administration and its judicial apparatus even when they did not marry according to the same substantive norms as their Zoroastrian co-subjects.

Much as in the Roman Empire, the fact that marriage as a legal relationship did not fall under the exclusive purview of East Syrian law does not mean that ecclesiastical figures played no role in its administration. It is entirely likely that priests attended and blessed marriages, although the earliest positive evidence for an East Syrian liturgical ceremony of betrothal is not earlier than the seventh century.[66] Furthermore, prohibitions of un-Christian marital practices form a significant part of East Syrian canon law from the Sasanian period. Mar Aba is exemplary in this respect; the distinctive Iranian forms of marriage enshrined in Sasanian law and common among some Iranian Christians—especially close-kin marriage and polygamy—compelled him to issue a substantial body of regulations for lay household life that became foundational to the later East Syrian legal tradition.[67] Like their contemporaries to the west, East Syrian bishops such as Mar Aba used the same techniques of pastoral censure and exclusion from Christian communion to promote their notions of Christian sexual morality among the laity; East Syrian law sometimes ventured beyond the territory of Roman canon law only because a greater range of household forms were lawful and customary in the Iranian empire.

On the administrative side, we can certainly expect that many of the communal judicial venues at which Christians contracted marriages according to common law traditions were ecclesiastical audiences and that many of the local notables who served their communities as scribes, as witnesses, and in other judicial capacities had positions in the church. A recent survey of Syriac and Middle Persian seals belonging to Sasanian Christians, for example, includes a number that identify the holder as a deacon, priest, or metropolitan.[68] In the late 600s, the *Judicial Decisions* of the East Syrian patriarch Hnanishoʿ I (r. 686–98) mention two marriage agreements that have been validated with the seals (Syriac singular *ṭabʿā*) of ecclesiastical officials, one a bishop and the other a traveling priest.[69] These are likely examples of clergymen carrying on the legal-administrative functions of their Sasanian-era predecessors.

In sum, ecclesiastical figures in the Sasanian Empire were no doubt involved in the civil-legal business of the communities under their purview, including contracting marriages. But ecclesiastical law itself retained for the East Syrians a more restricted role. Rather than functioning as a comprehensive system that sealed off East Syrians from imperial legal institutions, it promoted appropriately Christian modes of conduct by regulating individual believers' participation in Christian communion. Imperial and local civil traditions set the practical legal framework for marriage among Sasanian Christians in a manner similar to their Roman counterparts.

Religion, Magic, and Domesticity

Christian tradition put considerable claims on lay marriage and sexuality in the societies of late antiquity, but it ran up against other normative orders like imperial legal traditions, Greco-Roman sexual ethics, and Iranian marriage customs. As we have framed the story so far, much of this friction related to the public side of the institution of marriage: that is, the legal, moral, and theological statuses that those normative orders ascribed to men and women who had sex and cohabited with one another. For example, in the terms of Sasanian law a union between a woman and her nephew could be a valid marriage, while to East Syrian bishops it was unlawful fornication (*zānyutā*); sex between a man and a prostitute entailed no meaningful legal consequences in the Roman Empire, but it made the two into one flesh according to Christian theology. Before concluding, it is worth considering as well the relationship of Christian religiosity to some domestic aspects of late antique marriage, those that impinged less on public life. Late antique ecclesiastics prescribed norms for the private spaces of Christian households too; but again, practice varied considerably, and there is much evidence that the devotional side of household life was eclectic in ways that surreptitiously undermined the authority of Christian religious elites and their normative traditions.

Among the domestic activities that bore considerable attention from Christian theologians was sex itself, and we have seen that the prescription of monogamy and procreation characterized their traditions from an early date. Within the household, this translated into an emphasis on abstinence during fasting seasons and sexual restraint in general,[70] as well as condemnation of the sexual exploitation of slaves. How completely the Christian moral-theological vision impelled householders to reorganize domestic life in these terms, which occurred behind closed doors in ways that divorce or taking a third spouse did not, varied over time and space. But if the lawfulness of specific sexual practices within domestic spaces received a good deal of ecclesiastical concern, it is also as important to recognize that late antique societies knew an entire realm of ritual practices related to sexuality, domesticity, and the inner affairs of households, neighborhoods, and kin networks far different from the doctrines and modes of piety prescribed by ecclesiastics. Essentially, we are dealing with what modern scholars call, with an imprecise but heuristically useful term, "magic": a wide array of practices that tapped into the extra-human, unseen powers that filled the universe in order to effect healing, protect against personal and familial calamities, or visit negative effects on one's enemies.[71] Such practices typically included "amulets, recitations of incantations, and performance of adjurational rituals."[72] These were frequently administered by learned practitioners other than religious professionals like bishops; in such cases, the latter tended to denigrate and proscribe magic as unlawful, unholy "sorcery" (Syriac *ḥarrāshutā*). Yet magic remained ubiquitous in the late antique Mediterranean world and western Asia, and it was practiced and patronized across the religious spectrum. Some Christians must have understood that magic fell outside the bounds of what the bishops considered properly Christian,[73] but it remained an integral part of the life courses of untold numbers of laypeople formed less exclusively in the church's high doctrine. Talismans, amulets, and adjurations were a way to look after one's interests that coexisted largely unproblematically with one's religious affiliation.

For our purposes, the important point is that magical practices were deeply connected to domestic realms over which more institutionalized normative traditions also claimed authority.[74] If Christian soteriology was constructed around a particular ordering of human sexuality, much late antique magic was geared toward coping with the more immediate disorders and destructive possibilities of sex, as well as with other dangers that routinely beset ancient households—charming an indifferent beloved and attracting their desire, preventing against the dangers of childbirth, and warding off diseases that might befall loved ones are all common aims of late antique magical texts. Indeed, the fact that male religious professionals frequently conceptualized magic in negatively gendered terms—as arcane, unholy feminine knowledge—underscores its close connection to private, domestic spaces that bishops (as well as rabbis) could not always regulate so simply.[75]

The hundreds of Aramaic incantation bowls excavated from southern Iraq make for an evocative example of late antique domestic magic that involved religious-ritual practices and gender categories different from those of Christian orthodoxies. Dating to the sixth and seventh centuries (and perhaps to the fifth and eighth), the bowls are inscribed with incantations that seek healing or protection for the households of the clients who commissioned them: for themselves, their children, and their livestock and other property.[76]

The bowls are written in several scripts and dialects, including Jewish Aramaic, Mandaic, and Syriac. Client names indicate that individuals from across the religious spectrum—Zoroastrians, Jews, Christians, Mandaeans, Manicheans—made use of the bowls, and the incantations invoke a host of Hellenistic, Iranian, Jewish, and Christian deities, demons, and religious symbols.[77] The incantations are also gendered in idiosyncratic ways. Clients are usually identified by their matronymics—that is, descent in the maternal line—which is incongruous with the largely patrilineal social organization of the Sasanian Empire, and may speak to the incantations' connection to distinctly domestic realms understood in feminized terms.[78] We can take as an example a bowl inscribed for one Bar-Sahde, a Christian name meaning "son of martyrs," whom the inscription identifies further as the son of Ahata, a feminine Aramaic name. The magical practitioner who composed the incantation was presumably Jewish, to judge by its Hebrew script. The bowl's target is a lilith, a female demon who has taken up residence "upon the threshold of the house of Bar-Sahde" and "strikes [and smites and k]ills boys and girls." The lilith has effectively become a malevolent, unwanted member of Bar-Sahde's household: the incantation expels her from it by writing her a deed of divorce so that she can no longer harm her human fellow householders, Bar-Sahde, his wife Aywi, and especially their children. In order to accomplish the divorce, the incantation invokes "the name of Joshua bar Peraḥia," a rabbi whose demon-fighting powers appear often in bowl texts, as well as an Iranian entity, "Elisur Bagdana, the king of demons and *dēv*s, the great ruler of liliths."[79] After having the bowl inscribed, Bar-Sahde would have placed or buried it facedown in a corner of his house, the position in which excavations usually discovered the bowls, to trap or otherwise serve notice to the offending lilith.[80]

Bar-Sahde's bowl vividly evokes a sphere of late antique household religiosity, intimately connected to sexual and familial order but largely outside the purview of Christian orthodoxies and formal hierarchies. To protect his family and household, Bar-Sahde took recourse to a Jewish magician and received an incantation invoking Jewish and Iranian powers. Besides the religious boundary crossing involved, the conspicuous feminine gendering of certain elements of Bar-Sahde's incantation—its concern for matrilineal descent, the malevolent demon wife who must be divorced—evinces the domestic orientation of magical forms of ritual power and their difference

Figure 1. Syriac incantation bowl with an illustration of a magician. The incantation seeks protection against various demons for one Nuri and her house, husband, sons, and daughters. It invokes the Trinity, among other protective powers (see Moriggi, *Corpus of Syriac Incantation Bowls*, 27–31). The Catholic University of America, Semitics/ICOR Collections H156, with thanks to Dr. Monica Blanchard. Photo by author.

from the more public, institutionalized ritual practices of the church (although the figure of the lilith is suggestive of a concern for the destructive potential of uncontrolled female sexuality common to many high-normative traditions as well).[81] Late antique householders thus understood ritual practices like those surrounding Bar-Sahde's bowl as specially attuned to the uncertainties and problems of desire, domesticity, and family life. Christian powers could certainly be harnessed to similar ends; psalm-chanting priests ward off demons in the story of Rabban Bar ʿEdta, for example, and East Syrian synodal canons mention learned and even ordained Christians who compose incantations, amulets, and auguries—indeed, we have plenty of incantation bowls written in Syriac, a number of which invoke the power of Christ and the Trinity.[82] The telling point, however, is that high ecclesiastics condemned incantation writing, but not psalm chanting, as unlawful "demonic servitude" (*pulḥānā d-shēdē*): the former was part of a diverse tradition of ritual practice that bled out across the communal boundaries imagined by religious elites, operated outside the purview of more official hierarchies, and undermined Christian doctrine's claim to exclusive authority over sexuality and domestic life. To high ecclesiastics, salvation came only through their prescribed forms of Christian piety and the singular mysteries of the Eucharist and baptism. But many laypeople decided they could not afford to bank on such an exclusivist model, and domestic religiosity, sexuality, and familial order in the late antique world were thus much more heterogeneous affairs than the normative ecclesiastical vision.

Marriage was foundational to the social organization of the late ancient world, as it had been to human societies for millennia. It was the chief institution around which the practices of social reproduction were organized, rendering sex between a man and a woman legitimate and defining the familial and kinship relations that transmitted property, status, and social identity. In the late antique eastern Roman and Sasanian empires, marriage bore considerable cultural weight and sat at the intersection of multiple normative orders: the imperial legal traditions that regulated the public meaning of cohabitation, sex, and associated property relations; religious traditions that ascribed cosmological significance to human sexuality and sought to direct its practice accordingly; and any number of local customs (regional, tribal, magical, etc.) by which subjects throughout the two empires conducted their domestic affairs.

While there was much interpenetration among these moral-legal-practical orders, a foundational story of late antique societies was the major challenge posed by Christian theologies of sex to other, long-established systems. In societies that by the sixth century were majority Christian as far east as the foothills of the Iranian Plateau, Christian traditions valorized virginity, downgraded the moral and theological significance of marriage and childbearing, and condemned a host of ancient and legally recognized practices: divorce, sex outside marriage for men, and, in the Sasanian Empire, close-kin unions and polygamy. But the Christian vision was not hegemonic. Even as Christian principles made their way piecemeal into Roman legislation and Christian clerics became influential community leaders, ecclesiastical law never had the authority to determine the public validity of marriage and the kinship and property relations that it established. Clerics preached, prescribed penitential punishments, and catechized, and all this undoubtedly prodded the sexual lives of laypeople toward the orthodox ideal, especially in cities and other territories with thick ecclesiastical presences. But it is clear that many of those ostensibly un-Christian practices associated with ancient marriage persisted in late antique societies, not least because they remained generally lawful in the eyes of the empires. The same held true for the rituals of domestic life, love, and religiosity decried as sorcery by ecclesiastics. Marriage remained an institution that inducted late antique subjects into multiple loyalties: to spouse, kin, and imperium as well as to the religious community.

The imperial orders of late antiquity, however, were soon to change. In the first half of the seventh century, armies from the Arabian Peninsula conquered the entire eastern Mediterranean world south and east of the Taurus Mountains. They brought with them a new religious dispensation, particular attitudes toward sex and marriage, and quickly developing ideas about how their Christian, Jewish, Zoroastrian, and other subjects were supposed to relate to their rule. The encounter with this new empire, the Islamic caliphate, transformed the social and intellectual worlds of the Middle East's Christian communities over the course of its first three centuries. In particular, the articulation of caliphal structures motivated ecclesiastical leaders to reorganize Christian social patterns around the ancient institution of marriage in new and innovative ways.

CHAPTER 2

Christianizing Marriage Under Early Islam

For every land and for every nation, [God's diligence] [*bṭilutēh*] has put in order regulatory laws [*nāmosē mmashshḥē*] suitable to the times and the people of [those] times . . . through Moses, He established a book of diverse laws for the old nation which was a foreshadowing of the mystery of the new. Then, He granted the Gospel of life to His church through the glorious appearance of His beloved one. . . . In all times, however, the fickleness and great weakness of men . . . demands that those who have been entrusted by the grace of God with the instruction of [men's] souls take pains to zealously correct them.

—East Syrian patriarch George I, synodal address, 676

In 676, about a generation after Arabian armies proclaiming the message of the Prophet Muhammad first conquered much of the Sasanian and eastern Roman empires, the East Syrian patriarch George I (r. 660–80) journeyed from his see in central Iraq to a small island named Dayrin in the Persian Gulf. Though it may appear a marginal, unlikely destination for the chief bishop of the largest church in the caliphate's eastern domains, the Gulf's Arabian coastline and nearby islands—an area known in Syriac as Bet Qatraye, "the land of the Qataris"—had been home to a significant Christian community for several centuries.[1] The local Christians' deep roots gave George's visit its urgency, for he had inherited a problem from his patriarchal predecessor: the Christians of eastern Arabia had been going increasingly astray. The bishops of Bet Qatraye had declared themselves independent of the East Syrian patriarchate in the old Sasanian capital of Seleucia-Ctesiphon, while further down the Gulf coast whole communities had traded in their Christian affiliation for the new religion of the Arab conquerors. George, claiming the ecclesiastical mantle of "those who have been entrusted by the grace of God with the instruction of [men's] souls," set out to the Gulf to convene a synod with the local bishops, set the church's affairs aright, and attend to any local "practices in need of correction" (*suʿrānē da-sniqin ʿal turrāṣā*).[2]

While George's stated aim was to bring local life in line with the preestablished, authoritative standard of the central patriarchate, several of the canons he issued were completely unprecedented. Among them was one concerning marriage: "Women who have not [yet] been married or given in betrothal by their fathers shall be betrothed to men through Christian law, according to the custom of the faithful. [This shall be accomplished] through the consent of their parents, the mediation of the holy cross of our Savior, and a priestly blessing."[3] Marriages, according to this canon, would henceforth require sanctification by priests and Christian ritual to be valid. "Christian law" (*nāmosā krēsṭyānā*), rather than the law of the state or the custom of the village or tribe, was now the sole arbiter of the legitimacy of marital unions. In the traditions of Middle Eastern Christianity, this claim was strikingly new—and it underwrote a new conception of how marriage mediated the relationship between individuals, families, and households, on the one hand, and the larger social bodies to which they belonged, on the other.

Expanding claims over lay households in the name of Christian law were among the earliest, most striking responses of bishops like George to the Arab conquests, the establishment of the Islamic caliphate, and the social changes those events brought. Scholars often assert that in the seventh century, when the conquerors and the adherents of their new disposition were few in number and before the caliphate's techniques of rule had been formalized, life for the vast and diverse subject population of the new empire went on largely as it had before. But the clearing out of the former rulers in fact provided the subject elites who remained the opportunity to articulate new forms of authority, while the conquerors introduced new patterns of religious adherence to an already heterogeneous socioreligious landscape. In the absence of the old imperial orders, Christian religious elites began to make new claims concerning the authority of ecclesiastical law to set norms for laypeople; in conditions of religious diversity and shifting sociopolitical hierarchies, they took an increased interest in marriage and the household as sites for the elaboration of distinctively Christian social practices. Most notably, George I asserted the complete authority of Christian law over the public act of marrying, reformulating that foundational institution of social reproduction as an exclusively Christian one in order to secure the social boundaries of the Church of the East within the caliphate. In doing so, George and other contemporary Syriac bishops brought their Christian traditions in line with an established perspective among the other religions of late antiquity, including rabbinic Judaism, Zoroastrianism, and nascent Islam: that marriage was properly under the purview of religious law and constitutive of the religious community as a social body. In the seventh century, the halting establishment of a nascent Islamic empire thus effected the beginnings of a reformulation of Christian association centered on the link between ecclesiastical authority and believing households.

COMMUNAL INSTITUTIONS AND CHRISTIAN HOUSEHOLDS IN POSTCONQUEST IRAQ AND IRAN

When George I set off for the Persian Gulf in 676, the Islamic caliphate was ruled from Damascus by Muʿawiya, a scion of the Sufyanid branch of the Umayyad clan from Muhammad's hometown of Mecca. The caliph, leader of a small, mostly Arab political and military elite, presided over a vast subject population of Christians, Zoroastrians, Jews, and others. Contemporary Christian writers would remember Muʿawiya's long rule (661–80) as a time of stability and prosperity, bookended as it was by two civil wars among the ruling class.[4] Modern scholars take special note of Muʿawiya's caliphate for encompassing both the incipient formation of distinctive institutions of caliphal governance as well as strong continuities with the empires that the caliphate supplanted. On the one hand, Muʿawiya's fiscal administration appears to have been already quite systematized, and he held the centralized power to appoint members of the conquest elite to regional governorships throughout the lands under caliphal rule.[5] On the other, seventh-century Umayyad governance continued to rely on subject elites—scribes, urban notables, landowners, village headmen, and bishops and other religious elites—as administrators, local middlemen, and tax collectors. While later Umayyad caliphs beginning with ʿAbd al-Malik (r. 685–705) would reorganize this system and shift local fiscal and judicial authority away from non-Muslims, on the whole their elites played important roles in the administration of the caliphate throughout the seventh century.[6] The other side of this coin was that Umayyad governance left subject elites wide latitude to attend to the internal affairs of their own communities. This was both an administrative practice of convenience and a function, though not yet theorized in especially explicit terms, of Quranic theologies that understood God to have allotted different peoples their own particular legal regimes (as in Quran 5:47–49).[7]

While Umayyad governance has been framed frequently in terms of continuity, since local elites are thought to have carried on administering communal affairs much as they had before the conquests, it is also clear that the Arabs' overturning of the old imperial orders left room for considerable institutional innovation.[8] Among the Christian communities that made up the majority of the caliphate's population, East Syrian bishops in Iraq and Iran seized on this opportunity with special vigor to claim new forms of ecclesiastical judicial authority. Moreover, their efforts focused especially on regulating the practices of Christian household formation in new and more intensive ways.

These transformations are evident in the innovative Syriac legal texts produced by seventh-century East Syrian bishops. Immediately striking are the canons of George's synod in the Persian Gulf. In addition to its assertion that Christian law had constitutive authority over marriages between Christians (to which we will return below), it made another, even broader claim regarding the ecclesiastical judiciary: all litigation between Christians had to be adjudicated before ecclesiastics. East Syrian bishops had never claimed an authority this exclusive under the Sasanians. The fall of the dynasty to the Arab conquerors, however, likely entailed the loss of imperial prestige on the part of its judicial officials; though they no doubt continued to offer judicial services, they now lacked the backing of state power that had made their services attractive for Sasanian subjects of any religious affiliation. In response to this relative vacuum, as well as the permissive stance of caliphal governance, George took the opportunity to claim an entirely new ecclesiastical jurisdiction over laypeople's civil affairs.[9]

George's synod represents the most assertive example of this interest on the part of the East Syrian ecclesiastical hierarchy. Two unique East Syrian legal works from the latter half of the seventh century, both highly innovative in form, genre, and content, provide further evidence. These texts deal especially with the law of inheritance and succession: how property devolves from one generation to another and thereby reproduces the material wealth and social standing of lineages. Through them, we can observe how the establishment of the caliphate entailed not only continuities in Christian communal structures but efforts to strengthen those structures by formalizing an

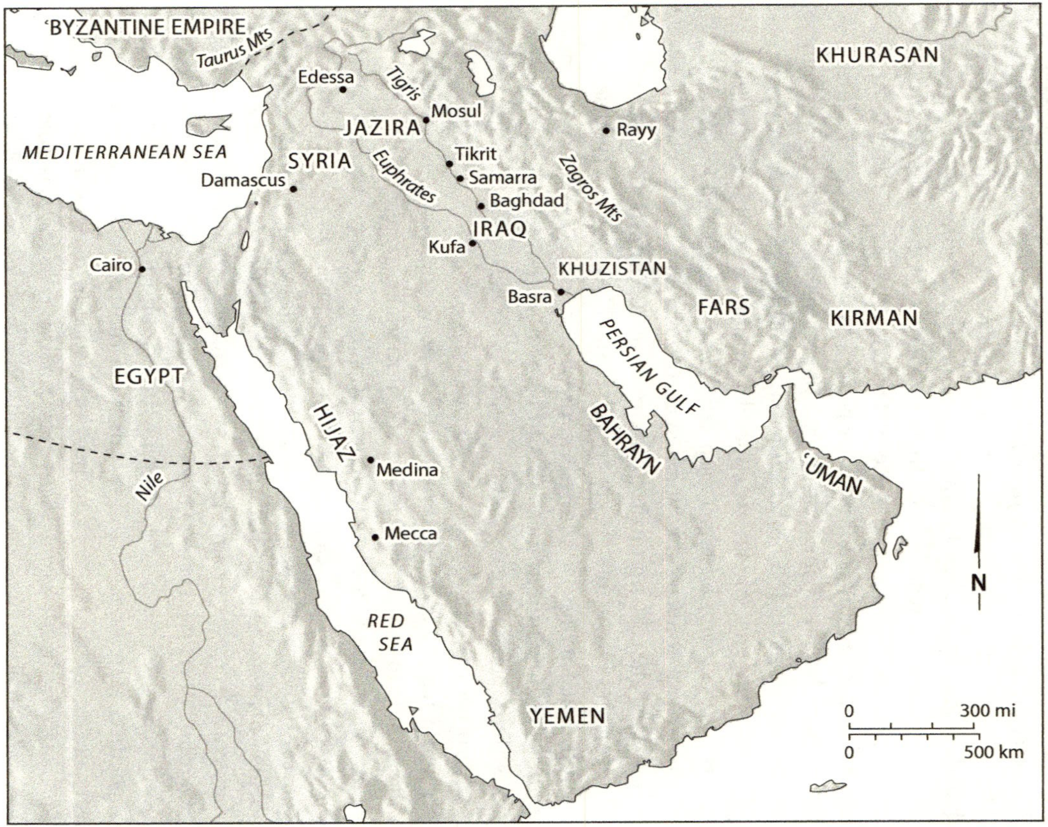

Map 2. The Medieval Islamic Caliphate

ecclesiastical role in the life of lay families. The first text in question is the *Law of Inheritance*, a treatise by Shemʿon (fl. mid-seventh century), bishop of Revardashir in Fars province in southwest Iran, composed originally in Middle Persian but extant in a Syriac translation. The second is the collected *Judicial Decisions* of Patriarch Hnanishoʿ I (r. 686–98, mentioned in Chapter 1). These cover a variety of topics, but the majority convey Hnanishoʿ's judicial decisions on inheritance disputes, many of which laypeople or lower clergy brought directly to the patriarch.[10] The significance of these texts rests in two features: the subjects they address and their genre. As we have seen, East Syrian bishops had cultivated a tradition of ecclesiastical law throughout the Sasanian period. The bulk of that tradition, however, consisted of the hoary genre of canons issued by bishops assembled at synods. By its nature, synodal legislation tended to address the broad areas of immediate concern for which synods were convened, which usually meant church organization more than the affairs of laypeople. Shemʿon and Hnanishoʿ's texts are different. They concern themselves with detailed points of family law, offering precise, casuistic considerations of how inheritances should be distributed. For example, the cases that Shemʿon treats include a man who dies with only his wife and brother as potential heirs and one who has only a granddaughter and a nephew.[11] One of Hnanishoʿ's decisions concerns a widow whose male in-laws have tried to appropriate her deceased husband's estate rather than let her son inherit it.[12] By contrast, one of the few Sasanian-era synodal canons to treat inheritance prescribes only a general principle: "every Christian who nullifies the will and testaments of the deceased" shall incur divine punishment, a far cry from the detail of Shemʿon's and Hnanishoʿ's rulings.[13] Furthermore, these seventh-century works differ from synodal canons in that they are not bodies of collective legislation but compositions by individual specialists—bishops who have taken on the role of jurist to delineate norms for civil life or to provide justice to laypeople in need.[14] Shemʿon's treatise gives a theoretical justification for this role: God has entrusted the "leaders of the church" (*mdabbrānē d-ʿēdtā*) with administering His "magnificent laws and teaching" (*nāmosē tmihē w-mallpānutā*) that guide human life.[15]

Shemʿon and Hnanishoʿ exemplify how East Syrian bishops stepped into expanded judicial roles after the fall of the Sasanian state and before the formation of a strong caliphal judiciary. Shemʿon's law book conceptualizes the intergenerational transfer of wealth as an area of social life newly subject to ecclesiastical pastoral care and repackages principles of Sasanian inheritance law as a Christian tradition. Similarly, Hnanishoʿ's decisions show how a high church official could take on a judicial role in regulating the disbursement of inheritances and, therefore, the reproduction of lineages, which had been one of the primary areas of activity of the Sasanian judiciary.[16] Shemʿon's and Hnanishoʿ's efforts in this regard were not entirely unprecedented; we have a few Sasanian-era canons that give guidelines for both intestate inheritance and bequests.[17] To judge by Shemʿon's discussion, however, those few precedents in no way added up to an authoritative, comprehensive body of communal law; the very problem from which his treatise followed was that the "teaching of our Lord [*mallpānutā d-Māran*] . . . did not determine a law for deciding civil judgments [*psāqā d-dinē*]."[18] In Hnanishoʿ's case, earlier patriarchs surely adjudicated comparable lay disputes; but there appears to have been no conception that such decisions might constitute a formal body of East Syrian civil law, and only in the seventh century did the ecclesiastical administration take an interest in preserving them.[19]

Shemʿon's and Hnanishoʿ's works, then, exemplify efforts to formalize ecclesiastical rulings as the substantive body of a more comprehensive, specifically Christian civil law tradition in a time of institutional transition effected by the Arab conquests. They point as well to the convergence of marriage, kinship relations, and property rights as the social arena for which laypeople most frequently sought ecclesiastical help and into which the new conditions of caliphal rule most facilitated the extension of ecclesiastical authority. Late antique canon law had enjoined chaste sexual practice within the ancient institution of marriage. The establishment of the Umayyad Caliphate provided bishops of the Church of the East the opportunity to begin bringing the material imperatives of household reproduction under the purview of Christian law as well.

MARRIAGE AND RELIGIOUS BELONGING IN GREATER SYRIA

Unlike their East Syrian contemporaries, bishops in formerly Roman Syria and western Mesopotamia (as well as in Egypt) were not as actively concerned with extending ecclesiastical law into lay civil and household affairs. This difference stems from the fact that the end of Roman rule and the fall of the Sasanians had different implications for the caliphate's Christian subjects. It is likely that the Christians of formerly Sasanian Iraq and Iran were less interested in going to the Zoroastrian judges of a no longer Zoroastrian state when they could turn to their own clerics instead, a grassroots impetus for the East Syrian ecclesiastical experimentations with communal law in the seventh century. In formerly Roman provinces, by contrast, the same Christian administrators, upper and lower clergymen, and others who served in judicial capacities remained more or less in place in the decades after the conquest (excluding those who fled with the Roman armies). Bishops in Syria thus did not have the same motivation as those in Iraq and Iran to emphasize new loci of judicial authority or to actively reconstitute their legal traditions to encompass inheritance law; they already had Roman law, or whatever was understood as Roman law in any given locale. What they did face was a shifting socioreligious landscape as the conquerors settled in the towns of Syria, bringing their new monotheistic message with them. Against this backdrop, the marital practices of Syrian Christians received heightened pastoral attention, evident in a range of episcopal letters, from bishops seeking to define social boundaries between their flocks and the conquerors.

The contrast between the institutional innovations undertaken by bishops in the eastern caliphate and in Syria is particularly evident among the Chalcedonians, those Christians who adhered to Roman imperial orthodoxy. In the first decades of the seventh century, jurist-bishops in Greek-speaking territories had continued the characteristically late Roman concern with legal codification, as inspired by Justinian, by composing the first nomocanons, novel collections of civil and ecclesiastical law;[20] but after the conquests, we have no evidence of comparable endeavors by Chalcedonian bishops living under the Medinan caliphs or the Umayyads. The Syriac Orthodox or West Syrian Church, defined in theological terms by its opposition to Chalcedonian orthodoxy and its adherence to miaphysite Christological doctrines, presents a somewhat different case. Some West Syrian bishops of the later seventh century invested considerable energy in consolidating a communal legal tradition particular to their church. The major figure in this development is Jacob of Edessa (d. 708), a monk and bishop originally from the region around Antioch and known for his reformer's zeal.[21] By Jacob's time, the West Syrian Church had achieved a degree of institutional distinctiveness in northern Syria and western Mesopotamia, with a hierarchy of bishops parallel to the region's Chalcedonian one and a network of closely associated monasteries.[22] In the late seventh century, Jacob took an interest in consolidating a specifically West Syrian ecclesiastical law that would both tie his church to the early Christian heritage and further define its institutional boundaries. To do so, he translated a variety of Greek pseudo-apostolic canonical works into Syriac. He then brought them together with Syriac versions of other works of canon law, especially ecumenical synods and the epistles of Church Fathers esteemed by miaphysites, into an authoritative collection of ecclesiastical legal texts.[23]

By and large, the texts in this collection were traditional ecclesiastical ones addressing church affairs. Jacob's goal was thus to define a West Syrian ecclesiastical canon rather than expand it to newly encompass lay civil matters. In seeking to increase the institutional distinctiveness of the miaphysite church in Syria and focusing on legal canonization, moreover, Jacob was perhaps continuing late Roman trends more than he was responding to immediately postconquest conditions. Importantly, however, canonization was not Jacob's only concern. He also penned a considerable number of responses to lower clerics on problems related to ritual and social dimensions of lay life.[24] These and similar responsa of other bishops in the former Roman east were very much addressed to the particularities of life under Umayyad rule; and they point us toward another central feature, alongside the communal administrative autonomy permitted to subject elites, of the seventh-century caliphate: highly heterogeneous patterns of religious practice and intensive social contacts of individuals across the religious spectrum, which added up to religious identities below the elite level very much at odds with the picture offered by normative, doctrinal texts. Furthermore, the episcopal responsa extant from early Umayyad Syria demonstrate the degree to which the household and marital practice became significant sites for the articulation of communal boundaries in the midst of this diversity. Caliphal rule did not impel bishops in Syria to claim innovative new jurisdictions for Christian law to the degree that their contemporaries did in Iraq and Iran. But they did take an interest in regulating specific marital practices in an effort to define the acceptable modes of interaction between Christians and others, especially the region's new rulers.

While the religious elites of the late antique and early medieval Middle East had vested interests in keeping their communities clearly differentiated in both social and religious terms, there is good reason to think that those boundaries were often much more fluid, at least from the sixth century into the eighth.[25] The sources of this period are littered with examples of less doctrinal, more capacious conceptions of religious belonging that allowed for many modes of social and ritual interaction between individuals of different religious affiliations. The mishmash of peoples, scripts, and magical spirits of the Aramaic incantation bowls—where it is unremarkable to find a Christian commissioning a protective incantation against Iranian demons from a Jewish magician—is one good example. To take a few others from Christian-authored texts, we find that a villager baptized in the Church of the East might feel no compunction receiving communion from miaphysites, or that Christian Arab tribesmen might readily join Muslims on raiding expeditions and slide into praying alongside them.[26] These individuals and countless others like them were embedded in any number of social networks, from villages to business partnerships to tribes and even marriages, not perfectly congruent with their confessional communities.[27] Especially in rural areas, where the vast majority of the region's population resided, hints in the sources suggest that loyalty to local leaders and local sources of sacred power could mean as much to conceptions of religious affiliation as the lettered elite's doctrines; the religious practices and social obligations that confessional belonging entailed thus look increasingly varied the further away any given community was from the instruction and oversight of literate, trained religious elites like bishops, rabbis, or Zoroastrian priests.[28] Overall, it appears that many subjects of the late antique empires did not understand religious belonging as an identity so exclusive as to determine all social ties, institutions, and ritual activities in which one could participate. The emergence of nascent Islam, moreover, likely intensified these already heterogeneous and hybrid socioreligious patterns. What were the faith commitments of the new ruling Arab tribesmen, whom their Christian subjects called *magaritai* and *mhaggrāyē* in reference to their self-designation as "militant emigrants" (*muhājirūn* in the seventh-century Arabic usage) who had come from Arabia to conquer the known world?[29] They proclaimed the God of Abraham and venerated Jesus the Messiah. In Syria they tended to settle in old urban centers (rather than found new garrison cities as in Egypt and Iraq), and in the early days after the conquests they sometimes performed their prayers in churches.[30] If some non-elites already did not know or care much about the distinctions between Chalcedonians, miaphysite West Syrians, and

Nestorians, what made these new Abrahamic monotheists so different? The general indeterminacy of the relationship between the Arabs' religious movement and other scriptured traditions likely rendered the boundaries between conquerors and conquered uncertain in the eyes of many.

That uncertainty should not be taken to imply that religion "on the ground" was a free-for-all, however, and here the responsa of bishops like Jacob enter the picture. Most late antique subjects must have understood themselves to belong to one religious community or another, whatever they understood the content of its traditions to be; there were certain actors for whom religious difference was very clear and to be enforced with violence;[31] and local institutions (such as kin networks and village leaders) created boundaries of their own that made religious difference socially concrete, as most assuredly did political hierarchies between conqueror and conquered. This, in fact, is where the writings of religious elites like bishops, rabbis, and Muslim ulama become especially instructive. They frequently focus on the specific contested practices around which elites and others made competing claims as to how religious belonging should impact social relations and how religious difference should be enacted; beyond simply attesting to fluid socioreligious boundaries, elite prescriptive texts identify the particular institutions through which they sought to solidify those boundaries. For our purposes, the responsa literature of seventh-century Syrian bishops underscores the significance of marriage in just this respect. The Arab conquerors, as a new element introduced to already diverse socioreligious environments, refocused ecclesiastical attention on defining the marital practices and attitudes toward sexuality that were a chief feature distinguishing Christians from others.

Two areas of concern are especially evident in the responsa: sexual contact between Christians and the new rulers and polygamous marriages. Regarding the former, for example, Jacob of Edessa responds in a letter to the priest Adday to the question of whether a Christian woman married to a Muslim (*mhaggrāyā*) can still receive communion—a concern especially pressing because, in this case, "her husband is threatening to kill the priest [*gāzem baʿlāh ʿal kāhnā d-qāṭel lēh*] if he does not give her the Eucharist."[32] Elsewhere, Jacob takes up the question of the appropriate penance for a Christian who commits adultery with a non-Christian.[33] An epistle of the West Syrian patriarch Athanasios II of Balad (r. 684–87) and a series of questions and answers by the Chalcedonian monk Anastasios of Sinai (fl. late seventh century) also address the permissibility of interreligious marriage.[34] Anastasios considers as well the spiritual status of enslaved Christian concubines of Muslim masters.[35] The ecclesiastics disapprove of all of these cases, though they accommodate them to differing degrees and to different ends that we will examine in detail in Chapter 8. For now, it suffices to note that household ties and sexual contact between the Arab conquerors and subject Christians were not uncommon in the first decades after the conquest, whether through marriage or because women among the considerable numbers of captives taken by the conquerors could be pressed into slave concubinage.[36] This spurred bishops to assert that religious difference required social separation: whatever they were, the Arab conquerors were not orthodox believers, and as such marriage with them was to be avoided.

Polygamy crops up conspicuously as well in bishops' responsa from seventh-century Syria, and it too has significant implications for the confessional stew of the Umayyad Caliphate. Polygamous household forms had no doubt been customary in many corners of pre-Islamic Arabia and were sanctioned by the Quranic passages understood to allow men four wives and any number of concubines that they could support (e.g., 4:3). When the conquests exported these practices to the conquered territories, the similarities between Christianity and the conquerors' scriptural religion appear to have made polygamy's lawfulness a newly live question for some lay Christians. So, a letter written by a mid-seventh-century West Syrian bishop named Yawnon counsels one Theodore, a traveling priest, on how to refute challenges to the Christian principle of monogamy that Theodore had been receiving. Anastasios also takes up the question as to why, when "those under the Law [i.e., the biblical forebears] often had two wives at the same time and were not condemned for it," Christians may not do the same. A ruling of Jacob of Edessa's prohibiting anyone from taking multiple spouses is salient here as well.[37] In the case of polygamy, the permeable socioreligious boundaries engendered by the conquerors' settlement in the lands of the old empires gave new currency to a marital practice long condemned by ecclesiastical tradition, and hence to the Christian household as an arena in which the bishops could prescribe differentiating practices.

The responsa of Jacob, Athanasios II, and Anastasios, which fit broadly into the genre of ecclesiastical law by virtue of their prescriptive nature, treat many ritual, liturgical, and administrative matters in addition to the family. The latter subject did not command the overwhelming attention of Chalcedonian and West Syrian bishops in the early caliphate, nor did they newly reshape their legal traditions to cover civil areas like inheritance in the manner of their contemporaries to the east. But in the context of the region's already varied religious landscape and the new uncertainties introduced by the conquerors' confession, marriage and the household came into renewed focus for Syrian bishops as institutions requiring ecclesiastical regulation and around which they could articulate the social obligations attendant to Christian belonging.

GEORGE I GOES TO QATAR: CREATING CHRISTIAN MARRIAGE

While social structures in the seventh-century caliphate exhibited strong continuities with the recent past, Christian clerical elites also responded to conditions brought on by the conquests in innovative ways. In Iraq and Iran, East Syrian bishops expanded ecclesiastical law and judicial activity to cover lay inheritance; in Syria, West Syrians and Chalcedonians sought to regulate newly contested lay marital practices as an already diverse indigenous population encountered its new ruling class. These themes—expanding Christian legal institutions, fluid socioreligious boundaries, and practices associated with the household—converge in the most potentially transformative social regulation enacted by a bishop in the seventh-century caliphate: George I's canon proclaiming that ecclesiastical law and priestly ritual granted unions between laypeople the status of marriage. In the late antique empires, a revisionist Christian sexual morality had coexisted with durable civil legal structures that regulated the public side of marriage; George's arrogation of the institution to the exclusive authority of ecclesiastical law at the Persian Gulf synod of 676 was therefore a radical move, one enabled by the wide latitude for communal administration that Umayyad rule granted ecclesiastics.[38] The canon had immediate and local concerns: it was geared toward securing the integrity of the church of eastern Arabia amid shifting political and socioreligious patterns that nascent Islam had introduced to the region. It also, however, had wider implications. In stressing a fundamental connection between marriage and the public shape of the religious community, George's canon set a precedent for how to conceive of and regulate Christian social groups within the Islamic empire that bishops in later centuries would develop in novel and significant directions.

The particular prescriptions of George's canon were several. They revolved around the steps unwed Christians would have to take in order to marry, and the role of priests and the church in that process:

> Women who have not [yet] been married[39] and are [fit to be] given in betrothal by their fathers' house[s] shall be betrothed to men through Christian law [*b-nāmosā krēsṭyānā*], according to the custom of the faithful. [This shall be accomplished] through the consent of their parents, the mediation of the holy cross of our Savior, and a priestly blessing [*burktā kāhnāytā*]. Because it is easy for Christians, unlike the rest of the nations, strangers to the fear of God, to err in lawful marriage [*shawtāputā d-zuwwāgā nāmosāyā*] and adhere to something else, it is necessary and all the more beneficial that a contract between the betrotheds [*tanway da-mkirē w-da-mkirātā*] be [confirmed] in the presence of the Creator of our life and the Giver of our salvation. [This is] so that if they break the pact of their union, *the sign of our victory* [*nishā d-zākutan*, cf. Philippians 3:14], through which all our hidden things are revealed and our deeds scrutinized before the tribunal of His fearsome glory, shall seek vindication of them [*it [h]u l-hon tāboʿā*]. Together and through a priestly blessing, then, [the betrothed ones] shall affirm faithfully that they conclude, by the blessing, the bond of their union [*assārā d-shawtāputhon*], according to their hope [for salvation in the world to come]. If, however, they transgress against these things because they want to marry in a new way and despise the established law, when they come to deceive each other they shall be left without vindication [*tbaʿtā*], for they have been deprived of the priestly blessing. They shall not deserve to be freed from the injustices [that they visited upon] each other through [ecclesiastical] decisions.[40] Along with these things, they shall also be anathematized from the church.[41]

In George's presentation, properly Christian marriage is demanding; the high standards of Christian sexual morality make it much easier for Christians to go astray than it is for adherents of other religions, with their looser sexual and marital norms. Therefore, it is only appropriate that ecclesiastical officials oversee marriages between Christians, ensuring that they have been contracted in the presence (*qarributā*) of God. Henceforth, the Church of the East shall recognize only betrothals blessed by a priest in a proper Christian ritual as legitimate; the priestly blessing, consent of the spouses' parents,[42] and a vocal affirmation of consent on the part of the spouses themselves are the constitutive elements that bring a valid betrothal contract (*tanway da-mkirē w-da-mkirātā*) into effect.[43] If some dispute arises over the contract or between the spouses, they may seek settlements from ecclesiastical judges. If Christians do not marry through a priestly blessing, however, not only will they be unable to have disputes adjudicated by ecclesiastics. They shall also be banned from the church—that is, from receiving the Eucharist and thereby participating in Christian communion, the path to salvation.

George's canon offers a considerable reformulation of marriage as a legal institution. There had been a variety of judicial avenues through which Christians in the late antique Middle East contracted marriages and formed households, and though ecclesiastical officials and blessings were often involved, the norms of civil law traditions were commonly understood to grant public recognition of a marital union's validity. In George's formulation, marriage is no longer a civil institution within which laypeople are expected to behave in appropriately Christian ways. The institution itself is now under the purview of Christian law (*nāmosā krēsṭyānā*); to marry requires correct ritual performance in conformity with that law; and as a contract and a legal relationship, marriage is constituted through its ritual elements, chiefly the priestly blessing, rather than consensual cohabitation or handing over a dowry. To fall short of this, moreover, means not only that one's marriage is not legally valid; it is to lose the right of participation in Christian communion. George, in other words, has remade getting married as a religious practice, an act through which the faithful embody their commitment to a specific divine tradition and its clerical custodians. This formulation is notable for its silence on the other modes of association that marriage traditionally mediated in the late antique Mediterranean world; it evinces no concern to invoke the authority of a king, assert citizenship or subjecthood in an empire, or acknowledge a civil tradition like the "Roman custom" of the Nessana contracts we saw in the previous chapter. If baptism and the Eucharist were the traditional rituals that initiated individuals into Christian communion, George's canon brings marriage to a similar level as a ritual practice that facilitates continued membership in that communion.

To those familiar with the sacrament of marriage of later Christian traditions, the idea that getting married is fundamentally a religious practice defined by religious law may seem unexceptional. Nothing, however, is necessary or natural about that idea. When George issued his canon in the late seventh century, there was no systematic sacramental theology of marriage in any major Christian tradition, including the Latin one; these would develop only later in the medieval period.[44] The notion that administering the formation of marriage bonds was exclusively the domain of the religious tradition and its clerics was decidedly novel. In fact, given that East Syrian synods of the Sasanian period routinely issued a smattering of canons related to marriage, it is all the more striking that only in 676, under the rule of the caliphate, did George make marriage the Church of the East's canonically delimited territory.[45]

Why did he do so when he did? Particular conditions arising from the Arab conquests and initial spread of Islam, concentrated in this case in eastern Arabia, provide the answer. These conditions included ecclesiastical schism, the specter of apostasy to Islam, and the unacceptable heterogeneity of local marital practices, especially the pattern of Christian women marrying non-Christian men. From the point of view of East Syrian bishops like George, these developments impinged alarmingly upon the social integrity of eastern Arabia's Christian communities and, ultimately, the Church of the East as a whole. One way to attend to this threat was to affirm a constitutive connection between the religious community and marriage, that ancient institution whose purpose was to facilitate the formation of households and the social reproduction of the human species. Bringing that institution under the purview of ecclesiastical law was an effort to ensure its proper practice in service to the religious community: reproducing not only the species in general but the true-believing individuals and households that together made up the church. By making marriage exclusively subject to the law of the religious tradition, George promoted a specific vision of East Syrian Christians as a distinct social collectivity within the caliphate.

Rebellion, Apostasy, and Polygamy on the Persian Gulf Coast

The immediate impetus for George's synod of 676 on the Persian Gulf island of Dayrin was ending a schism between the East Syrian patriarchate and the ecclesiastics of Bet Qatraye that had developed a generation earlier.[46] Under George's predecessor as patriarch, Ishoʿyahb III (r. 649–59), the bishops of Fars—the ecclesiastical province on the Iranian side of the Gulf to which the Qataris were subordinate—had declared their autonomy from the patriarchate in Seleucia-Ctesiphon, the former Sasanian capital in central Iraq. Fars was an old and venerable see that claimed apostolic foundation; it appears that when the Arabs overthrew the Sasanians, the ecclesiastics of Fars saw no reason to recognize the bishop of a now defunct imperial capital as their superior.[47] While they ultimately reconciled with Ishoʿyahb, their fellow bishops of Bet Qatraye continued to claim autonomy for themselves. Only under George did the various factions come to terms; he and six Qatari bishops convened the synod of 676 to formalize the reconciliation.

From Ishoʿyahb and George's perspective, an ecclesiastical schism like the Qataris' represented a major loss to the Church of the East. The bishops of Bet Qatraye severed an entire province from its ecclesiological structure when they removed themselves from communion with Seleucia-Ctesiphon. The laypeople of Bet Qatraye were in danger of losing their chance at salvation, as the ecclesiastical stewards who mediated their communion with the body of Christ had disconnected their link with the true church. The patriarchate, moreover, lost the spiritual, human, and material resources embodied in the region's Christian communities.[48] That loss was magnified, moreover, by the specter of apostasy occasioned by the Arab conquests and the spread of the Arabs' new religious movement. According to the Islamic tradition, the coastal regions of eastern Arabia (comprising the caliphal districts of al-Bahrayn, roughly equivalent to Bet Qatraye, and ʿUman) were incorporated into the Arab-Muslim polity fairly swiftly in the 630s.[49] However confessionally distinct Islam was or was not at that early date, the Arabs' new religious movement certainly spread in the region, at the very least among its Arab tribes—and at a cost to the Church of the East. We know from several of Ishoʿyahb's letters that the Christian inhabitants of Mazun, the Syriac name for the peninsula of ʿUman or a town thereon, had recently joined the religion of the Arabs (Syriac *ṭayyāyē*). The Mazunites did so to avoid paying a tax imposed by the conquerors: "They forsook the faith [*shbaq[w] haymānutā*] forever but held onto half [their] possessions [*pālgut qenyānē*] for a little while."[50] Mazun was a single bishopric, so its apostate Christian community was unlikely to have been large.[51] Nevertheless, Ishoʿyahb's reference demonstrates that losing believers in the Arabian Peninsula to the rulers' new religious movement was a real possibility in the eyes of the bishops. Significantly, Ishoʿyahb invoked the memory of the Mazunites' apostasy in his attempts to end the schism between the patriarchate and Bet Qatraye. "A single departure from the faith, like that of the Mazunites, would already have been enough for Satan," he wrote in a letter to the laypeople of eastern Arabia, "but the bishops of Fars and Bet Qatraye, zealous to forsake Christianity . . . even more than what Satan wanted [*āp yattir men mā d-ṣābē [h]wā sāṭānā*], have signed, sealed, and delivered [their] apostasy [*ktab[w] wa-ṭbaʿ[w] w-shaddar[w] kāporutā*]."[52] In the patriarch's eyes, the Qataris' ecclesiastical schism and the Mazunites' apostasy both contributed to the same problem: losing the very believers who constituted the church of eastern Arabia.

Against this background, George's synod assumed the task of securing the integrity of that social and institutional body. Besides ending the ecclesiastical schism, George's canons aimed to correct deviant local practices, which would put Bet Qatraye's Christians back on the path to salvation and simultaneously construct clear social boundaries between them and other locals of different religious affiliations. This aim is apparent in the synod's canons that regulate interactions with non-Christians, including prohibitions of litigating before non-ecclesiastical judges, socializing at Jewish taverns, and participating in ostentatiously "pagan" mourning rituals.[53] Marriage, however, had a special place in this effort. Among the Qataris' "practices in need of correction" condemned by George's canons were those same marital ones familiar to us from postconquest Syria: polygamy, concubinage, and marriages between Christian women and non-Christian men. In a region where the East Syrian patriarchate's hold on the local Christians was already tenuous, these marital practices threatened communal integrity in two distinct ways: by leading believers astray in the current generation and by perverting the divinely mandated, proper method for reproducing future ones. George's canon §16 states that men who take multiple wives or concubines, according to "pagan customs" (*ʿyādē ḥanpāyē*) and in contravention of the church's teachings, "have become estranged . . . from all Christian honor" (*hwaw mnakrēn . . . l-kul iqārā da-krēsṭyānē*).[54] Canon §14 castigates Christian women who marry unbelievers (*ḥanpē*), most likely meaning members of the Arab ruling class, since doing so introduces them to "customs of strangers to the fear of God" (*ʿyādē d-nukrāyin l-deḥlat Alāhā*)—that is, it pushes them toward apostasy.[55] In these respects, aberrant marital practices, like the other modes of interreligious contact addressed by George's canons, threatened to thin the ranks of believers in Bet Qatraye. George's prescription of ecclesiastical administration of marriage between Christians was an effort to tamp down this danger—to ensure that marital unions harmonized with ecclesiastical expectations and thereby kept laypeople within the communal fold, particularly in a region where ecclesiastical schism and apostasy had shaken the patriarchate's confidence in the local church's foundations.

More than other "practices in need of correction" among the Christians of Bet Qatraye, marriage was further significant because it had implications for future generations of believers in addition to the current one. Marriage was the institution that facilitated the reproduction of the human species in accordance with God's plan. The problem for George in seventh-century Bet Qatraye was that the institution itself was not necessarily reproducing good, true-believing Christians. This concern is especially evident in George's condemnation of interreligious marriage, which is gendered—it concerns only women, not men, who marry non-Christians—to a specific and significant end. As Chapter 8 discusses in greater detail, legal regimes that regulate the marriage of women across group boundaries are fundamentally efforts to manage the group's reproductive resources. It was a standard assumption of the patrilineal societies of the late antique and medieval Middle East that husbands and fathers defined the religious affiliation of their families.[56] Therefore, when a Christian woman married a non-Christian man, her reproductive potential was lost to her natal community, as her children would affiliate to her husband's religion. If ecclesiastical schism and apostasy represented immediate, collective losses to the Church of the East, marriages with the conquerors threatened its communal integrity by draining away potential believers from future generations.

George's marriage canon was a response to these conditions. Asserting Christian law's constitutive authority over marriage was an effort to secure the continued reproduction and integrity of the Church of the East as a socially embedded body of believers, particularly in a region with a recent history of ecclesiastical schism and Islamic expansion. Making the institution subject to Christian law and ecclesiastical oversight meant ensuring that marriage was put into proper practice producing future generations of faithful Christians, the very substance of the church as a discrete community within the caliphate's diverse society. Toward these ends, George took the novel step of redefining the social and legal institution of marriage as an exclusively Christian one.

Marriage and the Religious Community in Islamic Late Antiquity

George's canon, like other ecclesiastical efforts to regulate Christian households in Syria, Iraq, and Iran, was a response to a host of local contingencies. In this case, it was the unstable ecclesiastical politics and religious dynamics of seventh-century Bet Qatraye that demanded renewed attention to lay marital practices. George's formulation of Christian marriage, however, had implications that went beyond its local impetuses. Issued as it was by an ecclesiastical synod, George's canon was couched in a universalizing language that implied universal applicability. Christian women "shall be betrothed to men through Christian law"; anyone who transgresses this principle "shall also be anathematized from the church." By virtue of the form in which these strictures were issued, they theoretically applied not only to the Christians of Bet Qatraye but to all the laypeople under the purview of the Church of the East. It would take East Syrian bishops another century to revisit in a dedicated fashion the juridical implications of George's assertion that religious law, rather than that of the state, tribe, or other association, was the ultimate arbiter of the ancient institution of marriage. But already in the Umayyad Caliphate, it implied a reformulation of the social contours of the Christian community and brought East Syrian tradition into step with neighboring religions.

The idea that the law of the religious community had constitutive authority over marriages between its adherents had prevailed for some time among Jewish rabbis and Zoroastrian priests, and it was in the process of articulation as well among seventh-century Muslims. A distinctively Jewish law of marriage was already integral to the Mishnah and two Talmuds, the repositories of communal legal tradition around which rabbinic Judaism coalesced over the course of late antiquity.[57] The rabbis crafted a specifically Jewish law of contractual marriage that reshaped biblical prescriptions, aiming thereby to "creat[e] a collective memory, a formation of one Israel through the perception of continuous communal adherence to laws that stretch back to the primal myths."[58] While it is clear that many Jews in antiquity attended to their legal affairs, including contracting marriages, through a variety of civil legal orders,[59] the rabbis' tradition affirmed a fundamental connection between marriage and the wider religious community of their followers. Similar perspectives prevailed in the Zoroastrian priestly tradition: marrying was a meritorious act in the service of the Good Religion, while the prescriptions of Sasanian inheritance law encoded the Zoroastrian emphasis on reproducing male lineages in order to perpetuate the worship of the good deity Ohrmazd.[60] Finally, God's revelation to Muhammad in the Quran contained a considerable body of norms relating to the family and household life.[61] Quranic legislation reformed or systematized the marital practices of pre-Islamic Arabia, and in so doing affirmed the authority of God and His law over marriage as an Islamic institution.[62]

George's canon (and Shemʿon and Hnanishoʿ to a lesser extent) put forward the same notion for a Christian constituency. Like Quranic legislation, George's East Syrian law unmoored marriage from the civil frameworks—whether regional practice, tribal custom, or imperial law—that might also govern the institution and define its role in forming households and reproducing social relations. To what degree Christians actually followed his prescription is a different question that later chapters take up. But in normative terms, these seventh-century developments in East Syrian tradition asserted that the ancient human business of household formation and reproduction properly served and belonged under the purview of the religious community rather than any other human collectivity. The learned elite of late antiquity's exclusivist religions largely shared the perspective that confessional belonging was an all-encompassing identity that subsumed other loyalties. Christianizing marriage as a legal institution brought East Syrian tradition in line with its neighbors in propagating that notion; and it undergirded a conception of the church as one of many social bodies within the Islamic caliphate that bishops in later centuries were to amplify and refine.

While the establishment of the seventh-century caliphate did not explode the communal structures of the vast and varied subject populations under its rule, neither did it leave them untouched. The clearing out of former political elites and the accession of new ones interested in little more than tribute, taxes, and obedience from their subjects left room for subject elites to creatively reform their communal institutions. For Christian bishops in Iraq and Iran, that meant assuming more active judicial roles in their local communities, penning new corpora of ecclesiastical law, and asserting the independence of local ecclesiastical organizations from hierarchies established under the Sasanians. Into regions characterized by frequent interaction among individuals of different confessions and loose attitudes toward which religious rituals and communities any individual might participate in, the conquerors added nascent Islam to the mix. For bishops as for other subject religious elites, this created both a necessity and an opportunity to define more explicitly those social and ritual practices attendant to orthodox faith, especially in light of the sometimes uncomfortable proximity between Christian and early Muslim attitudes toward God, Jesus, and prayer.

Central to all of these adaptations to the new order of the seventh century was the Christian household. Bishops in Iraq and Iran mediated inheritance disputes and offered guidelines for the transmission of family property and thus the material constitution of Christian lineages, assuming more explicitly a role for ecclesiastical law that had belonged previously to the Sasanian judiciary. In Syria and Iraq, marriages between conquerors and Christians and a burgeoning interest in polygamy on the part of some laymen made marital practices a newly significant locus for the definition of Christian social distinctiveness. Most strikingly, George I responded to shifting socioreligious dynamics and fractious ecclesiastical politics in eastern Arabia by redefining marriage itself as an exclusively Christian institution. Bringing proper order to the institution that was the linchpin of social reproduction would secure the boundaries of the local Christian community in a changing corner of the caliphate. Thus, beyond the accession of a new political elite and the rising public predominance of a new religion, the establishment of the caliphate in the seventh-century Middle East set off reverberations that, in the form of ecclesiastical regulation, reached even into the households of Christian subjects.

The universalizing claims of George's synod notwithstanding, each of the creative adaptations by seventh-century Christian religious elites to postconquest conditions was piecemeal and responsive to particular, local circumstances. After the fall of the Umayyads, however, the increasing confidence and formalization of caliphal institutions of governance and Islamic traditions would elicit a different response from Christian elites. Under the rule of the early Abbasid caliphs, Christian bishops—especially West Syrians and East Syrians—undertook a more comprehensive effort at communal institutional reshaping: a reinvention of ecclesiastical law that placed marriage, the household, and the practices of social reproduction squarely at the foundation of Christian churches as non-Muslim social groups within the caliphate.

CHAPTER 3

Forming Households and Forging Religious Boundaries in the Abbasid Caliphate

Humans are distinct and separated from each other, in countries and lands, peoples and languages, customs and laws. Each of them desires a way of life in accordance with the customs and laws in which they have been habituated and raised. Indeed, they never depart from something when they have been habituated and raised in it. They accept change from something when they have been established in it only with difficulty and thousands of dangers; for custom is second nature, as the saying goes. . . . Who, then, can bring to a unity and gather together that which, a thousand times over, is separate and differentiated according to its [very] nature . . . ?

—East Syrian patriarch Timothy I, *Law Book*

In 805, Timothy I, the sitting patriarch (r. 780–823) of the Church of the East, composed the words above in the preface to a new book of civil regulations for East Syrian Christians. Although they are highly rhetorical, their sentiment contrasts notably with George I's remarks delivered to the synod of Bet Qatraye some 129 years earlier. While both concerned the rules that guide human beings' actions, Timothy expresses none of George's confidence in the power of bishops to put those rules into effect. Instead, he evokes a near bewildering diversity of peoples for whom God has established no single, unitary law. Human beings are a motley, mixed-up collection of creatures; trying to bring some order to mundane, messy human societies—that human condition "which, a thousand times over, is separate and differentiated according to its [very] nature"—is an unenviable task. Yet despite his protestations of the difficulty involved, this is precisely what Timothy set out to do with his new *Law Book*: to compile a single law for social practice to govern Christian believers, those peoples united by a shared faith but heretofore diverse in their "way of life." His interest in doing so was motivated by wider transformations in the institutional order and intellectual life of the caliphate in the late eighth and early ninth centuries. Timothy's *Law Book* exemplifies the response of many Christian elites living at the heart of the empire to those transformations: a reformulation of Christian communal belonging rooted in a new confessional law and a new conception of the Christian household.

The first century and a half of the Abbasid dynasty's rule, beginning in 750, is widely regarded as a crucial phase in the development of medieval Islamic society. Muslim caliphs, administrators, and scholars refined institutions of caliphal governance, from court ceremonial to taxation to the dispensing of justice; the Islamic dispensation realized its universal potential as non-Arab Muslims came to participate in the *umma*, the Muslim community, as fully as did descendants of the Arab conquerors; foundational intellectual traditions like Islamic law and theology took shape. Yet the early medieval caliphate remained a diverse, multiethnic, multireligious empire, and its vast numbers of non-Muslim subjects, especially the numerous Christians in its core territories west of Iran, both participated in and were affected by the transformations of Muslim state and society. Where early Umayyad rule had come with significant continuities in administration and social organization for the caliphate's subjects, developments in the Abbasid period spurred non-Muslim elites to rethink and reform their own communal institutions and traditions far beyond the concerns of their seventh-century predecessors. Their efforts to do so offer a vital vantage point—the intersecting interests of the empire and its subject elites—from which to trace the formation of the early Abbasid Caliphate's social order, so foundational a model of "medieval Islamic society."

Christian law and the Christian household lie at the center of this story. If bishops under the Umayyads had claimed new forms of legal authority in piecemeal fashion, the twin development in the late eighth and early ninth centuries of a reforming caliphal judiciary and vigorous traditions of Islamic law spurred bishops to cultivate Christian civil law as a holistic intellectual discipline. Abbasid-era bishops produced legal treatises, synodal legislation, and law books in Syriac and Arabic that sought to regulate an unprecedented array of lay affairs—marriage, inheritance, commercial transactions, even irrigation disputes. For West Syrians and especially East Syrians, the expansion of confessional civil law—and the corollary notion that religious belonging could be embodied in routine social practices—was a signal response to the emerging Abbasid order and an effort to define their place within it. This new Christian law, furthermore, focused on one area of social relations above all others: the family. Where bishops under the Umayyads had made new efforts to regulate marriage or inheritance, under the Abbasids they brought under their authority the full range of material practices by which households were formed and reproduced: marriage contracts, property exchanges and marital gift-giving, the disbursement of inheritances at a spouse's death. In doing so, the bishops effectively reimagined the Christian character of the institution of the household as resting not only in sexual discipline but in the particular material relationships and social hierarchies of which it was constituted. That triangulation between ecclesiastical authority, confessional law, and the Christian household would define the church as a social body—as a non-Muslim religious community in the emerging public order of an Islamic empire.

STATE AND SOCIETY UNDER THE EARLY ABBASIDS

When George I held his Persian Gulf synod in the second half of the seventh century, the Islamic caliphate's center was Syria, the powerbase of the Umayyad house whose rule Muʿawiya had established in the 660s. A century later, George's ecclesiastical successors lived in what was quickly becoming a very different empire. After political upheavals in the mid-eighth century led to the accession of a new ruling dynasty, the Abbasids, the caliphate's imperial center shifted to the cities of Iraq; and both state and social structures of the caliphate began to change in marked ways. Several interrelated developments underway in the new Iraqi heart of the caliphate had a special impact on its Christian subjects and spurred the significant transformations among them that are our primary concern. These developments included the growth of urban centers of enormous linguistic, ethnic, and religious heterogeneity; the withering of ethnic divisions between Arabs and others within the Muslim *umma*; the formation of Islamic intellectual disciplines like Hadith study, jurisprudence, and theology; and efforts to centralize or formalize key institutions of caliphal governance, including the courts, the norms of caliphal justice and their connection to Islamic jurisprudence, and the *dhimma* framework for regulating the caliphate's non-Muslim subjects.

The Abbasid dynasty came to power in the mid-eighth century on the back of religious and ideological opposition to the Umayyads, which had simmered within the Muslim *umma* for decades.[1] Since the first civil war from which Muʿawiya emerged the victor in 661, the Umayyads had faced frequent discontent from constituencies within the Arab-Muslim elite that saw their rule as tyrannical and hoped to replace it with a just regime led by relatives of the Prophet Muhammad. This politics became attractive as well to many non-Arab Muslims dissatisfied with their second-class status and what they saw as an exclusivist Arab chauvinism built into the Umayyad order. Among the several anti-Umayyad movements of the period, the most successful developed especially in Khurasan in northeast Iran in the 740s. With support from Arab nobles, Persian-speaking soldiers of mixed Arab and Iranian descent, and many more recent converts to Islam, this originally secret movement broke into open revolt in 747. After winning a series of battles against Umayyad armies and exterminating much of the Umayyad family itself, the rebels installed a new ruling clan of closer relation to Muhammad (though not nearly as close as many rebels had hoped): the Abbasids, so called by virtue of their descent from the Prophet's paternal uncle al-ʿAbbas. The Abbasids shortly moved their base of operations to central Iraq, which had long been a hotbed of support for the Prophet's family. The region's agricultural productivity and trade routes made it an economic powerhouse, and from 750 well into the ninth century the Abbasid Caliphate established itself as one of the most powerful states in Afro-Eurasia (rivaled only, perhaps, by Tang China).[2]

It is customary to speak of the Abbasids' rise to power as a "revolution," an image evoked by the fact that their movement began as a clandestine one and that it swept aside an old regime.[3] Just as important, the accession of the Abbasids created the conditions for significant changes in the social, religious, and political patterns of the caliphate. For one, the caliphate's urban centers became increasingly diverse homes to a wide range of peoples. How justly the Abbasids ruled is up for debate, but there is little doubt that an unprecedented degree of participation of non-Arabs in the political and cultural affairs of the caliphate characterized the new order. Iranian Muslims from the eastern provinces, the core of the Abbasids' supporters, filled the caliphate's high administrative posts, and the Khurasani soldiers settled in Baghdad were a new and very different demographic presence in the Fertile Crescent.[4] Besides the influx to Iraq of eastern

Iranians, the wealth and opportunities for patronage in the empire's main cities continued to attract the attention of a wide variety of individuals (almost always men) on the make. Civilian non-Arab Muslims, stigmatized in previous generations for their lack of pedigree, rose to prominence as religious scholars, state functionaries, and litterateurs as a matter of course in the early Abbasid period.[5] Ethnic and religious diversity had certainly already been characteristic of Umayyad cities, but it intensified in the Abbasid period as a result of the partial breakdown of the ethnic hierarchies of the Umayyad order, the magnetic pull of wealth, and the ongoing rise of Arabic as a lingua franca and thus a source of cultural capital irrespective of speakers' backgrounds. The conditions of Abbasid rule thus made the participation of an enormously diverse population in the high culture and governance of the caliphate increasingly unremarkable. Non-Muslims, especially East Syrian Christians whose demographic weight lay in Iraq but also Melkites, Harranian pagans, and others, gravitated toward the Abbasids' urban centers and served the empire conspicuously as administrators, physicians, and other professionals.[6]

This mixing of populations set the stage as well for the formation of a host of vital Islamic intellectual traditions. Islam's doctrinal content and the practical obligations of being Muslim were of course already at issue in the *umma*'s earliest days. But in the Abbasid Caliphate's mix of new Muslims, old Muslims, and non-Muslims, many new and different answers were on offer for how an adherent of any given religious tradition was supposed to act and what one was supposed to believe. That setting, combined with Arabic's growing literary prestige and the introduction of paper as a cheap, easy writing material, facilitated the initial coherence of several disciplines of study that would be foundational to the medieval Islamic tradition.[7] Scholars dedicated to rationalistic inquiry into metaphysical truth cultivated Arabic theology (*kalām*) and Arabic philosophy in the tradition of late antique Greek thought (*falsafa*). The collection, study, and emulation of Hadith, traditions of the Prophet's sayings and doings, continued among a very large subsection of pious Muslim scholars who had no patience for the speculations of theologians and philosophers. Most germane to our concerns is the formation of Islamic jurisprudence (*fiqh*).[8] In the second half of the eighth century, Muslim jurisprudents (or their students) increasingly committed to paper the legal norms and methods of legal analysis they devised through study of the Quran, the example of the Prophet, and various local traditions of legal practice going back to the Prophet's Companions. The later Sunni schools of law located their origins in the traditions and circles of the major Muslim jurisprudents of this era: Malik ibn Anas (d. 795) in Medina, Abu Hanifa (d. 767), Abu Yusuf (d. 795), and Muhammad ibn al-Hasan al-Shaybani (d. 805) in Iraq, and Muhammad ibn Idris al-Shafiʿi (d. 820) in the Hijaz, Iraq, and Egypt, not to mention other prominent jurists in Kufa, Basra, and Arabia whose traditions of study were subsumed by the other schools.

Closely related to the formation of Arabo-Islamic intellectual traditions was the reorganization and consolidation of institutions of caliphal governance, especially the judicial apparatus in Iraq and elsewhere, under the early Abbasids. In general, Abbasid caliphs and their advisors undertook a variety of projects aimed at centralizing legal, administrative, and religious authority in their hands. Al-Maʾmun's (r. 813–33) demand that the ulama assent to particular theological doctrines is perhaps the most well-known example,[9] but other, more nuts-and-bolts efforts were often more effective in the long run. Scribal formulas that are impressively consistent across tax documents from provinces as distant as Egypt and Khurasan point to a strongly centralized fiscal administration already under al-Mansur (r. 754–75).[10] Similarly significant were the Abbasid efforts to reform the caliphal judiciary. Judicial institutions in the caliphate had been relatively less centralized and systematized under the Medinan caliphs and the Umayyads. Judicial appointments were largely at the discretion of regional governors, and it was entirely unexceptional for individuals not appointed as agents of the ruling house, such as tribal arbitrators and the exceptionally pious, to be treated as figures of judicial authority and recourse.[11] Judicial procedure and the norms dispensed by judges, furthermore, appear to have varied considerably from city to city, as the Abbasid vizier Ibn al-Muqaffaʿ famously lamented.[12] While some of these patterns persisted for centuries—no premodern state as large as the caliphate could have put an end to all of them—the Abbasid caliphs nonetheless devoted significant energy to centralizing and adding a degree of systematization to the empire's diverse and diffuse judicial institutions, often with effective results. Principally, al-Mansur began the practice, brought to fruition under his successors, of centrally appointing the judges (*quḍāt*, singular *qāḍī*) of every major town in the caliphate. Harun al-Rashid (r. 786–809) is credited with establishing the office of chief judge (*qāḍī l-quḍāt*) as a member of the court and advisor to the caliph.[13] Overall, the Abbasids' projects brought new consistency to the learned judges' audiences that increasingly became the model Islamic judicial institution, particularly in populous, closely administered Iraq.[14] This meant, moreover, a degree of imperial patronage and support for the civilian religious scholars who developed the Islamic jurisprudence administered in the courts. While the ulama would long maintain a venerable tradition of reticence to accept state appointments in light of the injustice associated with rulers, the Abbasids appear to have had a hand in spurring the consolidation of the early Hanafi school of law, as caliphs beginning with al-Mahdi (r. 775–85) favored the students of Abu Hanifa for major judicial posts.[15] Caliphal judicial reform and the formation of Islamic jurisprudence thus ran in tandem and partially informed the other's success.

Such, then, is the view of the Abbasid revolution and its aftermath from an imperial metropolitan perspective: a diversifying Muslim ruling class and population, the formation of Arabo-Islamic intellectual disciplines, and caliphal institutional reform and centralization. If the crux of early Abbasid history is often presented as these forms of "classical" Islam first beginning to cohere, however, the majority of the Abbasids' subjects, certainly in the eighth and ninth centuries and perhaps a good deal later, were not Muslim and did not have a direct stake in the urban Muslim elite's creative wrangling over Islamic identity. But that does not mean that the empire had no impact on their worlds. The religious and political traditions of non-Muslims had informed Islam and the caliphate since their initial formation; in the Abbasid period, we can view the continued development of the caliphate's socioreligious order in non-Muslims' adaptations to new Abbasid institutions and trends in Arabo-Islamic intellectual culture. For the ecclesiastical elites of the Christian communities that lived at the heart of the caliphate, the West Syrians in northern Syria and the Jazira (the caliphate's northern Mesopotamian province) and especially the East Syrians in the Jazira, Iraq, and Iran, playing out the imperatives of Abbasid empire meant buttressing communal judicial institutions and creating newly expansive traditions of Christian law. Above all, that law aimed to extend the authority of the ecclesiastical hierarchy into Christian households and over the full range of practices by which Christians formed and reproduced families, kinship networks, and lineages. From the vantage point of the intellectual labors and administrative interests of contemporary Syriac bishops, the evolving Abbasid social order took shape at the intersection of empire, subject communal institutions, and the Christian household.

CREATING CHRISTIAN LAW AT THE HEART OF THE ISLAMIC EMPIRE

Christian Subjects in Muslim Courts

The formation of new traditions of Christian law and the communal reconfigurations they imagined were one response on the part of Christian elites to the increasing organization of the caliphate's institutions and the expectations that caliphal governance placed on non-Muslim subjects. If the early caliphate had tended to leave to subject elites the administration of their communities' civil affairs, in the Abbasid period Muslim jurists and state officials began to articulate this practice of convenience as a more explicit principle of Islamic governance. Their discussions revolved around the concept of the *dhimma* or "pact of protection." With roots in the Quran and the seventh-century administration of conquered territories,[16] in the eighth century the *dhimma* came to denote the legal status of non-Muslims in the Islamic polity. The caliphate granted each non-Muslim religious group the status of a "protected" (*dhimmī*) community and a certain degree of autonomy to regulate its own affairs; in return, dhimmis were obligated to recognize the caliphate's supreme authority, obey its commands, pay taxes, and follow regulations that distinguished Muslims from dhimmis and maintained the public predominance of Islam.[17] Muslim jurists and officials began to theorize and spell out in greater detail these strictures especially in the late eighth and ninth centuries, motivated in part by the socioreligious diversity of Abbasid cities and the centralizing interests of the Abbasid caliphs. A variety of treatments of the place of non-Muslims in caliphal state and society circulated or were promulgated in this period, such as the *Kitab al-Kharaj* of the Abbasid chief judge Abu Yusuf and the regulatory edicts of the caliph al-Mutawakkil (r. 847–61), among others.[18] No single approach to the public regulation of non-Muslims appears to have achieved canonical or official status in this period,[19] but the multiplicity of views on offer makes clear that defining the contours of *dhimma* governance was a priority for many Muslim jurists and officials in the first Abbasid century.

In certain respects, the *dhimma* framework worked in the favor of non-Muslim religious elites: it recognized a high degree of communal authority to rest with bishops, Jewish communal leaders like exilarchs and rabbis, and Zoroastrian priests. The institutional order of the early Abbasid Caliphate, however, presented distinct challenges to this vision even as Muslim officials more or less actively propagated it.[20] Caliphal judicial institutions, as they took a more organized form and as interreligious contact in the cities became more intensive under the early Abbasids, appear to have appealed to Christians, Jews, and others as well as Muslims. Principally, state courts were attractive because legal affairs transacted and rulings reached there had the backing of state (or at least local police) power. Contemporary sources contain numerous indications that Christians and Jews made frequent use of the services state courts provided; but this posed problems in turn for non-Muslim religious elites. Already in the seventh century, George I had asserted the exclusive authority of East Syrian bishops to adjudicate disputes among Christians; from the perspective of the caliph and many Muslim jurists too, that prerogative was the proper territory of non-Muslim religious elites. But George's competition had been a variegated array of lay notables, holy men, and Muslim officials. By the late eighth and ninth centuries, a town or city in the caliphate's central lands not only retained the local political authority as a figure of judicial recourse; increasingly, its judicial institution of recognizable prominence was the more formalized court of a Muslim *qadi*, a professional who administered a vigorously developing Islamic jurisprudence and had been favored by an appointment from a regional governor or the caliph himself. The fact of non-Muslim recourse to caliphal courts thus challenged elites' ideas of communal integrity, which prioritized discrete institutional spaces enclosing all true believers.

A range of responses to these conditions is discernible across the caliphate's non-Muslim subject populations. The geonim of central Iraq's Jewish academies, for example, followed rabbinic precedent in grudgingly tolerating the use of extraconfessional courts under limited circumstances.[21] Significantly, however, they already had the extensive, detailed law of the Babylonian Talmud, which they considered authoritative for Jewish communal life, to administer in their own rabbinic audiences.[22] The situation was different for the bishops of the caliphate, especially the East Syrians who lived in its central territories and were often closely connected to the caliphal court. Their inherited traditions of ecclesiastical law had never appropriated the full prerogatives of the late antique civil law systems alongside which they coexisted before the establishment of the caliphate. In spite of the new judicial territory that Umayyad-era bishops carved out for themselves, Christian writings of the early Abbasid period make clear that no church's ecclesiastical elite knew a tradition of law extensive enough to govern the full complement of civil affairs for which laypeople might seek the services of extraconfessional courts and officials. The East Syrian patriarch Timothy writes of laypeople "who, on account of lacking [Christian] judgments and laws [*laytāyutā da-psāqē d-dinē wa-d-nāmosē*], continually go to the audiences of the outsiders [*barrāyē*] and [their] courts."[23] Another eighth-century bishop tells his audience that "while Jews everywhere have one civil law [*dinā*]—as does the heresy of Magianism [Zoroastrianism] as well as those who rule over us now [i.e., Muslims]—among Christians, judgments are different . . . even from district to district and city to city."[24] The same Christian elites report receiving requests for guidance in the administration of civil affairs from bishops in major cities including Basra and Rayy and the provinces of Fars and the eastern Jazira.[25] Episcopal letters, of which exceedingly few have survived but of which there must have been many, show bishops responding to similar requests from humble priests in central Iraq, eastern Arabia, and even Yemen.[26]

In sum, unlike the geonim and contemporary Muslim jurists and in spite of developments under the Umayyads, Christian elites lacked a coherent communal law with which to engage the transforming institutions of the early Abbasid Caliphate. Their response was to create one. In Syria, Iraq, and Iran from the eighth to the tenth century, bishops composed a considerable number of new legal treatises, issued new bodies of synodal legislation, and translated important received texts into Syriac and Arabic. The elaboration of Abbasid imperial institutions thus spurred the formation of newly comprehensive traditions of communal law among the Middle Eastern churches.[27] This, moreover, proved an opportunity for bishops to redefine the social practices and obligations attendant to Christian belonging within caliphal society—which they did with special focus on the Christian household. Before we bring that operation into focus, however, we need a sense of the contours of the new traditions of Christian law crafted by Abbasid-era bishops: who the major figures were and what their major contributions were. The extent of bishops' engagements with law varied across the caliphate; for reasons we will examine, East Syrians cultivated law as an intellectual discipline most concertedly and creatively, while West Syrians and Melkites did so to lesser degrees. The following focuses on the East Syrians' response to the evolving Islamic empire and the transformations to law, community, and the lay household that it involved. Using East Syrian materials as a touchstone, we can then index other churches' engagements with communal law and, in turn, the differential impacts that the caliphate's institutions had on the shaping of its non-Muslim subject communities.

East Syrian Law in Abbasid Iraq and Iran

The emergence of East Syrian law as a newly dynamic intellectual tradition in the early Abbasid Caliphate is evident in the steady stream of innovative Syriac and Arabic legal treatises, compendia, and translations produced by East Syrian bishops beginning in the eighth century. The characteristic feature of this tradition is a novel textual genre: the law book or legal treatise composed by the individual jurist-bishop.[28] Shemʿon of Revardashir's mid-seventh-century *Law of Inheritance* had been an early step in this direction and a departure from the East Syrians' earlier ecclesiastical law. In the early Abbasid period, East Syrian bishops followed this precedent and composed many more such specialized jurisprudential treatises; but rather than treating a single topic, the East Syrian law books of the Abbasid period aimed for a greater degree of topical comprehensiveness. They thus became the base material of a wide-ranging Christian communal law meant to address the needs of dhimmi life in the caliphate.

The first, signal example of this new trend is the *Jurisprudential Corpus* of Ishoʿbokt, a later successor to Shemʿon as metropolitan bishop of Fars. We know little of Ishoʿbokt's life other than his Persian geographical and cultural background and the 770s as the probable time frame of his ordination as a bishop.[29] His *Jurisprudential Corpus*, composed in Middle Persian but extant in a Syriac translation, is a remarkable text: it draws on Sasanian law to bring an unprecedented breadth of practices under a single ecclesiastical legal regime. In an introductory discourse, Ishoʿbokt notes that he has received requests for a unified Christian law for his eparchy of Fars from his suffragan bishops. He tells the reader that he will create one by committing to writing the laws "adhered to in the tradition [*yubbālā*] of [our] ancestors in our area," supplemented with the customs of other orthodox Christians.[30] In other words, Ishoʿbokt set out to transmute the judicial custom (*ʿyādā*) of Fars, its churches, and its peoples into a Christian civil law (*dinā*, *dinē*) embodied in a written text.[31] Comparison of the *Corpus* to a late Sasanian juridical compendium, as well as Ishoʿbokt's use of technical Middle Persian terminology, demonstrates that the local traditions he drew on were essentially Iranian-Sasanian law, still familiar among non-Muslims in eighth-century Fars.[32] Further exceptional was the breadth of his interests: the *Corpus* comprises six extensive treatises covering legal theory, marriage and divorce, testate and intestate succession, various forms of contract, and judicial procedure. In a single work, Ishoʿbokt claimed the authority to cover practical topics as diverse as what makes for a legitimate betrothal contract, how to give loans and charge interest, and how to pay hired laborers.[33]

The *Jurisprudential Corpus* was highly innovative in the great range of legal subjects it brought under a single ecclesiastical regulatory regime. It was also fairly provincial in its connection to southwest Iran, having been written in Middle Persian rather than Syriac and taking local traditions as its focus. In fact, since we do not know exactly when in the eighth century Ishoʿbokt flourished, it is best to think of his work primarily as continuing a Persian Christian jurisprudential tradition in the vein of Shemʿon even as it responded to caliphate-wide legal developments. In Fars, ecclesiastics like Shemʿon and Ishoʿbokt were literate in Middle Persian, familiar with Sasanian law, and best situated to appropriate that law into their own, provincial sphere of judicial activity as caliphal institutions developed around them. Despite its provincialism, however, the sheer range of Ishoʿbokt's law book was exceptional; and when it circulated in the Church of the East's Iraqi heartlands, it became an influential model for East Syrian patriarchs and other jurist-bishops responding to the growing hegemony of Islamic law and the caliphal judiciary. Timothy I, the East Syrian patriarch from 780 to 823, approached Ishoʿbokt's work in just this manner. Timothy was a particularly prominent bishop whose long reign left an indelible mark on the intellectual culture of Abbasid Iraq and the historical trajectory of Syriac Christianity.[34] He was trained in the East Syrian schools of the hill country of the eastern Jazira, the Church of the East's demographic heartland and home to many monasteries and associated institutions of learning. Timothy is probably best known for his theological disputation with the caliph al-Mahdi dramatized in one of his letters and his Christian missionizing efforts in Central Asia. Just as significant were his more prosaic activities related to East Syrian law. In fact, Timothy stands out as the first patriarch on record to try both to consolidate the disparate, varied Christian legal works of earlier centuries and to bring the provincial concern for civil law evident in Ishoʿbokt's writings into the broader tradition of the Church of the East. In a word, his efforts mark the formation of East Syrian law as a comprehensive communal tradition encompassing both ecclesiastical and lay affairs.

These efforts are visible, again, in the textual record. Timothy commissioned the translation of Ishoʿbokt's *Corpus* from Middle Persian into Syriac; he may have been responsible for the translation of Shemʿon's legal treatise as well.[35] Furthermore, he was likely responsible for a redaction of the East Syrian *Synodicon*,[36] the collected proceedings of the Church of the East's late antique synods and related legal texts, as well as for incorporating into it the *Syro-Roman Law Book*,[37] a late antique Syriac translation of commentaries on Roman law. Overall, Timothy appears to have had a strong interest in identifying and collecting various received texts that could together define a canon of East Syrian law. But the majority of these received texts did not offer much guidance for regulating the social relations of laypeople, so just as significant are Timothy's own original legal writings. In addition to several epistles that treat family law,[38] Timothy collected ninety-nine of his judicial rulings, prescriptions, and legal responsa into a single composition, his *Law Book*. Much like Ishoʿbokt's work, Timothy's *Law Book* was a practical juristic collection intended to give ecclesiastical judges the material they might need to adjudicate lay civil affairs and obviate laypeople's interest in going to caliphal courts, an aim Timothy highlights in the work's preface.[39] To this end, the *Law Book* covers three major areas: the order and prerogatives of the ecclesiastical hierarchy; marriage and divorce; and inheritance. Though not as long or as systematic as Ishoʿbokt's *Corpus*, Timothy's *Law Book* thus represents a major evolution in the traditions of Christian law in the Islamic world. It is the first work we know of that not only sought to regulate both ecclesiastical and lay civil affairs in a detailed fashion but, by virtue of having been composed by a sitting patriarch, claimed the authority to do so for the entire Church of the East.

Timothy's interest in legal canonization and original composition mark the initial coherence of East Syrian law as a lettered tradition encompassing both ecclesiastical and civil affairs. Several other jurist-bishops active in Iraq throughout the ninth century refined that tradition further. Timothy's successor as patriarch, a monk from the Mosul region named Ishoʿbarnun (r. 823–28), continued the precedent set by Timothy that the Church of the East's chief bishop should also be a jurist. Ishoʿbarnun had studied with the same esteemed teacher as Timothy and subsequently took monastic vows at one of the eastern Jazira's most prominent East Syrian monasteries, but his patriarchal career was shorter and less spectacular than Timothy's—he is perhaps best known for his intense antipathy toward his predecessor and for trying to remove his name from the diptychs of the patriarchal church. Ishoʿbarnun did, however, compose a longer, substantial *Law Book* of his own on the model of Timothy's.[40] Ishoʿbarnun's work brings together the patriarch's decisions and responsa to lower ecclesiastics on legal topics, and it covers extensively lay civil affairs. The bulk of the *Law Book* treats marriage, divorce, and inheritance, while the remainder includes rulings on slavery, loans and debt, theft, and monastic and ecclesiastical order. After Ishoʿbarnun, succeeding generations of East Syrian jurist-bishops took up the task of synthesizing the episcopal law books and the earlier received materials into new treatises and civil law digests. In the mid-ninth century, ʿAbdishoʿ bar Bahriz of Mosul's *Order of Marriage and Inheritance* summarized the marriage law provisions of earlier works and offered a new system of inheritance law.[41] Not long after, Gabriel of Basra (fl. late ninth century) compiled excerpts from late antique canon law texts, East Syrian synodal canons, and rulings from the Islamic-period law books into treatises on distinct legal topics, creating the first systematic compendium of East Syrian law.[42]

ʿAbdishoʿ and Gabriel thus brought the tradition of East Syrian communal law to a clear stage of canonization. By the end of the ninth century, that tradition's corpus of texts was extensive enough to require new works to streamline its disparate rulings and doctrines. In matters of ecclesiastical law proper, the corpus stretched back to pseudo-apostolic writings from Christianity's early days and bishops' synods from the Roman and Sasanian empires. East Syrian civil law, on the other hand, was largely a recent creation of the Islamic period. The civil law sections of ʿAbdishoʿ's and Gabriel's systematizing works draw from the legal treatises of Shemʿon, Ishoʿbokt, Timothy, and Ishoʿbarnun but no comparable earlier or unknown sources.[43] A tradition of East Syrian communal law that sought to regulate not only ecclesiastical affairs but also the social, economic, and familial relations of lay Christians had thus taken shape as both a response to and a function of institutional conditions in the early Islamic caliphate. By the end of the ninth century, bishops in Fars and especially Iraq had developed that tradition into a coherent intellectual discipline cultivated by ecclesiastical jurists.

CHRISTIAN FAMILY LAW AND THE RELIGIOUS COMMUNITY

While the early Abbasid-era works of Christian jurisprudence were composed as resources for ecclesiastical judges, they were not merely a solution to an administrative problem. They also prescribed new norms of behavior for laypeople; creating Christian civil law was an opportunity for bishops to conceive in new ways of how Christian belonging was to be enacted and Christian communities constituted within caliphal society. To this end, the East Syrian legal works of the early Abbasid Caliphate show that the bishops had one principal area of social relations in view: the family. Where George I had prescribed ecclesiastical oversight of marriage contracts, Abbasid-era works of East Syrian law evince a broader concern to regulate the full range of practices and institutions associated with the formation and reproduction of households—marriage, inheritance, familial property rights. By gathering these into a single regulatory regime, the bishops put forward a new conception of the Christian household as a social institution. In doing so, moreover, they enjoined both a vertical solidarity between ecclesiastics and laypeople and a horizontal uniformity in the shape of lay households. Beyond giving ecclesiastics tools for judicial practice, Christian law marked out the linkage between ecclesiastical authority and the practices that formed laypeople into their most fundamental social units as the key element that constituted the Church of the East (and the West Syrians, as we will see later) as a social collectivity—a subject religious community—in the caliphate.

This operation of Christian law differed both from earlier Christian approaches to marriage and from strategies of socioreligious boundary drawing undertaken by other elites in the early Abbasid Caliphate. Abbasid-era East Syrian bishops focused on the economic relations and social hierarchies that made up households rather than their pious sexual discipline, the major concern of late antique Christian writing on the family, and they devoted far less attention to other realms of social interaction—marketplace commerce, for example—than did Muslim or Jewish jurisprudents. Crucially, the workings of Abbasid-era Christian law also exemplify the formation of the caliphate's social order at the dovetailing interests of an imperial and a subject elite. The prerogative for dhimmi elites to regulate their communities' internal affairs was a feature of caliphal governance; the interest in extending ecclesiastical authority further into Christian households and the very notion that there was such a thing as a household with a distinctively Christian material-social constitution were the result of subject elites playing out the imperatives of the circumstances of caliphal rule. Caliphal governance tacitly acknowledged the identities propounded by non-Muslim clerical classes and institutions as discrete social groups and left it to the clerics to fill in their substance; the clerics, for their part, had an interest in twinning theological identity with clear social boundaries and distinctive social practices. In the heartlands of the caliphate the result was a new formulation of Christian community rooted in ecclesiastical law's new definition of the Christian household. Like other Christian traditions, East Syrians already had distinct (though developing) doctrinal identities, clerical classes, and ecclesiastical institutions prior to the emergence of Islam. It was the extension of ecclesiastical authority into lay households and the prescription of uniform practices of lay social reproduction that newly defined them as a socioreligious group within the public life of the Islamic empire.

Creating the Christian Household

The scope of the East Syrian law produced by Ishoʿbokt, Timothy, and other jurist-bishops differed notably from the legal traditions cultivated by contemporary Muslims and Jews. Muslim ulama aimed to discern, to the best of their abilities, God's will for proper behavior in every facet of human life, including both ritual duties and social interactions (*ʿibādāt* and *muʿāmalāt*). The Babylonian Talmud comprised the rabbis' Oral Law of equally wide scope as well as centuries' worth of their dissections and analyses of it. While the East Syrian jurist-bishops sometimes give the impression that they aimed similarly to compile a comprehensive, "unified ecclesiastical legal code,"[44] the vast majority of their law's positive content focused on one sphere of social relations: the family.[45] It did so, moreover, in a particular way: going beyond the interests of earlier ecclesiastical law, its goal was regulating the full complement of material-social practices that formed and reproduced households and lineages.

A brief tour through Timothy's *Law Book* can give us a broad sense of this operation. Consisting of ninety-nine rulings in total, the work's first seventeen treat traditional ecclesiastical concerns like clerical duties. The rest of the law book is family law, and it is family law of a particular kind: its rulings regulate the material practices of social reproduction that are channeled through marriage as a legal institution. The work's first family law section defines how the marriage bond as a contractual relationship comes into public, legal effect: it details certain rituals that must be carried out (principally the priestly blessing) and conditions that must be met (e.g., that bride and groom not be of too close relation, which Timothy treats in a series of casuistic rulings).[46] The following section takes up cases in which the validity of the marriage bond is brought into question.[47] What happens, for example, if a man betrothed to a woman travels on business and disappears? What if a spouse is stricken with an illness that makes sex impossible? In answering these and similar questions, Timothy defines the ongoing obligations that marriage brings into effect: chiefly material support, owed by husband to wife, and mutual fidelity. Together, then, the first two sections of Timothy's treatment of family law define the creation, maintenance, and obligations of marriage as a legal relationship. The law book's final and most substantial sections revolve around what happens when a marriage ends—essentially, who has the right to inherit which kinds of property when a marital bond is dissolved due to a spouse's death.[48] The rulings explore a multitude of casuistic scenarios. For example, which of a deceased man's sons, married daughters, and unmarried daughters inherits his estate? May a deceased woman bequeath her property to her siblings rather than her husband? Two major concerns are evident throughout Timothy's inheritance law: establishing the primacy of sons' rights as heirs and providing guidelines for female relatives' inheritance rights and the disposal of their property.

The content of Timothy's law book is broadly representative of other Syriac works of civil law produced in the early Abbasid Caliphate, and it exemplifies what jurist-bishops were trying to accomplish when they expanded the scope of their confessional legal traditions. Where George I had used ecclesiastical law to Christianize marriage as a public institution, Abbasid-era bishops did so with the household itself in its material and social composition. The bulk of their law prescribes norms at two key nodes of the social reproductive cycle: the initial formation of the marriage bond and the transmission of property when death (or in certain cases, divorce) dissolves that bond. Those practices in turn produce a specific set of social relations among the spouses, their relatives, and their children. These relations are all hierarchical, ordered by age and gender. Fathers and uncles, for example, are granted a chief role in arranging marriages, which reinscribes the authority of the senior generation of males in new legal relationships.[49] Men are charged with providing their wives both an initial marriage payment and ongoing material support, the obligations constitutive of their patriarchal authority.[50] Sons are allotted the lion's share of their deceased fathers' estates because a male offspring "sustains the lineage and seed of his father" (*mqim gensā w-zarʿā l-abu[hy]*)—the son's inheritance embodies the social value of patrilineal descent in material terms and reproduces it in a new generation.[51]

The East Syrian jurist-bishops have a name for the web of material and social relations that their rulings produce: the *baytā*, the patriarchal, patrilineal household. A semantically broad Syriac word, *bayta* denotes a "house" in the sense of a physical abode as well as an estate or a patrimony—everything a man owns or has authority over, including but not limited to material possessions. Effectively, the bishops' law conceives of the Christian household as these intersecting senses of *bayta*: the set of relations of dependence upon a husband and father, the dependents living physically with and under the authority of that patriarch, and his patrimonial property. So, for example, a bride receives her dowry "from the *bayta* of her father" (*men bēt abuh*); when the marriage is finalized, she has "entered [the husband's] *bayta*" (*ʿellat l-bētēh*), her father having "sent her out of his *bayta*" (*shaddrāh men bētēh*) to "another guardian and *head*" (*yāṣopā ḥrēnā w-rēshā ḥrēnā*; cf. Ephesians 5:23).[52] Here, the father's *bayta* is the material estate of which his daughter receives a portion; but it is also his sphere of authority, and marrying for a woman means moving from one man's *bayta* to another. A *bayta*, furthermore, might be multigenerational—the patriarch's sons might have sons of their own who "work entirely in the *bayta* like their uncles." Eventually, the various male descendants establish their own households (*bātē dilhon*), each taking his portion (*mnātā*) of the original *bayta* as the material corollary to his inherited patriarchal authority.[53] Besides wives, female blood relations, and junior males, the bishops' conception of the *bayta* also includes slaves as another class of dependents.[54] More than a list of family members, the *bayta* connotes in sum the hierarchical relations among those members relative to a central male figure, as well as his material and symbolic capital—his property and family name.

There is nothing particularly exceptional about medieval male elites like the East Syrian bishops promoting a highly gendered, hierarchical conception of the household.[55] What is notable is that they did so in such comprehensive legal terms and in their capacity as religious authorities. By bringing under their purview the full range of social-reproductive practices for which marriage was the fulcrum, the Abbasid-era bishops defined a novel institution in the *bayta*: the Christian household as constituted not only by theological categories and sexual discipline but by particular material relations and social hierarchies. This was certainly innovative with respect to their received traditions. Seventh-century East Syrian bishops already defined marriage as a Christian legal institution; at least since Ephesians 5's instructions to wives to be submissive to husbands, major strands of Christian tradition routinely endorsed standard Mediterranean patriarchal norms. But the legal works of Ishoʿbokt, Timothy, and Ishoʿbarnun reached directly into the nitty-gritty practices that materially constituted patriarchal social orders; their detail and comprehensiveness were a departure from the general perspectives and piecemeal laws of the earlier tradition.

Furthermore, the East Syrian bishops' law differed from received Christian approaches that treated the household primarily as a site for disciplining sexuality or emulating the ecclesiological communion between Christ and church. Christian teachings are certainly evident in the bishops' law books when they strictly limit divorce and condemn extramarital sex, as we will see in detail later. But on the whole, the law books are decidedly uninterested in sexual ethics within the domestic sphere. Unlike classic Christian treatises on the household like Clement of Alexandria's *Pedagogue*, for example, they give no direction as to how Christian husbands and wives should speak to each other or lie down to have sex.[56] Furthermore, the Abbasid-era legal texts are largely devoid of language associating theological or typological meanings to marriage on the model of the relationship between Christ and the believers.[57] The bishops never refer to marriage as a *rāzā*, a "mystery" of divine union like baptism and the Eucharist. Furthermore, they use a wholly different, "secular" terminology of marriage to describe the groom and bride (*mkirā* and *mkirtā*) than that used in reference to Christ and church (*ḥatnā* and *kalltā*) in theological texts.[58] This does not mean that Syriac bishops had no conception of the theological import of marriage, and as liturgies for betrothal ceremonies developed they contained much church-as-bride imagery.[59] But the bishops' law had other goals. Rather than seeking to inculcate bodily piety or model cosmological meaning, its interests remained those moments when domestic affairs impinged on the public shape of wider communities and hierarchies: the formation and dissolution of marriage bonds and the concomitant rearrangement of familial connections and property interests. Bringing the full range of those practices under ecclesiastical purview was the chief concern of East Syrian law in the Abbasid Caliphate. Reformulating communal traditions in response to caliphal governance and Islamic law entailed a new definition of the household in its social and material configurations as a Christian institution.

The Dhimmi Community Between Christian Household and Islamic Empire

While the bishops' law undoubtedly had an intracommunal orientation as well as specifically Christian concerns in the marital practices it addressed, it also has broader implications for our understanding of the making of Abbasid society as a whole: it demonstrates the central role that subject elites and their traditions played in forging the normative model of the caliphate's multireligious, hierarchical social order. The *dhimma* framework of governance took for granted the clear boundaries of the non-Muslim religious communities it regulated. By the same token, much historiography takes that framework as descriptive of caliphal society, either presuming the essential coherence of Nestorians, Jacobites, Melkites, Rabbanite Jews, Qaraite Jews, and Zoroastrians as religious communities or implying that the propagation of the *dhimma* brought them into existence.[60] As we have emphasized, however, the caliphal social order should be understood not as an empirical fact but as the product of subjects' reception of and adaptation to the exigencies of living under caliphal rule. The early Abbasid period was decisive in this process, as its institutional consolidation and the newly intensive social mingling in its cities gave special motivation to subject elites to approach their communal institutions and traditions anew. The key point is that family law for East Syrians (and some other Christians) was the other side of the coin to the theological and ritual boundaries that communal elites were simultaneously invested in defining; East Syrian bishops' efforts to regulate lay households produced a particular notion of the Church of the East as an identifiable social group in the public life of the caliphate. The practical impact and lay reception of the new Christian family law were inevitably more complicated, as we will see in later chapters; but for the bishops, that law served as the chief social-regulatory means by which they could carve a discrete community out of the religiously and socially variegated Abbasid Caliphate.

By the early Abbasid period, the bishops of the various churches living under Muslim rule had generally strong, centuries-old "ecclesial identities" rooted in the particular Christologies and patristic authorities they studied in their schools and monasteries, although their doctrines would also be reformulated in the crucible of Arabo-Islamic theological discourse in the ninth and tenth centuries.[61] What those identities meant for the ritual participation and social relations of laypeople, however, could be much less clear; the magic bowls of Sasanian Iraq and Jacob of Edessa's Syria under the Umayyads have given us only two of many possible examples. If intensive social contacts and ritual participation across confessional boundaries characterized many corners of the late antique and early medieval Middle East, how were bishops to make their conceptions of religious affiliation concrete and meaningful for laypeople and lower ecclesiastics—how were they to translate the commitments formed in ecclesiastical settings such that they would define the boundaries of lay social relations and lay-ecclesiastical solidarities as well? The transformations of the Abbasid period provided East Syrian bishops the opportunity to do so through their new traditions of family law, pairing that mode of social regulation with an ongoing concern to enjoin orthodox ritual practice as the chief constitutive element of the religious community.

For the Church of the East, as for essentially all other Christian traditions, the mysteries of baptism and the Eucharist were the most foundational practices that integrated lay believers into a community of the faithful. This was both in a primary theological sense—by partaking of and becoming collectively the body of Christ—and through regular, bodily assembly as local congregations. From the high ecclesiastics' perspective, this communion—the theological and social constitution of the religious community—was only properly achieved through the mediation of ritual administrators of orthodox confession and ordination. This, however, was precisely one of the realms where fluid socioreligious boundaries threw a monkey wrench into their plans, as heterogeneous Eucharistic practices and ritual participation across confessional lines appear to have characterized much lay piety in the diverse socioreligious environments of Syria, Iraq, and the Jazira. In response, bishops invested considerable energy in enjoining ritual uniformity and orthodox communion, a concern that becomes especially evident in Syriac sources of the eighth and ninth centuries. West Syrian sources, for example, suggest an increasing focus on refining a distinctively West Syrian curriculum of study in order to better train priests, catechize the laity, and order lay ritual practices.[62] Among the East Syrians, a number of ecclesiastical and monastic figures in the first half of the eighth century put considerable effort into reforming and strengthening the network of East Syrian schools in the eastern Jazira, and thus increasing the learned religious elite's influence in local lay life.[63] The extant epistolary correspondence of early Abbasid-era East Syrian bishops, furthermore, shows that they frequently sought to reign in communion and baptism across confessional lines.[64]

Thus, across the diverse socioreligious landscape of the early medieval caliphate, high ecclesiastics intensified a long-standing concern to ensure that ritual practice mapped onto doctrinal identities, just as the conditions of Abbasid rule encouraged the formation of confessional laws that would draw Christian social boundaries in the public life of the caliphate outside the walls of churches and monasteries. Crucially, marriage and the household were the foundation of this effort. East Syrian law constituted the Church of the East as a socioreligious group in the Abbasid Caliphate by defining the Christian *bayta* as the preeminent lay social arena for the articulation of ecclesiastical authority and distinctively Christian practices, the corollary to orthodox belief and ritual participation. The Church of the East's historical roots stretched back to the Sasanian Empire, but it was neither an unchanging, static corporation now under Muslim rule nor one simply created by *dhimma* governance. Rather, confessional law made East Syrian Christians into the religious community that observers like al-Jahiz called the *nasṭūriyya*, the caliphate's Nestorians, at the intersection of ecclesiastical authority with the formative practices of Christian households.[65]

The degree to which the East Syrians grounded their notion of the religious community in the household is in some respects unsurprising.

Christian thought had a history of deep concern for sexuality; if the East Syrian bishops' focus on household reproduction departed from much received Christian teaching, it at least did so in a realm the bishops were used to scrutinizing. Familial disputes are also exactly the kind of endemic problem that we would expect laypeople to bring to ecclesiastics for adjudication, generating the rulings that made their way into written texts. Focusing attention on Christian households made further sense for the bishops, moreover, because of the circumscribed powers of sanction and enforcement they possessed as subordinate subjects of the caliph. We should not underestimate the degree to which the family appeared open to ecclesiastical instruction because this involved in part regulating the status of women and children—social actors who typically had less social capital and fewer avenues of recourse than men. Non-Muslim religious elites in the caliphate lacked authority over matters of public order and criminal law; but they were better positioned to establish it over their own subaltern communities' most subaltern members as defined by gender and age.[66] George I's concern at the synod of 676 to prevent Christian women from marrying non-Christian men is instructive here; the same gendered regulation of intermarriage appears in the eighth- and ninth-century Syriac legal sources as well,[67] which reminds us that the bishops saw regulating women's bodies and reproductive powers as one strategy for securing social boundaries that was actually within their grasp.

In other respects, however, the overriding focus of East Syrian law on the practices of household formation as constitutive of the religious community was quite singular, especially in comparison to developments in other contemporary legal traditions. While family law was unquestionably integral to contemporary Islamic and Jewish law, both delved equally into many other realms of social relations, like commercial transactions, funerary etiquette, and judicial procedure, which East Syrian jurist-bishops barely touched.[68] Where religious elites expected Muslims and Jews to embody their confessional affiliation in everything from their business contracts to the care for the dead and beyond, East Syrian law located Christian social distinctiveness squarely in the household. Furthermore, it is notable how little attention the bishops devoted to prescribing norms for the quotidian interactions with religious others that were routine throughout the Abbasid Caliphate. This was certainly a central preoccupation of formative Islamic law; in the same Baghdadi environments in which

Timothy and his successors lived, for example, Ahmad ibn Hanbal provided guidance to local Muslims on matters as minute as whether one might shake hands with a non-Muslim or address him familiarly with a respectful nickname.[69] When non-Christians show up in Timothy's *Law Book*, by contrast, it is in the context of general guidelines: whether Christians should go to Muslim courts (no), marry non-Christians (yes for men, no for women), appoint Muslims as guardians of their property (sometimes), or accept testimony from Muslims in ecclesiastical courts (sometimes).[70] East Syrian law did not ask of Christians to enact their confessional affiliation according to a script for mundane interactions with adherents of other religions; it associated the social contours of the religious community with particular marital practices much more narrowly and exclusively than did the normative traditions of contemporary Muslims and Jews.

If the East Syrian bishops took less interest in regulating other social relations, making marriage, the family, and the household the principal objects of their legal tradition was yet a particularly apt means to promote a notion of the Church of the East as a discrete social body—as one coherent religious community among the many that made up the caliphate's social order in the vision of religious elites. A conception of the church as an assembly of pious households had deep roots in Christian tradition, but the Abbasid-era bishops' focus on the material and social relations that constituted them had different implications. In the bishops' definition of the Christian household, their chief preoccupation was the points at which domesticity intersected with public, economic, and material affairs: when marriages bound individuals and families into new relationships and when their dissolution reaffirmed social bonds by transmitting property to the appropriate relatives. In prescribing norms in this realm, East Syrian law (or at least each individual jurist-bishop) flattened out any diversity of practice into a singular Christian model: it asserted that Christians had their own, particularly Christian way of coming to exist in the world and passing on material goods and social identity from one generation to the next.[71] Moreover, the bishops' definition of the *bayta* as the patriarchal household modeled the social hierarchies that would make up a broader Christian community. The *bayta* encompassed a foundational set of such hierarchies—gender, age, free/slave status—that were largely typical of the premodern Mediterranean world but which the bishops now put forward as normatively Christian by encoding them in their laws. Their gendered rulings on marriage and inheritance further imagined each *bayta* as bound into wider associations and solidarities—agnatic kinship (common descent in the male line) tied groups of patriarchal households into multigenerational patrilineages (Syriac singular *gensā*, *sharbtā*).[72] A Christian law of marriage and inheritance thus plotted households as nodal points and drew the connections between them that mapped a wider social body: the "holy Church of the orthodox Easterners" (*ʿēdtā qaddishtā da-triṣē da-bnay madnḥā*),[73] distinguished from Muslims, Jews, and others not only in doctrinal and ritual terms but also as the collectivity of believing households formed in their distinctively Christian way.

Finally, as bishops at the heart of the caliphate redefined the Christian household in response to caliphal judicial reform and Islamic law, they outlined not only Christian communal boundaries but a whole subsection of the empire's social order. It was their encounter with empire that engendered the bishops' consolidation of communal institutions and the new vision of Christian community their efforts produced. From this perspective, Christian law and the Christian household were functions of Islamic empire; their redefinition was a major facet of the experience of imperial rule for non-Muslims like the East Syrians who lived at its heart. On the one hand, caliphal rule meant restrictions on the public, political, and economic life of dhimmis in ways that were only becoming more formalized under the Abbasids. The proscription of public displays of non-Muslim religiosity and the prescription of differentiating physical signs were part of the normative order put forward by the *dhimma* tracts penned by Muslim scholars; the *jizya* poll tax was a basic, recurrent way in which non-Muslims experienced tangibly the differential legal status assigned to them by Muslim rulers. But discriminatory measures imposed from above are only part of the process by which the hierarchical, religiously differentiated societies of the medieval caliphate took shape. For all the pressures that caliphal governance placed on subject non-Muslims, it also offered the potential for the consolidation and even the strengthening of their communal institutions. For the East Syrians, those institutions were the ecclesiastical judiciary and the Christian household itself, the latter a product of the bishops' regulations for how laypeople were to form marriage bonds and transmit family property. While clerics had worked toward Christianizing lay sexuality for centuries, Islamic governance enabled the new link between ecclesiastics and lay households that defined the East Syrians as a religious community in the public order of the caliphate.

LEGAL TRADITIONS, HOUSEHOLDS, AND RELIGIOUS COMMUNITIES ACROSS THE CALIPHATE

The East Syrians are but one example of a non-Muslim community that not only "owed [its] institutional development to the kinds of changes wrought by Islamic rule" but whose development contributed to forging the social structures of the Islamic empire.[74] Indeed, the same holds true to one degree or another for each of the caliphate's dhimmi communities. Confessional lawmaking and the redefinition of the household, however, were not the only possible responses to the development of the Abbasids' empire by its subject populations; their efforts to retool their communal traditions differed depending on their respective intellectual resources and the character of their interaction with the agents and institutions of the Abbasid state. A comparison of the East Syrian case to the West Syrians, Jews, Zoroastrians, Melkites, and Copts will bring into starker relief the spectrum of roles played by non-Muslim elites in building the caliphate's social and institutional order and, for some of them, the special place of confessional law and the household in that process.

East Syrians and West Syrians

The East Syrians' concerted focus on reforming law and the household was in good part a function of the proximity between the bishops, Muslim jurists, and evolving caliphal institutions in Iraq and Iran. The East Syrians were concentrated in the caliphate's Iraqi heartlands, where Kufa, Basra, and Baghdad were centers of formative Islamic jurisprudence. Ecclesiastical interest in an expanded confessional law came especially from cities home to caliph-appointed judges, including Baghdad, Basra, Rayy, and Mosul.[75] Timothy and his patriarchal successors resided in the Abbasid capital from which the caliphs promulgated judicial reform and where the empire's chief judge had his seat. Timothy himself, whose activities were so influential in the expansion of the Church of the East's legal tradition, was well acquainted with the caliph's court.[76] The strength and pull of caliphal judicial institutions and emergent Islamic law were thus especially conspicuous from the vantage point of East Syrian bishops and laypeople. Additionally, several factors particular to East Syrian history and tradition contributed to their ecclesiastical elites' special focus on law. The East Syrians already had some elements of a distinctive communal law going back to late antiquity, a result of their status as the Christian subjects of a diverse, non-Christian empire even before the Arab conquests. Of further significance is the fact that the works of Theodore of Mopsuestia, the late antique exegete whose thought served as the foundation of the East Syrian doctrinal and scholarly tradition, evince a strikingly "positive notion of law."[77] Theodoran teachings accorded law a significant place in God's plan for humanity, a rationale from within East Syrian tradition that legitimated law as an intellectual discipline and gave bishops a language to define their role as Christian jurists. These factors, in addition to proximity to the centers of Abbasid power, the caliphal judiciary, and Islamic legal creativity, facilitated the special interest of East Syrian bishops in redefining the Church of the East through law and rooting its social profile in the composition of lay households.

The West Syrian case offers both telling similarities and contrasts. Other than the East Syrians, the West Syrian bishops of Iraq and the Jazira were the Christian elites of the early Abbasid Caliphate most invested in creating a confessional legal tradition, and they significantly expanded the content of West Syrian ecclesiastical law in Syriac. But differing intellectual resources and distance from the centers of Islamic legal thought meant that they did not cultivate law as an ecclesiastical discipline to the same extent as their East Syrian counterparts. Precisely contemporary to the uptick of East Syrian jurisprudential works produced in the late eighth to ninth century, a series of patriarchal synods convened in 785, 794, 812/13, 817/18, 846, 878, and 896 issued a new, substantial body of legislation for the West Syrian Church.[78] Two short jurisprudential tracts written by individual bishops survive from the ninth century as well.[79] While much of the synodal material covers the traditional, strictly ecclesiastical areas of canon law, it includes as well new regulations for civil matters, of which about two-thirds relates to marriage, divorce, and inheritance.[80] So, the synods assert for the first time in West Syrian tradition that only betrothals administered by ecclesiastical officials are valid; spend considerable time on the conditions that determine whether or not two individuals are eligible to marry; and regulate the exchanges of property between spouses that occur at marriage.[81] Thus, West Syrian civil legislation in the early Abbasid Caliphate was primarily focused on regulating the practices that constituted marriage as a public institution, and the other social bonds this entailed. Like their East Syrian contemporaries, West Syrian bishops took the opportunity afforded by caliphal rule to expand their legal tradition, and they focused especially on the intersection of ecclesiastical authority with marriage and the practices of lay household formation.

They did not do so to the same degree as the East Syrians, however, which illustrates the differing impacts that the caliphate's institutional reordering and the formation of Islamic intellectual traditions had on subject populations. Notably, the West Syrians simultaneously engaged those transformations less intensively than did the East Syrians while receiving their influence in the substance of West Syrian communal law. West Syrian bishops were certainly cognizant of Abbasid judicial consolidation; lay recourse to non-ecclesiastical courts appears as a prominent motivation for new ecclesiastical legislation in the synodal materials.[82] The confessional law the bishops produced in response, however, was simply never as extensive as that of the East Syrians. As far as we can tell, no West Syrians in the eighth and ninth centuries wrote dedicated jurisprudential treatises like their East Syrian contemporaries; their synodal legislation treated novel subjects but never as comprehensively or with the same casuistic detail as the East Syrians' law books. This probably does not have much to do with the character of the received tradition that the West Syrians had to draw on. While East Syrian bishops like Timothy could take inspiration from Middle Persian jurisprudence that the West Syrians could not access, East Syrian civil law prior to the eighth century was neither systematic nor comprehensive; and had they wanted to codify a more extensive Christian civil law, West Syrian bishops had the *Syro-Roman Law Book* (translated from Greek to Syriac by the eighth century) as a model.[83] Instead, their contentedness with traditional forms of synodal legislation was likely a result of physical and intellectual distance from the urban hubs of legal study and socioreligious diversity to the southeast. The West Syrian population centers were the western Jazira (northern Syro-Mesopotamia) and central Iraq, but the eighth- and ninth-century patriarchs responsible for expanding West Syrian law received their formation and tended to reside in the rural monasteries of the former region.[84] They interacted often with state figures, but the towns of the Jazira were never hotbeds of Islamic law or caliphal administrative experimentation comparable to Kufa, Basra, and Baghdad. West Syrian bishops thus responded to caliphal institutions by consolidating communal regulations and bringing the practice of lay household formation more fully under ecclesiastical authority. But the different character of their relationship to Islamic

Figure 2. The monasteries and schools of the Jaziran hill country were centers of learning and intellectual formation for future bishops. While the East Syrian patriarch sat in Baghdad, West Syrian patriarchs tended to reside in the monasteries. Monastery of Mor Awgen, north of ancient Nisibis, modern Nusaybin, Turkey, 2013. Photo copyright the author.

thought meant that they did so as an administrative reform and with less concern to cultivate a high tradition of jurisprudence.

Paradoxically, however, the West Syrians' distance from the centers of legal study in Iraq left their law open to Islamization from a different angle. Both East Syrian and West Syrian family law were very Christian in many unsurprising respects; it consistently prohibited divorce, polygamy, and marriage to non-Christians, for example. In other ways, however, the West Syrians more readily adopted norms and procedures from Islamic law, such as those relating to the betrothal contract, male guardianship of female relatives, and inheritance. We will explore these in detail in Chapters 4 and 9. For now, the point to note is that the less systematic character of the West Syrians' civil law tradition, a product of their less intensive engagement with the judicial and legal reforms of the early Abbasid Caliphate, left a vacuum that the bishops readily filled with customary practices and norms, which were often Islamic ones. The East Syrians' closer interaction with caliphal institutions and Islamic law, conversely, produced a more autonomous tradition of Christian law in the long run.

Jews and Zoroastrians

Syriac Christians were not the only non-Muslims concentrated in the Abbasid Caliphate's core Iraqi and Iranian territories. The religious elites of these regions' significant Jewish and Zoroastrian populations likewise retooled certain of their communal institutions in response to political and religious developments within the caliphate. As in the case of the East Syrians and West Syrians, a reformed legal tradition was centrally important to Jewish rabbis and Zoroastrian priests as they carved out the social-institutional spaces of their respective subject communities.

There is no question that interactions with the Islamic empire were crucial to the development of Jewish communal institutions and to the formation of the very scholarly traditions that defined Judaism for centuries: Rabbanism, centered on study of the Babylonian Talmud, and Qaraism, which rejected the rabbinic tradition in favor of a greater focus on the Hebrew Bible. When the Abbasids came to power, Jewish intellectual life in Iraq was centered in the rabbinic academies of Sura and Pumbedita, small towns on the middle Euphrates, where the heads of the academies—the geonim—cultivated the oral transmission and study of the Babylonian Talmud.[85] By the early tenth century, the academies had moved to Baghdad and become "cosmopolitan and outward-looking institutions" whose members engaged in the wider political and intellectual trends of the caliphate.[86] Over the course of the ninth and tenth centuries, Jewish intellectual disciplines evolved in entirely new directions, as Qaraites and then Rabbanites began to write in Arabic and to adopt many of the strategies of discourse and the "book culture" characteristic of Arabo-Islamic learning.[87] Of special significance for our purposes are the new efforts evident among the geonim of this period to make Babylonian Talmudic law the definitive communal tradition of Jewish life. In the tenth century, Iraqi geonim composed for the first time individually authored, stand-alone treatises that summarized or commented on various facets of the Talmudic corpus. These, as well as written copies of portions of the Talmud, which had always been transmitted orally in Babylonia itself, circulated among Jewish communities in the Mediterranean world and encouraged the recognition of the special authority of the Babylonian tradition.[88] It is only in the Abbasid context, in other words, that we see clear evidence of Jewish learned elites in Iraq "transform[ing] the Babylonian Talmud, the great compendium of rabbinic teachings compiled over the course of the pre-Islamic centuries, into the principal legal text of rabbinic Judaism."[89] The foundations of the tradition that the geonim worked with were much more ancient than East Syrian law; but they too developed their tradition in response to exigencies in the Abbasid Caliphate, reconstruing its character and promoting it, through new textual methods, as a communal law proper to a geographically dispersed, subject religious community. For their part, Qaraite authors writing in Hebrew and Arabic in the ninth and tenth centuries produced their own body of communal law, always with an eye toward deriving it from or justifying it with reference to the Hebrew Bible.[90]

These formative developments in medieval Rabbanite and Qaraite legal traditions appear to have begun slightly later than the East Syrians' concern for confessional law, evident already in the second half of the eighth century. It may be significant in this regard that while the East Syrian patriarch was already based in Baghdad and attending the caliph's court in the 770s, the duty of representing the Jews to the caliph appears to have been filled not by the geonim but by the exilarch, a communal leader whose position came from his claim to descent from the Davidic monarchy.[91] Despite residing in central Iraq, the geonim of the late eighth century were thus perhaps at a slightly farther remove from the caliphate's legal and institutional developments than their East Syrian ecclesiastical contemporaries.[92] We do have at least one responsum attributed to an eighth-century gaon, Rav Haninai (d. 769), that takes note of Jews making recourse to extracommunal courts,[93] and two of the earliest extra-Talmudic legal codes have been dated to circa 800 and 850.[94] But overall, there is little evidence that the judicial consolidation or Islamic legal developments of the very earliest Abbasid period spurred immediate adjustments in geonic institutions and jurisdictions. In many ways, Abbasid fragmentation in the later ninth and tenth centuries had greater implications for Jewish communal organization: westward-migrating Iraqi and Iranian Jews helped entrench Babylonian Rabbanism outside of Iraq, while connections with the newly powerful Muslim courts that emerged in the former Abbasid provinces encouraged Jews throughout the eastern Mediterranean to "[organize] themselves into territorial administrations run by local leaders."[95]

Interactions with the evolving institutions of Islamic polities thus encouraged Jews to reconfigure their communal legal traditions, but those traditions were already quite ancient and their developmental trajectories differed from that of Syriac Christian law. Similarly, family law and the regulation of household ritual and reproductive practices had long been of fundamental importance to Jewish law, and they remained so; the geonim were not in a position of having to build a largely new family law as were the East Syrians of the early Abbasid Caliphate. Family law subjects figured prominently in the new treatises on Talmudic law that the geonim of the tenth and eleventh centuries began to author in Judeo-Arabic,[96] and the norms governing marital unions between relatives made up one of the practical legal arenas most contested between Qaraites and Rabbanites.[97] But given the much greater topical breadth of Jewish law in comparison to that of Christian traditions, it is not surprising that many more ritual, commercial, and other subjects occupied the literary attentions of Jewish thinkers in the Abbasid Caliphate as well.[98]

In a manner similar to the experience of East Syrians and Rabbanite Jews, the consolidation of an inherited legal tradition and its propagation as a dhimmi law was a clear response on the part of the Zoroastrian communities of Iraq and southwest Iran to the development of the Abbasids' Islamic empire. Arguably, the Zoroastrians were the non-Muslims for whom the establishment of the caliphate had been the most immediately impactful. The elimination of the Sasanian state over the first few decades of the conquests meant the end of imperial patronage for the Zoroastrian priestly elite and its institutions, and scholars tend to view conversion to Islam and Zoroastrian impoverishment as proceeding relatively quickly on the Iranian Plateau.[99] Yet we also have indications of the persistence of fire temples and robust Zoroastrian communities, especially in southwest Iran, into the tenth century.[100] Significantly, the same period witnessed a burst of Middle Persian literary production by Zoroastrian high priests in Iraq, Fars, and Kirman, through which they transformed what had been an imperially sponsored cult into a religious tradition proper to a subject community of the Islamic caliphate. Middle Persian texts of the ninth and tenth centuries show the priests consolidating in written form a vast amount of Zoroastrian learning, as well as deploying that learning in the form of instructions to petitioners and local communities as to how they should carry on their ritual duties, organize their internal social relations, and manage their interactions with Muslims.[101] In reordering their received tradition in this manner, the Zoroastrian priests were in many respects responding to Islamic expectations of what a religious community was supposed to look like—they produced a textual corpus that laid out the scope of their high religious tradition and functioned as a repository of knowledge for how Zoroastrians should behave within a non-Zoroastrian polity. Indeed, Zoroastrians themselves began to explicitly describe their tradition as a scriptural religion—complete with a founding prophet, Zarathushtra, and a holy book, the Avesta—in the same period.[102]

One major theme of the Abbasid-era priests' Middle Persian literature was to define clearly the institutions most fundamental to Zoroastrian communal belonging, among which ritual and the household were especially prominent. The Zoroastrian family law of the Sasanian state had been both complex and highly distinctive in comparison to other regional traditions;[103] the Middle Persian works of the early Abbasid period, particularly question-and-answer texts between Zoroastrian high priests and various petitioners, seek to streamline this Sasanian heritage and impress it upon the laity as constitutive of Zoroastrian affiliation.[104] Family law is hardly these texts' only concern; matters of ritual purity are central, as is the related subject of interactions with non-Zoroastrians. But endeavors on the part of the priesthood to strengthen its authority over Zoroastrian households and to regulate their practices of reproduction in distinctively Zoroastrian terms were certainly significant facets of the reconstituted Zoroastrian religious tradition in the Abbasid Caliphate. Much as East Syrian and West Syrian bishops did, Zoroastrian priests emphasized the connection between priestly authority and the household in order to demarcate the boundaries of the Zoroastrians as a religious community.

Melkites and Copts

From the Jazira to Iraq to Iran, non-Muslim religious elites responded to the methods of governance and social settings of the early Abbasid Caliphate by creating, reforming, and consolidating communal legal traditions. To varying degrees, they also took the household as one of the most important sites for the projection of their regulatory authority and the prescription of differentiating practices. We can see the character of these particular responses to empire in sharper relief if we move west to Syria and Egypt. While the early Abbasids' innovations in Islamic empire encouraged Melkite religious elites in greater Syria to assemble a newly Arabicized canon of Christian legal texts, distance from the centers of Islamic legal thought meant that neither they nor the Copts of Egypt cultivated civil law to the same extent as their contemporaries to the east. They turned to other literary strategies and focused on other social institutions as they constituted their churches as dhimmi communities.

Among the most significant developments within the Chalcedonian communities of Muslim-ruled Syria and Palestine was their adoption of Arabic as a literary and liturgical language in the eighth century, earlier than other Christians in the caliphate. This development was largely responsible for defining them as a distinctive ecclesial body that, though in communion with the Byzantine Church, maintained its own traditions and identity: by the early ninth century, the Arabaphone Chalcedonian subjects of the caliphate had come to be known as Melkites ("king's men," i.e., followers of the Byzantine emperor's confession, from the Syriac and Arabic root *m-l-k*).[105] The monasteries of Palestine were the centers of Melkite intellectual activity; there, Chalcedonian monks began in the eighth century to translate their Greek Christian heritage into Arabic.[106] Law was a significant part of this endeavor. The Melkites translated a wide range of late antique Greek ecclesiastical legal texts, including synodal canons, pseudo-apostolic works, and patristic writings, and compiled them into comprehensive manuscript codices.[107] Thus, one way that Melkites constituted themselves as a subject religious community was to demonstrate that they too had a confessional law. They showed little interest, however, in expanding its purview to cover lay civil affairs the way West Syrian and East Syrian bishops did. Perhaps our only example of Melkites using law to draw social boundaries for laypeople is a chapter from a ninth-century Arabic theological treatise, which collects several pre-Islamic canons "on what has been forbidden to Christians concerning food, marriage, and mixing with non-Christians [*al-ma'kal wa-l-tazwīj wa-l-khalṭa bi-l-ghurabā'*]."[108]

While this text is an example of Melkite elites seeking to regulate lay social relations in terms similar to those set down by their contemporaries elsewhere in Syria, Iraq, and Iran, it is a small and essentially unique one. This is likely a result of the distance of those Melkite elites, especially the monks of Palestine, from the centers of caliphal judicial reform and Islamic law in Iraq. Significantly, Melkites in the eighth, ninth, and tenth centuries developed other literary strategies for defining the social obligations that went along with religious affiliation. In the towns of Syria, where Arabic was already commonly used or had overtaken Aramaic and Greek faster than it did elsewhere, establishing ritual distinctiveness between Christians and Muslims looks to have been a priority for Melkite ecclesiastics.[109] Melkite authors also produced martyrologies commemorating Christians executed by Muslim authorities that have no substantial parallels among the literatures of other Christians in the caliphate (with the exception of the Iberian Peninsula in the far west). Martyrologies were a means for Melkite monks to protest "more accommodating attitudes towards Arabo-Muslim culture" common among laypeople in the multireligious settings of Syrian towns.[110]

It is worthwhile to note that household dynamics are often important to the religiocommunal solidarity that the martyrologies promote. Some martyrs are converts from Islam who shed their non-Christian family ties along with false religion—in one case, it is the martyr's Muslim family that delivers him to the authorities for execution. Other martyrs receive aid from their Christian relatives.[111] Christian family and household bonds are thus presented as coterminous with Christian faith. But otherwise, Melkite elites did not concern themselves with the formal extension of ecclesiastical authority over the material and social composition of lay households as West Syrian or East Syrian bishops (or Zoroastrian priests) did. Linguistic acculturation and social interactions appear to have loomed larger for Syrian Chalcedonians than the caliphate's reforming judiciary, and their elites focused on social arenas other than the household as they defined the requisites of Melkite belonging.

An interest in communal definition through law and new modes of regulating the household is even less in evidence among the Christians of Egypt. Coptic religious elites of the early Abbasid period did not consolidate or create anew any communal legal tradition as Christians in Syria, Iraq, and Iran did. On the whole, Coptic bishops were slower to take on new intellectual genres and disciplines of study in response to the establishment of the caliphate and the emergence of Arabo-Islamic intellectual culture. We should interpret this again as an outcome of the particular nature of the contacts between Christians, Muslims, and the institutions of Muslim governance in Egypt. Egypt appears to have maintained more consistently unmixed, heavily Christian areas of the countryside longer than other core regions of the caliphate; Coptic patriarchs generally stayed away from Muslim urban centers, tending to reside in small Delta settlements and only moving to the Fatimid capital of Cairo in the late eleventh century.[112] Coptic elites did begin to narrate their history differently with the arrival of Muslim rule, gradually coming to contrast their tradition with the perfidy of the Byzantines and thereby producing the idea of Egyptian miaphysites as an indigenous Coptic Church.[113] But overall, Egyptian Christians experienced Islamic empire differently in our period, with a slower pace of conversion to Islam and less intensive interactions of Christians and Muslims in urban centers relative to elsewhere in the caliphate. As a result, there is little indication of Egyptian Christian elites of the eighth and ninth centuries engaging in radically new forms of intellectual production comparable to the new legal and theological idioms employed by Melkites, West Syrians, East Syrians, and Qaraite and Rabbanite Jews.

In later centuries when Egypt's Muslim population expanded and its Christian elites interacted more closely with the currents of Islamic intellectual culture, however, the Copts' religious traditions were transformed. Coptic elites produced a large body of new Arabic literature, including much law focused on regulating Christian households in changing social and institutional contexts. This production began around the eleventh century and expanded greatly in the thirteenth.[114] Because it is outside the time frame of comparable developments to the east, the transformation of Coptic legal traditions and institutions as a result of Egyptian Christians' encounter with Islamic polities will be largely out of view in the rest of this book. The many similarities between it and the East Syrians' in the heartlands of the eighth- and ninth-century Abbasid Caliphate are noteworthy, however. In both cases, interreligious social contact and the imperatives of Islamic governance spurred the consolidation of communal legal traditions and new claims of ecclesiastical authority over the material and social constitution of Christian households. These were among the key institution-building practices by which religious elites sought to shape the non-Muslim subjects of medieval Islamic polities as distinct religious communities.

Christian Law in the Making of Islamic Society

Our focus on those practices has been guided by a concern to put the vast numbers of non-Muslims who lived under the medieval caliphate at the center of its story. Christian lawmaking illustrates that the multireligious social order of the medieval caliphate was neither a simple reality inherited from late antiquity nor the top-down institution of the *dhimma* system by Muslim lawyers and rulers. Rather, it was an ongoing "coproduction" of Christians, Jews, Zoroastrians, and Muslims, as the former actively responded to the imperatives of the latter's rule by reordering their own traditions and institutions.[115] In emphasizing agency among subjects who are often at the margins of Islamic history, however, we should not lose sight of the asymmetries that characterized their relationships with the ruling religion. The Christian legal traditions of the early Abbasid Caliphate point us toward the central role of non-Muslim elites in imagining and building the caliphate's social order; the circumstances of their production also remind us that it was Islamic institutions that set the parameters within which those elites operated. In that very fact, however, non-Muslim developments like the ones we have been following remain indispensable to the historiography of the medieval Middle East: they show us the structures that will eventually appear characteristic of the region's societies not as accomplished facts but in the uneven, uncertain processes of their formation. In this vein, we will close this chapter by considering the ambivalent relationship of the Abbasid-era jurist-bishops to their own legal traditions and the Islamic contexts that informed them. In seeking to bound their community by a law attendant to mundane social affairs and material transactions, East Syrian bishops adopted the very terms by which Islamic discourse defined a religion: "a law and a path" (*shiraʿtan wa-minhājan*, Quran 5:48) bestowed by God as a function of His scripture. At the same time, their legal writings evince efforts to undermine the theological foundations of this perspective. At these moments of dissonance—of simultaneous adoption and refusal of Islamic categories of cosmology and social organization—we can see a characteristically medieval Middle Eastern conception of the religious community taking shape.

The bishops of the Syriac churches would not have disputed the notion that God created laws to guide humanity, but their Christian tradition differed starkly from Islam in making sharper theological distinctions between God's Law, on the one hand, and the norms by which humans govern life in the present world, on the other. The former consisted of the Creator's exalted plan and principles for His creation, "amazing laws [*nāmosē tmihē*] [that] correct and order our way of life here . . . a teaching [*mallpānutā*] that is appropriate and does not hinder us from heavenly ways of conduct, but aids and enriches us."[116] Ever since the Pauline denial that any human might be "justified" through the Mosaic law (e.g., Galatians 3:11), however, the mainstream of Christian thought had been skeptical at best of the notion that precise regulations for worldly life were part of God's plan—in marked contrast to Jewish tradition and later to Islam.[117] In the perspective of the Syriac bishops of the early medieval caliphate, God's great Laws provided moral guidance toward the ultimate goal of salvation in the perfect world to come; He did not get bogged down in details in the present, fleeting one by "institut[ing] laws for insignificant, human civil affairs" (*da-nsim nāmosē ʿal dinē daqdaqē w-nāshāyē*).[118]

Because God's plan for salvation through Christ was too exalted to concern itself with mundane civil transactions, the bishops say, Christian association had never consisted in a singular, identifiable model of social practice. While Jews, Zoroastrians, and Muslims each had a tradition of judgment according to a single civil law, "among Christians civil rulings [*dinē*] are different in the land of the Romans from those in the land of the Persians; they differ again from those in the land of the Aramaeans [central Iraq], from Khuzistan, and from Mayshan [southern Iraq], and similarly in other places."[119] One might profess adherence to Christianity while simultaneously being an Iraqi, a Persian, or even a resident of one or another neighboring village who keeps to whatever local customs prevail in civil transactions. For an even more striking formulation of this idea, we can return to the preface to Timothy's *Law Book* with which we began: "Humans are distinct and separated from each other, in countries and lands, peoples and languages, customs and laws. Each of them desires a way of life [*huppākā w-duyyārā*] in accordance with the customs and laws [*ba-ʿyādē wa-b-nāmosē*] in which they have been habituated and raised. . . . They accept change from something when they have been established in it only with difficulty and thousands of dangers; for custom is second nature, as the saying goes."[120] It is precisely to this state of affairs, in which social customs and laws vary from locale to locale, that the *dhimma* framework and its underlying Quranic theology assumed that religion would bring some degree of uniformity. In creating their traditions of confessional civil law, the Syriac bishops of the early Abbasid Caliphate were effectively recasting their communities according to that Islamic model. Christian law would distinguish Christians from Muslims, but in practice it simultaneously constituted Christianity as a religion in the Quranic mold—a scripture plus a law. The power of Islamic categories to reshape the other religious traditions of the caliphate is starkly in evidence here. In its origins Islam had taken shape in a milieu of established late antique monotheisms; its formative traditions owed much to Jewish and Christian models.[121] But by the Abbasid period, the very existence of Christian law is testament to a caliphate-wide intellectual culture increasingly defined by Islamic paradigms, even in an empire that remained highly religiously diverse and probably mostly non-Muslim.

Yet those paradigms were not so hegemonic as to make other perspectives inconceivable. As the bishops of the early Abbasid period adapted their intellectual labor to an Islamic framework, they simultaneously attempted to resist its theological implications. To continue with Timothy: "Alone among all things on the earth, man . . . is distinct in his properties and actions [*b-dilāywātēh wa-b-suʿrānaw*] because of the power of knowledge and free will that he has received from his Creator. Who, then, can bring to a unity and gather together that which, a thousand times over, is separate and differentiated according to its [very] nature, other than that Sign that [first] brought it into being and creation?"[122] Here, Timothy affirms that the diversity of customs and practices among human beings, even those who adhere to a single religion, is a function of the faculty of free will with which God has endowed them. It is by nature impossible, then, to bind a motley cross-section of humanity together with a single body of worldly law. Despite this protestation, in practical terms this is exactly the project that Timothy and other Abbasid-era jurist-bishops undertook. But by posing the question rhetorically and implying that only God who created humanity in the first place is truly capable of such a feat, Timothy undermines in this passage the theological foundation of the law-bounded religious community. Ultimately, he avers, "worldly judgments" proposed by human jurists "are superfluous and useless [*yattirē enon wa-d-lā ḥāshḥu psāqā d-dinē ʿālmānāyē*]. For rulings and prescriptions are useful to the men of this world [alone]."[123] The invention of a confessional law in the mold of the Islamic Shariʿa may have been necessary to define Christian communal boundaries in the caliphate. But it was not integral to the Christian dispensation in the manner that Muslims (and Jews) would have it; it was only a man-made stopgap measure for the present, imperfect world. However much the bishops imbibed the notion that specific civil transactions defined participation in a religious community, the Christian social groups that were now constituted by those practices were ultimately ephemeral. True Christian association, Timothy maintained, would be realized in the world to come.

That gap between Christian theology and Islamic thought is a useful end point at which to index the development of an early Abbasid social order that was at once multireligious but also Islamic in increasingly significant ways. Rather than positing the medieval caliphate's "segmented society composed of separate religious communities" as an accomplished fact of Islamic thought and governance,[124] the friction between Christian and Islamic perspectives draws our attention to the historical processes of its production. Significantly, the very fact that Timothy composed his *Law Book* demonstrates the centrality and power of the Islamic perspective in setting the parameters of the issue; as much as he protested about the ultimate uselessness of a worldly law, Timothy still had to create one in order to demarcate his religious community within the caliphate. At the same time, Timothy's protests express a conception of the relationship between revelation and social organization that rejects the overriding normativity of the Islamic model; he renders it something less than common knowledge about the way the world works even if he more or less accepted it in practice.

Ultimately, it is fissures like this—in which the representative of a subject population adapts to but simultaneously refuses dominant categories of thought and behavior—that show us Islamization as a contested process at a particular historical moment rather than flattening it out into an inevitable reality. That viewpoint reminds us that, even when the subject is the growing hegemony of Islamic thought, non-Muslim communities, traditions, and transformations must be integral to any narrative of the culture and society of the medieval Islamic empire.

By any account, the early period of Abbasid rule was a crucial one for the making of the medieval caliphate. Conditions under the Abbasids made for interreligious and interethnic social contacts more intensive than ever in the Islamic empire's urban centers. New Arabic intellectual traditions like law, theology, philosophy, and belles lettres cohered in the scholarly circles and salons of those cities. Caliphs sought to centralize their power over key institutions of governance like the judiciary; caliphs and civilian Muslim jurists alike refined the *dhimma* framework that defined the place of subject non-Muslims in an Islamic state and society. The confident emergence of these Islamic traditions, institutions, and identities—formative stages building toward a "classical Islam"—is frequently the beginning and end of scholarly accounts of early medieval Middle Eastern history. Instead, we have emphasized a different perspective: that the making of the society and culture of a multireligious, multiethnic empire like the medieval caliphate can only be understood as the processes by which its subjects encountered imperial structures and, in adopting, contesting, and reproducing them, transformed their own institutions and traditions.

The nature of that encounter among Middle Eastern Christians—who comprised the majority of regional populations well into the ninth century and perhaps beyond—varied across the caliphate. From Syria to Iran, caliphal judicial reform, the formalization of norms of dhimmi governance, and the emergence of Islamic law spurred bishops to expand and consolidate new communal legal traditions of their own. Many had the immediately practical aims of providing a workable civil law for ecclesiastical courts and keeping laypeople away from Islamic ones. But new Christian confessional law was also a means for jurist-bishops to define the social obligations attendant to religious belonging within interlocked and overlapping social environments. For those Christians living at the caliphate's heart—the West Syrians and especially the East Syrians—this meant above all a new definition of the Christian household and a new vision of Christian communal integrity at the link between ecclesiastics and lay households. Where ecclesiastics had always approached the household as a site for enjoining domestic moral behavior and disciplining sexuality, Christian law in the caliphate prescribed norms for the material practices that constituted and reproduced it as a social institution: the contracting of betrothals, the attendant financial obligations between spouses, and the devolution of property to relatives when a spouse's death ended a marriage. Christian law would demarcate East Syrians and West Syrians as dhimmi communities by ordering the practices that formed households and inscribing in them the basic elements of wider social hierarchies: patriarchal authority, patrilineal property and identity, the primacy of agnatic kin networks. Although these principles would already have been taken for granted by many laypeople, they were presented now as cumulatively constitutive of the church as a social body.

Significantly, the redefinition of Christian belonging undertaken by Abbasid-era elites entailed as well the adoption and reproduction of Islamic discourses concerning the very nature of religion and religious communities. East Syrian legal writings asserted that confessional civil law was not a function of God's will as Muslim ulama might have it; but they still propagated a notion of the law-bounded Christian community that fell largely into line with Quranic cosmology. In these transformations—as subject Christian elites mediated the expectations and imperatives of Abbasid governance and Islamic thought—we can see the caliphate's socioreligious order in the immanence of its making.

Our story to this point has been a largely top-down one of institutional overhaul at the link between empire and subject elites. But reform does not simply follow from elite prescription; in practical terms, the structure of the medieval caliphate's subject Christian communities owed just as much to negotiations among laypeople, Christian law, and Islamic institutions over the ecclesiastics' new social regulations. The following chapters chart those negotiations with a focus on a few interlocking themes. One is the question of what made the bishops' law distinctively Christian in comparison to the other traditions around which it grew. Throughout the Syriac and Arabic Christian legal writings of the Abbasid period, several marital practices and institutions figure conspicuously as the facets of family life that the jurist-bishops were most concerned to regulate in light of received teachings: the betrothal contract, divorce, close-kin unions, polygamy, and interreligious marriage. A considerable diversity of practice in these areas among the populous and geographically diffuse Christian peoples living under Muslim rule was an ongoing challenge to the bishops' vision of Christian association. A second theme is the significance of Islamic norms and institutions in delimiting patterns of lay social behavior, the categories of Christian law as an intellectual tradition, and the practical shape of Christian communities. Caliphal courts remained open to non-Muslim litigants; non-Muslims were fixtures of elite social circles where sexual mores very different from the bishops' ideas predominated; Islamic legal thought was always in the bishops' rearview mirrors as they developed their own confessional law. These realities suggest that the Christian communities of the medieval caliphate should not be understood as autonomous of Islam and the caliphal state, which is how dhimmi social groups are often depicted. Rather, they were shaped precisely by the tensions between communal institutions and extracommunal Islamic ones, and by the ways that bishops positioned the former in response to the latter. Our final theme of emphasis is the utility of Christian materials and traditions in expanding the historiographical scope through which we view the early medieval caliphate's intellectual culture. Put in comparative perspective with Islamic law, Syriac and Arabic Christian legal works display the diversity of ancient traditions of learning in the Abbasid world that contributed to but were not simply subsumed by Islamic thought. Furthermore, they allow us to see how certain historiographical narratives related to the formation of Islamic thought might be more illuminatingly cast in terms of the interaction between multiple traditions producing transformations in each.

PART II

Christian Family Law in the Making of Caliphal Society and Intellectual Culture

CHAPTER 4

The Ancient Roots and Islamic Milieu of Syriac Family Law

There is a man betrothed to a woman in the same city, and for various reasons he does not want to hold a banquet and take her as a bride. Her father and brothers, whether on a pretext or truthfully, say, "We want to leave this city and this region, and we cannot take a virgin girl with us and go around in many places; but neither is it proper to leave her and go." They dispute with her betrothed in court [*lābkin la-mkirāh b-dinā*] so that he will either marry his betrothed according to custom [*ṭaksā d-rādē*] or leave her. The groom says, "I will not leave [*shābeq*] my betrothed, but I am not able to marry her." The bride says, "I cannot remain betrothed any longer." Her groom, whether on a pretext or truthfully, says, "I cannot marry her this year."

—Timothy I, *Law Book*

Around the year 805, Timothy I sat down in Baghdad to write a response to the scenario described above. It gives the picture of a contentious but fairly typical family squabble: a young woman and her family complain that her prospective groom is not following through on the marriage in good time, to which the man responds by pleading poverty. The combination of detail and mundaneness in the description suggests that this was a real case presented to the patriarch as a request for a ruling. What, then, did Christian law have to say on the matter? Was the young man obligated to follow through with the betrothal? Could the prospective bride's family break the agreement and find a new match somewhere else? What about the young woman herself—did she have any say, or did her father and brothers decide whom she was to marry? How, precisely, did a marriage contract come into effect, and what rights and obligations did it entail? Timothy's received ecclesiastical tradition offered no real precedents for solving these concrete problems. Now that bishops in the Abbasid Caliphate had sought to bring family and other civil affairs under their purview, however, they had to assemble a body of legal knowledge to be able to do so—to attend to the legal mechanics and minutiae of marital relationships that civil traditions in past ages had traditionally governed.

The Abbasid-era Syriac law books that contain the answers of Timothy and other bishops to questions like those posed above evoke for us the multifarious legal culture of the early medieval Middle East—the diverse mix of legal customs and institutions that the people of the region had been using for centuries, if not millennia, to structure their social relations, as well as the newer disciplines of confessional jurisprudence into which those customs and institutions were now cohering. Indeed, East Syrian and West Syrian jurist-bishops engaged with a range of ancient and contemporary legal traditions as they assembled and fixed in place the nuts and bolts of their newly expansive Christian family law. Those nuts and bolts consisted of several basic legal instruments and institutions: the betrothal contract and the rights, duties, statuses, and relationships it brought into effect. Institutions of these kinds were common to essentially all ancient Middle Eastern legal cultures; but the bishops drew the specific forms that they included in their law books and treatises principally from the regional customs of Iraq and Iran, and secondarily from Islamic judicial practice. The substantive content of Syriac family law thus attests to the burgeoning influence of Islamic law as a normative model across the early Abbasid Caliphate's non-Muslim religious communities. Simultaneously, however, it shows us the continuing diversity of the caliphate's legal cultures, as Christian jurisprudence consolidated the still vital elements of ancient, pre-Islamic ones into new learned traditions.

SYRIAC CHRISTIAN FAMILY LAW: NUTS AND BOLTS

Marriage as Contract

The principal goal of Syriac Christian law in the Abbasid Caliphate was to regulate the material practices through which households were formed and reproduced. It did so by ordering those practices around several key legal institutions, with which we need a closer acquaintance in order to examine their genealogy and the light it sheds on the legal cultures of the early medieval Middle East. The most foundational of those institutions was the marriage contract. In legal rather than theological terms, marriage for both East Syrian and West Syrian ecclesiastics (as for jurists of other traditions) was a contractual relationship: an agreement between parties that conferred a new legal status on each and entailed specific rights and obligations. This perspective is evident already in George I's canon of 676, which requires "a contract between the betrothed ones" (*tanway da-mkirē w-da-mkirātā*) to ensure clarity in any future disputes.[1] The East Syrian law books of the eighth and ninth centuries frequently use the same Syriac term for contract, *tanway*, to refer to marriage agreements.[2]

What brought a Christian marriage contract into effect according to the bishops? George's canon mentions several constitutive elements. First is the "priestly blessing" (*burktā kāhnāytā*), the clerically administered ritual we encountered in Chapter 2, as well as the "mediation of the holy cross of our salvation" (*meṣʿāyutā da-ṣlibā qaddishā d-purqānan*), which we should probably interpret as the sign of the cross made as part of the ritual. Evidently due to its proclamation by a patriarchal synod, George's formulation spread and became widely accepted among East Syrian bishops; Ishoʿbokt, Timothy, Ishoʿbarnun, and ʿAbdishoʿ bar Bahriz all prescribe iterations, with minor differences, of the same ritual.[3] By the late eighth century, the West Syrians had adopted a similar doctrine; the canons of a synod convened in 794 by the patriarch Kyriakos require a clerically administered ritual and blessing to render a marriage between Christians valid.[4]

Other than the priest's ministrations, George's canon requires the consent of the spouses' parents (*shalmutā d-ābāhayhēn*) and of the spouses themselves to bring a marriage agreement into effect. The consent of various parties is a pillar of later Syriac legal sources' doctrine of contractual marriage as well, although their details differ. One of Ishoʿbarnun's decisions, for example, recognizes that a young man's parents might enter into a betrothal agreement for him without his consent (*d-lā b-ṣebyānēh*); if the young man refuses to go through with the marriage, his parents should disinherit him.[5] Timothy's *Law Book*, by contrast, emphasizes the consent of the spouses themselves; in one decision treating an orphan whose parents had betrothed her as a child, Timothy declares that "her will shall stand" (*ṣebyānāh nehwē*) as to whether to go through with the marriage once she reaches legal majority (*mshuḥtā d-purshānā d-idaʿtā*, "age of discretion").[6] In all the East Syrian and West Syrian sources, however, the consent of the spouses' parents or fathers remains essential.

To this point, we have referred to the agreement that created a union between two spouses as a marriage contract. This designation is convenient but does not capture all the intricacies of how the Abbasid-era jurist-bishops understood marriage as a legal relationship. More precisely, the bishops saw it as a two-step process: the contract effected a "betrothal" (*mkirutā*, *mkurē*, *mkuryā*), which would be finalized as "full union" (*shawtāputā*, *zuwwāgā*) through consummation and the beginning of cohabitation at a later date.[7] The particular conception of betrothal here is not merely a promise to marry at some future time; it initiates the change in legal status in which most of the rights and duties of husband and wife obtain. Timothy, for example, considers it possible that a man might already be providing financial support (*nepqātā*) to a woman to whom he is only betrothed, making the betrothal as indissoluble as full marriage. He further allows a betrothal to be broken only in the same limited circumstances in which divorce is permissible.[8] Legal historians call this two-step form of marriage in which betrothal already confers a new legal status "inchoate marriage," an idea we will return to.[9] While the jurist-bishops made a distinctively Christian ritual one of the constitutive elements of the betrothal, they attached less importance to the finalization of the union; the sources mention that some type of banquet (*ḥlulā*, *meshtutā*) should be held to mark the occasion but do not detail any ritual elements.[10] The bishops presumably expected consummation and the spouses' cohabitation to follow. We can infer that Timothy, at least, did not consider a marriage finalized until it was consummated, or until the couple had been alone together such that consummation could be presumed; a woman becomes eligible to inherit from her betrothed—in other words, the full bond of marriage is established—only when "he has seen her [*ḥzāh*] or had intercourse with her [*etʿni ʿamāh*]."[11]

The Indissolubility of the Contract

A signal feature of Christian sexual morality from its earliest days was a heavy stigmatization of divorce, a perspective rooted in several well-known teachings of the Gospels and Pauline epistles: husband and wife become one flesh (Genesis 2:24); the marriage bond is affirmed by God such that no human can undo it (Matthew 19:6, Mark 10:8–9). The exception to this perspective is Matthew 5:32, which gives adultery on the part of the wife as the single legitimate cause for a husband to leave a marriage. According to the late antique Christian teachings that followed from this scriptural foundation, divorce was fundamentally unlawful and immoral. Unsurprisingly, the jurist-bishops of the Abbasid Caliphate largely translated this perspective into their civil law traditions: they maintained that the contractual relationship of marriage was indissoluble outside of certain limited circumstances. The West Syrian synods straightforwardly decree that adultery (*gawrā*, *zānyutā*) is the only grounds on which a spouse may leave his or her partner (and presumably remarry, though they do not specify this). Notably, this restriction applies to unconsummated betrothals just as much as to full marriages.[12] The only respect in which this doctrine departs from earlier Christian tradition is its notion that adultery is a gender-neutral transgression. Roman law as well many other ancient legal orders considered only a wife's infidelity to be adultery entailing harsh punishments—patrilineal societies tend to hold in special horror sexual liaisons that render paternity uncertain.[13] Accommodating that customary Roman perspective, some late antique Christian thinkers construed a husband's infidelity as a dire moral transgression but not acceptable grounds for the wife to seek a new spouse.[14] Abbasid-era West Syrian law favored the response found in other patristic writings, which understood extramarital sex on the part of men and women as equally consequential.[15]

The East Syrian jurist-bishops viewed the contractual relationship of marriage as similarly indissoluble, although they recognized a few grounds for divorce beyond adultery. Ishoʿbokt's *Jurisprudential Corpus* describes the acceptable reasons for which a man might leave his wife as "exactly three": "The first is rejection of God [*kpuryā da-b-Alāhā*], the second is adultery [*gawrā*], and the third is murder [*qeṭlā*]; it being known that sorcery [*ḥarrāshutā*] is also rejection of God, for no man is able to attempt this abomination without rejecting God first."[16] We should understand "rejection of God" to mean apostasy. "Sorcery" denotes practices related to extrahuman powers unsanctioned by the church—"demonic servitude" (*pulḥānā shēdānāyā*) as another Syriac law book has it.[17] In further rulings, Ishoʿbokt's text adds that a man might also leave a marriage to live a life of holy continence (*myattrutā*, "virtuousness") or, in rare cases, because his wife is extremely disobedient (*paknitā wa-mṣaʿʿrānitā*). A wife may leave her husband only for rejection of God, sorcery, or murder.[18]

Ishoʿbokt thus expanded the grounds for the dissolution of marriage beyond adultery to include apostasy, sorcery, murder, desire for the holy continent life, and, in rare cases, wifely disobedience. His formulation appears to have been the basis of the doctrines in later East Syrian legal works. Timothy and Ishoʿbarnun give largely overlapping grounds for divorce using much the same terminology, the main differences being that they leave aside wifely disobedience and recognize no gender differentiation; men and women are equally capable of the transgressions that lead to marital dissolution.[19] As the penalty for divorcing one's spouse without recognized cause, the bishops usually prescribe exclusion from receiving the Eucharist—that is, placing the offender outside of the Christian community altogether.

The Effects of Marriage: Financial Obligations

The nigh indissoluble marriage bond was a contractual arrangement that conferred a new legal status—"married"—on the man and woman who were party to it. This status entailed specific rights and obligations, which in turn produced the web of hierarchical social relations that constituted a household. In the Syriac legal sources, most of those obligations are financial ones. The East Syrian jurist-bishops take it for granted that when a marriage is finalized the bride will bring a dowry (*pernitā*), provided by her father or his heirs, to her conjugal household.[20] Generally, this remains the wife's property that she can bequeath to whomever she wishes at her death, though her husband might have usufructory rights in it.[21] Both the East Syrian and the West Syrian legal sources also presume that a husband must pay his wife a marriage portion (*mahrā*).[22]

The *pernita* and *mahra* are essentially one-time financial obligations that either the betrothal contract or consummation of the marriage brings into effect.[23] The East Syrian bishops also mention a further, ongoing obligation that falls on husbands: providing their wives with maintenance (*tursāyā*, *nepqātā*).[24] The bishops do not specify whether they imagine this maintenance to be in cash or in kind, but it is presumably meant to cover food and shelter at minimum. What reciprocal duties do wives bear? Shemʿon of Revardashir in the mid-seventh century had specified that they owed their husbands obedience: a man is obliged to "fulfill the support [*purnāsā*] of his wife, and a wife is obligated as long as she lives to serve and be subject to her husband [*la-mshammāshu wa-l-meshtaʿbādu l-baʿlāh*]."[25] The Abbasid-era sources do not repeat this obligation explicitly, but they certainly expect the same. Ephesians 5:22–24, which enjoins wives to be submissive to their husbands just as the church submits to Christ, was a standard ecclesiastical point of reference on proper marital relations, and it accorded closely with the patriarchal presumptions of medieval Middle Eastern societies. In this respect, the obligations attendant to the marriage contract put into practice the gendered hierarchy expected of the household, with the husband as provider and bearer of authority over his wife.

The Effects of Marriage: Reproduction, Succession, and Inheritance

Marriage in the Syriac legal sources not only confers reciprocal obligations on husband and wife; as in essentially all ancient Middle Eastern legal orders, it also renders sexual intercourse between them licit and affiliates to them any progeny that issue from the union. In this manner, marriage facilitates not only biological but also social reproduction: legitimate children carry the social identity of their natal households into new generations. The material terms of that social reproduction are encoded in the bishops' rulings on inheritance—the devolution of wealth from one generation to the next.

Inheritance law makes up the bulk of each of the Abbasid-era East Syrian law books, and though their details differ they share several key principles. They all agree that in an ideal world, living sons will be around to inherit their father's property when he dies (and has not left a will). The law books are unanimous in seeing the patrilineage as the archetypical, most important line of descent down which property flows. As Ishoʿbokt puts it, a son has the greatest right to inherit because he "sustains the lineage and seed of his father" (*mqim gensā w-zarʿā l-abu[hy]*).[26] After a man's daughter marries, her children will affiliate to her husband's family; because she participates in the reproduction of her husband's lineage rather than her father's, she does not have the same claim on his estate as her brother does. Social identity depends chiefly on who one's father is, and as such, property ideally passes from father to son.[27] This does not mean that no other relatives receive property from a deceased man's patrimony. Ishoʿbokt, Timothy, and Ishoʿbarnun all recognize that wives and daughters are entitled to specific, limited pieces of men's estates—we will consider some of the details—and the question of heirs changes greatly when a man has no living sons. But the overriding principle is that sons should inherit their father's property because they will carry on his lineage.

What happens to the property of a married woman when she dies? The bishops treat this question as well but with less concern than they give to a man's estate. In Ishoʿbokt's words, a woman has "no [role in] perpetuating a lineage . . . other than that of her husband" (*lā yubbālā d-gensā . . . ṣṭar men hāy d-baʿlāh*).[28] Since children do not affiliate to their mothers' lineages, in other words, there is less of a question of ensuring that their property remains in a particular line of descent. Generally, the East Syrian jurist-bishops assign a deceased woman's property to her children without distinguishing between the claims of sons and daughters.[29]

The West Syrian synods of the eighth and ninth centuries prescribe no norms concerning inheritance, although in later centuries Syriac treatises containing Islamic inheritance laws would circulate among the West Syrians. The East Syrian sources, however, provide an abundance of rulings on the subject that make the general views of contemporary ecclesiastics very clear. If marriage facilitated procreation, in more precise terms its purpose was to produce sons who carried on their fathers' lineages as well as daughters who would assist other men in carrying on theirs. The fundamental rule of the bishops' systems of inheritance—sons' preeminent claims on their fathers' estates—materially and symbolically perpetuated the patrilineal ideal.

CHRISTIAN FAMILY LAW BETWEEN REGIONAL CUSTOM AND ISLAM

When Syriac bishops of the eighth and ninth centuries wrote about marriage as jurists rather than theologians, they sought to define the core practices, institutions, and instruments that would make it identifiable in legal terms and subject to regulation. These included the betrothal contract, the two-stage system of marriage, the exchange of marital gifts, other financial and reciprocal obligations, and the rights of inheritance accorded to offspring. While the bishops' treatises and synodal canons present their law as specifically Christian, many of its constituent elements would have been familiar and intelligible to non-Christian contemporaries throughout the caliphate; Syriac family law underwrote an entirely typical vision of the ancient world's archetypical mode of familial organization, the patriarchal household. Yet the ubiquity of patriarchy does not mean that all regional legal traditions were simply equivalent; despite a common emphasis on patrilineality, for example, the law of inheritance elaborated by Zoroastrian priests was distinctive in comparison to rabbinic law, which differed again from the idiosyncratic rules spelled out by the Quran and its commentators.[30] All of this begs the question: If civil subjects had been largely outside the purview of ecclesiastical tradition until the early Abbasid period, where did East Syrian and West Syrian bishops come up with the substantive content of their new family law? A close analysis of the core elements surveyed in the foregoing indicates that all are iterations of common regional practices and institutions; crafting a Christian civil law in the caliphate was thus largely a process of turning pieces of what we might think of as Middle Eastern common law into a high, written tradition. For the East Syrians, this meant adopting elements common to pre-Islamic Mesopotamian and Iranian legal traditions. West Syrian bishops, on the other hand, appear also to have taken the Islamic law administered in caliphal courts as a model. Christian marriage law thus testifies to the continued vitality and diversity of legal cultures in the caliphate even as its distinctively Islamic traditions and institutions were growing ever more prominent.

Mesopotamian and Iranian Law in East Syrian Tradition

We can begin with the foundational institution of Syriac Christian family law: the marriage contract.[31] The notion of marriage as a legal relationship effected by contract was more or less ubiquitous in the legal traditions of the ancient and medieval Middle East. In Mesopotamia, we have examples of Akkadian marriage contracts that record the mutual obligations of the spouses dating back as far as the second millennium BCE.[32] We have already seen examples from late Roman Egypt and Palestine, as well as a model Middle Persian contract reflecting Sasanian practice. In the Abbasid-era bishops' more immediate milieu, both Islamic and rabbinic law maintained the familiar contractual notion of marriage; numerous documentary examples are extant from Egypt.[33] Similarly, the bishops' conception of the two successive stages through which a marriage comes into effect—betrothal conferring a new legal status followed by full union—is quite evidently a version of "inchoate marriage," a widespread Fertile Crescent institution. Ancient iterations of it stretch back as far as the law of the Babylonians, the Assyrians, and the Hebrew Bible.[34] Inchoate marriage is characteristic of rabbinic and Islamic law as well: the *qiddushin* and *nissu'in* of Talmudic law and the Islamic marriage contract (*ʿaqd al-nikāḥ*) and later consummation correlate to the bishops' *mkure* and *shawtaputa*.[35] In the case of the marriage contract and the two stages of inchoate marriage, then, the jurist-bishops have clearly adopted into their Christian tradition customary legal instruments represented in a range of regional legal cultures.

More distinctive sources of the East Syrians' law are discernible in the financial obligations, including marital gifts and inheritance rights, that the marriage contract brings into effect. That marrying entails the transfer of property between the individuals and families involved is another essentially ubiquitous characteristic of eastern Mediterranean and Middle Eastern legal systems. But the East Syrian sources show the bishops to have adopted more specifically Mesopotamian and Iranian dowry and inheritance practices. Because patrilineal societies are always concerned to ensure that sons carry on their fathers' estates, the way any legal system treats the transfer of patrimonial property to women in the form of dowry is often closely connected to how it treats the disbursement of inheritances. One approach is to consider the dowry to be a daughter's share of her father's estate in case of intestate succession; in other words, when a man dies without a will his daughter has a right to some piece of his property that will serve as her dowry, but only his sons count as his full heirs and receive the bulk of the estate. This model of dowry and inheritance is generally characteristic of the legal traditions of the Fertile Crescent and Iran, including ancient Mesopotamian, Sasanian, and rabbinic law.[36] Roman law is a major outlier, as it gives sons and daughters equal shares in their fathers' estates regardless of the dowries that daughters receive.[37] Islamic law gives daughters lesser shares than sons, but the amounts are not dependent on dowries, which Islamic law does not require.[38] Quite notably, the East Syrian law books contain forms of the pre-Islamic eastern pattern.[39] Ishoʿbokt's treatment of dowry and inheritance corresponds largely to Sasanian law: when a man dies, his married daughters receive no inheritance, as their dowries represent their share of his estate; his unmarried daughters receive half the share of his sons.[40] Timothy and Ishoʿbarnun similarly treat a daughter's dowry and/or the maintenance provided by her natal household as her share of her father's patrimony (although Ishoʿbarnun allows that customs might differ in this respect from region to region).[41] The patriarchs' law does not appear to be Sasanian, as they do not give unmarried daughters the Sasanian half share. Timothy suggests instead one-tenth of the father's estate, a standard opinion found as well in the Palestinian and Babylonian Talmuds.[42] This correspondence indicates either that Timothy was familiar with this rabbinic tradition or that both represent a common regional practice. Overall, Timothy and Ishoʿbarnun look to have adopted Mesopotamian practices as their Christian law of dowry and inheritance, while Ishoʿbokt drew from a similar, Iranian tradition.

Strikingly, even the East Syrians' treatment of divorce—an area of their family law one might expect to be uniquely formed by Christian perspectives—appears to have incorporated some distinctively Iranian elements. We know that Ishoʿbokt made use of Sasanian sources for his *Jurisprudential Corpus*, and there are noteworthy similarities between his extension of the grounds for divorce beyond adultery and the treatment of the subject found in Zoroastrian priestly writings. These allow for divorce by mutual consent, but otherwise they permit the dissolution of marriage only when a wife has committed a grievous sin (one that renders her *margarzān*, "deserving of death").[43] The classification of sin in Zoroastrian thought is complex, but murder, sorcery, adultery, and wifely disobedience figure prominently in lists of grievous sins and transgressions that allow for divorce in the Middle Persian writings of the Abbasid period.[44] Also worth mentioning is an eleventh-century Arabic account of Zarathushtra's teachings on divorce, according to which "there can be no divorce other than for one of [the following] three [reasons]: adultery, sorcery, and apostasy [*al-zināʾ wa-l-siḥr wa-l-tark al-dīn*]."[45] These formulations parallel Ishoʿbokt's very closely; they are also gendered in the same way, allowing men to end their marriages for the causes enumerated but limiting women's prerogatives to do so. Given that Ishoʿbokt was closely conversant with Sasanian law, it is not a stretch to suggest that he was inspired by Zoroastrian thought or by the regional background that he shared with it when he put his Christian doctrine of divorce to paper. Timothy and Ishoʿbarnun reworked his formulations in their own law books, and the treatment of legitimate grounds for divorce in East Syrian law thus incorporated several typically Zoroastrian-Iranian perspectives.

All these congruencies between East Syrian and other regional traditions—in inheritance, dowry, and divorce law—remind us of the continuing diversity of Abbasid society and culture even in the "formative period" of Islamic history. While Islamic law was becoming increasingly integral to caliphal judicial practice and intellectual culture, the East Syrian jurist-bishops of the eighth and ninth centuries pointedly turned to other resources to create their Christian legal tradition; their law books reveal the durability of ancient legal orders that persisted alongside caliphal administration and Islamic law. The fact that the roots of Islamic law also lay in regional traditions meant that many of those legal orders did not always differ from one another very substantively, at least in the realm of the family; from the vantage point of widely shared expectations of patriarchal social organization, for example, it is not surprising to find Timothy having no problem with a Christian "appoint[ing] a Muslim [as guardian] over his sons and house" (*pqad ʿal bnaw w-ʿal bētēh gabrā mashlmānā*) when no suitable Christians are to be found and the Muslim is pious and God-fearing (*dāḥel l-Alāhā*).[46] Despite such areas of overlap, it is nonetheless striking that the East Syrian bishops turned to a variety of customary, ancient legal materials to repackage as Christian tradition when Islamic law might seem an obvious resource and when the conditions of caliphal rule spurred their concern for communal law in the first place.

West Syrians: The Question of Islamic Law

The West Syrian synodal legislation of the eighth and ninth centuries is a converse example. While it is built out of many of the same regional institutions as East Syrian law, such as the system of two-stage inchoate marriage, several of its key features appear to have taken shape under the influence of Islamic legal norms and practice. One is the *mahra*, the marriage portion the groom owes to the bride, which in the West Syrian treatment exhibits many affinities with the cognate Islamic institution, the *mahr* (or *ṣadāq*). Islamic law enjoins the payment of the *mahr* by the groom; dowries might still be gifted in practice, but Islamic law does not require them.[47] While the East Syrian sources devote much attention to regulating the amounts and disposal of dowries, the marriage portion is the only nuptial gift that the West Syrian canons comment on.[48] Dowries were no doubt standard among many Christians in early Abbasid Syria and the Jazira, so the fact that West Syrian jurist-bishops took an interest in regulating only the marriage portion suggests an accommodation to Islamic legal practice. Their use of the term *mahra* is further relevant. The *Syro-Roman Law Book*, a Syriac translation of Roman law that circulated among West Syrians in territories where provincial Roman law had held sway before Islam, uses the Roman term *dorā*, from Greek *dōrea*, to render the marriage portion paid by groom to bride.[49] The fact that Abbasid-era West Syrians eschewed that readily available Roman terminology in favor of *mahra* suggests again that the Islamic *mahr* was their model.

A similar situation holds for the understanding of the constitutive elements of a valid betrothal contract found in West Syrian synodal legislation. One such element, the active consent of both prospective spouses, is suggestive of a Roman legal background.[50] In the case of a bride whose parents have died, however, practices characteristic of Islamic law come into the picture. The main canon treating this matter specifies that an orphaned bride must have a guardian (*mamkrānā*) to give her in marriage and two further male witnesses (*trēn gabrē*) to testify that she has given her explicit, vocal consent to the union (*men pumāh*, literally "from her mouth").[51] These provisions accord closely with Islamic law, which requires precisely the bride's guardian (*walī*) and two additional witnesses to render a marriage contract valid.[52] Furthermore, although Muslim jurists tended to allow fathers the authority to marry off their virgin daughters whether or not they consented to the match, a girl's consent was necessary if someone else acted as the guardian.[53] In addition to these congruencies with Islamic law, the West Syrian canon again eschews the Roman terminology for the guardian (*epiṭropā*, *quraṭor*) found in the *Syro-Roman Law Book*.[54] Together, these factors suggest that the West Syrian doctrine of the marriage contract accommodated Islamic norms as much as it continued pre-Islamic provincial Roman practices.

Despite the differing relationship to Islamic norms between West Syrians and East Syrians, we should still understand the former to have been adopting regional customs into their ecclesiastical tradition much as the latter did. The distinction is that, where the East Syrian bishops stuck more closely to regional traditions of civil law whose roots predated the establishment of the caliphate, the West Syrians accommodated their law to Muslim judicial practice. Indeed, the very fact that the West Syrian provisions look more or less Islamic is a strong indication that Islamic law and caliphal courts were familiar resources to Christians in northern Syria and the Jazira. The best explanation for why West Syrian bishops would adopt norms of Islamic provenance more readily than the East Syrians lies in the latter's greater interest in cultivating law as a full-fledged ecclesiastical discipline. When East Syrian bishops turned to local Mesopotamian and Iranian traditions, they mined them fully; the West Syrians, on the other hand, were concerned with establishing a more general set of guidelines, so adapting to what locals were already doing, even if this was the practice of Muslim judges, was an expedient solution. Where the content of the East Syrians' family law demonstrates the continued vitality of diverse ancient traditions in the legal culture of the early Abbasid Caliphate, the West Syrians' indicates the simultaneous, growing hegemony of the Islamic model. In both cases, Christian law as a learned tradition took shape through interactions with a range of resources beyond the Syriac ecclesiastical heritage proper.

If jurist-bishops in the early Abbasid Caliphate promoted a conception of Christian community centered on the connection between ecclesiastical authority and the lay household, several key doctrines and institutions provided its legal architecture. Chief among these was the marriage contract, the instrument that established the statuses, rights, and duties that defined the social relations of the household. Although the bishops presented these doctrines as a specifically Christian law, they cobbled them together from a range of regional legal practices still rich and varied some 150 years after the Arab-Muslim conquests. The nuts and bolts of East Syrian family law represent Mesopotamian and Iranian practices that largely predated Islam and shared similarities with rabbinic and Sasanian law. West Syrian law appears to have adopted a few standard elements of Islamic practice related to the marriage contract and shows relatively little continuity with Roman law. As a new learned tradition produced out of the institutional and intellectual transformations of the early Abbasid Caliphate, Syriac Christian family law attests both to the great variety of legal cultures still vital in the early medieval Middle East and to the increasing importance of Islamic law as a model for organizing the social relations of the region's religious communities.

CHAPTER 5

Islamic Institutions, Ecclesiastical Justice, and the Practical Shape of Christian Communities

When a Christian man makes a betrothal contract [*tanway da-mkirutā*] without the mediation of priests and lay believers, [but] through a written document or the mediation of the pagans [*ḥanpē*], and takes a Christian wife, and later he does not want to keep her, we do not compel a man like this to keep that wife by the law of Christianity, because he did not marry her through Christian law [*nāmosā krēsṭyānāyā*].

—Ishoʿbokt, *Jurisprudential Corpus*

When the bishops of the early Abbasid Caliphate composed the treatises and issued the synodal canons that made up their new legal traditions, they sought to carve a distinctively Christian institutional space out of the multireligious society in which they and their lay flocks lived. They could not, however, make that society and its nonecclesiastical institutions simply disappear. Ishoʿbokt's ruling above describes laypeople using the services of non-Christians ("pagans," almost assuredly Muslims) to order their legal affairs—specifically, to contract marriages—and raises the question of whether Christian law and its prohibition of divorce still apply to such individuals. More broadly, we might ask: What does the fact that a Christian could engage with extracommunal marital institutions, like the "pagan" betrothal contract in Ishoʿbokt's ruling, say about the nature of religious affiliation in the early Abbasid Caliphate? How did the imbrication of Christian family law in the Islamic institutional order of the caliphate affect Christian social relations?

Seeking answers to these questions allows us to leaven our focus on the normative content of Syriac Christian family law with greater attention to practice—to consider how Christian marital institutions facilitated particular interactions between laypeople and ecclesiastics that shaped the practical boundaries of Christians as dhimmi communities. The bishops' law imagined a Christian community centered on ecclesiastical regulation of the household; this required chiefly laypeople's participation in ecclesiastical judicial venues where clerics contracted marriages and administered justice. But the non-ecclesiastical legal arenas open to all subjects of the caliphate exerted a constant pressure on this ideal picture. How might laypeople have navigated these options when they contracted marriages, and how did the bishops seek to manage and restrict them? A close examination of the Abbasid-era Syriac legal sources indicates that while the bishops construed lay participation in the institution of Christian marriage as a requirement of communal belonging, they simultaneously accommodated in theory lay recourse to comparable, non-ecclesiastical judicial and marital institutions—Ishoʿbokt chastised the laypeople in the ruling above, but he did not try to expel them from Christian communion altogether. Divorce, on the other hand, presented a more intractable problem for the bishops' vision of Christian community in the plural legal setting of the caliphate. Here, ecclesiastical law drew a hard boundary, emphasizing that if confessional belonging required participation in Christian marriage, that institution was by definition unbreakable. That boundary was under constant pressure in practice, however, as a result of the fact that Islamic law offered both male and female caliphal subjects of any religious affiliation a variety of ways out of unwanted marriages. The strictures of Christian divorce law thus produced a structural tension in Christian communal integrity, as a result of which particular circumstances might conspire to pull individuals outside the purview of ecclesiastical justice or out of the religious community altogether.

Ultimately, the common image of the institutionally autonomous, internally sufficient dhimmi community does not adequately describe the Church of the East (or other non-Muslim social groups) in the early Abbasid Caliphate. Lay-ecclesiastical interactions around the Christian marriage contract made confessional affiliation a more gradated affair, enacted through the necessary participation in particular communal institutions but with the potential of engagement with certain outside ones as well. Furthermore, the potential for lay recourse to Islamic judicial institutions meant that the indissolubility of Christian marriage as a communal boundary would always be contested and up for lay-ecclesiastical negotiation.

CHRISTIAN MARRIAGE IN PRACTICE: COMMUNAL PARTICIPATION BETWEEN ECCLESIASTICAL AND CALIPHAL INSTITUTIONS

The practical negotiation of Christian communal boundaries among ecclesiastical law, laypeople, and the Islamic institutional context will concern us in this chapter and the following three. Our overriding interest in this avenue of investigation is its potential to lead us to a sociological description of a "religious community," commonly considered the basic building block of the caliphate's social order, that accounts for both the social behavior of the community's members and the limitations set by elite norms. The classic scholarly approach to the medieval caliphate's religious communities views them as autonomous "social corporations," a view founded on a particular understanding of the nature of their communal institutions.[1] According to this model, a collection of people with a shared religious affiliation effectively becomes a "community" when they acquire a set of institutions sufficient to organize all their religious affairs and social relations, and which they participate in to the exclusion of equivalent institutions associated with other religions. To take one classic account of the East Syrians as an example, the Church of the East's distinctive theological doctrines, schools, monasteries, and legal institutions make it "possible to describe [analytically] a Nestorian religious community already in existence in Iraq toward the end of the Sasanian period."[2] While this generally reflects the image of the enclosed, self-sufficient community that religious elites projected in their normative texts, as we have seen from our overviews of the Abbasid-era Syriac legal sources, we also know that medieval subjects in fact participated in many institutions—legal, ritual/religious, commercial—beyond the narrow confines of their own religious affiliations.[3] This does not mean that communal boundaries were simply ephemeral, however, and the question then becomes not whether boundaries were crossed but which internal and external institutions, and which modes of participation therein, structured a community at particular historical moments, and how and why these changed over time.[4]

In this connection, examining the marital institutions that medieval Christians themselves understood as closely tied to religious identity is an avenue by which we might describe in greater detail the practical constitution of the medieval caliphate's confessional communities. The Christian marriage contract, as the foundational legal instrument from which the rest of the bishops' family law proceeded, is key here. Negotiations between ecclesiastics and laypeople around this institution, hints of which are visible in the bishops' written rulings, reveal a practice of Christian communal belonging founded on the necessary but not exclusive participation in the ecclesiastical administration of marriage—a model in which marriage was a Christian institution and a pillar of lay-ecclesiastical solidarities but was not understood to produce an unbreachable boundary against the comparable institutions of the dominant Islamic legal order.

The Eucharist and the Anathema

To illustrate this, we first need to revisit one other, particularly definitive Christian institution: the Eucharist. From almost any perspective, participation in key Christian rituals including baptism, festivals, and communion to the exclusion of the rituals of other traditions (or at least greater devotion to the Christian ones) made one a Christian in the medieval world; partaking of the body of Christ especially was the ultimate arbiter securing one's belonging to the church. Because clerics administered the communion ritual, regulating access to it was a key means by which they could mark who should and should not be considered to belong to the community. The anathema—a public decree issued by an ecclesiastic of "suspension," "estrangement," or "excommunication" (*kelyānā*, *nukrāyutā*, *ḥermā*) from receiving the Eucharist and from social mixing with Christians—put those who engaged in ecclesiastically disapproved practices beyond the communal pale.[5] We can imagine the strategy behind the anathema to have been twofold: to trouble offenders' consciences with the possibility of being cut off from salvation, and to subject them to social stigmatization through exclusion from the public rituals in which their peers and neighbors participated. Generally, the goal was to compel offenders to cease whatever behavior ecclesiastics identified as transgressive and to accept some form of penance, after which they would be readmitted to communion.

Because of the constitutive significance of the Eucharist to most any Christian association, examining the deployment of the anathema is a good way to track other practices around which questions of communal boundaries coalesced. For example, both the East Syrian law books and West Syrian synods prescribe the anathema for any layperson who brings a dispute before a non-ecclesiastical judge or figure of authority.[6] This was an intervention in many laypeople's tendency to patronize caliphal courts, both for the legal services they provided and because the decisions they reached had the backing of the state.[7] The bishops' prescription of anathema for litigating before non-ecclesiastics promoted an institutionally exclusivist vision of the community: to seek justice away from the ecclesiastical hierarchy was to forfeit access to communion and therefore one's standing as a Christian. In practice, many laypeople must have continued to bring disputes to Muslim judges (and to other non-ecclesiastics, like lay notables); perhaps some were suspended from communion for specific amounts of time for doing so, but it is impossible to imagine that every Christian who litigated in a non-ecclesiastical venue was definitively pushed out of the community. The deployment of the anathema in this context, then, points us toward the practical organization of Christian social relations around the institution of ecclesiastical justice; the bishops' expectation of exclusive participation existed in tension with a structural tendency for laypeople to do otherwise while continuing to claim Christian affiliation.

Communal Participation Through Christian Marriage

At first glance, Christian marriage as defined by the jurist-bishops of the early Abbasid Caliphate appears to have been a communal institution similarly exclusivist in design and unrealizable in practice. Since the East Syrian synod of 676 and the West Syrian synod of 794, bishops had asserted that only Christian law and ritual turned cohabitation between a man and a woman into lawful marriage. Both our scanty evidence for lay practice and the normative Christian legal sources themselves, however, suggest a partial accommodation to lay participation in non-ecclesiastical institutions in these realms. If Syriac law imagined the connection between ecclesiastical authority and lay households as the backbone of Christian social groups in the caliphate, they could be flexible enough to expect participation in Christian marriage without demanding exclusivity.

This becomes evident if we return to the question of the anathema. While the Syriac sources specify the anathema for Christians who bring disputes to non-ecclesiastical judges, litigation was not the only reason for medieval subjects to seek out figures of judicial authority. Drawing up documents that recorded agreements and transactions—such as marriages—was another standard judicial service that had been the domain of literate and scribal classes in Middle Eastern societies for millennia. Notably, the East Syrian legal sources say nothing explicit about Christians going outside of ecclesiastical circles for document-drafting services. While Timothy, for example, enjoins suspension from the Eucharist for Christians who take their disputes to non-ecclesiastics, he mentions only "repentance" (*tyābutā*) for going to "outside judges" (*dayyānē d-barrāyē*) in general.[8] Participating in a non-ecclesiastical judicial institution for reasons other than dispute resolution, in other words, is not as hard a boundary; the bishops disapprove of such practices, but they do not preclude one from communal belonging.

In theory, drawing up a marriage contract is just such a transactional legal service, as opposed to a litigious procedure. The Syriac sources clearly expect clerics to be able to render that service to laypeople. But in keeping with their general silence on non-litigious activities outside the ecclesiastical judicial sphere, the East Syrian jurist-bishops do not draw as hard a line on the subject as they might. The patriarch George's canon of 676 suggested the anathema for Christians who contracted marriage through non-ecclesiastical venues, but the Abbasid-era law books stress only that ecclesiastical law does not recognize such marriages and that therefore ecclesiastical judges cannot adjudicate disputes involving them.[9] This, for example, is the thrust of Ishoʿbokt's decision mentioned above; it states that if a couple has contracted a marriage through the law of the Muslims (*ḥanpē*, literally "pagans"), ecclesiastics should not recognize it as a true, indissoluble union "because [the couple] did not establish their pact [*qyāmhon*] before us."[10] Two points are noteworthy. One is the positive indication that some Christians did indeed contract marriages through non-Christian judicial channels. The second is that Ishoʿbokt does not understand the Christians in question to have forfeited their membership in the community; rather, spurning Christian law has left them without recourse to ecclesiastical adjudication if a dispute arises.

A ruling of Ishoʿbarnun's is similarly instructive: "There are people who have said simple, unsanctified words [*mellē shḥimātā*] to each other concerning their children, young women and men, in order to marry them to each other. They have not administered the betrothal through the witnessing of priests and their fellow believers, and have not given a cross, holy oil, or ring. Later, they do not want [to adhere to] something they had spoken of; [but] they receive no judgment [*lā ṣābēn b-meddem d-mallel[w] ʿam ḥdādē: layt ʿlayhon gzārdinā*]."[11] This ruling indicates that, beyond the perceived threat of Islamic courts to communal solidarity, bishops also reacted against lay tendencies to arrange legal affairs before prominent community members and among themselves.[12] But Ishoʿbarnun's approach, much like Ishoʿbokt's, is further notable in that it tacitly recognizes the continued Christian affiliation of laypeople who have married without using ecclesiastical judicial channels, even as it evidently disapproves of them.[13]

Together, these rulings evince a gradated conception of communal belonging facilitated by the institution of Christian marriage. On the one hand, the bishops asserted that only a Christian ritual and adherence to ecclesiastical law could turn cohabitation between a man and a woman into a valid marital union. On the other, they did not preclude laypeople who engaged with non-ecclesiastical legal orders in this domain from access to the Eucharist and Christian society in general. In fact, further evidence suggests that the bishops had an interest in accommodating such laypeople and bringing them into the sphere of Christian law. Ishoʿbokt's *Jurisprudential Corpus* offers a variety of simple means by which laypeople who have been living in "irregular" unions can have them recognized as legitimate by the church. If a man and woman have been cohabiting and claim to be married, for example, they may simply present themselves before priests and lay witnesses at a later date. If no priests are available, two or three lay witnesses are sufficient to make the union valid. Even more striking, a man who "has taken a slave or other woman into his bed" (*amtā aw anttā ḥrētā aḥid b-teshwitēh*) may simply acknowledge her as his wife.[14] Here, Ishoʿbokt allows an unlawful sexual relationship to be brought into the realm of legitimate unions recognized by the church; like the other cases, the ruling provides a mechanism to acknowledge irregular relationships in an ecclesiastical framework rather than penalizing them as unlawful.

Although our evidence is too thin for a definitive statement, the overall picture that emerges is that ecclesiastics imagined the Christian household as a foundational communal institution and expected that the practices of its formation and reproduction would pass through ecclesiastical channels; but as long as that condition was met, they did not level the anathema at lay engagement with other judicial avenues, thus tacitly, if grudgingly, accommodating them. One wonders whether lay patronage of both ecclesiastical and extracommunal legal orders for matters related to marriage was relatively common, at least in cities where Christians and Muslims lived in close quarters. What would have prevented a layperson from drawing up one marriage contract with ecclesiastical officials and receiving a blessing, then walking down the street to register the union and the associated property transfers with a Muslim judge according to Shariʿa norms? As the terms of the latter contract would have been more readily enforceable, covering one's bases in this manner may have been attractive; perhaps laypeople were willing to weather whatever grief the ecclesiastics gave them in the off-chance that they needed a Muslim judge to reach a settlement on a dispute. Relevant here is comparative evidence from Egypt, from where we have several ninth- and tenth-century marriage contracts drawn up by Muslim scribes, according to Islamic scribal conventions and with Muslim formulas like the *basmala*, for Christian parties. A document of 885 from the Upper Egyptian town of Ashmun, for example, records the marriage portion one Yuhannis ibn Shanudah promised to his wife, Darwa bint Shanudah, both manifestly Coptic names.[15] Egypt is not Iraq or the Jazira, of course, but this and other contracts like it are striking examples of Christians making use of non-ecclesiastical institutions to contract marriages even in regions, like Upper Egypt, with large Christian populations and ecclesiastical infrastructures.

What did Yuhannis's and Darwa's priest think of their Islamic marriage contract? He likely would have grumbled disapprovingly, but had he shared the perspectives of East Syrian jurist-bishops he may well have let it slide as long as the couple also contracted a proper Christian marriage with a priest's blessing. In this respect, the East Syrian doctrine of contractual marriage as elaborated by Abbasid-era jurist-bishops allowed for practices of communal participation more gradated than the exclusivist, institutionally autonomous model we typically expect from dhimmi religious elites. They demanded lay participation in Christian marriage as a foundational communal institution; but when laypeople went elsewhere, as many no doubt did in the pluralistic legal arena of the medieval caliphate, the bishops sought to extend legitimation to their activities rather than exclude them from the community altogether. In this respect, a shaded Venn diagram rather than a closed, separate circle might better represent the Church of the East as a social group within the caliphate. Different degrees of affiliation were conceivable and practicable; these ranged from exclusive patronage of East Syrian institutions—keeping to the center of the community's circle—to participation in the church's necessary ritual and social institutions while simultaneously engaging in certain extracommunal ones—moving toward the circumference of the circle where it overlapped with others.

It is also of the utmost importance to emphasize that, because extracommunal institutions like Islamic marriage contracts administered by Muslim judges conditioned the possibilities for lay practice and elicited ecclesiastical responses, those institutions too were constitutive of Christian communal boundaries. Even to the extent that fully exclusive lay participation in Christian social institutions was realizable in practice, communal autonomy was still illusory insofar as it was only conceivable in response to an external order—the caliphal institutions against which communal ones were supposed to be a bulwark. In this respect, East Syrians constituted themselves as a community not purely through their own autonomous institutions but in the triangulation between lay social practice and the competing limits placed on it by both ecclesiastical and extracommunal norms.

CHRISTIAN DIVORCE LAW AND ISLAMIC INSTITUTIONS

The role of extracommunal institutions in shaping the early Abbasid Caliphate's Christian communities is even more conspicuous in another, related realm of ecclesiastical judicial practice: divorce. Syriac family law adopted a typically Christian perspective that the bond of marriage was essentially indissoluble. Only for a few, especially grievous transgressions—chiefly adultery and apostasy—could a spouse lawfully forsake his or her partner and seek to marry another. (Strictly speaking, it was remarriage rather than divorce itself that most troubled Christian thinkers; since sex and marriage rendered two individuals one indivisible flesh, for one of them to unite with another was an affront to God's order.) From the bishops' perspective, complete fidelity to these principles was a requisite of Christian communal affiliation: the default punishment for leaving a marriage without recognized cause was anathematization from receiving the Eucharist and from social intercourse with other Christians.[16] Communal participation through the institution of Christian marriage, then, not only meant having one's union blessed by and contracted before clerics; it also meant adhering in practice to the Christian principle of marital indissolubility.

Islamic law, on the other hand, offered generally permissive rules of divorce that contrasted starkly with those of the ecclesiastics. Significantly, this had the potential to make Islamic judicial institutions an attractive resource for laypeople seeking divorces that ecclesiastical judges were loath to grant. Caliphal institutions were thus a strong practical challenge to the ecclesiastics' ideal of indissoluble marriage and the form of communal participation it facilitated. If laypeople went outside the sphere of ecclesiastical justice to end their marriages, did this put them outside the bounds of Christian community altogether? How did the bishops respond to that challenge? What was the impact of Islamic divorce law on Christian social bonds in the early medieval caliphate? Divorce law in Islamic and other medieval legal traditions is strongly gendered; as such, we will consider in turn its structuring effects on the practices available to non-Muslim men and women, and thus its interaction with Christian institutions in creating specific, gendered boundaries of communal participation.

Men Divorcing Women

The Islamic law administered by state-appointed judges offered wide latitude to adult male subjects of the medieval caliphate to end their marriages as they saw fit, as long as their financial circumstances were secure enough. Islamic law's doctrine of divorce is rooted in the Quran, and Muslim jurists had already well delineated its basic outlines by the eighth and ninth centuries.[17] In all the major Islamic schools of law, a husband has the right to unilaterally repudiate his wife, a divorce procedure known as *ṭalāq*.[18] He is obligated to hand over any marriage payment he owes as required by the original marriage contract and, according to some jurists, to support his wife during her *ʿidda*, the waiting period intended to ensure that she is not pregnant before the divorce becomes final. Otherwise, *talaq* is a broad and largely unrestricted institution. According to medieval Muslim jurists, men could effect *talaq* simply by pronouncing one of a number of acceptable formulas; courts had no necessary role to play, and written documentation was not required. Nonetheless, divorces were also brought before judges to be recorded and witnessed in documents, especially in order to keep track of whether the debt of the marriage payment that *talaq* entailed had been fulfilled.[19]

The caliphate's legally pluralistic environment, in which state judicial venues were open to subjects of any religion, undoubtedly posed challenges to the bishops in this realm. Theoretically, a Christian man who wanted to end his marriage for any reason unsanctioned by the bishops' norms had to do no more than go before a Muslim judge and witnesses and pronounce the requisite divorce formulas. This is what one Sawirah (Severus, a thoroughly Christian name) did in an Arabic document of 909 from Egypt's Fayyum Oasis, for example: the papyrus records Sawirah's affirmation that he "has divorced his wife Qasidaq, daughter of George the monk, triply [and] irrevocably" according to the standards of Islamic jurisprudence (*ṭallaqa mraʾatahu Qsydq ibnat Jrjh al-rāhib thalāthat al-batta lā rajʿa lahu ʿalayhā*).[20] At issue for us is how ecclesiastics might have responded to such situations. East Syrian and West Syrian bishops of the early Abbasid Caliphate prescribed the anathema for any Christians who left their spouses for unrecognized causes, suspending them from communal participation in order to pressure them to return to both spouse and Christian community. The other side of the coin, however, was that the offender might apostatize; if his ties to Christian social networks were not otherwise strong enough to compel him to return to the fold, he might opt instead to cut his losses and convert to Islam, obtaining the desired divorce and accruing the potential benefits of being a Muslim subject of a Muslim state. We lack the data to be able to say how often this occurred. But the key point is that the intersection of caliphal judicial institutions (which allowed men a simple path to divorce) with the Syriac bishops' law (which prescribed the anathema for ecclesiastically unsanctioned divorce) could create the structural effect of draining Christian men away from the community. The same scenario did not apply, by contrast, to Jewish men, who according to rabbinic law already had prerogatives to divorce their wives not dissimilar from *talaq*.[21]

If they did not want to risk losing believers in this manner, the bishops' other option would have been to accommodate lay divorce by not strictly enforcing the anathema. Notably, the Syriac legal sources show little sign of budging in this respect. In addition to offering systematic descriptions of the grounds that allow for divorce and remarriage, the bishops' law books treat a range of marital hardships—poverty, impotence, infertility, abandonment—for which dissolution of the union might appear to be an expedient solution. These represent very real problems, and the casuistic nature of the rulings and the detail involved suggest that they came often to the attention of ecclesiastical judges. Consider, for example, the following question addressed to Timothy: "A man took a wife and lived with her. After a while she was struck by a long-lasting illness, and it has prevented her from union [*shawtāputā*, i.e., sexual intercourse] with the man. She has no hope of recovery. The man says, 'I am young, and I cannot remain continent [*eṭṭor qaddishutā*].' How should we answer him?"[22] One can easily imagine a distressed (and callous) Christian husband appearing before an ecclesiastical judge and looking for a way out of a marriage the circumstances of which had become untenable for him. If the judge followed the rules laid out in East Syrian legal writings, however, the man would have been disappointed. A finalized marriage in which the wife (or husband) falls chronically ill such that sex and childbearing become impossible is still a Christian union, and divorce is impermissible.[23] The same holds when a wife turns out to be infertile.[24] Other than a few exceptions made by individual jurist-bishops—if one spouse is "tried by Satan" (*metnassyā men sāṭānā*, probably meaning epileptic) or if a wife is "disobedient" (*paknitā wa-mṣaʿʿrānitā*) to an extreme degree—the indissolubility of the marriage bond remains the rule even in cases of hardship.[25]

On the whole, then, the jurist-bishops of the early Abbasid Caliphate understood participation in the institution of Christian marriage to mean adhering strictly to its indissolubility. Conflict over laymen's desires for divorce and remarriage is an entirely familiar feature of other Christian societies, but the crucial difference here is the caliphate's institutional setting. The easy path for male subjects to a "civil-law divorce" through Islamic judicial practice was a structural incentive that, in particular circumstances, could pull Christian men beyond the sphere of ecclesiastical justice and away from the Christian community altogether. We might speculate schematically that in areas with large Christian populations, overseen by bishops and with the regular service of priests, communal pressures and the stigma of the anathema were strong enough to counteract this incentive. Without overstating its evidentiary value, al-Jahiz's anecdote that opened this book is instructive: according to its (highly rhetorical) description of the urban Christians with whom al-Jahiz was familiar, the impermissibility of divorce was a fully accepted norm.[26] But the structural tension between Christian divorce law and Islamic judicial practice was a constant, and it therefore put stresses on the bonds of Christian communities and laymen's communal affiliation different from those attending other socioreligious groups in the caliphate.

Women Dissolving Marriages

Talaq, divorce by unilateral repudiation, is an exclusively male right in Islamic law. The medieval jurisprudential tradition, however, recognized a variety of other means by which women—and in one case, non-Muslim women specifically—could seek the dissolution of their marriages. When comparable cases came before Syriac Christian jurist-bishops, on the other hand, they continued to uphold the general indissolubility of the marriage bond. Caliphal judicial practice thus created potential tensions in laywomen's religiocommunal allegiance, different from those that affected Christian men but still significant.

The principal Islamic doctrine by which women could seek to end their marriages, and probably the best documented in practice, is *khulʿ*, a judicial procedure in which a wife requests her husband's consent to dissolve the union in return for giving up some compensation, usually her marriage portion.[27] Muslim jurists also developed mechanisms to free women from marriages made untenable by particular hardships, which, because *khulʿ* required the husband's consent, they would have been unable to do otherwise. These doctrines were not always unanimously accepted across the legal schools, but they are already present in the earliest Islamic legal texts of the eighth and ninth centuries. Because the jurists understood sexual intercourse to be a wife's conjugal right, for example, her marriage to an impotent man (*ʿinnīn*) unable to consummate the union could be dissolved by judicial decree a year after she raised the issue with a recognized authority.[28] Al-Shafiʿi, as well as Malik ibn Anas in Medina, gave women the right to dissolve marriages to men stricken with chronic, debilitating illnesses including insanity (*junūn*), elephantiasis (*judhām*), and leprosy (*baraṣ*), on the grounds that these make sexual contact impossible.[29] The jurists of Kufa, including Abu Hanifa, tended to disagree on this point; but there was also support among the early Hanafi authorities of Iraq for the Shafiʿi and Maliki position, as Muhammad ibn al-Hasan al-Shaybani is reported to have considered a husband with an "unbearable [bodily] flaw" (*ʿayb lā yuḥtamal*) equivalent to one unable to consummate a marriage, and so ruled that his wife should be given the option to leave him.[30]

Thus, despite the fact that Islamic law did not allow women the prerogative of *talaq*, the jurisprudential traditions offered a variety of other means by which they could seek to dissolve their marriages.

The contrast with the Syriac bishops' law is predictably stark. Timothy, for example, does not allow a woman to leave her husband even if he has been unable to consummate his marriage for twenty years.[31] As discussed in the previous section, chronic illnesses in either spouse are not legitimate grounds for divorce either. Ishoʿbokt offers a few exceptions to this general strictness. If a man is unable to consummate his marriage due to his "natural defects" (*mumē kyānāyē*), his wife can request judicial dissolution after remaining in the union for one year and waiting another in "widowhood" (*armlutā*).[32] Ishoʿbokt also allows for the dissolution of betrothals by mutual consent in extreme circumstances—if the couple "hate each other" (*sānēn la-ḥdādē*), they may pay various financial penalties and separate with no claim on each other's property (*metparshin men ḥdādē w-lā shalliṭin ʿal qenyānā da-ḥdādē*).[33] These more lenient rulings, however, apply only to unconsummated marriages—that is, when sex has not established singleness of flesh, and separation thus does not pose acute theological problems.

Overall, the bishops' law maintained the principle of the indissolubility of marriage, in contrast to a caliphal judiciary that did offer limited means for women, otherwise disadvantaged by Islamic divorce law, to get out of untenable marriages. Which Christian women in our period would have had the legal literacy to go outside of ecclesiastical justice to seek *khulʿ* and other Islamic forms of judicial divorce? We lack the evidence to answer that question, but there is another judicial practice that further makes clear how restrictions on women's divorce options could pose a structural danger, from the bishops' perspective, to the integrity of Christian communities. Because Islamic legal traditions maintained unanimously that a Muslim woman could not be married to a non-Muslim man, converting to Islam before a Muslim judge and witnesses was a means by which non-Muslim women could acquire divorces that their own communal leaders would not allow. We have no way to evaluate the scale or frequency of this practice, but it is clear that non-Muslim women did pursue it at times.[34] Even if they did not go through with conversion, non-Muslim litigants who were disadvantaged within their own communal judicial settings could use the threat of apostasy in order to secure leverage in negotiations; the Genizah documents of medieval Cairo's Jewish community, for example, occasionally show women in domestic disputes doing just this.[35] The early Abbasid-era Syriac bishops were certainly aware of the opportunities that conversion to Islam afforded to laypeople, and especially laywomen, who faced domestic difficulties; one ruling attributed to an East Syrian patriarch Yohannan (probably Yohannan IV bar Abgare, r. 900–905), for example, expresses concern that a couple who have been unable to consummate their marriage for several years will "go pagan" (*neḥnpun*)—that is, convert to Islam—if they are not released from their bond.[36]

While the prospect that women seeking divorce might apostatize confronted all non-Muslim communities, we can once again imagine it posing a greater problem to Christian religious elites than Jews, much as the tension between ecclesiastical divorce law and the prerogative of *talaq* was a structural danger to laymen's Christian affiliation. The highly gendered character of premodern Middle Eastern legal traditions meant that women were invariably disadvantaged in the divorce options open to them; but rabbinic law, both in antiquity and the Islamic period, developed a number of mechanisms by which women could request the dissolution of their marriages. These, such as the "ransom divorce" (Arabic *iftidāʾ* or *ikhtilāʿ*) attested in geonic writings and the responsa of Egyptian rabbis, were often comparable in procedural terms to *khulʿ* and other Islamic forms of judicial divorce.[37] We should not interpret these legal institutions too simplistically as unequivocal sources of power for Jewish women; besides the fact that class and social connections must have conditioned their feasibility, there are strong indications in the documentary record that men more often coerced their wives into ransom divorces, in which the latter gave up any claim to the marriage portions they were owed, than women initiated such divorces to free themselves from unwanted men.[38] It is conceivable that a similarly unequal balance of power often obtained among medieval Muslim men and women with respect to the practice of *khulʿ*.[39] Nonetheless, the fact remains that in medieval Islamic polities, Jewish women with the necessary material and social resources to seek divorce had their own communal institutions through which to do so; East Syrian Christians, as far as we can tell, did not, at least as long as ecclesiastical judges hewed to the principle of marital indissolubility encoded in their legal tradition. Insofar as threats of apostasy or recourse to Muslim courts were strategies available to any non-Muslim woman caught in difficult domestic circumstances, caliphal judicial practice in this area constituted a significant limit on the shape of all non-Muslim communities. But bishops expected laywomen to participate in the uniquely indissoluble institution of Christian marriage; when their marriages became untenable,

Islamic law offered them even greater incentives than it did to Jewish women to make use of extracommunal judicial institutions and, in dire situations, to leave their religious community altogether.

Men Gone Missing: A Case Study in Ecclesiastical Justice

While Christian divorce law had the potential to compromise communal integrity, it could also support and affirm it in particular, distinctive ways. We can see how this was so by examining the bishops' treatment of a conjugal problem endemic to medieval societies across the Mediterranean world and the Middle East: men's prolonged absence from or abandonment of their households. The traveling, missing, or runaway husband is a conspicuous figure in medieval Middle Eastern literary and documentary sources; his treatment in the Syriac Christian law books offers a useful case study of how bishops imagined their divorce law to buttress Christian institutions and community in the face of Islamic law and mores. The latter offered female subjects of the caliphate a variety of ways out of the untenable conjugal conditions that a missing or runaway husband might lead to. Christian law generally maintained the indissolubility of even those problematic unions; but it emphasized bishops' duties to correspond across the networks of the ecclesiastical hierarchy, track down missing men, and set lay household affairs aright. Strict divorce law could thus facilitate ecclesiastical-lay solidarities, produced in this case by the ecclesiastical administration of justice to laywomen and their families in times of hardship.

S. D. Goitein called absent and runaway husbands the single most common "family problem" to surface in the Genizah documents of medieval Cairo, and it must have appeared much the same in other corners of the medieval caliphate and the eastern Mediterranean.[40] Specific economic conditions and cultural practices, including the role of regional and long-distance trade in the medieval economy and the prominence of geographically diffuse centers of pilgrimage and religious study, meant that travel outside of local communities was both imaginable and practicable—especially for men of certain classes, to whom these activities were primarily open.[41] The Genizah documents—in which merchants ply trade routes from the Mediterranean basin to Cairo to India while humbler craftsmen make the rounds of the Egyptian Delta countryside—illustrate this reality well.[42] Its potentially detrimental effects on families' material circumstances, however, are readily apparent. Technologies of communication were no faster than human and animal messengers; what were a wife and household to do if a traveling man seemed to drop off the face of the earth or ceased sending maintenance back home, or if a husband fallen on hard times simply departed for greener pastures elsewhere? The social problems associated with men's travel are evident in varied attestations across the literatures and documents of the early medieval caliphate. In one early Islamic legal tradition, for example, a man who had been abducted by *jinn* excoriates the caliph ʿUmar ibn al-Khattab for allowing his wife to marry someone else in his absence.[43] The interconnected breadth of the early medieval caliphate made years of disappearance a distinct possibility, abduction by malicious spirits a reasonable explanation, and marital problems a predictable result.

The legal traditions of the early medieval caliphate devised a variety of means to free women from marriages to missing men and thus mitigate the problematic effects of spousal disappearance. One early Islamic juridical opinion, widely known across the caliphate, allowed a man's death to be presumed if no news of him was heard for four full years; after waiting an appropriate *ʿidda*, his wife could remarry.[44] The early Hanafi jurists of Iraq stuck to a more formalist position according to which only certain news of a missing man's death, or his pronouncement of a divorce formula, could end his marriage.[45] Al-Shafiʿi and his followers, however, offered a way around this impasse by allowing a woman whose husband did not supply her with proper maintenance to request the judicial dissolution of her marriage, which certainly covered cases of spousal abandonment or disappearance.[46] The Hanafis then made a standard practice (evident in later fatwa collections) of instructing wives of missing or negligent husbands to go to judges belonging to the other legal schools to receive more favorable rulings.[47] Thus Muslim jurists developed a number of legal mechanisms to ease the potential hardship caused by men's disappearance or abandonment. Jewish rabbis made similar efforts. Missing husbands are well known as one of the thorniest issues in rabbinic family law throughout the centuries; since a marriage could only be dissolved by the husband issuing a bill of divorce, the wives of Jewish men who disappeared became *ʿaggunot*, "anchored" to their husbands and unable to remarry.[48] Rabbis of the medieval period attempted to mitigate this difficulty by relaxing the criteria according to which a missing man's death might be proven or presumed. The Genizah attests to further methods, such as a husband leaving a conditional bill of divorce before he traveled with stipulations for freeing his wife from the marriage bond should no news of him arrive for a specified amount of time.[49]

Muslim and Jewish jurisprudents thus recognized exceptions to the general restrictions they put on women's prerogatives to divorce that could free them from untenable conjugal situations created by missing husbands. The same problems appear conspicuously in Syriac legal texts (Timothy's *Law Book*, for example, includes five lengthy rulings on the subject);[50] but rather than offer alternative solutions, the jurist-bishops tend to double down on the indissolubility of the marriage bond. Consider, for example, the following case: "A man takes a wife and remains with her for some amount of time, then goes to work somewhere else. He is [there] three or four years and sends no maintenance to his wife. In another instance, a man takes a wife and goes to a distant place [*atrā raḥḥiqā*] for five years and sends her no letter, nothing that brings her news of him, [nor maintenance]. She wants to marry another man, but she has not been released [*lā eshtaryat*] from that [first] one. What is the woman's answer?"[51] The question conveys the sense that considering the missing man's marriage dissolved and allowing the wife to remarry might be the most expedient solution. Timothy's answer, however, is unequivocal: a man may have obligations to his wife, but a consummated marriage cannot be undone by a husband's disappearance; only sure news of his death can release the woman from the marital bond; if she remarries without receiving that news, she has done so unlawfully (*lā nāmosā'it*) and committed adultery, and should therefore be anathematized. With no news of the first husband's death, the marriage cannot be considered dissolved.[52]

What about a runaway husband who has simply abandoned his wife and children? Another question addressed to Timothy depicts the issue well: "Someone was [resident] in some city from which he did not hail and married the [daughter] of a local [*anttā men nāsh bar mdintā*]. He stayed with her for some time, then went elsewhere for business and sent no maintenance to his wife. The woman's father wrote to her husband in order that he send maintenance to her. He did not, and informed him through word of mouth [*shlaḥ lēh b-melltā d-pumā*], 'I consider your daughter divorced, and I am not married to her' [*shbiqā li bartāk w-layt li shawtāputā lwātāh*]. He went elsewhere and no news of him has been heard. The father wants to marry [his daughter] to another man."[53] Timothy's answer maintains that in spite of the lack of maintenance payments, the bond of marriage remains fundamentally indissoluble; the wayward husband should be sought out and compelled to return to his wife.[54]

In cases of spousal disappearance or abandonment, Timothy's rulings thus maintain a strict, formalist adherence to the indissolubility of the Christian marriage bond. One might easily imagine Islamic judicial institutions coming into play here; if material support from family, community, or ecclesiastical institutions was not forthcoming, seeking a ruling or even converting before a Muslim judge might have been a reasonable alternative for Christian women backed into a corner. In spite of its strictness, however, Timothy's Christian divorce law might also work to uphold communal integrity in certain respects. Regarding runaway husbands, Timothy's ruling maintains that divorce is impermissible; but it also declares that a recalcitrant man who refuses to return to his wife should be anathematized. Since his abandonment of his wife has placed him outside the bounds of Christian community, his marriage is dissolved and his wife may remarry.[55] Although this ruling effectively gives up the offending husband as lost, Timothy in this case manages to uphold the theological opposition to divorce while simultaneously releasing the wife from an untenable marriage—obviating the incentive to seek a ruling of marital dissolution from, say, a Shafiʿi judge or to apostatize herself.

In other respects, the legal and social problems caused by missing husbands served as a platform for the bishops to promote a vision of communal integrity revolving around the link between ecclesiastical justice and lay households. Consider, for example, the following response of Timothy's: "It is not right that [the wife of a missing husband] turn toward another marriage until she knows exactly whether her husband has died or not. For the matter is not hidden, not [even] if he is among the Indians or Chinese. Bishops, metropolitans, and even patriarchs should correspond and investigate [concerning] the matter. Anywhere the man may be, he is compelled by the strictures [*tḥumē*] of the Word of God and the canons until he returns to his wife or sends her maintenance, as is right."[56] Although his requirements for divorce are strict, Timothy suggests here that a missing husband is not in fact likely to cause hardship. When someone goes missing, the East Syrian hierarchy, a network stretching as far as India and China, will always be able to find either news of his death or the man himself, and then lay God's law before him. The Church of the East is an integrated whole, with ecclesiastical custodians working to ease the way for their lay flocks; recourse to resources outside of the church need not enter the picture. Timothy puts forward a similarly bold claim in another response on a runaway husband: "The matter should be investigated and the man's whereabouts sought. The bishop of the wife's city shall correspond with the bishop who has jurisdiction [*uḥdānā*] where the man is, and he shall be anathematized until he turns to what is right. There is no jurisdiction in which we have no bishop or metropolitan. If the man dares to stand in dispute against both the canons and strictures and his directors and advisors [*matrṣānē w-mallpānē dilēh*], he shall be a stranger to the catholic church as one who transgresses the commandment of our Lord."[57] Here again, Timothy's rhetoric offers a vision of the Church of the East working like a well-oiled machine, with ecclesiastical manpower present in every corner of the world ready either to return a wayward husband to the straight and narrow or to anathematize him and allow his wife to get on with her life. Marital hardship need not require turning away from Christian tradition for solutions. To the contrary, it facilitates communal integrity, as ecclesiastics use the necessary resources to ensure the well-being of abandoned women and other afflicted members of their flock.

Pastoral duties of this kind had always been part of bishops' calling, but the sheer breadth of ecclesiastical reach and the intimacy of its entanglement with lay life that Timothy's rulings envision are striking. In his presentation, a network of bishops stretching as far from Iraq as China and India are linked together and coordinate resources (under the ultimate authority of the Baghdad patriarchate) so as to solve lay problems and ensure obedience to Christian norms. Timothy communicated by letter across the Abbasid Caliphate and as far as Turkic Central Asia and India's Malabar Coast, which illustrates that those great distances were imaginatively traversable to him; it is highly doubtful, however, that ecclesiastical power was ever as geographically prevalent and deep as his rhetoric imagines.[58] Nonetheless, even if the church's custodians could never ensure the well-being of every Christian household confronted by hardship, Timothy's rulings declared that they should try. He thus affirmed a vision of an integral Christian community founded on vertical solidarities between laypeople and clerics. Islamic judicial institutions and conversion to Islam always offered the prospect of draining believers away from the Christian community. Rather than loosen the strictures of Christian divorce or cede any ground to Islamic law and the options it offered to women in untenable conjugal circumstances, Timothy doubled down on traditional doctrine and the expectation that Christian belonging required participation in the indissoluble institution of Christian marriage. This necessitated ever-closer connections between ecclesiastical justice and lay households, as bishops would expend all efforts to alleviate the difficulties in the present life to which the moral rigor of Christian law might lead. The administration of ecclesiastical justice in lay households would thus produce the ecclesiastical-lay solidarities that defined the church as a socioreligious community, a distinct group embedded in but marked off from the caliphate's social landscape.

Despite its highly prescriptive character, Syriac family law provides important insights into the practical constitution of non-Muslim communities in the early Abbasid Caliphate, especially when put in comparison with Islamic texts and traditions. Scholarship on the caliphate's dhimmi communities tends to depict these as either fully autonomous or with highly fluid boundaries; our examination of East Syrian family law, on the other hand, has been concerned to identify more specifically which communal and extracommunal institutions, and which modes of participation therein, defined the Church of the East's social boundaries.

Christian marriage as outlined by the bishops' law was unquestionably a foundational communal institution. Their legal writings stress that lay participation in it—that is, lay deferral to the authority of ecclesiastics to validate, administer, and bless marriage contracts—was a requisite of Christian affiliation. Interestingly, however, East Syrian law also appears to have accommodated laypeople who contracted marriages in non-ecclesiastical venues like caliphal courts. It either extended legitimation to their "non-Christian" unions or looked the other way as long as laypeople also had their marriages blessed by a priest. In this regard, Christian marriage did not represent an impassable boundary that cut community members off from non-ecclesiastical institutions. In practice and in the bishops' law, Christian marriage facilitated a range of forms of communal participation; having a priest bless one's betrothal was expected of anyone who claimed Christian affiliation, but engagement with extracommunal institutions in other corners of the early Abbasid Caliphate's pluralistic legal order was possible as well.

In the area of divorce, however, Islamic judicial practice posed significant challenges to the bishops' model of a community integrated through lay participation in the institutions of Christian marriage and ecclesiastical justice. Generally, Syriac family law maintained a typically Christian perspective prohibiting divorce; ending a marriage for any cause unrecognized by the bishops was a transgression deserving of anathematization and thus put the offender outside the bounds of Christian communion. Islamic law, on the other hand, offered a variety of means for men and women to end their marriages. The Islamic institutional context thus created structural incentives with the potential to pull laypeople seeking divorce outside the bounds of Christian community—laymen might register a divorce before a Muslim judge and receive the anathema in response, laywomen could convert to Islam to get out of untenable marriages from which their own communal authorities would not release them. While the latter prospect confronted essentially all non-Muslims in the caliphate, both posed problems that were particularly acute for Christian communities, since other non-Muslim legal traditions tended to give men wide latitude to end their marriages and women at least some avenues to do the same. For the most part, the jurist-bishops did not compromise their opposition to divorce in response to these challenges. Instead, they viewed difficult unions in which laypeople were forced to remain as an opportunity to practice Christian fidelity and to build lay-ecclesiastical solidarity, as priests and bishops were charged with seeking reconciliation and alleviating hardship in lay households.

On the whole, the indissolubility of marriage was a hard boundary between Christians and others but one on which Islamic institutions exerted structural pressure owing to the very peculiarity of Christian law. That fact reminds us that it is never sufficient to describe the social form of non-Muslim communities in the medieval Middle East solely in terms of their own institutions; certainly by the Abbasid period, their boundaries were always negotiated against Islamic institutions and the practices that these enabled.

CHAPTER 6

Can Christians Marry Their Cousins?

Kinship, Legal Reasoning, and Islamic Intellectual Culture

Hashim ibn al-Muttalib ibn ʿAbd Manaf married al-Shifaʾ bint Hashim [ibn ʿAbd Manaf], and she bore him Yazid ibn Hashim. He was pure with no imperfection in him, for that is what they would call someone whose mother was the paternal cousin of his father.

—al-Baladhuri, *Ansab al-ashraf*, on cousin marriage among the Arabs

What fault is there for a man to marry a woman of close relation, whether [he and she are] the children of brothers or the children of sisters, or whether she is a more distant relative?

—Makarios, deacon of Hira, to Patriarch Ishoʿbarnun

Sometime after acceding to the East Syrian patriarchate in 823, Ishoʿbarnun sent a letter to the deacon Makarios of Hira, a town on the lower Euphrates adjacent to Kufa. The letter contained answers to a series of questions that Makarios had sent previously to the patriarch. Most of them revolved around liturgical practice and the proper administration of the Eucharist, but one was poignantly concerned with the problem of unlawful marriages—particularly, marriage between first cousins ("the children of brothers or the children of sisters"). Ishoʿbarnun replied that in fact there was no problem with cousin marriage, and its lawfulness was a divine mandate that "God commanded to Moses." The patriarch did not leave it at that, however. He went on to offer some choice words about his patriarchal predecessor, whom he blamed for putting in Makarios's head the mixed-up notion that there was anything wrong with cousins marrying each other: "Timothy, however, trying to undo God's commandment [*kad nassi d-neshrē puqdānā d-Alāhā*] . . . established himself against God and his saints and forbade this thing [cousin marriage]."[1]

This exchange between Ishoʿbarnun and Makarios is intriguing and unexpected. It is surprising to find a patriarch condemn his peer and predecessor in such stark terms, in a letter to a lowly deacon, no less, and over as seemingly mundane an issue as whether two cousins might marry each other. In fact, marriage between cousins was an ancient practice, common enough throughout the Middle East that we might describe it as a social institution, as suggested by the statement of the Muslim historian al-Baladhuri (d. 892) quoted above. Timothy, however, had indeed attempted to prohibit the practice among East Syrian Christians. The dispute this touched off with his successor, Ishoʿbarnun, offers a unique view of the role of distinctive conceptions of kinship in defining the Christian communities of the early Abbasid Caliphate, as well as the place of Christian law in the intellectual culture of the time.

Just as important as the legal and judicial institutions related to the family that the jurist-bishops enjoined laypeople to participate in were those that they proscribed. We focus on these in this chapter and the following two—and on how ecclesiastical prohibitions outlined distinctively Christian patterns of social reproduction that distinguished Christians as a social body from Muslims and others. In this connection, defining the range of kin relationships that made two individuals unmarriageable emerges as a common concern in late antique ecclesiastical legal writings in both the Roman and Sasanian empires. Influenced by their readings of key biblical passages and by Roman social norms, bishops throughout the late antique world sought to prohibit a variety of forms of close-kin marriage that were either customary in certain locales or characteristic of other religious traditions. Kin-marriage prohibitions thus became a well-worn ecclesiastical tool to imagine a Christian community distinguished by a distinctive model of kinship, one more rigorous, virtuous, and in line with the divine economy than the kin relations undergirding other social groups. In the caliphate, West Syrian and East Syrian jurist-bishops systematized more and more the theoretical web of kin marriages that they considered unlawful for faithful Christians. The resistance to Timothy's attempt to prohibit cousin marriage in the ninth century, however, is a reminder that some social institutions were sturdy enough to trump religious identity; cousin marriage remained a feature of kinship patterns across the Middle East's religious communities in the *longue durée*.

The Abbasid-era bishops' treatment of kin marriage not only concerned questions of communal boundary drawing; it also brought the bishops and their legal traditions into the mainstream of key developments in the caliphate's intellectual culture. Ishoʿbarnun's disagreement with Timothy regarding the permissibility of cousin marriage represented a contestation over legal authority—specifically, over the degree to which the discretionary reasoning of specialist jurist-bishops on the one hand and received tradition on the other should determine the norms of East Syrian law. Notably, a similar "reason/tradition" dialectic lies at the heart of the historiography of the formation of Islamic law; debates comparable to that between the East Syrian patriarchs definitively shaped Islamic (as well as Jewish) traditions in the same milieu of early Abbasid Iraq. The cousin-marriage dispute thus exemplifies how the concerns of wider scholarly circles informed the region's Christian traditions and communities. More significantly, it is another example of the necessity of incorporating non-Muslim materials into the historiography of medieval Islam—the reason/tradition dialectic not only was formative to Islamic law but represents a much wider transformation impacting multiple religious traditions in a highly diverse medieval empire.

KINSHIP, MARRIAGE, AND COMMUNITY FROM LATE ANTIQUITY TO THE ABBASID CALIPHATE

Timothy's prohibition of cousin marriage—"It is not permissible [*lā yajūz*] for a man to marry the daughter of his paternal uncle, paternal aunt, maternal aunt, or maternal uncle"—was only one of a series of rulings in his *Law Book* detailing unmarriageable relatives, ranging from sisters-in-law to uncles' widows to nephews and nieces.[2] It is not an exaggeration to say that essentially all human societies have espoused a set of norms like these: rules that govern who counts as an individual's kin, and who within and outside of that group qualifies as a legitimate prospect for marriage. The study of the intersection of kinship and marriage practices is one of the oldest subfields of social anthropology, which has long recognized that how human collectivities conceive kinship and how they use marriage to tie different kin groups together are fundamental to their overall social organization.[3] Are young people of marriageable age expected to marry residents of another town in order to ensure peaceful relations with neighbors? Are more closely related spouses preferable in order to consolidate lineages and family properties? Though questions like these no longer receive the scholarly attention that they did in the heyday of structural anthropology, there is no doubt that normative ideas of how kin are supposed to relate to each other set constraints on marriage in every human social order.

For our purposes, it is further important to recognize that those constraints are often valorized in culturally specific terms. When Timothy's *Law Book* prohibits marriage between a man and his sister-in-law, for example, it not only labels the practice impermissible but calls it a "custom of the pagans and Zoroastrians" (*ʿādat al-ḥunafāʾ wa-l-majūsiyya*).[4] Much more than a social faux pas, the practice in question is an affront to the Christian moral order. Whatever the social-structural functions of kin marriages, in other words, legal regimes frequently construe such practices as constitutive of cultural affiliations. This was true across the multireligious societies of the late antique and medieval Middle East. In the Roman and Sasanian empires, bishops promoted kin-marriage regulations that accorded with their distinctive readings of scripture and produced Christian difference from non-Romans, Jews, and Zoroastrians. For Abbasid-era jurist-bishops, kin marriage was one of the few areas of family law that had a strong basis in the ecclesiastical traditions of late antiquity, which the bishops expanded into ever more systematic schema of kinship impediments to marriage in their Syriac legal writings. The most striking of their novel regulations is Timothy's prohibition of cousin marriage, which, not unlike those of earlier periods, constructed a notion of distinctively Christian kinship by flying radically in the face of regional customs and practices common to other religious traditions.

Kin Marriage in the Roman East and Islamic Syria

A wide array of attitudes toward the relationship between marriage and kinship characterized the societies of the ancient Middle East and Mediterranean world. The Romans are known for a general aversion to kin marriage; at the other end of the spectrum, the Zoroastrian traditions of Iran esteemed close-kin unions in a manner that routinely horrified outside observers. Christian law on either side of the frontier between the two empires responded to these realities and made the avoidance of certain close-kin marriages a mark of Christian belonging. Though ecclesiastical law in the Roman Empire treated marriage relatively little, it did at times incorporate Roman perspectives on kin marriage, largely in response to practices in the eastern provinces and to those associated with Judaism. In the Sasanian Empire the situation was much different. The high value that the imperial religion placed on particular types of close-kin marriage, and their incompatibility with biblical teachings, led the fifth-century East Syrian patriarch Mar Aba to issue the first substantial body of Christian family law: a series of prohibitions of close-kin unions associated with Zoroastrianism.

Scattered throughout the sources of ecclesiastical law of the later Roman Empire are a variety of prohibitions and prescriptions of penance for certain types of marriage between relatives. Though never very systematically enumerated, there were several organizing principles behind them. One was the doctrine of the "oneness of flesh" (Genesis 2:24) created by the marital bond and its implications for marriages with affine relations (i.e., in-laws—people one is related to through marriage). If a husband and wife are one flesh, then the blood relatives of each are effectively the blood relatives of the other. So, from this perspective, if a woman's husband dies and she later marries his brother, the union might be considered an unlawful brother-sister one. Besides the "oneness of flesh" principle, the other major impetus behind ecclesiastical regulation of kin marriage was Roman law. In general, scholars believe that the peoples of Rome and the Romanized territories of the western Mediterranean tended toward exogamy: marriage outside of an individual's broader kin group appears to have been the norm.[5] As such, the classical Roman legal order prohibited a variety of kin marriages. These included unions between parents and children and between siblings, the core "incest taboo" that anthropologists see as nearly universal across human societies. But they extended further as well, most significantly to prohibiting unions between uncles and nieces and between aunts and nephews.[6] As the relationship between Christianity and the Roman state grew ever closer, late antique ecclesiastical law incorporated some of those standard Roman perspectives on the degrees of relationship that made marriage between two people unacceptable.

Ecclesiastical law, moreover, did not adopt these strictures as hypothetical exercises. Rather, it did so in response to the Christianization and Romanization of the empire's eastern provinces. In many corners of Egypt, Syria, Mesopotamia, and Arabia, customs prevailed that were quite distinct from the Roman tendency toward exogamy, and preferences for certain types of marriage within kin groups were old and deeply rooted. Although their origins are essentially unknowable, a common assumption is that kin marriages became customary among certain peoples because they have the benefit of consolidating family properties—the fragmentation of a man's estate upon his death can be avoided or mitigated if some of his heirs are married to each other. With the extension of Roman citizenship to all the empire's inhabitants in 212 and the steady pace of Christianization beginning in the fourth century, confronting these forms of kin marriage became important to efforts at Christian self-definition.[7] Several practices stand out notably in this respect: marriage between uncles and nieces and between widows and their deceased husbands' relatives.

Uncle-niece marriage is the chief union between kin related by consanguinity (i.e., by shared ancestry or "blood") that receives condemnation in late antique Christian legal sources. According to the pseudepigraphical *Canons of the Apostles*, for example, a man married to his niece may not serve in the clergy, while epistles and canons issued by bishops including Ambrose of Milan (d. 397), Rabbula of Edessa (d. 435), and Theodoret of Cyrrhus (d. c. 457) denounce the practice.[8] This likely reflects the promotion of Roman kinship norms as proper Christian practice; the Bible includes no prohibition of uncle-niece marriage, but classical Roman law as well as later edicts of the third and fourth centuries frequently condemned it.[9] There is little doubt that both emperors and bishops were concerned to issue this legislation because uncle-niece marriage was common or at least unremarkable in stretches of Syria and Mesopotamia. For example, Theodoret's letter castigates the magistrates of Zeugma, a city on the Euphrates, where "uncles have taken the opportunity to marry their nieces."[10] It is also worth noting that Jewish rabbis were known to promote uncle-niece marriage as meritorious.[11] Ecclesiastical condemnation, then, was an effort to promote Roman social mores in the eastern provinces and, perhaps, to distinguish Christian from Jewish marriage patterns.

In addition to marriage between blood relations, late antique ecclesiastical law also targeted at times unions between affine relatives. For example, the *Canons of the Apostles* decree that a man who "marries two sisters" cannot become a clergyman—in other words, a widower should not marry his deceased wife's sister.[12] As noted above, one of the primary rationales behind these prohibitions was the theological principle of oneness of flesh created by the marriage bond: if husband and wife are a single flesh, their respective in-laws are actually blood relatives and therefore unmarriageable. Affine unions were also offensive to Roman mores, evidenced by their condemnation by a number of imperial edicts.[13] It is again likely that late antique ecclesiastics and Roman officials actively addressed these practices because they were current in certain regions of the Roman east. Affine marriage as an institution is probably most well known in the form of the biblical levirate, according to which the brother of a man who died sonless was obliged to marry the widow (his sister-in-law) in order to produce a fictive heir for the deceased to carry on his lineage.[14] Affine marriages could also serve to cement ties, political or otherwise, between families; if a man's wife died but he wanted to retain connections to her natal family, one way to do so was to marry her sister. While the levirate itself may no longer have been current among Jews in the late ancient empire, analogous practices in the eastern provinces likely elicited the official condemnations. An imperial law of 475, for example, calls marriage between a man and his brother's virgin widow an Egyptian practice.[15] This and other evidence suggest that various forms of marriage between affine relatives in order to perpetuate the lineages of childless men or consolidate ties between families could be found in the late antique Roman east. Contrary as these practices were to Christian theological principles, bishops made efforts to restrict them.

Unsurprisingly, that ecclesiastical perspective carried through to West Syrian law in the caliphate. Canons issued by synods in 785, 794, and 846 enumerate the traditional kinship impediments to marriage, with some additions we will examine later.[16] One new norm is worth noting now: a prohibition on marriage between people related by baptismal sponsorship (*shāwshbinutā*). Synodal canons of the eighth and ninth centuries specify that marriage between a godparent and godchild is unlawful. Moreover, they make baptismal sponsorship essentially a third category of impediment to marriage equivalent to affinity and consanguinity: a godparent's relatives are prohibited to his or her godchild, and vice versa.[17] Interestingly, Jacob of Edessa notes in one of his responsa of the late seventh century to the priest Adday that "in the canons of the Apostles or Fathers [*b-qānonē mān da-shliḥē aw d-abāhātā*], nothing is written concerning this matter. . . . According to custom, however, especially in the entire province of Syria [*ba-ʿyādā dēn w-yattirāʾit b-kulēh purnāsā d-Suriya*]," marrying someone related through sponsorship is a "grave, incurable sin" (*ḥṭāhā meddem qashyā w-lā metasyānā*).[18] We seem to have, then, a practical concern of the church in Syria that made its way formally into West Syrian legislation only under the rule of the caliphs.

To an outside observer baptismal sponsorship may appear entirely different from consanguinity or affinity, but that difference underscores how culturally determined any kinship system is. Whom individuals may marry and whom they are encouraged to marry fundamentally affects any human society's overall patterns of social reproduction and organization. West Syrian ecclesiastical traditions asserted effectively that Christianity had its own such system, constituted especially of the spiritual kinship created by Christian ritual and Roman preferences for exogamy, which was specifically different from Jewish practices and other ancient conceptions of kinship in the eastern stretches of the Roman world.

Kin Marriage, Zoroastrianism, and Christianity in Iraq and Iran

While a limited range of forms of marriage between kin caught the attention of ecclesiastics in the Roman Empire, circumstances to the east were different. To Romans and most other outsiders, the Iranian empire of the Persians was a hotbed of incest—a place where impure and unnatural unions between family members were allowed or even celebrated.[19] In the words of the early Christian theologian Tatian (d. c. 180), "Greeks at any rate think that intercourse with one's mother is to be avoided, but such a practice is most honourable among the Persian magi."[20] Although the Roman perspective was value laden, it was not entirely incorrect. Bishops in the Sasanian Empire and its successor provinces of the early caliphate had to reckon with the practice of close-kin marriage on a larger scale than did their counterparts to the west.

In Sasanian Iran, Zoroastrian thought and the importance of aristocratic lineage combined to produce a system of values and practices in which many close-kin marriages were acceptable, religiously laudable, and sometimes economically advantageous. In brief, Zoroastrian cosmology understood certain "next-of-kin" unions (Middle Persian *khwēdōdah*)—specifically between a man and his mother, sister, or daughter—as virtuous emulation of the creative coupling of the gods. On the basis of this divine model, human practitioners of *khwedodah* marriage acquired great religious merit.[21] Zoroastrian tradition also placed high importance on human fertility, particularly the perpetuation of male lines of descent, to guarantee humanity's continued worship of the deities and to counteract the destructive forces of the evil god Ahreman. This priestly orientation accorded well with the concerns of Iranian aristocrats to maintain their family lineages. The result was a distinctive Zoroastrian-Sasanian law of inheritance that often encouraged unions between kin to ensure that every lineage had a male heir, a system similar to but much more complex than the biblical levirate. Modern scholars refer to these practices as intermediate and substitute successorship.[22] According to several key Middle Persian legal texts, when a man of a certain socioeconomic standing died without any living sons his estate was to be transferred to an intermediate or substitute successor—usually one of his relatives—for temporary safekeeping. The substitute successor was charged with entering a temporary marital relationship to produce a male child. That child then became the full legal heir of the deceased, the true successor, and inherited his patrimony and family identity. The sources expect that it often would have been a sonless man's relatives who would have taken up the task of producing this heir; it appears, therefore, that temporary unions for the purpose of intermediate and substitute successorship were often contracted between kin of some form. For example, a daughter could have been called upon to provide a male heir for her deceased father by entering into a union with his brother—resulting in an uncle-niece union—or a nephew for his deceased uncle with the uncle's widow.

For our purposes, the principal point of interest is that Christians in the Iranian empire were certainly among the practitioners of these institutions: late antique East Syrian sources indicate that some Christians in Sasanian Iraq and Iran made use of the close-kin marital strategies for lineage reproduction encoded in the law of the Zoroastrian priests.[23] In the view of a monastically trained, reformist East Syrian episcopacy emerging in the sixth century, however, those practices were fundamentally disconsonant with the teachings of Christian scripture. This opposition is evident above all in the writings of the patriarch Mar Aba. Mar Aba's concerns revolved around Leviticus 18:6–18, which prohibits sex between a man and a specific set of consanguine and affine relations (mother, father's wife, sister, granddaughter, aunt, paternal uncle's wife, son's wife, brother's wife, wife's descendants [from a previous marriage], wife's sister). Mar Aba understood these sexual prohibitions as impediments to marriage that should apply to all Christians; as such, they precluded many of the temporary unions between kin facilitated by the institution of substitute successorship to produce heirs for sonless, deceased men. Mar Aba singled out these practices as characteristically Zoroastrian and un-Christian in an exhortative exegetical treatise on Leviticus and a widely circulated synodal letter. The latter, for example, suspends from communion any Christian man who "dares to approach his father's wife, his paternal uncle's wife, his maternal uncle's wife, his paternal aunt, his maternal aunt, his sister, his daughter-in-law, his daughter, his wife's daughter, his son's daughter, his daughter's daughter, or the daughter of his wife's daughter like the Magians [*mgushē*]."[24] The fact that Mar Aba found the need to explicitly condemn these unions indicates that they were current to some degree in Sasanian Christian communities. It is also important to emphasize that the patriarch's letter suggests not some arbitrary predilection among laypeople for what the bishops see as incest but the practice of the specific, characteristically Iranian institution of substitute successorship.[25] The man Mar Aba targets who has sex with his uncle's wife, for example, would have been doing so because that uncle died sonless; he and the widow married temporarily because they had been charged with producing a fictive male heir. To Mar Aba, the union itself was unacceptable and impure because it violated biblical prescriptions; in the context of Sasanian society, on the other hand, it was simply one step in the practice of substitute successorship, a lawful and accepted way to perpetuate a male lineage that was in danger of dying out.

Mar Aba's kin-marriage prohibitions made up the first discrete body of East Syrian ecclesiastical law related to marriage and the family; insofar as laypeople followed them, their effect was to distinguish Christian patterns of reproduction from Zoroastrian-Iranian ones.[26] Notably, the practices that Mar Aba targeted persisted into the early Abbasid period in formerly Sasanian regions, where they continued to draw the attention of ecclesiastics. Two of Timothy's letters of the late eighth century attest to a conflict between the patriarchal center and the Christians of Khuzistan over whether Christian affiliation precluded the Iranian customs of lineage reproduction facilitated by close-kin marriages. Warning the region's Christians to stay away from the "unlawful marriage of the Magians" (*zuwwāgā b-lā nāmosāyutā da-mgushē*) and the "Magian laws of Zarathushtra" (*nāmosē mgushāyē d-Zardosht*), the letters cite several legal texts of Roman provenance that prohibit marriage between a man and his wife's sister, brother's wife, niece, aunt, and father's wife. Timothy adds further that children born of these unlawful unions may not receive inheritance; this confirms the connection to substitute successorship, as passing on inheritance to the fictive heirs of deceased men was usually the point of contracting marriages between kin in an Iranian cultural setting.[27] Close-kin marriage, a function of Iranian institutions of lineage reproduction but which the ecclesiastical hierarchy associated with Zoroastrianism, thus persisted among the East Syrians of Khuzistan, and perhaps elsewhere, into Abbasid times.

In view of the practical constitution of Christian communities, Timothy's letters also underscore how locals might contest the patriarchal center's definitions of which marital practices fell outside the bounds of Christian belonging. Khuzistan was an ancient and prominent eparchy that looks to have had a strong sense of regional identity and interests, attested not only by the persistence of close-kin marriage but also by local resistance to Timothy's ecclesiastical appointees, evident in other letters of his.[28] Timothy's arguments to the Khuzistanis offer the canons from the Roman texts as authoritative; they also use admonitory language, saying, for example, that transgressors of his strictures against close-kin marriage "shall be strangers to the exalted gloriousness of the Kingdom of Heaven until they repent."[29] But one has the sense that having those strictures accepted across an entire region like Khuzistan was not a simple matter, and that the patriarch's vision of Christian community modeled on biblical notions of kinship had to be negotiated with regional actors to some degree.

From Mar Aba to the Abbasid Caliphate, then, the idiosyncrasies of Zoroastrian-Iranian marriage and inheritance practices and their currency among some Christians spurred the articulation of a set of kin-marriage prohibitions as part of the Church of the East's ecclesiastical law. These proscriptions were more extensive than the kin-marriage legislation of West Syrian bishops and their Roman predecessors, but all viewed kin marriage as an arena in which scripture had established definite guidelines for faithful Christian practice—guidelines that it was an ecclesiastical duty to expound and that produced Christian distinctiveness when set beside the norms of other religious communities. Where West Syrian bishops largely prescribed Roman norms as ecclesiastical law, East Syrian kin-marriage prohibitions would specifically differentiate Christian practices of lineage reproduction from those of Iranian aristocrats and Zoroastrian teachings.

The Curious Case of Cousin Marriage in the Caliphate

The common denominator of those prescriptive traditions is that they were issued in direct response to social practices. In the Abbasid period, West Syrian and East Syrian bishops interested in building a more systematic communal law expanded on these foundations considerably, identifying ever more distant relatives whom good Christians should not marry. Other than the specter of Zoroastrian customs in the Church of the East's Iranian jurisdictions, however, the early Abbasid sources give the impression of being less interested in legislating against current social practices when they tackle kin marriages. Neither the West Syrian nor the East Syrian sources, for example, rail against Islamic kinship patterns the way that Sasanian-era bishops did against Zoroastrian "impure marriage" (*zuwwāgā ṭanpā*).[30]

At first glance, Timothy's prohibition of cousin marriage (quoted in the following from the shorter Arabic translation of the Syriac original) would seem to fit this pattern: "It is not permitted for a man to marry the daughter of his paternal uncle, paternal aunt, maternal aunt, or maternal uncle, because they are analogous to [*yujrawna majrā*] his father and mother, brothers and sisters, and their children. If it is not permissible to marry those who are more distantly related, how [can it be permissible to marry] them [i.e., cousins]? For if we consider the paternal uncle's wife and maternal uncle's wife analogous [*nujrī . . . majrā*] to the mother [in terms of prohibition], how much more so [*kam awlā*] should we consider the paternal uncle analogous to the father and paternal aunt analogous to the mother?"[31] We will return to the details of this passage, but for now the point worth noting is that Timothy makes no mention of actual practices or of non-Christians. His justification for the prohibition of cousin marriage is rather a reasoned argument—essentially, cousins as relatives are similar to siblings; since siblings are unmarriageable, so should be cousins.

Despite the apparent abstraction, however, Timothy's prohibition represented in fact a radical intervention, as marriage between first cousins was a nearly ubiquitous feature of kinship patterns in the medieval Middle East. For Timothy to prohibit it was therefore to assert a conspicuous Christian exception to practices of social reproduction and organization common to Muslims, Jews, and others throughout the central lands of the Abbasid Caliphate. In this respect, Timothy continued the precedent set by pre-Islamic bishops like Mar Aba—he located Christian distinctiveness from the wider society in which laypeople were embedded at the intersection of kinship and marriage. Notably, however, this Christian norm did not last, as Makarios's appeal and Ishoʿbarnun's repeal of the prohibition demonstrate, and this is where the greater interest lies. The East Syrian dispute over cousin marriage is another example of how illuminating non-Muslim materials and traditions can be to the history of the medieval Middle East more widely. If cousin marriage might easily appear emblematic of a timeless, reified Middle Eastern kinship system, the East Syrian sources show us that foundational social institution as it was contested, reproduced, and reconfigured as part of a religious tradition.

That a preference for marriage between first cousins, especially parallel paternal ones (i.e., the children of two brothers), has characterized many kinship systems of the eastern Mediterranean and western Asia was a running theme of twentieth-century structural anthropology.[32] Diffuse but numerous attestations throughout premodern literary traditions demonstrate that the practice was ancient and widespread. According to a Hadith attributed to the Prophet Muhammad, for example, an indication that the Day of Judgment has come will be when "a man seeks an Aramaean peasant [*nabaṭiyya*], marries her at his expense, and leaves aside his cousin [*bint ʿammih*], not looking at her"; in other words, it is a true sign of the apocalypse when men choose to not marry their cousins.[33] The extensive sources from medieval Egypt show parallel cousin marriage to have been common in the Jewish community represented in the Cairo Genizah and among Copts.[34] Writing in the mid-ninth century not long after Timothy's patriarchate, ʿAbdishoʿ bar Bahriz called marriage to one's paternal uncle's daughter (*mkirtā bart dādēh*) "a custom that is held to and is current among the people" (*ʿyādā d-aḥid wa-rdē bēt bnay nāshā*).[35] We might list any number of further examples from both late antiquity and the Islamic period.[36]

If cousin marriage was an entirely mundane feature of social relations in the medieval Middle East, Timothy's ruling betrays no concern for this. Rather, he presents the prohibition as a corrective to a logical hole in East Syrian law, a necessity to maintain the internal coherence of the system of legal norms he considers authoritative for

East Syrian Christians—if you cannot marry your sibling, you cannot marry your cousin. While a concern for intellectual consistency of this kind is unsurprising for a learned, celibate bishop, banning cousin marriage had very material implications for the lay householders among whom it had long been an unremarkable marital strategy. In this light, although Timothy never says that he is prohibiting cousin marriage simply because Muslims, Jews, or any other non-Christians do it, his ruling asserts a specifically Christian form of kinship sharply distinct from that of the general milieu of the Middle East. Much like Mar Aba's polemics against Iranian substitute successorship, Timothy's prohibition rendered cousin marriage no longer just something many subjects of the caliphate did; the imperatives of legal reasoning made a regional practice into one that denoted non-Christian belonging.

Unlike Mar Aba's kin-marriage prohibitions, however, Timothy's did not remain part of the East Syrians' normative tradition. In Makarios's question to Ishoʿbarnun regarding the lawfulness of cousin marriage, we can glimpse some tentative local resistance. Lower clergymen had daily commerce with laymen and were well positioned to encourage practice to conform to the ecclesiastical hierarchy's norms; the fact that a deacon appealed Timothy's prohibition to his successor suggests not only that Timothy's laws had circulated in Makarios's Hira, a brief overland trip from Baghdad, but that the locals had had a hard time accepting the unlawfulness of a practice as customary as cousin marriage. Ultimately, Ishoʿbarnun repealed Timothy's prohibition, deeming cousin marriage permissible in both his letter to Makarios and his *Law Book*.

The final point of interest here is that Timothy's prohibition, even if it lasted only a few years, is a telling moment in the making of a medieval Middle Eastern social institution. On the one hand, the dispute over cousin marriage is suggestive of the *longue durée* of certain aspects of premodern social organization. For all that the establishment of the caliphate inaugurates a new political and religious era in the standard periodization, the fact that a religious elite like Timothy could not get his prohibition of cousin marriage to stick betrays deep continuities in regional patterns of social reproduction. On the other hand, the dispute also reminds us that those patterns were not eternal, immutable facts.[37] Conditions in the Abbasid Caliphate spurred new articulations of Christian communal belonging through law, and these reconstrued cousin marriage as something other than a routine domestic practice; after contestation over its suitability for good Christians, it was inscribed in East Syrian legal tradition and rendered lawful in Christian terms. A standard, regional feature of kin relations was thus redefined explicitly as an element of Christian kinship—one of the central methods by which Christian law constructed difference between Christian social collectivities and others in the caliphate.

REASON, TRADITION, AND LAW, OR, WHY CAN'T AN EAST SYRIAN MARRY HER COUSIN?

If Makarios found Timothy's prohibition of cousin marriage a considerable burden on the average households of his congregation, he must have been pleased to receive Ishoʿbarnun's letter, delivered some twenty years after the original ruling, rescinding it. But like Timothy, Ishoʿbarnun showed little interest in cousin marriage as it was actually practiced. He took issue instead with the justification that Timothy put forward to ban it—a reasoned argument hinging on Timothy's intellectual authority as a bishop. Where Timothy turned to reason, Ishoʿbarnun offered up a different form of proof for the permissibility of cousin marriage: he turned to scripture.

The negotiation between these two modes of authority is a key feature of the Abbasid-era bishops' approach to kin marriage and their broader ideas of Christian community shaped by lawful practice. It has significant implications, moreover, for our understanding of the place of Christian law in the developing intellectual culture of the Abbasid Caliphate. Ishoʿbarnun's response to his predecessor's stance on cousin marriage brought to the fore the fundamental question of the relative authority of individual, reasoned opinion versus received tradition—the question of what, precisely, the sources of Christian communal law should be. Most revealingly, this was not a problem that only Christian bishops in the Abbasid Caliphate confronted. Islamic law was taking shape in the same milieu around precisely the same question, as were Rabbanite and Qaraite Judaism. The East Syrian dispute over cousin marriage, then, shows us how the emergence of Christian law in the caliphate was part of a wider renegotiation of the role of reason and received tradition in the religions of the early medieval Middle East. In this case, legislating about Christian marriage did more than define the shape of Christian communities; it also exemplified the key place of Christian traditions in the caliphate's transreligious intellectual culture.

Analogical Reasoning and Law in Abbasid Intellectual Culture

To situate Timothy and Ishoʿbarnun's dispute in the intellectual context of the time, let us return to Timothy's ruling (quoted here in the original Syriac) and draw out the justification behind it in greater detail.[38]

> Is it right for a man to marry his paternal uncle's daughter, his paternal aunt's daughter, or his maternal aunt's daughter?
>
> It is not right for a man to marry [*lā zādeq d-nessab*] either his paternal uncle's wife or his maternal uncle's wife. The paternal uncle is like a man's father; the paternal uncle's wife, therefore, is like a man's mother. And a man's maternal aunt is like his mother. If, therefore, we may not marry [*lā shalliṭ lan d-neshtawtep*] the paternal uncle's wife or the maternal uncle's wife, even though they are not related to us [*w-hādē kad lā qarribin* (read *qarribān*) *lan b-gensā*], how can one marry the paternal uncle's daughter or the maternal uncle's daughter? We have spoken [of uncles' wives] as "like the mother," and we have spoken of the paternal uncle and maternal uncle as "like the father." God forbids one *to lie with his sister, the daughter of his father or the daughter of his mother* (Deuteronomy 27:22, cf. Leviticus 18:9). Therefore, it is not right for a man to lie with the daughters of the mother's [and father's] brothers and sisters who are related by flesh [*bnāt aḥē w-aḥwātā d-emmā* (*wa-d-abā*) *d-qarribin ba-bsar*]; [this is so especially] since divine law forbids and admonishes us from uniting with the paternal uncle's wife or the maternal uncle's wife and from *revealing their shame* (Leviticus 18:14), though they are not related to us by flesh [*w-lā qarribin* (read *qarribān*) *lan ba-bsar*]. Those who do these things [i.e., marry cousins] are transgressors of the law [*ʿābray ʿal nāmosā*].

Though the passage may appear somewhat convoluted, Timothy is in fact employing a fairly straightforward method of analogical reasoning to arrive at his prohibition of cousin marriage. In essence, he identifies a general prohibitive principle in several recognized impediments to marriage, then builds an analogy on this rule to derive his new norm. Timothy begins from the premise that any sexual contact between a man and his aunts or his uncles' wives is prohibited. These norms, familiar from Leviticus 18:12–14, were already an established part of East Syrian law thanks to Mar Aba.[39] Timothy argues that these prohibitions obtain because a man's relationship with his uncles and aunts is analogous to that with his father and mother. In the case of a man's blood aunts, for example, a prohibition of marriage to consanguine female relations applies to them just as it does to his mother. In the case of his uncles, the same prohibitions apply to the women of their households as to the women of his father's; if a man may not marry his father's wife, he also may not marry his uncle's. Since the marriage prohibitions that apply to one's parents are thus analogous to those that apply to one's uncles and aunts, Timothy comes to the conclusion that the prohibitions that apply to the children of one's parents—that is, one's siblings—should likewise cover the children of one's aunts and uncles—that is, one's cousins. If uncles and aunts are like one's parents, then cousins are like one's siblings, and marriage with them is equally unlawful.

This ruling is notable for the fact that Timothy spells out fully the reasoning behind it, which is not his standard practice elsewhere in the *Law Book*. The mode of analogical reasoning itself, on the other hand, is not so unique. In fact, the prohibition of cousin marriage is only one example of jurist-bishops in the early Abbasid period approaching kinship impediments to marriage as a theoretical field to which they could apply tools of legal reasoning to spin a wider, systematic doctrine out of established norms and principles. This is interesting for two reasons. In aiming for greater systematicity, this orientation exemplifies the emerging sense among Abbasid-era bishops that law was an intellectual discipline to be cultivated, rather than merely the sum total of the community's rules issued on an ad hoc basis. It also fits into a wider regional interest, evident in the Islamic law taking shape in Iraq, in several Jewish movements, and in theological and philosophical inquiry, in the power of human reason to determine metaphysical truth and reveal God's will.

Impediments to marriage based on kinship were already part of the ecclesiastical law that bishops in the caliphate inherited from late antiquity. Abbasid-era bishops, however, were invested in compiling newly comprehensive communal legal traditions embodied in authoritative texts. When they approached their traditions as jurists more than as ad hoc legislators, kin-marriage prohibition was a topic that lent itself well to extrapolating theoretically a more systematic legal doctrine. It is not difficult to see why this was so—impediments to kin marriage derive from fundamental principles like consanguinity and affinity, and new ones can be calculated based on degrees within a closed system (i.e., the set of all possible relationships to any given individual). This is precisely what Timothy did with respect to cousin marriage: he saw that the logical coherence of the East Syrians' scheme of kin marriage prohibitions required ruling out marriage between cousins as well.[40]

Timothy's ruling is only one example of a steady expansion of kin-marriage prohibitions in the Syriac legal sources of the eighth and ninth centuries. Among the West Syrians, a good example is the short treatise *On Unlawful Marriages* composed in the circle of Patriarch Yuhanon III (r. 847–74). It lists fifteen fundamental affine kin-marriage prohibitions, then details the web of problematic interrelations that would result from each prohibited union. For example, if a man married a woman and his son her daughter, it would mean that the man had married the mother-in-law of his son and the woman had married the father of her son-in-law; their children would be both siblings and uncles/aunts to the man's son and woman's daughter.[41] The treatise goes on at some length in this manner, but the point to note is that we are not dealing with an individual ruling targeting a conspicuous social practice. Rather, Yuhanon's treatise is an example of ecclesiastics as jurists taking their received norms and spinning them out into a more systematic, comprehensive legal doctrine. A comparable East Syrian example is the treatment of kin-marriage prohibitions in ʿAbdishoʿ bar Bahriz's ninth-century *Order of Marriage and Inheritance*. ʿAbdishoʿ begins with a discussion of the fundamental Levitical principle that no man should "reveal the shame" (*maglāyu pursāyā*) of his relative (*qarrib besrēh*).[42] He then lists seven categories of relationship into which all kin-marriage prohibitions fit, such as ascendants, descendants, lateral relations, and various forms of affinity. Finally, he gives a systematic list of forty-one prohibited unions. Many betray the theoretical nature of the exercise; it is unlikely, for example, that ʿAbdishoʿ was actually concerned that many Christian men would dare to marry their paternal uncles' wives' siblings' mothers (*abāhay aḥay shotāpay dādaw*).[43]

ʿAbdishoʿ's treatment of kin marriage both identifies fundamental principles and details a comprehensive list of specific cases. In that combination we see that what was once a few norms issued by Mar Aba in response to transgressive social practices has become a more systematic statement of legal doctrine. The West Syrian treatise fits the same pattern. The greater systematicity evident in these works is emblematic of the degree to which bishops in the caliphate had come to see law as a learned tradition to be cultivated by specialists rather than a collection of ad hoc legislation. That change in perspective was due largely to the institutional and intellectual conditions of the Abbasid Caliphate. The authorities of each religious tradition were both expected to attend to their community's affairs and interested in keeping laypeople out of Muslim-staffed courts. Expanding Christian law to fit those needs could require treating it as a "jurists' law" in the manner of Muslim *fiqh*—as a comprehensive tradition to be delineated, organized, and managed by specialists.[44]

Especially germane are the more specific intellectual contexts of Abbasid Iraq and Iran. The quantitative, calculable principles underlying kin-marriage prohibitions lent themselves well to systematization and expansion through the application of analogical reasoning. Significantly, interest in the power of human reason to discern truth was a major feature of several distinctive intellectual trends in early Abbasid Iraq. Beginning in the late eighth century, Muslim courtiers in Baghdad began to invest a considerable amount of patronage in the translation into Arabic of ancient scientific and philosophical texts; the disciplines of Arabic philosophy (*falsafa*) and Islamic theology (*kalām*), the primary aim of which was investigating the nature of God and creation through reasoned argumentation, became prominent in the scholarly circles of Basra and Baghdad.[45] In the realm of law, analogical reasoning as a method of producing legal doctrine is closely associated with Islamic legal study in Kufa as well as with several Jewish groups in Iraq and Iran. Muslim jurists in Kufa were known especially for their use of *ra'y*—personal, discretionary reasoning—to decide new norms and rule on cases.[46] Among Iraq's Jewish communities, ʿAnan ben David (fl. c. 770) drew the ire of the geonim for publishing his own legal interpretations that rejected much Talmudic tradition. A major feature of ʿAnan's teaching was his use of the exegetical principle of analogy (Hebrew *heqqesh*) in a manner far beyond what the rabbis would allow to derive legal norms directly from the biblical text.[47] Further significant is early Qaraism, whose major thinkers lived in later ninth-century Iran and Iraq. Qaraite thought was defined by its rejection of the absolute authority of rabbinic tradition in favor of "a commitment to reason as an interpretive tool" (by the tenth century many Qaraites viewed ʿAnan as a founding figure, but originally the two movements were unrelated).[48] Notably, both ʿAnan and early Qaraites like Benjamin al-Nahawandi (fl. c. 850) took an interest in applying systematic and analogical reasoning to the incest prohibitions of Leviticus 18; extensive kinship impediments to marriage are a prominent feature of their writings.[49]

The treatment of kin marriage in the Syriac legal sources, then, exemplifies an approach to confessional law that is consonant with developments in other religious traditions of Abbasid Iraq and Iran.

From one perspective, there may be nothing particularly remarkable about this. Any body of positive law will be constructed by extrapolating in some fashion from accepted foundations, be they the Quran, the Bible, judicial precedents, or the French Civil Code. In the East Syrian case, however, the Abbasid context is certainly relevant. Timothy is well known to have been closely involved in the intellectual and court life of Abbasid Baghdad; he is reported to have translated Aristotle's *Topics* into Arabic and engaged in theological and philosophical debates with an Aristotelian philosopher and al-Mahdi himself at the caliph's court.[50] Muslim jurists of the Kufan tradition moved in those courtly circles as well, as the Abbasid caliphs beginning with al-Mahdi tended to favor the followers of the Kufan Abu Hanifa (d. 767) for major judicial positions.[51] We should see Timothy's explicit interest in using analogy to extrapolate God's law for Christians as a function of his engagement with this intellectual milieu. Importantly, this does not mean that he (or any other jurist-bishop) borrowed Islamic analytical methods in some mechanistic fashion. Timothy was learned in Aristotelian logic; he did not need anyone outside of East Syrian scholastic culture to tell him that syllogism and analogy were basic tools of reasoning. Furthermore, Islamic law in Timothy's day was still largely the provenance of study circles and had yet to develop a canon of texts that we might imagine non-Muslim scholars getting ahold of to study, as they would in later centuries. Rather, the focus on human reason characteristic of intellectual discourse in Abbasid Iraq pushed Timothy to deploy the argumentative resources of his own tradition in a new pursuit—confessional law—and in a manner that accorded closely with what his Muslim contemporaries were doing.

While Timothy did not simply appropriate legal analogy from Muslim jurists, his analogically derived prohibition of cousin marriage is emblematic of how Islamic thought was beginning to set the parameters of discourse of other traditions in its orbit. We have seen that the nuts and bolts of East Syrian law derived largely from non-Islamic sources; a diversity of traditions remained current in Abbasid Iraq, and Islam was not the only or even the most significant reference point. But because the potential for patronage was concentrated in the caliphate's major cities and the hands of Muslim elites, their interests were increasingly influential in determining prestige disciplines and methods of intellectual inquiry. The caliphate's institutional arrangement had already necessitated the production of Christian law and the rethinking of Christian community it entailed; Timothy's prohibition of cousin marriage is an example of Muslim scholars' intellectual agenda shaping the mode of discourse in a non-Muslim tradition.

Analogy Versus Exegesis, Reason Versus Tradition

If Timothy gives us a glimpse of Islamization—in the sense of the rising influence of Muslim scholars' intellectual preoccupations—Ishoʿbarnun's response points us in a different direction. For the latter, Timothy's interest in using reason to discern correct guidelines for human action conflicted with the normative authority of biblical scripture and other received traditions recognized by the Church of the East. In this respect, Timothy and Ishoʿbarnun's dispute over cousin marriage resembles the dialectic between reason and tradition commonly seen as the focal point of the development of Islamic law. But the East Syrian case suggests that that dialectic, rather than being a narrowly Islamic story, is in fact the backbone of a wider, longer-term realignment in regional intellectual culture.

Timothy's prohibition of cousin marriage by way of analogy implied that his position as chief bishop of the Church of the East gave him the authority to issue new norms on the basis of already accepted ones. When Ishoʿbarnun wrote his response to Makarios maintaining the permissibility of cousin marriage, he argued from a different source of authority: scripture. "That a man may marry the daughter of his father's brother, or a woman the son of her father's brother, God commanded to Moses. For He said, 'let the daughters of Zelophehad marry the sons of their paternal uncles.' And just as the children of brothers may [marry each other], so also may the children of sisters."[52] Ishoʿbarnun cites the story of Zelophehad's daughters from Numbers 36—in which the women in question were married to their paternal cousins in order to keep their father's patrimony in the tribe of Manasseh—as a scriptural proof that God has sanctioned marriage between cousins. He expands this line of reasoning in his *Law Book*, where the approval of cousin marriage communicated in the epistle to Makarios features as a ruling.[53] Here, Ishoʿbarnun adds an East Syrian exegetical tradition according to which Abraham and Sarah were cousins, the son of Terah and the daughter of Terah's brother. We learn from another of Ishoʿbarnun's treatises, moreover, that this understanding of Abraham and Sarah's kinship was propounded by no less than Theodore of Mopsuestia (d. 428), the late antique theologian whose exegesis and Christology formed the core of East Syrian ecclesiastical identity.[54]

From Ishoʿbarnun's perspective, this added up to a significant accumulation of received tradition weighing heavily in favor of the lawfulness of cousin marriage: God allowed the first biblical patriarch to marry his cousin, no apostle or church father afterward said anything to the contrary, and we know these facts of scriptural and ecclesiastical history from the East Syrians' chief intellectual authority. On what basis, then, could Timothy claim to outlaw cousin marriage? What we have here is contestation over the authoritative sources and methods that should determine Christian law. Where Timothy looked to extrapolate analogically a new ruling from established ones, Ishoʿbarnun held that any such derivation had to accord with God's prescriptions and the practices of the biblical forebears as found in scriptural narrative. Significantly, East Syrian ecclesiastics were heir to a late antique exegetical tradition, associated with the city of Antioch, that stressed the historical integrity of the biblical narrative.[55] If scripture and its authoritative Christian exegetes said that God had permitted cousin marriage to the patriarchs, that is indeed what happened, and it had to be understood as normative; Ishoʿbarnun, as a dedicated exponent of Antiochene exegesis, could not ignore this fact of scriptural history or explain it away as an allegory concealing some esoteric meaning.[56] From Ishoʿbarnun's perspective, therefore, Timothy's personal use of legal reasoning to arrive at a prohibition of cousin marriage had no precedence over the higher authority of received tradition, including God's scripture and its faithful interpreters.[57] The latter clearly substantiated that marriage between first cousins was lawful in Christian terms.

With Ishoʿbarnun's invocation of the authority of received teachings, we reenter the wider intellectual arena of the early Abbasid Caliphate. Anyone familiar with the history of medieval Islamic thought will notice an immediate parallel to the East Syrian cousin-marriage dispute: the standard narrative of the formation of Islamic law from the eighth century into the tenth revolves precisely around a "reason/tradition" dialectic, as Muslim jurists opposed to *raʾy* located greater legal authority in the normative example of the Prophet Muhammad. The rough consensus this debate ultimately produced—the "Great Rationalist-Traditionalist Synthesis" in the words of one leading scholar—is understood as a turning point in the development of Islamic law toward its standard, later medieval form.[58] What relationship did Ishoʿbarnun's recourse to exegetical tradition bear to this similar, but much more historiographically prominent, debate among contemporary Muslim jurists? It was not merely a pale reflection of Muslim concerns. Rather, the East Syrian cousin-marriage dispute helps us to see the "Great Rationalist-Traditionalist Synthesis" as a wider transformation in regional intellectual culture than the essentially Islamic story it is commonly presented as. The interests of Muslim scholars were a driving force behind this transformation, but its greater breadth becomes visible when we put the Islamic narrative into conversation with Jewish and Christian materials—like the East Syrian cousin-marriage dispute—and into a longer time frame. The heart of the early medieval caliphate's intellectual history, like that of its society and institutions, lies in the encounters of multiple religious traditions, not only in the specifically Islamic forms that these produced.

In the standard narrative, the reason/tradition dialectic at the heart of formative Islamic law involved a back-and-forth between the proponents of *raʾy*, chiefly the early Hanafis of Iraq, and those who sought to position the growing body of Hadith—records of the sayings and practices of the Prophet Muhammad—as the more authoritative source of Shariʿa norms. Ultimately, a general consensus among Sunni Muslim jurists emerged in the centuries following the pioneering work in legal theory of Muhammad ibn Idris al-Shafiʿi (d. 820).[59] This consensus recognized prophetic Hadith, in newly canonized textual form, as a source of Islamic law second only to the Quran; a limited form of analogical reasoning (*qiyās*) became the third source, to be applied to the first two by specialists in order to derive new norms. At first glance, one might suspect that the "tradition" side of the Muslim jurists' debate inspired Ishoʿbarnun's invocation of the authority of traditional exegesis, much as the intellectual climate of early Abbasid Baghdad conditioned Timothy's interest in analogy. This, however, would be a misinterpretation. Antiochene exegesis, central to East Syrian thought since at least the sixth century, had always stressed the integrity of the biblical narrative; it was a structural, normative limit within East Syrian tradition that would necessarily come into play whenever bishops began to reconsider the laws that bound Christian conduct in the present world. Taking the normative force of biblical narrative seriously, for example, drove Mar Aba's determination to apply Leviticus to Christian kinship in the Sasanian period.[60] As another example, the same imperative required Ishoʿbokt to explain why certain regulations found in scripture obtained for contemporary Christians while others no longer did.[61] The key point is that Ishoʿbarnun's invocation of exegetical tradition was in no way an attempt to whip up a Christian equivalent to prophetic *sunna*, carried out under the influence of Islam; it was a reaction from within East Syrian tradition to the challenges posed by the expansion of communal law and to Timothy's "reckless" use of analogical reasoning.

A comparison to the Qaraite case is apt here. The Qaraites rejected the special authority of the rabbis' Oral Law as embodied in the Mishnah and Talmud; they sought to derive new legal norms from the text of the Bible by way of analogy and reasoned argumentation. Because Qaraite hermeneutic principles accord very closely with those of Muslim jurists and certain early Shiite trends, scholars have devoted significant attention to the question of Qaraism's "Islamic origins." Recent studies have stressed, however, that the Qaraites' methods and scriptural focus are just as easily explained as outgrowths of traditional Jewish reading practices and epistemological problems in rabbinic thought.[62] There is little question that when the Qaraites began to write in Arabic, they employed terminology and idioms characteristic of Islamic law and theology, and these structured their modes of discourse in significant ways. But the debate over the normative authority of received tradition at the heart of Qaraite and Rabbanite efforts to define their traditions against one another was not simply the trickle-down residue of Muslim concerns.

Read in tandem with the East Syrian and Jewish examples, then, the Muslim jurists' "Great Rationalist-Traditionalist Synthesis" looks to be one strand of a wider reorientation of scriptural religious traditions in the early Abbasid heartlands. Each responded to the central problem of what role received, authoritative traditions should play in defining communal laws and practices, and each did so on the basis of internal imperatives—the prophetic example, Antiochene exegesis, rabbinic hermeneutics. In certain crucial respects, it was Muslim concerns that set this reorientation in motion. Muslim thinkers and Muslim patronage in Iraq made the role of human reason a central preoccupation of intellectual discourse, encouraging the forays into legal analogy of Timothy (and perhaps of ʿAnan ben David) and providing the Arabo-Islamic idioms in which the Qaraites discussed law. Here too, however, there is a significant background of interreligious encounter. It is clear that the focus on reason characteristic of Islamic thought in early medieval Iraq emerged in part out of

Christian methods of dialectical argumentation and rabbinic legal hermeneutics; early Muslim *kalam* texts follow the dialogic structure of Syriac theological works, for example, while scholars have long seen the roots of Islamic legal analogy (*qiyās*) in the rabbinic principle of *heqqesh*.[63] The point here is not to deny the originality of Islamic thought; rather, it is to illustrate that the "Great Rationalist-Traditionalist Synthesis" depended on longer-term interactions among Christians, Jews, and Muslims just as much as Islamic rationalism was later the catalyst to which Christians and Jews had to respond. We might schematize the overall process as follows. First, Muslim thinkers absorbed and repurposed features of Christian and Jewish reasoned discourse to their own ends. Then, as Arabo-Islamic thought in Iraq became increasingly influential and refracted its preoccupations with human reason across the region's intellectual landscape, Christians and Jews began to incorporate its methods into their repertoires as well. Finally, they, like al-Shafiʿi or Muslim traditionists, were compelled by the distinctive imperatives of their respective heritages to reconsider the normative standing of scripture and received tradition vis-à-vis reason and its newly central place in scholarly study.

Among Muslims, this process resulted eventually in the wide acceptance of a new legal theory, as well as the special niches occupied by theology and philosophy in medieval Islamic education. Among Jews, the debate over the authority of the Oral Law was foundational to the emergence of Rabbanism and Qaraism as distinct scholarly traditions (though not, at first, as distinct social groups).[64] Among Christians, the effects were more muted. The reason/tradition debate does not show up obviously outside of East Syrian law; and despite the emphasis that Antiochene exegesis placed on the literal-historical meaning of the Bible, Christians simply did not have to reckon with a body of received legal teachings as massive or as overwhelmingly central to their social and intellectual life as prophetic *sunna* or the Talmud. Nonetheless, reckon they did with the Bible, the exegesis of Theodore of Mopsuestia, and the faculty of human reason as they crafted a communal law necessary for life in the caliphate; and they did so in a manner not dissimilar from that of their Muslim and Jewish contemporaries.

From this angle, a small dispute between two Christian bishops over the permissibility of cousin marriage underlines again the interconnected religious diversity that was fundamental to the early medieval caliphate but is too often neglected in scholarly narratives. Contestation over the authority of reason and tradition was unquestionably central to the formation of Islam, and Islamic intellectual paradigms would only grow in influence as the centuries went by. But in the early medieval period, that contestation and the intellectual syntheses it produced were enabled by the multireligious setting of the Abbasid Caliphate, and they shaped traditions across that spectrum.

Whether or not Makarios knew it, his seemingly innocuous question to Ishoʿbarnun on the permissibility of cousin marriage cut to the heart of communal belonging and the intellectual makeup of religious traditions in the Abbasid Caliphate. Since late antiquity, ecclesiastics had sought to regulate the intersection of kinship and marriage in light of their readings of God's prescriptions in scripture and to distinguish Christian conceptions of endogamy and exogamy from those of other religions. In the Roman Empire, bishops tended to promote Roman perspectives on kinship as Christian law. In Sasanian lands, they sought to cut Christians off from the strategies of lineage reproduction that were characteristic of Zoroastrian preferences but conflicted with the norms of Leviticus 18. Timothy's prohibition of cousin marriage would likewise have strongly differentiated Christian practices of social reproduction from those of Muslims, Jews, and others; cousin marriage was an entirely ubiquitous feature of Middle Eastern patterns of kinship across religious boundaries.

One of the lessons of our investigation is the long-term durability of those patterns, even in the face of attempted regulation. Timothy's prohibition of an ancient household strategy did not last long, as Ishoʿbarnun rescinded it only twenty years later (and it never reappears in East Syrian legal sources of the later medieval period). Even the Zoroastrian-style kin marriages against which Mar Aba polemicized so strongly in the Sasanian period seem to have persisted for centuries, judging by Timothy's letters to the Christians of Khuzistan. Articulating a distinctively Christian notion of kinship required engaging with deeply embedded social practices whose connection to religious belonging was not necessarily evident to regular believers; drawing that connection was precisely the point of communal law, but its record in affecting or changing those practices was highly varied. Cousin marriage persisted well; in territories where the East Syrian patriarch's orders were not so keenly felt, Zoroastrian-style kinship patterns seem to have wholly ended only after Sasanian institutional structures faded away and conversion to Islam ramped up. Much like the patriarchal household, kin-marriage patterns as illustrated by Christian source materials represent deep continuities in Middle Eastern social history beneath the grander periodizations of political and religious change.

An equally significant context that those sources illuminate is the intellectual culture of the early Abbasid Caliphate. Timothy reasoned analogically to arrive at his prohibition of cousin marriage in the interest of making East Syrian law more systematic. Ishoʿbarnun rejected that prohibition because it conflicted with East Syrian biblical exegesis, which understood God to have sanctioned marriage between cousins for the biblical patriarchs. Where Timothy foregrounded personal ecclesiastical authority and discretionary reasoning, Ishoʿbarnun gave precedence to authoritative textual traditions. Effectively, the East Syrian patriarchs played out a Christian version of a parallel dispute taking place among Jews and Muslims in the early Abbasid Caliphate; exponents of each tradition sought to define the authority of received texts and teachings against the centrality of human reason that characterized much learned discourse in Kufa, Basra, and Baghdad. The East Syrian example has several important implications for the intellectual history of the early Abbasid period. On the one hand, it demonstrates the rising influence of Islamic thought on other traditions in its orbit; the Islamic disciplines cultivated in the cities of Iraq under the patronage of Muslim political elites encouraged a wider, newly acute interest in the epistemological power of reason. From this vantage point, East Syrian law formed as an intellectual tradition in response to parameters of inquiry increasingly set by Islamic thought, even as its goal was defining a distinctively Christian social practice in caliphal society. On the other hand, the East Syrian dispute over cousin marriage suggests that the reason/tradition dialectic was not simply internal to Islam and definitive of Islamic law, as one might suppose from many accounts of early Islamic history. Rather, it was constitutive of a broader realignment of the caliphate's major religious traditions; staking a position on the reason/tradition question was central to determining the characteristic shapes of Islam, Judaism, and even East Syrian Christianity as intellectual traditions in the medieval Middle East. A richer account of the early Middle East's history is dependent once again on giving due acknowledgment to the intersections of its many religious communities.

CHAPTER 7

The Many Wives of Ahona

Christian Polygamy in Islamic Society

Recall how we settled the dispute that occurred between Daniel the deacon with his lay brothers, the sons of Ahona of Karka d-Bet Slok, and that woman whom Ahona married in Kufa unlawfully. . . . We honored the fear of God, insofar as the ecclesiastical laws command that everything that was left by that man Ahona, whether real estate or cash, and all [his] property should be the inheritance of his lawful wife and sons.

—East Syrian patriarch Hnanishoʿ I to a clergyman in Kufa

In the last decade of the seventh century, a wealthy Christian man of Karka d-Bet Slok (modern Kirkuk) named Ahona passed away. What happened next was predictable enough, given that Ahona was a man of some means: his relatives got in a fight over how to split up his property. In this case, however, those relatives included wives and children from two separate—but apparently simultaneous—marriages. The clerical hierarchy of the Church of the East was none too happy about this situation, a fact that was to have a decisive impact on the outcome of the case when it came before the patriarch Hnanishoʿ.

This case of Christian polygamy brings us back to the theme of how laypeople, ecclesiastical regulation, and caliphal institutions interacted to shape in practice the Christian communities of the early medieval caliphate. Polygamous arrangements like Ahona's had deep roots in the patriarchal and patrilineal societies of the ancient and medieval Middle East but were anathema to Christian tradition. Polygamy thus became a locus of contestation between ecclesiastics and laypeople over the social commitments required by Christian belonging within non-Christian empires. Impressing upon laypeople the Christian ideal of monogamous marriage was a consistent concern on the part of bishops from the Sasanian Empire of the sixth century to the Abbasid Caliphate of the tenth. In particular, the prevalence of polygamy in the upper echelons of caliphal society created opportunities for jurist-bishops to articulate their vision of communal boundaries defined by a distinctively Christian household form—one fashioned by a monogamous mode of social reproduction sharply differentiated from that of Zoroastrians, Muslims, and others. Simultaneously, caliphal institutions provided resources for polygamous laymen to challenge that ecclesiastical understanding of the community, pointing again to the role of extracommunal institutions in shaping the caliphate's ostensibly autonomous dhimmi social groups.

Syriac legal texts from late antiquity demonstrate that customary forms of polygamous household organization persisted among certain classes of Christians in the eastern Fertile Crescent and Iran, despite well-established ecclesiastical opposition. Contemporary bishops both declared polygamy unlawful and sought a variety of practical means to discourage and restrict it. Banning those who transgressed their laws from participating in communal rituals was their chief tool. Conditions in the caliphate, however, gave new symbolic import to the practice of polygamy among Christians and spurred the development of new communal institutions to regulate it. The permissibility of polygamy under Islamic law and the opportunities of Muslim courtly society encouraged its practice by elite laymen. Beginning in the seventh century, jurist-bishops' efforts to expand their confessional legal traditions resulted in new strategies to combat lay polygamy, particularly by regulating the inheritance practices of Christians ever more closely and deciding who among their children was legitimate and who was not, as in Ahona's case. By denying inheritance to the Christian sons of second wives and concubines, the bishops promoted a Christian model of lineage reproduction starkly distinct from that of elite Muslim households.

In addition to legal texts, a variety of Arabic and Syriac narrative sources detail conflicts over polygamy between ecclesiastics and laypeople in the Abbasid Caliphate. These allow us to posit an informed outline for the practical effects of ecclesiastical regulation on lay practice and the constitution of Christian communities within the Islamic empire. In broadest terms, ecclesiastical tools like the anathema could persuade some laypeople to follow ecclesiastical prescriptions. The same elite status that encouraged others to practice polygamy, however, also allowed them to use their connections to state power in order to circumvent or nullify ecclesiastical sanctions.

Ecclesiastics had a better chance of enforcing their rules on inheritance: these materially affected women and children as potential heirs rather than powerful polygamous laymen themselves. Much like the case of divorce, however, the strictness of Christian law could also render communal integrity more precarious; punishing individuals because they belonged to polygamous households might push them to seek redress outside the communal fold or even through conversion to Islam. In these respects, caliphal institutions played a significant role alongside ecclesiastical regulation and lay interests in shaping the caliphate's Christian subjects as dhimmi social groups.[1]

ANCIENT POLYGAMY IN COMPARATIVE PERSPECTIVE

Much like close-kin marriage, a variety of polygamous practices were a routine part of many societies of the ancient and medieval Middle East; these constitute the sociohistorical backdrop to the forms of polygamy contested among Christians, Muslims, and others in the early medieval caliphate. In strict terms, our subject here is "polygyny": the practice of a man having multiple wives simultaneously. We will use the more idiomatic "polygamy" to cover a looser, wider range of situations in which a man cohabits with multiple women to whom he has sexual access, whether or not they are all lawful wives; some may be slave concubines, for example. "One man, multiple women" is thus the basic definition of polygamy we will work with, but it is important to note that it brings under its umbrella a wide array of household formations with distinct social functions.

Polygamous practices of one form or another have been characteristic of a wide swath of the typically patriarchal societies of premodern Afro-Eurasia. Anywhere under Islamic political dominion, for example, the lawfulness of polygamy was a given; the Quran was essentially unanimously understood to allow men to marry up to four wives and to have as many concubines as they could support.[2] But the lawfulness of polygamy should not be taken to imply that its practice was necessarily frequent or common. By all accounts, most ostensibly polygamous societies actually see very low rates of polygamy, since only a small social stratum has the resources to afford it. The polygamy premodern sources usually allow us to see is that of social and political elites: situations in which men who, by virtue of wealth and status, have the prerogative to keep multiple wives and/or concubines in their households. Royal polygamy, for example, was entirely typical in the Middle East from the Sasanians to the Abbasids to the Ottomans, as indeed it had been centuries and millennia earlier.[3] Sub-royal elites, including military officers, administrators, and merchants, might also have multiple wives or concubines in their households. Nor were these forms of elite polygamy restricted to the Middle East. Early medieval sources for Ireland and northern Europe, for example, attest that polygamy and concubinage remained common as a prerogative of elite status until the eleventh and twelfth centuries, well after Christianization.[4]

While polygamy was frequently a marker of status, it was also a reproductive strategy. In largely patrilineal societies, the more women bear children for a man, the better chance he has of continuing the family name. Reproductive concerns became especially important to the practice of polygamy at elite levels in the Islamic caliphate. From the early ninth century the Abbasid family began to prefer concubinage as a strategy for reproduction; Abbasid sons of concubines made up most of the potential heirs for succession to the caliphal seat.[5] In Sasanian Iran, polygamous arrangements could provide the more specific reproductive purposes required by the institution of substitute successorship—an already married man might be called to enter a second, temporary marriage to provide an heir for a deceased kinsman.[6] Also worth noting are the productive potentials of polygamy. If we move outside the cities to rural populations—the people who produced the agricultural wealth on which all preindustrial economies were based—polygamy could make for larger households and, therefore, more labor, more production, and more wealth.[7] The nature of the surviving sources makes it notoriously difficult to know anything about the peasantry in the premodern Middle East, but we should not rule out that polygamy might have been possible for landowning and more prosperous peasants where it was lawful.

The Roman Empire and, especially, its Christian successor territories are the major exception among other premodern Eurasian societies in which polygamy was largely normal and accepted, if not especially common. Scholars usually think of Roman society as fundamentally monogamous, and in strict terms it was. Roman law allowed only one wife to each man, and only children born to lawful unions were considered legitimate.[8] Roman public life thus allowed no room for the ostentatious elite polygamy common in other corners of the eastern Mediterranean world, and it certainly precluded polygamy as a reproductive strategy. At the same time, elite Roman households by their nature included multiple women to whom the family patriarch had sexual access: domestic slaves.[9] The sexual availability of slaves to their masters was understood as given; there would have been no clear line between the sexual and other labors a slave was expected to perform in the household. From this vantage point, Roman monogamous marriage differed strongly from the polygamy found elsewhere in Eurasia, where multiple wives or concubines might be kept for reproductive purposes; but Roman household forms still allowed for elite men's sexual access to multiple women.

From Ireland to Rome to Iran, the major challenge to all these practices in late antiquity and the medieval period was Christianity. Christian lettered traditions understood monogamy as the only acceptable kind of marriage.[10] Any sexual activity outside of monogamous marriage was fundamentally immoral and unlawful, contradictory as it was to the "singleness of flesh" and indissolubility of the marriage bond; polygamy could never be more than willful, ongoing adultery. A major facet of the process of Christianization in the heartlands of the Roman Empire was bishops' efforts to condemn and stigmatize the extramarital sexual outlets open to men within their own households; in parts of northern Europe, elite polygamy was a major target. Christian bishops in the Sasanian Empire acted on the same concerns. As they expanded Christian law under the rule of the Islamic caliphate, furthermore, they developed new methods to regulate polygamy and thereby structure Christian lineages and communities.

CHRISTIAN ELITES, POLYGAMY, AND THE SASANIAN COURT

If polygamous practices were broadly characteristic of many ancient Eurasian societies, it is unsurprising to find bishops in the late antique Sasanian Empire condemning them. Canons published by East Syrian synods in 410, 484, and 585, as well as Mar Aba's influential legal writings in the sixth century, generally agree that any layman who takes multiple wives or concubines "should be cast out of the community" (*neshtdē men gawwā*).[11] The fact that Sasanian bishops had to explicitly condemn such practices suggests that some Christian strata in the empire engaged in them much as did their non-Christian neighbors. If Sasanian-era bishops affirmed that affiliation to the church was to be realized through not only ritual participation in church on

Sundays but also the abandonment of social practices and commitments deemed unlawful, how did laypeople receive the prohibition of polygamy? Although the evidence is predictably meager, a few high-profile cases of polygamous laymen stand out in Syriac and Arabic chronicles covering the reign of Shah Khusraw II Parviz (r. 590–628). These give us a finer picture of the social contexts of polygamy among Christians in the Sasanian Empire. Furthermore, they reveal strong lay opposition to ecclesiastical regulation, as well as extracommunal solidarities—in this case, between laymen and the shah's court—that undermined the ecclesiastical monopoly on the definition of Christian communal boundaries, a dynamic that would continue into the medieval caliphate.

The cases in question revolve around anathemas pronounced by the patriarch Sabrishoʿ I (r. 596–604) and bishop Gregory of Nisibis (d. 611/12) against several prominent Christians associated with Khusraw's court who took multiple wives. Gregory, originally from Kashkar in lower Mesopotamia, is remembered in the sources for having tried zealously to reform the deviant practices of Christian clergy and laity in his see. As part of this project, he banned polygamy and anathematized several Nisibene physicians in Khusraw's service for persisting in keeping multiple wives. The Nisibenes, for their part, were not particularly happy with an outsider coming in and attempting to change their ways; they denounced Gregory to Khusraw, who subsequently forced him to leave his diocese and retire to a monastery.[12] Around the same time, Sabrishoʿ anathematized another of Khusraw's physicians, Gabriel of Shiggar, for taking multiple wives in addition to his first.[13] Gabriel's hometown of Shiggar (Arabic Sinjar) was near Nisibis and fell in the cultural orbit of that major city;[14] Sabrishoʿ, like Gregory, is thus remembered for issuing an anathema in an attempt to end the polygamous practices of the Nisibene elite associated with the shah's court. At Sabrishoʿ's death in 604, the bishops of the Sasanian Empire supported Gregory to succeed to the patriarchate. Gregory's old physician opponents from Nisibis, however, were not interested in seeing him take the Church of the East's highest office, so they obtained the support of Khusraw's Christian wife Shirin, a close confidant of Gabriel, for an alternate candidate who was ultimately consecrated patriarch.[15]

There are several noteworthy aspects of Sabrishoʿ and Gregory's conflict with the Nisibene physicians. First is the form of lay polygamy evident in it. We are dealing not with a ubiquitous, generalized social practice but an elite one. The polygamous physicians all had ties outside the strongly Christian city of Nisibis; they were lay Christians but also functionaries of the emperor's court, precisely a social setting in which we can expect polygamy and concubinage to have been elite prerogatives and markers of status. For the Nisibene physicians, embodying their affiliation to an aristocratic class through polygamous practices did not contradict their religious belonging. These Christians, and not others, practiced polygamy precisely because they moved in social worlds in which ecclesiastical expectations were not normative.

Following from this point, these cases demonstrate how asymmetrical negotiations over the Christian household among laypeople, ecclesiastics, and extracommunal institutions could determine the practical shape of Christian communities. Ecclesiastics like Gregory and Sabrishoʿ sought the disciplinary reform and ultimate salvation of their lay flocks but required recognition by those laypeople of their authority to direct the patterns of lay life. The lay elite, on the other hand, was interested in maintaining its influence over local affairs (hence the Nisibenes' rejection of the outsider Gregory), a say in electing ecclesiastics favorable to its interests, and the accustomed social practices of elite life, like polygamy, that reformer bishops sought to ban. In these conditions, Sabrishoʿ and Gregory appear to have overplayed their hands. The bishops could deploy the anathema to prod laypeople to follow ecclesiastical rules. This may have worked frequently when the offenders had no recourse outside their local Christian networks, but this was precisely not the case with the Nisibene physicians. They had ties of patronage to the Sasanian court, which they used to remove Gregory from his position as metropolitan bishop, prevent him from becoming patriarch after Sabrishoʿ's death, and further influence ecclesiastical politics for the following years.[16] In this case, at least, the Nisibenes were able to depose their ecclesiastical opponents and presumably retain both their polygamous ways and access to the Eucharistic ritual through which they enacted their belonging to the body of Christ. Ecclesiastical institutions, in other words, were not powerful enough to enforce ecclesiastical law on those who could go above the bishops' heads to the shah. In practical terms, the Nisibene lay elites rejected the bishops' claim that following their prescriptions for marital practice was exclusively constitutive of Christian belonging.

While the obstinate laymen of Gregory and Sabrishoʿ's day refused to admit of any discord between their polygamous marital practices and their Christian affiliation, a unique document dated to the late sixth or early seventh century shows other lay East Syrians taking ecclesiastical marriage law to heart.[17] The document in question is a collection of statutes for an artisans' association from an unknown city. Besides various stipulations on sharing expenses and other professional matters, the pact asserts that the members "shall obey without dispute all the holy laws laid down by the leaders of the church." Among these are specified Mar Aba's marriage-related prohibitions, including "the foul practice of having two wives."[18] The document thus shows lay Christians acknowledging ecclesiastical laws as "the distinguishing marks of the pious, the symbolic boundaries of a particular vision of Christian unity," and vowing to implement those strictures in practice.[19] These anonymous town artisans were presumably outside the Nisibene physicians' world of elite power and privilege, and, in contrast to those elites, pledged to order their social affiliations in accordance with the notion of community propagated by the bishops.

ECCLESIASTICAL JURISDICTION, INHERITANCE, AND POLYGAMY AFTER THE CONQUESTS

Polygamy was lawful in the Sasanian Empire and likely customarily practiced throughout its territories, including among some Christians. Roman attitudes toward polygamous household arrangements were different. The Arab conquests of the seventh century, however, upended the legal order of Rome's eastern provinces as well as the Sasanian Empire, and one outcome was the heightened prominence of polygamy as a locus of contestation over the requisites of Christian belonging. To many observers in the immediate aftermath of the conquests, the distinctions between Judaism, Christianity, and the conquerors' scriptural, monotheistic dispensation, which permitted polygamy, were not immediately evident. Moreover, the conquerors not only made polygamy newly lawful in formerly Roman provinces like Syria and Egypt; they practiced it on a wide scale, as many women among the great numbers of captives they took wound up as slave concubines in conquerors' households.[20] Together, these factors made polygamy a newly conspicuous matter for the empire's Christian subjects. The relative frequency with which seventh-century Christian legal sources emphasize the unlawfulness of polygamy suggests that some of the caliphate's lay subjects were newly questioning why polygamy was out of bounds, and perhaps sought to practice it themselves.[21]

The bishops predictably maintained that polygamy was incompatible with Christian belonging and that transgressors of this stricture deserved the anathema. Notably, however, postconquest conditions—the fall of the former imperial orders and bishops' concomitant claims to expanded judicial authority over lay civil affairs—allowed the bishops to employ another method for regulating lay polygamy not attested in earlier sources: inheritance law. Rather than pressuring male transgressors to give up their polygamous ways, judicially active bishops could seek to disinherit children born of unlawful, polygamous unions, sculpting Christian lineages in succeeding generations according to the ecclesiastics' monogamous ideal. Lay polygamy was thus an opportunity for jurist-bishops to define a distinctively Christian model of the material and social practices of lineage reproduction. Their efforts in this regard exemplify the increasing emphasis on the connection between ecclesiastical justice and lay households as definitive of Christian communities in the early caliphate. We can see this strategy in operation by returning to the case of Ahona and his feuding heirs in the 690s.

The East Syrian patriarch Hnanishoʿ lays out the details of the case in an epistle to an unnamed local priest charged with carrying out his ruling on it.[22] The recently deceased Ahona had a number of sons by his wife in Karka d-Bet Slok while also maintaining a second wife and at least one child on his properties in Kufa, Syriac ʿAqula, adjacent to the old Christian settlement of Hira on the Euphrates. At his death, Ahona's Kufan wife apparently attempted to secure a share of the patrimony for herself and her unwed daughter (we do not know whether she had other children by Ahona) that would be proportionate, in some respect, to that of the wife and sons in Karka, who contested her claim. Hnanishoʿ rules that only Ahona's first wife and sons can be considered his legitimate heirs; the Kufan wife, having been married unlawfully (*lā nāmosāʾit*), has no rightful claim on Ahona's estate. Hnanishoʿ does allow the Kufan wife and her daughter to remain on one of Ahona's properties and to receive a minimal amount of maintenance and clothing. However, even this will be cut off if and when the wife chooses to remarry and the daughter is old enough to earn her keep "by the labor of her own hands" (*men pulḥānā d-idēh*). If the Kufan wife further contests Hnanishoʿ's ruling, he tells the unnamed priest to bar her from "mixing with Christians in all of the churches in both Kufa and Hira" (*ḥulṭānā d-ʿam krēsṭyānē b-ʿēdātā kulhēn wa-b-ʿĀqulā wa-b-Ḥirtā*).

The case of Ahona's multiple households is revealing of both a particular style of lay polygamy and techniques for regulating it available to judicially active bishops like Hnanishoʿ. Ahona, whose multiple properties show him to have been wealthy, maintained two separate households in Karka, at the foothills of the Zagros Mountains east of the middle Tigris, and Kufa, on the Euphrates in Iraq. These locations are significant. We would expect both of these regions to have had large Christian populations and thick ecclesiastical presences in the seventh century. It is worth raising the possibility, speculative though it may be, that this had something to do with Ahona keeping his multiple wives apart, rather than in a single location. For a polygamous layman, separate households might be better kept away from the prying eyes of local clergies and other concerned parties—at least until someone died and estates came into the picture. If this reading is correct, it is indicative of a particular socioeconomic model of polygamy: men who traveled regularly between a few set locations and supported households in each one. We hear hints of similar arrangements elsewhere in Christian sources, and there is some evidence for them as well among the merchants of the Cairo Genizah.[23] If this mode of polygamous practice was an option for a certain class of geographically mobile men in the early medieval Middle East, it may have been more manageable for elite Christians than single-household polygamy—it was less subject to the scrutiny and pressures of local Christian communities and church officials.

While the exact details of Ahona's arrangement elude us, Hnanishoʿ's determination of inheritance allotments is certainly notable as a distinctive strategy for polygamy regulation. The Church of the East's well-established canons banning polygamy were not enough to prevent Ahona from marrying multiple women. However, Hnanishoʿ saw to it that Christian law would order Ahona's household affairs after his death by excluding his second family from any real share of inheritance. In doing so, Hnanishoʿ prescribed both social stigmatization and economic marginalization of that second family. Passing on inheritance not only transfers wealth but facilitates the reproduction of family identity and social status in successive generations. Divesting Ahona's second family of inheritance excluded them from any material stake in, and therefore symbolic belonging to, Ahona's lineage.

This strategy for regulating polygamy is very different from issuing the anathema in order to pressure a polygamous man into obedience. Rather than affecting the transgressor himself, disinheritance puts material constraints on much socially weaker figures—women and children of the second family. Since the deceased offender Ahona was now beyond his reach, what did Hnanishoʿ seek to achieve in this? The patriarch seems to have been aware that his ruling could be viewed as overly harsh; his letter notes that concerned parties tried to persuade him to allot the second wife an inheritance, but he went ahead with disinheriting her anyway.[24] Perhaps Hnanishoʿ intended to punish publicly the transgressor's (unwitting?) abettors and progeny in order to discourage other Christian men from such practices. But more significantly, disinheriting a polygamous family was a means for Hnanishoʿ to set Christian social relations to right, from his perspective, in starkly material terms. If Hnanishoʿ thought that Ahona never should have had two households in the first place, his inheritance law would prune Ahona's family tree according to a monogamous, properly Christian ideal after his death; disinheriting the second family meant that, in terms of economic status and social recognition, only the first continued his family line.

Of further significance is what this ruling suggests concerning the ecclesiastical hierarchy's practical means to enforce its laws, and the shape of Christian communities in the Umayyad Caliphate these defined. It is not unreasonable to think that the division of Ahona's estate was carried out as Hnanishoʿ instructed. The patriarch's letters record numerous disputes among Christians that laypeople and clergymen brought directly before him for adjudication; the very fact that they did so suggests that his rulings were viewed as authoritative by many at a time when Muslim authorities were largely uninterested in non-Muslim affairs that did not impinge on public order. More significantly, inheritance regulations of the kind that Hnanishoʿ prescribed disadvantaged individuals who would have been less likely to have alternative reserves of social power. This contrasts with the Nisibene physicians, who used their ties to the Sasanian court to oppose the ecclesiastics who anathematized them. In the Ahona case, the second wife and daughter were up against the patriarch and three sons from the first marriage. While it is not inconceivable that the wife could have sought adjudication from a Muslim authority, or could have threatened to do so, such a course of action appears much less probable in the seventh century—before the growth and consolidation of

Islamic law and administrative justice—than in later ones. Perhaps the second wife had relatives from her natal family of some influence to whom she could turn. But otherwise, this case has precisely the features—socially weak defendants, no obvious extracommunal means to pressure the ecclesiastics who issued the rulings—to suggest that communal officials would have carried out the patriarch's instructions.

Hnanishoʿ's treatment of Ahona's two families is thus suggestive of a case in which ecclesiastical institutions were robust enough to shape Christian communities in practical terms according to the ecclesiastical vision. This was enabled, moreover, by caliphal rule—the expanded judicial authority claimed by bishops after the fall of the Sasanians produced more intensive connections between ecclesiastical justice and lay households, in this case the regulation of inheritances. If polygamy would invariably be a contentious practice between ecclesiastics and lay elites, "laissez-faire" Umayyad rule allowed the bishops new tools for defining Christian social distinctiveness around it.

What was the ultimate fate of Ahona's second wife and her daughter? Was the maintenance provided by Ahona's estate sufficient for their needs? Would the daughter have been able to marry carrying the stigma of illegitimacy? No immediate answers are available. But it is worth emphasizing again that disinheritance as a strategy for polygamy regulation had the potential to leave individuals of relatively weak social position even more marginalized within Christian communities. Whether this might lead them to cut their losses and apostatize is a possible further effect to keep in mind.

CONCUBINAGE AND CHRISTIAN POLYGAMY AT THE ABBASID COURT

Hnanishoʿ's forays into inheritance law exemplify how the institutional transformations inaugurated by the establishment of the early caliphate allowed for new forms of ecclesiastical regulation of lay households. As Christians in the Abbasid period interacted ever more frequently with Muslims and the Muslim ruling class propagated new social norms, polygamy became an especially prominent locus around which bishops defined a distinctively Christian model of the household. Abbasid-era Syriac legal texts and Arabic biographical dictionaries reveal an increasing interest among urban Christian lay elites in a particular form of polygamy: slave concubinage. This interest is especially evident among certain East Syrians who were well integrated into the upper echelons of Baghdad's courtly society. Their connections to the caliphal court, moreover, served often as leverage against the protestations of ecclesiastics and allowed them to maintain both polygamous households and their Christian affiliation; much like Muslim judges and Islamic law, the caliphal court was an extracommunal institution that had a significant impact on the practical boundaries of Christian communities. The bishops' response was to further codify a law of inheritance meant to sculpt Christian lineages as strictly monogamous ones. The shared practices between elite Christians and Muslims in Abbasid society thus gave the bishops a further opportunity to articulate their vision of Christian social groups constituted through their own, distinctive practices of household formation and reproduction. Much as in the case of divorce, however, ecclesiastical condemnation of household sexual practices that Islamic law allowed may also have posed problems for Christian communal integrity.

Slaves and Concubines

Unsurprisingly, the newly extensive Syriac Christian legal treatises and canonical legislation of the eighth and ninth centuries reaffirm the traditional prohibition of polygamy.[25] More interesting is a conspicuous concern with sexual relationships between married Christian men and their female slaves, which features in several law books, canons, and epistles. A West Syrian canon of 817, for example, anathematizes any man who "keeps a concubine or handmaiden alongside his wife" (*druktā meddem aw amtā ʿam anttā dilēh nēḥod*), while ʿAbdishoʿ bar Bahriz spells out the only circumstances in which a relationship between a man and his slave becomes licit (he has to free her, marry her, and not already have a wife).[26] While it was a basic reality of institutionalized household slavery in the eastern Mediterranean that masters freely exercised sexual dominion over slaves' bodies, several developments in Abbasid society likely contributed to the growing concern with such practices on the part of the bishops. For one, the Islamic legal traditions that took shape in the early Abbasid period defined master-slave sexuality quite clearly as a particular institution of concubinage (basing their definitions on Quran 4:3). Men were entitled to maintain households that included, in addition to their wife or wives, as many slave women as they could support and to whom they had sexual access.[27] Modern scholars typically refer to slave women kept mainly for sexual purposes, as opposed to other forms of labor, as concubines; medieval Middle Easterners also tended to recognize social distinctions among slaves based on their labor and economic roles, although these made no difference to a slave's legal status unless a slave woman bore her master a child.[28] Islamic norms thus in no way introduced the sexual exploitation of household slaves to Christian subjects in the premodern Middle East, but they did reconfigure it as a particular model of household polygamy open to elite males with sufficient resources.[29] This legal and social context applied throughout the caliphate, but it was particularly significant for the Church of the East now that the imperial capital had returned to central Iraq. Similar to the Nisibene physicians at the Sasanian shah's court, East Syrian physicians, scribes, and other prominent laymen moved conspicuously in the elite circles of the Abbasid capitals at Baghdad and Samarra beginning in the second half of the eighth century. Wealthy and intimately enmeshed in the capitals' goings on and politics, these Christian men were participants in the elite male culture of the Muslim caliphal court. There, keeping concubines was a mark of status. The courtly culture of early Abbasid Baghdad, for example, is well-known for the special place it accorded the "singing slave girls" (*qiyān*) trained in music and poetry and prized as consorts by the city's wealthiest men. The enormous wealth flowing into the imperial capital and coffers, moreover, gave the courtly elite considerable resources to spend on their households and entourages. The harems of the caliphs are routinely reported to have included thousands of slaves, but many administrative and military elites were not far behind; even the wife of Yahya al-Barmaki, Harun al-Rashid's vizier, is said to have owned one hundred slave girls.[30]

Notably, narrative sources of the early Abbasid Caliphate show Christian courtiers partaking in the elite prerogative of concubinage as well. The most prominent Christian courtiers of early Abbasid Baghdad came from a number of lineages of East Syrian physicians ministering to caliphs, viziers, and other members of caliphal entourages. These included the families of Bukhtishuʿ, Masawayh, al-Tayfuri, and others, most of whom hailed originally from the towns of Khuzistan or southern Iraq.[31] A number of biographical dictionaries and chronicles preserve information on the lives and careers of these figures. Their anecdotes offer insight into the effects of courtly mores on ecclesiastical-lay contestation over concubinage and on the shape of urban Christian communities living at the heart of the Abbasid Caliphate.

Stories About Doctors

The protagonist of our first such narrative is Jurjiyus ibn Bukhtishuʿ (d. 769), the first member of his family to leave Khuzistan for Baghdad and enter caliphal service. In this narrative, the caliph al-Mansur (754–75) becomes concerned for Jurjiyus, having heard that he has no wife. Jurjiyus informs the caliph, "I have an old, weak wife [*zawja kabīra ḍaʿīfa*] who is unable to move from her spot." In consideration of his favored physician's no doubt difficult sex life, the caliph sends him a gift of three Byzantine slave women. When Jurjiyus returns home, he is incensed to find that his Christian pupil ʿIsa ibn Shahlafa has allowed the women into his house. The physician returns them to the caliph and explains that "we, the community [*maʿshar*] of Christians, do not marry more than one woman, and as long as she lives we do not take any other than her."[32]

A second anecdote in an East Syrian patriarchal history begins with Timothy I scolding Jibraʾil ibn Bukhtishuʿ (d. 828), Jurjiyus's grandson and the richest and most prominent physician in Harun al-Rashid's service, for taking slave concubines. Jibraʾil does not mend his ways, so Timothy anathematizes him. Jibraʾil confronts the patriarch angrily and calls him a pederast (*lūṭī*), outraging Timothy and his entourage. Not long afterward, Jibraʾil receives divine retribution for the insult when he is trampled in the street by a horse. Timothy keeps away from the offender for two days even after his mother's pleadings, but then gives Jibraʾil communion; Jibraʾil heals. The narrative ends there, but the implication is that Jibraʾil subsequently gave up his concubines.[33]

Jibraʾil's son Bukhtishuʿ (d. 870), who for a time was the caliph al-Mutawakkil's (847–61) chief physician, has a similar reputation in the narrative sources. He is said to have worked for the appointment of the patriarch Theodosios (r. 853–58) because he was afraid that another aspirant to the patriarchate "would anathematize him for taking concubines" (*yuḥarrimuhu li-tasarrīhi*).[34] Another chronicle specifies that Bukhtishuʿ had two concubines (*amhātā*), each of whom bore him a son.[35]

اليسود ولدت واحدا والولد تخرم رحم امه

اظفاره فمخرج منها ع

ن

سكم وعسد الله بن يحيىنوع الله لما امرى

۸؛

Figure 3. The physician ʿUbaydallah Ibn Bukhtishuʿ (d. c. 1058), great-great-grandson of Jibraʾil, and a pupil. The Arabic text to which this illumination was added includes zoological knowledge that Ibn Bukhtishuʿ compiled at the behest of the amir Saʿd al-Din (see Contadini, *World of Beasts*), which illustrates well the long history of Christian medical dynasties serving Muslim elites in Islamic Iraq. *Kitab Naʿt al-hayawan*, MS BL Or. 2784, fol. 101v, British Library, London. Copyright the British Library Board. All rights reserved/Bridgeman Images.

A final anecdote takes us to a different family of elite Christian doctors. Yuhanna ibn Masawayh (d. 857) was another physician in the service of Harun al-Rashid and several of his successors. The biographical sources tell us that Yuhanna was known for keeping slave concubines and was often upbraided for it. The situation was further complicated because the physician served in church as a deacon. At one point, a group of Christians tells him that he has to either restrict himself to one woman or leave the deaconate. Yuhanna responds defiantly, "We are commanded [by scripture] to take neither two women nor two garments (cf. Luke 3:11). So who gave the catholicos, that biter of his mother's clitoris [*al-ʿāḍḍ baẓr ummih*], more of a right to have twenty garments than wretched Yuhanna to take four concubines? Go tell your catholicos to adhere to the laws of his religion [*qawānīn dīnih*] in order for us to do so with him. If he disobeys [them], we will disobey him."[36]

Patriarchs and Lay Elites Negotiating Christian Polygamy

These narratives are valuable sources for the cultural history of the Abbasid Caliphate. While the veracity of reports from medieval historiographical works is always at issue, there is no reason not to accept these as more or less historical; they had to have been believable to medieval audiences, and therefore their subtexts and literary tropes betray cultural assumptions of Abbasid society whether or not every last detail is perfectly accurate. As such, these anecdotes of conflicts over polygamy show us the practical negotiation of Christian communal boundaries among ecclesiastical law, lay elites, and the latter's connections to the caliphal court.

First of all, the anecdotes demonstrate the perceived normalcy of polygamous concubinage as an elite male privilege in Abbasid court circles, regardless of religious affiliation. In the Jurjiyus story, a gift of slave women is a simple caliphal gesture to a favored member of his entourage. The caliph shows no hesitation in giving such a gift to a Christian and has to be told afterward that it is religiously inappropriate; the presumption underlying the narrative is that any normal male would welcome adding concubines to his household. Jurjiyus is unique in having an explicit reputation for avoiding concubinage, and it may be significant that he was already an adult by the time he had become the first prominent Christian physician at the Abbasid court in Baghdad. Later generations of his family likely grew up much closer to the court and were thus more likely to have been shaped by its norms and etiquette. As a case in point, Jibraʾil's anecdote shows the physician so incensed that anyone would claim to deny him the polygamous privileges of his social position that he calls the chief bishop of his church a pederast for trying to do so.

The stories of Bukhtishuʿ, Yuhanna, and Jibraʾil are further notable for their depiction of elite laymen fighting back against the patriarchs' claim of sole authority to decide which marital practices preclude communion with the Christian social and theological body, and for the fact that they sometimes do so in the very language of their shared religious tradition (or at least in a flippant version thereof). Bukhtishuʿ wades into ecclesiastical politics to install a patriarch who promises to overlook his predilection for concubines. Yuhanna ibn Masawayh's retort to his Christian opponents references Luke 3:11 (that anyone with two tunics should give one away) in order to assert that the patriarch has ignored the Christian ethic of compassion for the poor by comporting himself extravagantly. Jibraʾil's insult against Timothy evokes the Arabic literary trope that celibate Christian monks often indulge in pederasty;[37] he thus implies that if the church's spiritual custodians transgress its canons on sexual conduct, the patriarch is in no place to call a layman un-Christian. Together, the narratives demonstrate how powerful laymen, like the Nisibene physicians before them, might contest the patriarchs' authority to declare that the privileges customary to their social networks were incompatible with their identity as Christians. In Yuhanna's allusion to scripture, especially, we see a layman claiming a bit of interpretive authority himself to assert that he can live as both a Christian and an elite functionary of the caliphal court.

Yuhanna was fooling no one, of course; that polygamy and concubinage were out of bounds for good Christians was an entirely well-known principle by the ninth century. Nonetheless, in practical terms, did the elite physicians of early Abbasid Baghdad keep their polygamous households while still participating in the institutions that signified Christian belonging? The evidence is thin, but we should venture a speculative yes—again like the Nisibene physicians, men like Jibraʾil, Bukhtishuʿ, and Yuhanna had reserves of social power and extracommunal patronage connections that they could use to ensure that they continued to receive the Eucharist and take part in Christian communal life in spite of ecclesiastical opposition. In our narratives, only Jibraʾil faces an anathema over his polygamous practices.

Because of the moralized and miraculous way that the story wraps up, however, we may doubt its historicity. Moreover, the anathema is not actually effective in subjecting Jibraʾil to social pressure and stigmatization so that he follows ecclesiastical instruction; only being trampled by a horse, an event either providential or completely random depending on one's perspective, does that. In general, lay elites, including both physicians and administrators in the caliphal bureaucracy, were routinely involved in maneuvering their favored candidates to the patriarchal see in order to preserve their own interests. Bukhtishuʿ got Theodosios the patriarchate, for example, by petitioning the caliph al-Mutawakkil to decree that Theodosios was the man for the job (*fa-amara bi-taqlīdih*) over the favorite of the Christian scribe Abu Nuh al-Anbari.[38] Again, this structural pattern recalls the Sasanian evidence. Ecclesiastical tradition said that Bukhtishuʿ could not keep concubines and his Christian affiliation; he did so, however, because he was among an extremely limited group of men with access to caliphal power that could pressure ecclesiastics to keep participation in communal rituals open. That practical power of social position is evident as well in the Yuhanna story. The physician's Christian opponents never try to bar him fully from the church; they say he can keep his concubines as long as he steps down from the deaconate. The text implies that it is too much of an affront to have a known polygamist aiding in the administration of church services, but it still allows his participation in the assemblies and rituals constitutive of communal belonging.

The anathema was the main institution available to ecclesiastics in the Abbasid Caliphate to compel social practices to accord with their instructions; bishops do not frequently appear to have influenced caliphal appointments and proclamations. This form of extracommunal power was more readily available to Baghdad's lay elite and could frequently override ecclesiastical prerogatives. Lay elites thus influenced the bounds of Christian community to accommodate their positions and investment in the elite Muslim society of the caliphal court. Along similar lines, the caliph and his court emerge from this tableau as another example of an extracommunal institution that had a significant structural check on the practical constitution of Christian social groups. We have already considered the role that Muslim judges and judicial institutions might have played in structuring how laypeople actually practiced ostensibly indissoluble Christian marriage. Here, we see the caliph and his ability to affect ecclesiastical politics facilitating a particular model of Christian belonging: one in which elite lay domesticity and household structures are outside the sphere of ecclesiastical regulatory authority.

Trimming Christian Family Trees: Illegitimacy and Inheritance

Islamic law and elite mores in the Abbasid Caliphate meant that polygamy, especially in the form of concubinage, was both conceivable and attractive to an elite class of Christians with close connections to Muslim courtly circles. If the anathema was an ineffective tool of dissuasion, the law books show us another ecclesiastical strategy for dissociating concubinage from Christian household life that follows on Hnanishoʿ's precedent: prescribing the exclusion of children born to married men and their slaves from inheritance in order to marginalize economically and socially the unlawful branches of Christian family trees. The Christian practice of concubinage thus provided the bishops the opportunity to articulate through inheritance law a distinctively Christian household form and model of lineage reproduction.

The law books of Ishoʿbokt, Timothy, and Ishoʿbarnun include multiple rulings that address the status of children born of relationships between married men and their slaves. Each disadvantages those children in the amount of inheritance they receive from their fathers. According to Ishoʿbokt, for example, a man who fathers a son with his slave should "raise him" and "give him something from his property in a just manner [*zādqāʾit*]"; but "he cannot make heirs of unlawful [*d-lā nāmos*] [offspring]."[39] Timothy's legal language is less precise, but his ruling is also instructive in this regard: "[What is the ruling concerning] a man who falls upon his female slave, she bears a son, and [the man] does not acknowledge him during his life; but [then] stipulates at the time of his death that inheritance be given to him like one of his [lawful] sons, and acknowledges that he is his own son? He is considered [one] of the sons. But not like freeborn sons [*bnay ḥērutā*]; rather, as the son of a slave woman he shall be given a one-twentieth share out of kindness [*netyheb lēh b-ṭaybu men yārtutā d-abu[hy] ḥad men ʿesrin mnawātā*], as a warning that no one should be defiled [and] that no offspring should be excluded from inheritance."[40] Though Timothy calls the portion of the father's estate going to the slave's son inheritance, it is a small sum meant only for his maintenance; the child has no right to a share equal to that of his legitimate brothers. One of Ishoʿbarnun's two rulings on the illegitimate children of slaves goes even further in promoting their social marginalization. It specifies that the son of a married man and his slave "should be raised as a slave for the shame of his adulterer father" (*netrbē ʿabdāʾit l-behttā d-abu[hy] d-zanni*) and that the slave mother should be sold and cast out of the household.[41]

This treatment of slaves' children in the East Syrian law books is comparable to many of the premodern Mediterranean world's other legal traditions, according to which only the progeny of marriages qualified as legitimate and with full rights of succession. In medieval Europe, for example, clerical reformers put a good deal of effort over the course of centuries into convincing laypeople of just this notion.[42] In the context of the Islamic Middle East, however, the East Syrian bishops' rulings radically differentiated Christian from Islamic law and the patterns of social reproduction that the latter facilitated. In Islamic legal traditions, not only may men keep as many slave concubines as they can support, but any children born of those unions are free, affiliated to their fathers, and entitled to normal shares in their fathers' estates. The concubine acquires a new legal status as well as an *umm walad*: she may not be sold, and she becomes free upon her master's death.[43] The legitimacy accorded to concubines' children and the status of *umm walad* hinged in practice on men acknowledging paternity, which surely did not always happen.[44] But on the whole, the special status of concubines' children in Islamic law meant that concubinage became a standard strategy of social reproduction in elite Muslim echelons. Islamic history is full of prominent men born of concubines; it is particularly noteworthy that by the time of Ishoʿbarnun's death in 828, four Abbasid caliphs (al-Mansur, al-Hadi, Harun al-Rashid, and al-Maʾmun) had been sons of concubines, as had been the last three Umayyads (Yazid III, Ibrahim ibn al-Walid, and Marwan II).[45] The maternal descent and therefore the reproductive strategies of sub-royal elites are more difficult to recover, but there are enough examples to indicate that having children with concubines was a pattern in those strata too, if not on the same scale as in the Abbasid house itself.[46]

We should understand the East Syrian bishops' rulings on the inheritance of slaves' children against this backdrop. They are an attempt to interdict concubinage as a social reproductive practice available to Christian elites in Abbasid society and an effort to sculpt Christian lineages in a manner radically distinct from Islamic household patterns. East Syrian law divests the children born of concubines of a meaningful role in the intergenerational transfer of wealth and, therefore, the reproduction of patrilineages. This stands in direct opposition to the function that Islamic law gives to concubinage and the exact use to which it was put by many elites. This regulatory strategy could serve a function for the Abbasid-era bishops similar to what it did for Hnanishoʿ: shape Christian social relations according to the ecclesiastical vision after the laymen who had been powerful (or devious) enough to do something transgressive had died. Disinheritance marginalized concubines and their children both economically and socially; it cut them out of the group of individuals whose shared material and symbolic interests made them a family. It could thus mold families' social formation according to a monogamous Christian ideal, in spite of both biological realities and Islamic norms. Even though laypeople might engage in concubinage, inheritance regulation could make socially concrete the institution's un-Christianness by denying recognition to lineages that grew from it. If Islamic law and mores gave Christian elites the opportunity to flout ecclesiastical prescriptions on marriage and sexuality, the bishops devised a confessional inheritance law to reinscribe both Christian ethics and religious difference in the multigenerational shape of Christian families.

A Slave Woman and Her Son: Two Cases

The foregoing suggests that the bishops might have been better able to influence the disbursement of inheritances after an elite layman's death than to enforce an anathema against him while he lived. This supposition rests on the fact that inheritance regulation as an anti-polygamy strategy directly affected slaves and children, individuals with far fewer resources to counteract ecclesiastical decrees than a courtier. But can we recover anything more definite of the prospects for enforcement and the effects of disinheritance on the unfree and the illegitimate? A major question is whether ecclesiastical regulation would have marginalized Christian children of concubines enough that conversion to Islam became attractive. The short answer is that we cannot know, given our meager evidence. Nonetheless, it is worth considering a range of possibilities, speculative though they may be, on the basis of two cases of Christian men siring children by slave women for which we do have some evidence: the first concerning the estate of Bukhtishuʿ ibn Jibraʾil, one of the polygamous physicians we met above, in ninth-century Iraq, the second an anonymous household in Yemen around 900.

Bukhtishuʿ died in 870 having attained, lost, and reattained both riches and caliphal favor during his decades of service in the Abbasid capitals. His extensive notices in Arabic biographical dictionaries specify that he left behind a son named ʿUbaydallah and three daughters. Unfortunately for the heirs, rapacious Abbasid functionaries extorted from them (*yuṣādirūnahum wa-yuṭālibūnahum bi-l-amwāl*) the considerable wealth they had inherited from Bukhtishuʿ, a not uncommon fate in the precarious world of Abbasid court politics.[47] ʿUbaydallah recovered enough status to serve the caliph al-Muqtadir (908–32) as a financial official (*mutaṣarrif*), and his descendants returned to the family profession as physicians.[48] Bukhtishuʿ's family tree does not end there, however. As noted earlier, Christian chronicles record his reputation for keeping concubines, and one tells us that two of his female slaves bore him sons: a Gabriel and a Yohannan, Yuhanna in Arabic.[49] Interestingly, neither is mentioned among Bukhtishuʿ's heirs in the Arabic biographical dictionaries. It is possible that this represents an instance in which the bishops' inheritance law had been applied in practice. Gabriel and Yuhanna escaped the biographers' notice and do not appear as the target of powerful imperial servants' predations; given that they were the sons of concubines, it is plausible that this was so because they had received no share in Bukhtishuʿ's estate worth extorting.

Whether or not this was the case, Bukhtishuʿ's family is of further interest because we have some fragmentary hints of how life turned out for his concubine's son Yuhanna.[50] Despite his illegitimacy, Yuhanna was able to achieve prominence in the East Syrian episcopacy as the metropolitan bishop of Mosul.[51] He even made a play for the patriarchate, throwing his hat in the ring to contest the succession when the sitting patriarch died in 899. Many bishops were loath to accept Yuhanna as head of the Church of the East, however, because of "his being born of a concubine as a result of adultery" (*wilādatuhu min surriyya ʿalā sabīl al-zināʾ*).[52] Before his episcopal career, the concubine's son appears to have been a high-ranking layman as well. One Yuhanna ibn Bukhtishuʿ appears in a Muslim-authored biographical dictionary as a physician serving the Abbasid regent al-Muwaffaq (d. 891). Was this the same individual as Yuhanna the bishop? The entry does not associate Yuhanna the physician with the family of the famous Bukhtishuʿ ibn Jibraʾil, which is less odd if the former was indeed a concubine's son who had been tagged as illegitimate through disinheritance.[53] Furthermore, although East Syrian bishops were normally drawn from monastic ranks rather than the lay elite, reports that Yuhanna the bishop had children indicate that he entered the episcopacy only later in life.[54] Fragmentary though the evidence may be, the best reading looks to be that Bukhtishuʿ indeed had a son named Yuhanna by one of his concubines, and that Yuhanna rose high in Abbasid society as a physician and later a bishop despite the stigma of illegitimacy he carried. It is distinctly possible that he had even been excluded from sharing in his father's estate because of his mother's status.

Whatever its details, Yuhanna's story is instructive as an example of how, even as ecclesiastics sought to marginalize the offspring of polygamous unions, communal institutions could work to keep those individuals within the Christian fold. Yuhanna hardly seems to have faced the prospect of conversion, for example, to make it in life. He was able to follow his father's path studying medicine and find a place in the ecclesiastical establishment. Christian communal institutions in the late ninth century provided a place for an illegitimate son of a prominent father; disinheritance, if that is indeed what Yuhanna experienced, did not necessarily translate into complete exclusion. In this case, it may have served as an adequate compromise between ecclesiastics and lay elites. Bukhtishuʿ had his concubines; Yuhanna was marked as illegitimate in some regard, perhaps through disinheritance and certainly through restrictions from achieving the patriarchate; but he acquired an elite status befitting his paternal descent.

Yuhanna, of course, was male and came from a rich family based in the urban centers of the Abbasid heartlands. What about illegitimate daughters or sons from less prominent backgrounds? Would local communities have found the means to provide for such individuals, or would they have been compelled to seek well-being in social networks beyond their blood relatives and other Christians? What about their slave mothers? Again, we lack solid evidence, but we can use one more case to posit some informed guesses. The case is mentioned in an epistle of Yohannan bar Abgare, the bishop who beat out Yuhanna for the East Syrian patriarchate, in which capacity he served from 900 to 905. The letter responds to a priest in Yemen named al-Hasan ibn Yusuf who had previously sent the patriarch a number of questions related to ritual and family law.[55] One described a case that had arisen concerning a slave woman's child: "A man had a wife and a slave woman [*jāriya*]. When the slave died, he acknowledged her son and said that he was his. But when this man died, his cousin [*ibn ʿammih*] came and also declared that the son was his. Is [the boy] entitled to inheritance [*hal yajib lahu l-mīrāth*]?"[56] This question is suggestive of a household situation perhaps more common than that of the courtiers of Baghdad and Samarra and their cultured concubines: a domestic slave whose unfree status made her available to her master.

When al-Hasan turned to the patriarch for advice on this quandary, the issue at stake was in part the confused paternity of the slave woman's child. Was a rapacious man taking advantage of the weak position of his cousin's illegitimate son and trying to secure the deceased's estate for himself by claiming paternity? Patriarch Yohannan's response, however, did not concern itself with the paternity issue or the cousin's counterclaim; instead, it went about upholding East Syrian legal doctrine. The patriarch's letter emphasizes first that extramarital sex between men and their slaves is unlawful; no Christians should be getting themselves into this situation in the first place. If, however, reliable witnesses in the community (*jamāʿa maqbūla*) affirm that the deceased indeed fathered the child, there are two possibilities. If the man does not have a legitimate son, half of his estate should go to the slave's son and the other half to the rest of his relatives. If the man did sire sons by his lawful wife, the slave's son receives one-twentieth of the estate (*niṣf al-ʿushr*) while the rest goes to the lawful descendants.[57]

Yohannan's allowance of inheritance to the slave's son if he is an only child evidently stems from the principle that property devolves more or less naturally through patrilineages, even illegitimate ones if no others are available. But more significantly, Yohannan's ruling of the one-twentieth share is a reaffirmation of the standard that Timothy set in his law book in the early ninth century. It is thus a concrete example of an East Syrian patriarch communicating the ecclesiastical concern to trim the polygamous branches of Christian family trees directly to a local community. What effects might we imagine these rulings to have had? The case appears to have come directly before the priest, so he may well have had some ability to carry out the patriarch's directives. Furthermore, this case suggests again why clergymen might have been able to follow through with rulings of disinheritance: the potential loser was the fatherless son of a slave for whom other avenues of recourse may have been slim. If we assume that the paternity of the deceased was accepted, the case could have taken several directions. If the slave's son was the only surviving child, perhaps receiving half of the estate positioned him well enough to carry on with life in the local community in spite of any stigma associated with his illegitimacy. Considerable questions arise, however, when we consider the possibility that the slave's

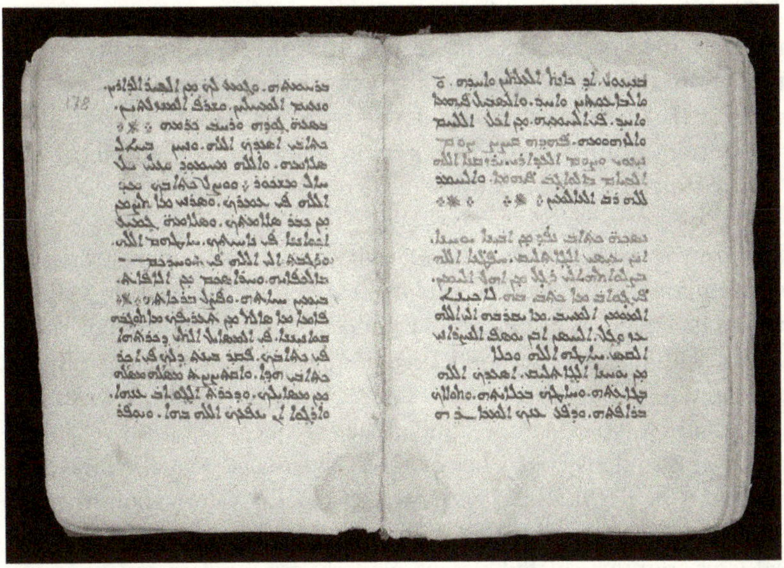

Figure 4. Manuscript copy written in Garshuni, Arabic in Syriac script, of Yohannan bar Abgare's letter to Yemen. Chaldean Cathedral of Mardin, Turkey, MS 333 (olim Diyarbakır 157), fols. 177v–178r, reproduced with permission. Image supplied by the Hill Museum & Manuscript Library.

son received only a minor piece of inheritance. Yuhanna ibn Bukhtishuʿ was from a prominent family and was well integrated in elite East Syrian communal institutions: schools and the episcopacy. Would anything comparable have been available to the unnamed Yemeni? Might he have been able to enter a monastery? Could he have found a spouse in spite of his unfree parentage? What would the prospects have been for a daughter in a comparable position? This is the line at which the social effects of disinheritance and illegitimacy might become acute. There are two possibilities worth mentioning if social and institutional relations within Christian communities could not tolerably integrate someone like the unnamed slave's son. One is that he might convert to Islam and seek a livelihood in Muslim social networks, or perhaps eligibility for charity from Muslim institutions. In such a case, Christian law would realize the ideal of monogamous descent in social relations at the cost of pushing marginalized individuals out of the communal fold. Another possibility is that someone might bring the slave's son's case before a Muslim court; if witnesses confirmed that the deceased slave owner had acknowledged paternity, the slave's son would inherit fully under Islamic law. Muslim courts thus represented an extracommunal source of leverage that could overrule the Christian institution of disinheritance by according rights to concubines' children. But whether the Christian child of a slave—or the slave mother herself after her master's death—would have had the ability and the social literacy to take the case before a Muslim judge remains speculation.

Polygamy is unlikely to have been overly common among the Christian communities of the medieval Middle East, certainly not on the scale of cousin marriage, as a contrastive example. Various forms of polygamy and concubinage had certainly been familiar to societies east of Rome since antiquity, but the resources required to support multiple wives and concubines was a structural limit on their frequency of practice. Polygamy was also flatly contradictory to the most basic sexual ethics—the singleness of flesh created by marriage and the valorization of strict monogamy—of the Christian tradition, which late antique ecclesiastical legislation articulated clearly. Nonetheless, polygamous practices persisted in particular strata of Middle Eastern Christian communities precisely because those strata were embedded in networks and legal orders in which Christian perspectives were not hegemonic. We have seen this most clearly among Christian civilian elites attached to rulers' courts. The physicians of sixth-century Nisibis and ninth-century Baghdad and Samarra moved in courtly circles in which relatively public forms of concubinage and polygamy were status prerogatives. For these laymen, their religious affiliation, their social-professional identity, and the household forms through which they enacted their elite status were reconcilable and unproblematic.

For the bishops, on the other hand, they were not. Narratives sources have allowed us to suggest an outline for how ecclesiastical institutions sought to restrict lay polygamy and by extension other social practices of which the bishops disapproved. The anathema was the principal tool of persuasion available to ecclesiastics who lacked any powers of physical sanction. Ecclesiastical law affirmed that polygamy was un-Christian; proclaiming the anathema against a polygamist and preventing him from receiving the Eucharist cut him off from the core ritual practice that facilitated both salvation and communal assembly. The pressures brought on by the anathema may have been frequently effective in securing obedience to ecclesiastical norms among laypeople whose primary social ties were within Christian networks. The picture gets more complicated, however, with lay elites who had access to other forms of power and influence. The Nisibene physicians and Bukhtishuʿ ibn Jibraʾil, for example, were able to go over bishops' heads to ruling court circles and see to the installation of bishops who were favorable to their interests and willing to look the other way from their polygamous proclivities. Yuhanna ibn Masawayh appeared to strike a similar balance. This suggests a heuristic model for how the intersection of Christian communal institutions with those of the state produced communal boundaries in practice in the early medieval caliphate: laypeople who could mobilize royal-caliphal power were able to realize simultaneously their Christian affiliation through ritual participation and their other social commitments that ran contrary to ecclesiastical expectations. In these specific situations, the lay elite's understanding of the shape of the community effectively won out over the ecclesiastical one familiar from normative texts. In practice, the dhimmi community was not simply autonomous—its boundaries were created through competition between different constituencies, a competition conditioned by the limitations and possibilities offered by extracommunal, caliphal institutions.

If Christian integration in elite Muslim circles allowed some laymen to maintain polygamous households and bend the shape of the religious community accordingly, bishops used inheritance law to reshape lay lineages in appropriately Christian terms. Beginning in the seventh century and continuing into the Abbasid period, the sources show bishops expanding their judicial horizons and seeking to order the intergenerational transfer of wealth in Christian lineages in a manner that excluded the children of polygamous arrangements from any meaningful share in their fathers' patrimonies. In doing so, the bishops aimed to marginalize unlawful progeny and deny to Christians a standard practice of lineage reproduction in elite Muslim society: Islamic law accorded full inheritance rights and paternal affiliation to the children of polygamous marriages and relationships of concubinage. Ecclesiastics were likely better able to enforce these rules than anathemas against powerful laymen. Disinheritance affected materially second wives, children, and slave mothers precisely after the troublesome family patriarchs had died. It is possible that free second wives and their children could have taken their cases before Muslim judges to secure recognition and inheritance; it is likely, however, that the pressures of clerical and neighborly surveillance made public, polygamous marriage less common among Christians than concubinage. For their part, slaves and their children are much less likely to have been able to muster alternative forms of pressure to counteract the bishops' rulings or seek other modes of redress. Yuhanna ibn Bukhtishuʿ's career and Yohannan bar Abgare's letter to Yemen give us potential examples of the ecclesiastical strategy of disinheritance playing out in practice. When it did, the marginalization of unlawful progeny realized in social and economic terms the ecclesiastical ideal of monogamous Christian lineages, starkly distinct from elite Muslim ones, even when the bishops had not been able to prevent the practice of polygamy in the first place.

What were the further effects of ecclesiastical regulation on the individuals it sought to marginalize and on the shape of Christian communities more broadly? Yuhanna ibn Bukhtishuʿ offered an intriguing case in which the unlawful son of a Christian man may have been divested of inheritance in line with the bishop's prescriptions but remained a prominent member of the community. However, we can readily imagine that others—disinherited second wives, less prominent concubines' sons, daughters stigmatized as illegitimate—might have faced more difficulties. Would ecclesiastical regulation have pushed them to conversion, to seeking economic and social well-being outside of Christian social circles? The same is conceivable for elite laymen fed up with ecclesiastical pressures to abandon the polygamous prerogatives of their status in a social order governed by Muslim law and mores.

From this perspective, the ecclesiastical effort to restrict polygamous practices, lawful in the caliphate overall, conceivably contributed over time to the thinning of Christian ranks through conversion to Islam. It is not likely to have had a major effect on Christian communal integrity on its own, however. The resources required to sustain polygamy meant that its practice was never ubiquitous. It was only subject to regulation, moreover, when it was public in some manner. Indeed, we can analyze forms of polygamy like the concubinage of enormously rich doctors' households in imperial capitals precisely because the individuals concerned were prominent enough that they show up in our sources. Yet polygamous practices in the premodern world were varied, and many other arrangements in which men cohabited with multiple women who were sexually available to them remained current. The societies of the medieval caliphate were slaveholding, and in that context it was countless domestic slave women subject to their masters' desires, like the unnamed mother in the patriarch Yohannan's epistle, whose experiences of polygamous households are least visible to us but were likely the most representative.

CHAPTER 8

Interreligious Marriage and the Multiconfessional Social Order

Concerning a Christian woman who by her own will marries a Muslim [*mhaggrāyā*]: is it suitable for priests to give her the Eucharist? Is there a canon concerning this? If her husband threatens to kill the priest if he does not give her the Eucharist [*w-en gāzem baʿlāh ʿal kāhnā d-qāṭel lēh en lā yāheb lāh qurbānā*], is it right for him to assent during the time when [the husband] is seeking to have him killed? Or does he sin by assenting? Or is it better to give her the Eucharist so that she does not apostatize [*thaggar*, literally "go Hagarene"], since her husband likes Christians?

—Adday, West Syrian priest, to Jacob of Edessa, circa 680s

The question above takes us back to the period of Umayyad rule, some fifty years after the Arab conquests of Syria and Iraq. Adday, a miaphysite priest serving somewhere in Syria, had apparently heard of a case of a Christian woman married to a member of the new ruling class (in the seventh century Syriac writers called the conquest elite *mhaggrāyē*, a reference to the early Muslim self-designation as "Emigrants," Arabic *muhājirūn*). Established Christian tradition held that those who married adherents of other religions gave up their right to Christian communion, but this case had a twist—denying Christian ritual participation to the woman in question might cause even more trouble if her overly solicitous husband tried to kill her priest. Adday turned to Jacob of Edessa for advice on this tricky situation, and Jacob's answer tried to steer a pragmatic course: assign the woman penance if appropriate but keep giving her the Eucharist. Jacob's answer illustrates well the fundamental concerns that religious elites had with interreligious marriage. Of all the practices we have examined so far, this one challenged most obviously and explicitly the communal boundaries that bishops, ulama, and rabbis built around the institution of marriage. Demanding unmixed households, however, might also do no more than push adherents of one's own tradition across the internal household divide and into the spouse's religion. For elites, regulating interreligious marriage came down to managing the affiliations of individuals embedded in households whose very composition questioned the bounds of religious communities as distinct social bodies.

In the multiconfessional societies of the medieval caliphate, marriage and other sexual relationships like concubinage across religious lines were not uncommon. Christian thought maintained a consistent theological principle of opposition to these forms of interreligious contact, but the legal traditions it inspired developed different emphases in response to changing social and political conditions from the late antique empires to the caliphate. In particular, Muslim political dominion in the early medieval period motivated jurist-bishops to regulate especially the marriage of Christian women to non-Christian men. From the bishops' perspective, women's reproductive potential was key to the integrity of the church as a theological and social collectivity and therefore required special regulation to prevent its loss through interreligious marriage—hence the concerns in Adday's question and Jacob's response. This was especially so because Islamic law and political authority prohibited Muslim women from marrying into non-Muslim families but allowed Muslim men to take Christian and Jewish wives and concubines. Norms governing interreligious marriage thus represent another facet of the challenge that Islamic law posed to the social boundaries of Christian communities and that affected the particular form that Christian law took in response.

INTERRELIGIOUS MARRIAGE FROM LATE ANTIQUITY TO THE MEDIEVAL CALIPHATE

The Roman Empire

Among the most foundational ways that systems of family law structure the boundaries of wider social groups is by defining whether and in what circumstances a member of the group may marry outside of it. The very act of identifying some feature that makes a set of individuals unmarriageable does the cultural work of creating in-groups and out-groups—those individuals do not have what defines "us" and therefore become "them" instead. Thus, essentially any legal regime addressed to human social behavior will necessarily formulate a notion of intermarriage as part of the process of distinguishing who constitutes the in-group subject to its rules. Because norms such as these have consequences for procreation, furthermore, they work to manage and ensure the reproduction of the in-group across time: "injunctions against intermarriage, together with clerical control or influence over marriage," in the words of one sociologist, "have often helped reproduce socioreligious segmentation. This, in turn, has helped reproduce religious, ethnic, and national communities over the long run and has worked to prevent their dissolution through assimilation."[1] The nature of the intermarriage boundary will not be congruent in all contexts, however, as methods of regulation and the culturally determined values associated with the notion of intermarriage differ. In this connection, the Christian traditions of late antiquity on either side of the Roman-Sasanian frontier exhibit distinctions in the forms of social difference they created between Christians and others, including pagans, Jews, and Zoroastrians, even as they shared the same theological concerns. Later, intermarriage with the first generations of Arab-Muslim conquerors posed new problems to Christian bishops. Their responses coalesced into one distinctive approach to the subject, evident in the Syriac legal texts of the Abbasid Caliphate, which imagined a particular, gendered social boundary enclosing Christian communities.

The question of whether believers might marry unbelievers goes back to the earliest days of the Christian movement. When bishops of later centuries like Jacob of Edessa took it up, their perspectives were at least partially rooted in the guidance offered by the Pauline epistles. Paul's consideration of intermarriage in 2 Corinthians 6:14—"Do not be bound to those who do not believe" (*w-lā tehwon bnay zawgā l-aylēn d-lā mhaymnin*), in the standard Syriac Peshitta Bible—became the locus classicus of the issue. Though scholars continue to debate the precise theological and, perhaps, Jewish legal background to Paul's directive, most agree that the basic understanding that he and the patristic tradition developed centered on a concern for purity and defilement. Marriage between believers and unbelievers was unacceptable because the bodies of believers, as partakers of the body of Christ, were holy, while the bodies of unbelievers were necessarily impure and defiled.[2] For a believer to marry, have sex with, and become one flesh with an unbeliever was thus to introduce that defilement into the church. Though 1 Corinthians 7:12–15 granted an exception in allowing a convert to remain married to his or her pagan spouse, the patristic tradition was largely unanimous in understanding interreligious marriage as a form of *porneia*, unlawful sexual practice, on the basis of 2 Corinthians.[3]

This basic theological perspective came to structure both canonical and civil legislation in the Christian Roman Empire. Marriage to pagans was at issue for the earliest community; but with the growth of Christianity in the Roman world and the ongoing efforts to define and promote orthodoxy, intermarriage with two groups, Jews and Christian heretics, became of chief concern. So, the canons of several late antique church councils forbade variously clergymen and laypeople from marrying heretics, Jews, and pagans.[4] Meanwhile, a 388 constitution of Theodosios made marriage between Christians and Jews a public crime on par with adultery, introducing to Roman law the entirely novel concept that disparity of cult was grounds for dissolving marriages.[5] Already in late antique Rome, then, ecclesiastical and imperial traditions construed interreligious marriage as a hard, impassable boundary separating Christians from other socioreligious groups.

Christians and Zoroastrians in the Sasanian Empire

Across the frontier in the Sasanian Empire, bishops were well acquainted with the teachings of Paul and the Church Fathers according to which interreligious marriage undermined the ecclesiological integrity of the Christian community. But the very different circumstances of the Iranian empire, where Christianity was not the state religion, gave a material urgency to the prospect of interreligious marriage and led a discourse on the matter to develop with subtly different emphases. This discourse was gendered: it specified that Christian women should not marry across religious boundaries but paid little attention to men. Its purpose was to uphold the material and social bonds of Christian communion in addition to the indispensable theological ones. This perspective is evident already in a set of canons accepted by Sasanian bishops at the synod of 410 convened under the patronage of Shah Yazdgird I, which first formally organized the disparate Christians of the empire into the Church of the East. Several canons treat interreligious marriage, which was clearly a topic of concern, but they do so in conspicuously gendered terms. One, for instance, allows Christian men to marry "women of all nations" (*neshē men kul ʿammin*) in order that they might "instruct them" in the ways of Christianity.[6] Women, however, may not marry non-Christians; and according to another canon, fathers or brothers who give their female charges in marriage to non-Christians "shall be cast out from the entire community of believers [*kulēh ḥulṭānā da-mhaymnē*]."[7] Underlying these rules is a standard assumption characteristic of patriarchal social organization: head males define the religious identities of their families. For men to marry non-Christian women, then, brings those women into the communal fold. But when Christian women marry outside the community they are essentially lost to it: "through their laxity [*rapyutā*], they become attracted to the doctrines [*reʿyānē*] of their husbands, leave their Christianity, and go near to paganism and Judaism."[8]

The concern for apostasy is telling, and it points to the different logic behind the gendered regulation of intermarriage versus its blanket prohibition on theological grounds: the former is concerned also with managing human reproductive powers and social resources. Forbidding Christian women to marry outside the religious community preserves their powers of reproduction for its service. Allowing the intermarriage of Christian men brings in greater reproductive capacity. Regulating intermarriage in this manner is unsurprising in a largely patrilineal society, but it is significant in the Sasanian context in that the social group whose boundaries it aims to secure is the religious community: it defines the Church of the East as a distinct social body within the empire's religiopolitical hierarchy. Sasanian Mesopotamia was home to a variety of religious groups, including Christians, Jews, Zoroastrians, Mandaeans, Manichaeans, pagans, and others, while the ruling dynasty acknowledged and supported Zoroastrianism as the cult of Iran and its people. Marriage was certainly one form of interaction among adherents of these different religions.[9] Sasanian shahs, for example, had Christian wives and concubines, such as Khusraw II's influential wife Shirin; a Christian craftsman in the shah's service might marry a Persian wife; East Syrian canons speak of "priests, deacons, and sons of the covenant who marry pagan women [*ḥanpātā*]" and "pagans who espouse the women and daughters" of clergymen.[10] Marriage between Christians and others may not have appeared transgressive to everyone; but ecclesiastical law identified it as a distinct category of practice, and by prescribing norms for it in terms of the strategic, gendered allocation of communal resources, the bishops defined the church as a distinct social group beholden to the exigencies of generational reproduction. This was a discourse less overtly concerned with the theological status of believers' bodies than with the social coherence of the church in the present world.

The gendered discourse on interreligious marriage in East Syrian law developed further in the sixth century. An example from the synod of the patriarch Yosep held in 554 illustrates in starkly material terms just how central female reproductive potential was to the bishops' notion of communal integrity. Yosep's canon §11 addresses the problem of bishops who wrongfully appropriate monastic and church properties (*qenyānē d-ʿēdātā wa-d-dayrātā*, likely meaning land) and bequeath it to their descendants as private property. When their female heirs marry Zoroastrians, the latter end up inheriting what had once belonged to the church, which is thus lost to the "entire community of Christianity" (*kulēh gawwā da-krēsṭyānutā*).[11] The canon's solution is that all wills and testaments must be public knowledge; it does not mention any prohibition of interreligious marriages. But its perspective is grounded in a gendered notion of household religious affiliation and speaks precisely to the central importance, from the bishops' perspectives, of female reproductive power to the social and material integrity of the church. Christian women in this context are carriers of the religious community's material property, repositories of its potential for social reproduction, and in danger of being lost to its service. When Christian women marry non-Christian men, their property alongside their reproductive capacity is siphoned away from the Church of the East as they facilitate the generational reproduction and material well-being of their non-Christian families. Even more dangerous is that some such women might be holding wrongfully appropriated ecclesiastical property, which represents an acutely material loss to the religious community.

Overall, East Syrian bishops in the Sasanian Empire developed a legal discourse on interreligious marriage that put surprisingly little explicit emphasis on the theological necessity to attend to the purity of the body of Christ; it was informed instead by a concern for the management of resources in the Sasanian Empire's multiconfessional social hierarchy. Regulating intermarriage in those terms meant managing chiefly women's reproductive potential: prohibiting marriage between Christian women and non-Christian men but allowing Christian men to bring other women into the fold in order to increase the community's material and reproductive capacities. It is important to note that the bishops presumed that non-Christian wives would be converted, and so technically there would be no "interreligious marriage" posing ecclesiological problems.[12] In this they maintained the traditional theological opposition to bringing unbelievers into the body of Christ. But the gendering of the bishops' regulations demonstrates that their fundamental purpose was to secure women's reproductive potential to the service of the religious community.

This discourse's concern for "resource allocation" at points of interreligious contact produced, in turn, the very notion of discrete religious communities that it presented as natural. On the face of things, a Christian and a Zoroastrian might have married, begotten children, and passed on their property to those children without any sense of owing those acts to any community beyond the family or lineage. The bishops' regulations, on the other hand, affirmed that resources, whether material, human, or social, necessarily functioned in the service of the religious community to which their possessors belonged. When property devolved from a believing parent to a non-Christian heir, therefore, or when a Christian father gave his daughter in marriage to a Zoroastrian, those resources were lost to the community. Regulating interreligious marriage in this manner asserted that the religious community had rightful claims on the material and reproductive services of its adherents; those claims in turn gave the religious community a material and social tangibility through property and reproduction. Rather than penalizing the infraction of a supposedly natural marital-sexual boundary between communities, this discourse created that boundary to secure the immanence of the religious community itself.

Christian Women and Muslim Men in the Umayyad Caliphate

The Arab conquests of the seventh century made the Christians of Syria (as well as of Egypt and North Africa) the subjects of a non-Christian polity, much as their coreligionists to the east had been for centuries. It is evident that bonds of marriage and concubinage between conquerors and subjects subsequently became relatively common in the period of the Medinan and the early Umayyad caliphs. As a result, contemporary episcopal letters and other Christian legal sources from the former Roman provinces exhibit a conspicuous concern for managing the implications of marriage across religious lines; they trend away from simply restating the patristic tradition's blanket prohibition and focus instead on strategies for keeping Christian women who have married into the conquerors' households within the

Christian fold. East Syrian legislation, for its part, reemphasizes the gendered regulations of the Sasanian-era canons.

The convergence of several conditions in the immediate aftermath of the conquests suggests that marriage between conquerors and their subjects, Christians as well as others, occurred with a good degree of frequency. For one, Islamic teachings were more or less unanimous in allowing marriage between Muslim men and free women of the People of the Book (*ahl al-kitāb*), that is, Jews and Christians as described in the Quran.[13] Various early Muslim leaders, including Muhammad himself and the third caliph ʿUthman, set important precedents by taking Christian wives and concubines.[14] Furthermore, since the earliest phases of the conquests involved the movement and settlement of large numbers of fighting men, it is unremarkable to find indications in the sources that the conquerors sometimes established households by taking wives and concubines from the local conquered populations.[15] Anastasios of Sinai's responsa, for example, deal with the spiritual status of enslaved Christian women who have been compelled into fornication (from Anastasios's perspective) with their Muslim masters; Arabic chronicles report that the conquerors of the Sawad, the populous breadbasket region of central Iraq, married local Jewish and Christian women because there were no Muslim women settled there yet.[16] It is also significant that many such local people may not have understood marrying the conquerors as an impermissible form of intermarriage at all. Not only did the doctrinal content of the conquerors' religious movement remain fairly fluid for much of the seventh century;[17] its immediately recognizable elements included a scripture, a strong focus on monotheism, and esteem for Jesus and Mary, and so early Islam may have appeared to be within the bounds of "us" in the socioreligious imagination of some Christian communities, particularly rural ones that were less exposed to the doctrinal fine points of high clergymen.[18] Additionally, many of the Christian communities of the Fertile Crescent's desert fringes were Arabic speaking and interacted regularly with pastoralists; some were tribal pastoralists themselves, including those like the Taghlib who wound up fighting alongside the early Muslims against the Romans and Sasanians.[19] Many such Arabophone and Arab Christians may not have considered marrying the conquerors to have been crossing any momentous religious boundary. These circumstances, combined with the Quranic approval of marriage to People of the Book and the fact that the first waves of Muslim settlers were predominantly male soldiers, explain why the integration of conquered peoples into the conquerors' households was likely fairly common in the caliphate's first century.

For Christian religious elites, however, this situation was problematic. In the eyes of the bishops, the followers of the Quranic dispensation were heretics at best, and a variety of seventh-century Christian legal works express disapproval of marriage between the conquerors and Christian women. This disapproval took several forms. Some synodal legislation and responsa from the period of Umayyad rule continue the two strands of late antique discourse on interreligious marriage. George I's Persian Gulf synod of 676, for example, speaks against women marrying non-Christian men and so carries on the East Syrian concern to maintain female reproductive potential within the community. The relevant canon also recognizes the potential for marriage with Muslims to lead to apostasy: "marriage to [*ḥanpē*] brings [Christian] women to the customs of strangers to the fear of God."[20] In Egypt, the responsa of the Chalcedonian Anastasios of Sinai repeat the traditional blanket prohibition of interreligious marriage.[21]

Two West Syrian ecclesiastical epistles, on the other hand, show the bishops adopting imperfect but practical methods of accommodating the reality that some Christian women were marrying Muslims and trying to keep the former within the communal fold. One, a letter of the patriarch Athanasios II of Balad, responds to the "wicked news" (*ṭebbā bishā*) that Christian women have been "marry[ing] pagans [i.e., Muslims] unlawfully and inappropriately" (*mezdawwgān l-ḥanpē lā nāmosā'it w-lā wālyā'it*). Athanasios's letter is addressed to traveling bishops and priests (*kor episqopē w-sā'orē*) and instructs them on how to handle the matter: they should continue giving the Eucharist to Christian women married to Muslims and see to it that they baptize their children and avoid participating in Muslim festivals. Rather than denying women married to Muslims the Eucharist and therefore participation in ecclesiological and social communion, Athanasios seeks to keep them in the fold and ultimately keep Christian salvation open to their children.[22] Jacob of Edessa offers a similar perspective in his response to Adday's question with which this chapter began. If a Christian woman marries a Muslim, Adday asks, is it right for a priest to give her the Eucharist? What if her husband threatens to kill the priest if he will not include his wife in communion? Jacob advises Adday to allow the woman's continued participation in Christian ritual: whether or not the husband threatens the priest, he should continue giving her communion in order to keep her from apostatizing. If there is no danger of this happening, he should prescribe an appropriate penance for the woman for marrying outside of the church.[23] Like Athanasios, however, Jacob envisions keeping her within the community rather than proclaiming an anathema against her.

Athanasios's and Jacob's letters are examples of ecclesiastics betting on the long run: despite the common assumption they no doubt shared that a husband determined the religion of his household, the two bishops still looked to secure the Christian affiliation of women married to Muslim men—and perhaps later generations of their descendants—rather than give them up as lost to the church. In this respect, their letters exemplify again how the regulation of interreligious marriage in gendered terms—essentially, managing women's marriage across group boundaries—was key to structuring socioreligious groups in the patrilineal societies of the late antique Middle East. At the establishment of the caliphate, the region's Christian traditions were heir to a generally clear patristic and legal discourse on interreligious marriage that enjoined marriage within group boundaries; for a Christian to join with an unbeliever introduced the defilement of that person's false belief into the body of Christ. Integral, unmixed households should form the theological, moral, and social boundaries of the church. In the Sasanian Empire, Zoroastrian political power had made the prospect of the loss of communal resources through interreligious marriage of immediate concern; in response, ecclesiastics put special emphasis on preventing Christian women from marrying non-Christian men, as by doing so they would facilitate the reproduction of unbelievers at the church's expense. This perspective took on new urgency for bishops throughout the territories of the former Sasanian and eastern Roman empires after the Arab conquests, when many non-Muslim women were brought into the households of the conquerors by way of marriage or concubinage. In the absence of Christian state power, Athanasios and Jacob could not prevent these situations from happening. Instead, they aimed to facilitate Christian women's participation in the community's ritual institutions even when they had married outside of it.

Confessional Law and Christian-Muslim Marriage in the Abbasid Caliphate

If Athanasios's and Jacob's epistles represent relatively pragmatic attempts to salvage something out of less than ideal circumstances, the civil law traditions of the Syriac churches that took shape in the early Abbasid period adopted stricter rules on interreligious marriage overall—usually, the gendered perspective prohibiting women's marriage across religious lines. In doing so, Christian law in the caliphate put less emphasis on the theological rationale, though that was still present; instead, it came to mirror Islamic law and promoted the same conception of a social order of discrete religious communities segmented by gendered regulations for marriage and reproduction.

The various schools of Islamic law were essentially unanimous in allowing Muslim men to marry Jewish and Christian women. They based this perspective on Quran 5:5: "Today all good things have been made lawful for you. . . . So are chaste, believing women as well as chaste women of the people who were given the Scripture before you." The Islamic tradition wholly rejected, however, any notion that non-Muslim men might marry Muslim women. This norm was an outgrowth of the idea that Islam was exalted above all other religions and that wives were subordinate members of the household; to have a Muslim woman in a position of subordination to a non-Muslim husband would thus upend the proper socioreligious hierarchy.[24] According to a tradition of the Companion Ibn ʿAbbas (d. 686/87), "Our religion is the best of the religions [*fa-dīnunā khayr al-adyān*]. . . . Our men are above their women, but their men shall not be above our women."[25]

Islamic thought had little concern for theological purity of the kind that undergirded the Christian tradition's opposition to interreligious marriage. It focused instead on restricting women's potential husbands to those within the *umma*, securing group boundaries in a manner by now familiar to us. Notably, as the bishops of the Abbasid Caliphate consolidated their legal traditions in the eighth and ninth centuries, they too tended to adopt more definitively that gendered approach to regulating interreligious marriage. West Syrian synods of 785, 794, and 846 and the law books of Timothy and Ishoʿbarnun are unanimous in stating that anyone responsible for a Christian woman marrying a non-believer should be anathematized—the woman's family members if they arranged the marriage, the woman herself if she consented to it willingly.[26] The East Syrian sources tend to specify that Christian men might marry other women in order to convert them;[27] the West Syrian sources do not comment on this possibility, but their prohibition of only female interreligious marriage implies that it is acceptable. In another respect, the West Syrian sources are particularly explicit as to how regulating women's marriage options secures the boundaries of the religious community: their synodal canons specify the anathema for marriage to Jewish men and Christian heretics, including Nestorians and Chalcedonians (*nesṭoryānē* and *kalqidonāyē*), in addition to Muslims.[28] Christian women whose marriages shirk their commitment to the unmixed, integral church lose the right of participation in the community's constitutive ritual institutions.

The West Syrian bishops surely presume, just as the East Syrians prescribe explicitly, that a non-Christian wife will convert to her husband's religion. They thus avoid the theological problem of introducing an unbeliever into the body of Christ through marital union. In this their law differs from Islamic tradition, which took no fundamental issue with allowing non-Muslim women married to Muslim men to retain their religion (though Muslim scholars debated the degree to which those wives' freedom to practice took precedence over their husbands' rights and objections).[29] But the bishops' discourse is still gendered, and its approach to intermarriage thus revolves around managing reproductive resources in the service of the religious community.

THE STRUCTURAL IMPLICATIONS OF INTERRELIGIOUS MARRIAGE

We should interpret Abbasid-era Christian legal texts' adoption of gendered norms on interreligious marriage, rather than the blanket prohibition, as a response to both the parallel Islamic perspective and the very real prospect of Christian women marrying across religious boundaries. Bishops throughout the caliphate were in largely the same position that their Iraqi and Iranian predecessors had been under the Sasanians. Religious elites understood the material and reproductive resources of individual households to maintain the integrity of their communities. This meant regulating especially female reproductive powers and keeping Christian women within the marital bounds of the community. Insofar as this perspective ran precisely parallel to the rules of Muslim *fiqh*, ecclesiastical law in the caliphate promoted the same vision of the social order that Islamic law rendered normative: discrete religious communities, built of patriarchal households and segmented from one another through marital regimes organized around securing female reproductive potential. Encoding these norms of patrilineal social organization as ecclesiastical law was a response to conditions in the caliphate and, unlike the prohibition of divorce or polygamy, had little specifically Christian precedent.

If the East Syrians' and West Syrians' gendered regime of interreligious marriage regulation essentially mirrored the Islamic position, however, the institutional apparatuses to enforce them were highly unequal. This represents clearly another instance in which caliphal institutions produced a structural tension in the practical shape of Christian communities, as it did for other non-Muslims. The various schools of Islamic law denied the possibility that non-Muslim social groups might benefit from Muslim women's reproductive powers by prescribing harsh penalties, from corporal punishment to death, for non-Muslim men who had sexual contact with or married Muslim women. They further mandated the annulment of marriages contracted between two non-Muslims if the wife subsequently converted to Islam.[30] Historians have tended to presume that these harsh sentences meant that unions between Muslim women and non-Muslim men were rare indeed. Christian regulations allowing Christian men to bring unbelievers into the community would then have had little real bearing on social relations between Christians and Muslims, although they still would have been relevant if Christian men married members of other subject religious communities. It is conceivable that we simply lack documentation for marriages between Muslim women and non-Muslim men, which may have occurred at least occasionally. But in general, marriage in the medieval caliphate was a public institution, open to the scrutiny of authorities, neighbors, and others beyond the spouses themselves. As such, we have much greater reason to think that social pressures and the very real capacity of state functionaries to practice coercive violence limited marriage between Muslim women and non-Muslim men. The official stance of Christian law as developed by Abbasid-era jurist-bishops, for its part, effectively gave up Christian women who married men of other religions by anathematizing them. Overall, then, the fact that the Islamic and Christian discourses on interreligious marriage paralleled each other strongly favored the apportionment of reproductive capacity to Muslims in the long term, since Muslim political power was better situated to actually prevent Muslim women from marrying outside the community.

In the face of that structural limitation, the options open to non-Muslim religious elites were few. We saw Athanasios and Jacob of

Edessa in the seventh century skirt the nominally official church line and continue to give women married to Muslim men the Eucharist in order to keep them in ritual communion. It is difficult to imagine later ecclesiastics doing much more than this to try to counteract the loss to Christian communities represented by interreligious marriage. Perhaps the best they could hope for was that the children of Christian women and Muslim men might fall through the cracks of the caliphate's judicial apparatus and accept Christianity in the future. Comparable examples of non-Muslim religious elites employing flexible approaches from their disadvantaged legal position are evident in other religious literatures as well. For example, a Middle Persian responsa text of Adurfarrbay-i Farrokhzadan, the Zoroastrian high priest of Fars circa 815–33, evinces a concern to stem the tide of the loss of female reproductive capacity when it allows a man to remain married to a wife who has committed adultery with a non-Zoroastrian.[31]

How might subject religious elites have dealt with situations in which the husband of a non-Muslim couple converted to Islam while his wife kept to her birth religion, another potentially common form of interreligious marriage in the medieval caliphate? One possible strategy to lessen the negative impact of men's apostasy on non-Muslim communities was "single-generation conversion," which one scholar has identified in the abundant source material dealing with Coptic conversion to Islam in late medieval Egypt.[32] In the fourteenth century, activist ulama and Egypt's Mamluk regime put considerable pressure on Coptic government functionaries to convert to Islam; one way that Copts tried to accede to those pressures while still keeping human and material resources within Christian communities was for the functionaries themselves to convert while their wives and children remained Christian. This strategy appears to have been somewhat effective until the Mamluk sultan decreed that entire families had to convert when their patriarchs did. The practice of single-generation conversion is of interest for our period as well; around 850, the Abbasid caliph al-Mutawakkil issued what was likely the first edict in Islamic history prohibiting the employment of non-Muslims in government bureaucracies.[33] The decree provoked a good number of conversions among the Christian ranks of government clerks (*kuttāb*) who wanted to keep their jobs, likely resulting in at least some multireligious households.[34] It is conceivable that the men in question practiced single-generation conversions, as in the later setting of Mamluk Egypt, in order to keep both the families and the property of convert husbands within the communal fold—that is, by maneuvering to have still Christian wives or children inherit from their newly Muslim fathers.[35] We lack positive evidence for this practice comparable to that available for the Mamluk period, however. Perhaps the only hint is an anecdote concerning ʿUbaydallah ibn Sulayman ibn Wahb (d. 901), a vizier to the caliph al-Muʿtadid (r. 892–902) and convert to Islam from an East Syrian secretarial family.[36] In the narrative, a cross falls from ʿUbaydallah's person, presumably when he is present at a courtly setting; his excuse to the onlookers is, "This is something our old women seek blessings with, so they put it in our clothes without us knowing" (*hādhā shayʾ tatabarrak bihi ʿajāʾizunā fa-tajʿaluhu fī thiyābinā min ḥaythu lā naʿlim*).[37] The anecdote indicates that ʿUbaydallah's household included Christian family members even after his conversion, as well as hinting that he himself carried on Christian practices in private, domestic spaces; whether his wife and children remained Christian is unclear.

If they were ever effectively practiced, strategies like single-generation conversion, maintaining the Christian ritual participation of laywomen married to Muslim men, or seeking to baptize children of religiously mixed parentage were stopgap measures. The capacity of caliphal power and judicial institutions to enforce Islamic norms afforded the *umma* a distinct advantage in acquiring reproductive potential through interreligious marriage. Similar to the prospect of Christian women apostatizing to acquire divorces or men seeking recourse to Muslim courts in opposition to ecclesiastical law, this is another example of Islamic institutions exerting pressure on Christian and other non-Muslim communities at their edges—and, therefore, defining the structure of those communities as social groups within the medieval caliphate.

It is unsurprising that interreligious marriage was a topic of considerable concern to the bishops of the Abbasid Caliphate, and one they frequently sought to regulate in their law books, letters, and synodal rulings. Bishops, like rabbis, ulama, and Zoroastrian priests, looked out on a social landscape that they understood to be divided fundamentally along religious lines. Managing marriage and thus reproduction at points of intergroup contact was vital to securing the integrity of the in-group—their own religious community—as they understood it. In fact, labeling marriage between two individuals of different confessional affiliations as a distinct, proscribed category of practice did much to produce the very notion of religious communities as discrete social groups. Christianity had a long tradition of condemning interreligious marriage in any form on the grounds that it introduced unbelievers' impurity into Christian communion. In the multiconfessional setting of the Islamic caliphate, however, bishops put a higher priority on regulating marriage between Christian women and non-Christian men. When Christian men took non-Christian wives, the latter could always convert, and so ecclesiological purity was not at issue. When Christian women married non-Christian men, especially Muslims, however, their reproductive services were lost to the church. The bishops thus adopted a gendered regulatory regime of interreligious marriage organized especially around preventing women from marrying outside of the community.

In broad view, this approach paralleled Islamic law (and other regional religious traditions), and it promoted the same vision of a social order segmented into discrete religious communities through patrilineal reproduction. In this respect the jurist-bishops reframed ancient and enduring models of social organization as the teaching and prescriptions of their religious tradition, in a manner not dissimilar to their adoption of other ancient practices related to the family into Christian law—inchoate betrothal, dowry customs, first-cousin marriage. More significantly, the problem of interreligious marriage provides another example of the role of Islamic institutions in reshaping Christian traditions and communities in the caliphate. Muslim political dominion and its ability to proscribe and physically punish sexual contact between Muslim women and non-Muslim men favored the greater apportionment over time of reproductive powers to Muslim communities. That fact was a structural challenge to Christian numbers, and it spurred the bishops to adopt the gendered regulatory regime of interreligious marriage themselves.

Those regulations, alongside lay-ecclesiastical negotiations over the marriage contract, divorce, kin marriage, and polygamy, illustrate how Syriac Christians in the early medieval Abbasid Caliphate organized themselves as dhimmi social groups around the foundational communal institutions of marriage and the household. Two concluding points are worth emphasizing, both of which have implications for our overarching concern to integrate the histories of Christians, Muslims, and others into a narrative of the medieval caliphate attentive to its character as a multiconfessional empire.

First, the transformations in intellectual culture of the eighth- and ninth-century Middle East should not be understood solely as the triumphal emergence of the classical Arabo-Islamic tradition, in whose wake all other religions then followed. Rather, it is at the points of contact among the region's various traditions that we often get a clearer picture of contemporary intellectual developments as a whole. We have seen, for example, that the basic instruments of East Syrian family law were built out of a range of local Mesopotamian and Iranian practices, which remained vital even as Islamic law was beginning to cohere as the region's predominant legal tradition. Islamic institutions provided the context in which Syriac law developed; but the ancient, autochthonous resources it drew on remind us that the caliphate's intellectual culture was not yet obviously, overridingly Arabo-Islamic. In a similar vein, the jurist-bishops' debate over cousin marriage suggests that the reason/tradition dialectic, so central to accounts of early Islamic law, theology, and traditionism, was not simply an Islamic story; it was informed by the interplay of multiple religious traditions and shaped medieval Judaism and eastern Christianity just as it did Islam. There is no question that Arabo-Islamic literary genres and intellectual categories were soon to become highly influential models that Jewish and Christian thinkers readily adopted. But the non-Muslim majority of the caliphate's subject population continued to vigorously cultivate its ancient traditions; into the tenth century (and perhaps beyond), many of those had larger audiences and communities of dedicated custodians than did Islamic ones. Treating non-Muslim traditions as the special preserve of Syriac studies or Jewish studies, rather than as the very substance of Middle Eastern intellectual history, thus effaces the region's essential cultural and religious heterogeneity as well as key facets of the major transformations that certainly occurred under the rule of the early caliphate. Frequently, new and creative trajectories of all the region's traditions emerged from their contacts with one other—Islamic judicial practice encouraged the formation of Syriac Christian civil law, for example, while the latter allows us to see the depth and breadth of the role of the reason/tradition dialectic beyond Islamic law. In these respects, our studies of Syriac family law point to the fruitfulness of putting the contacts between religious traditions—rather than Islam alone—at the center of the early medieval Middle East's intellectual history.

The second concluding point relates to the character of the caliphate's religious communities. Where older historiography tended to emphasize the autonomous dhimmi social group, more recent studies have focused on the fluidity of religious boundaries; but it is also essential to be able to account for how particular communal and extracommunal institutions facilitated different practices of religious belonging across the medieval Middle East's social landscape. In the Christian case, caliphal rule spurred West Syrian and East Syrian bishops to push for a newly formalized and intensive connection between ecclesiastical law and believing households. When it came down to precisely how lay Christians were supposed to participate in the foundational institution of ecclesiastically sanctioned marriage, however, the bishops often faced resistance and competition. Laypeople made use of extracommunal courts; they sought to retain accustomed practices of social reproduction like cousin marriage; keeping polygamous households appealed to some as an embodiment of elite status in caliphal society. In many such cases, Islamic institutions—courts, *fiqh* norms, the caliph himself—delimited the range of practices open to laypeople and even functioned as leverage against ecclesiastical laws. Dhimmi communities were therefore not autonomous of caliphal institutions but were in fact constituted in part through them; Christian communal boundaries took shape precisely through lay practice in conversation and competition with the claims of ecclesiastical regulation and the possibilities and limitations imposed by Islamic and caliphal norms. Crucially, these new modes of religious association among Syriac Christians in the early Abbasid Caliphate exemplify the transformative impact of caliphal rule on the communal institutions of its subject populations. As such, the reorganization of Syriac Christian communities around law and the household is not a narrow story relevant only to eastern Christian history or Syriac studies; it is the very making of medieval Middle Eastern society from the perspective of the empire's non-Muslim subjects.

This account of the early medieval caliphate's history differs greatly from the image one might get from a teleological vantage point in the later Middle Ages, when Muslims were a clear majority throughout Iran, the lowlands of the Fertile Crescent, and Egypt, and when Islamic traditions defined the region's intellectual culture more completely. Yet despite the early medieval socioreligious diversity to which Syriac Christian law attests, certain of its preoccupations—interreligious marriage chief among them—have significant implications in the direction of later developments as well. If the Islamic law of interreligious marriage gave to Muslim communities a "demographic advantage" in the apportionment of reproductive resources, this is surely relevant to the region's long-term Islamization. This reminds us that the extraordinary heterogeneity of the caliphate's religious demography and lettered traditions, which certainly characterized the ninth century, did not last forever, at least not in the same forms; indeed, the notion of a transition in the tenth or eleventh century toward a more straightforwardly Islamic society is a scholarly commonplace.[38] Whether or not we accept all the implications of this model, it is certainly true that Arabicization was proceeding apace, that Arabo-Islamic idioms were becoming ever more predominant in intellectual discourse, and that characteristic Sunni institutions like the *madrasa* were rising to prominence in this period.[39] These points beg a historiographical question: Does Islamization in the later medieval period render the Middle East's non-Muslims and their traditions historiographically insignificant, fit to be abandoned to their respective, specialized scholarly niches?

In fact, they remain essential to a comprehensive account of the medieval Islamic world's social and cultural history, as the following chapter and conclusion argue. Because long-term changes like Islamization could be uneven, contested, and even overturned within shorter time frames, it is imperative not to couch our narratives in terms that depict those changes as inevitable. The perception of non-Muslim decline, in demographic or cultural terms, would have been intelligible to historical actors themselves at particular times but not at others. Timothy in the early ninth century looked out on a Church of the East that stretched from Syria to India and Tibet; he was surrounded by doctors and scribes who counted as some of the richest men in Eurasia's largest empire while remaining generally secure in their Christian affiliation. Conversion and interreligious marriage must have eaten away at Christian numbers, resources, and probably confidence, but that does not mean that everyone had to have seen these trends as portending imminent collapse. Nor would Christian decline have been on the minds of many who saw the Byzantine conquests of the tenth and eleventh centuries in Anatolia and northern Syria and the subsequent settlement of large numbers of Armenians and West Syrians in the region.[40] A similar scenario obtained even in the early decades of Mongol rule, when many among the new political elite showed a good deal of favor to their Christian subjects.[41]

Ultimately, it is precisely because the various facets of long-term Islamization were fraught and uneven that non-Muslim traditions remain historiographically vital to understanding the formation of

Islamic societies in the later medieval period: they can serve as gauges of those overall changes, as evolving standards against which to check the steady progress of Islamic traditions and institutions that one typically finds in the historiography. It is from this perspective that the final section of this book traces the development of Christian family law in the Muslim-ruled Middle East from the fragmentation of Abbasid power to the early fourteenth century. Throughout the final phases of intensive Christian literary production in medieval Syria, the Jazira, and Iraq, Syriac legal traditions exhibit ever more consistently the influence of Islamic law—a strong testament to the Islamization of regional intellectual culture in the later medieval period. At the same time, jurist-bishops continued to mine their ancient, inherited intellectual resources, maintaining their currency in the face of increasingly predominant Islamic models.

PART III

Islamic Law and Christian Jurists After Imperial Fragmentation

CHAPTER 9

"Christian Shariʿa" in Confrontation and Accommodation with Islamic Law in the Later Medieval Period

To marry a virgin is most excellent. *Rejoice with the wife of your youth, a loving doe, an ibex. Learn her ways at all times and be content in her love* (Proverbs 5:18–19). One should choose a woman from a lineage known for childbearing [*gensā d-yallādātā*], because *being fruitful* was [God's] first command (Genesis 1:28). And [it is good] to form a household with those who are unrelated by kinship [*d-lā ḥyānin*].

—Bar ʿEbroyo (d. 1286), *Nomocanon*

The passage above comes from an extensive legal treatise composed by Bar ʿEbroyo, a polymath of enormous erudition active in the thirteenth century and one of the greatest scholars in the history of the Syriac Orthodox Church. Here, toward the beginning of his exposition of the West Syrian law of marriage, Bar ʿEbroyo offers some sage advice on the ideal qualities a man seeking to marry should look for in a bride. No doubt the Christian prospective householders in his audience appreciated his words of wisdom. They might have been surprised to know, however, that Bar ʿEbroyo did not draw inspiration for this formulation directly from the scriptural passages he dressed it up with but from the writings of the Muslim thinker Abu Hamid al-Ghazali (d. 1111).[1] Bar ʿEbroyo's entire treatise on Christian law, in fact, was modeled on al-Ghazali's works of Islamic *fiqh*, and the wifely qualities recommended here—virginity, fertility, and the absence of close kinship—constitute one of numerous instances in which Bar ʿEbroyo reconfigured norms of Islamic provenance for his Christian audience.

Bar ʿEbroyo's *Nomocanon* is the most striking example of the accommodation of Syriac Christian family law to Islamic thought in the later medieval period. But it is not the only one; and accommodation was not the only posture that ecclesiastical jurists took as Islamic law and institutions became ever more predominant in Middle Eastern societies. From the tenth century to the early fourteenth, Christian jurist-bishops in Syria, the Jazira, and Iraq interacted with the learned traditions of Islamic law in many ways and to many ends. The most significant such developments include the adoption of Islamic inheritance law by West Syrians; the Arabicization of the East Syrian legal heritage; and the starkly different approaches to Islamic family law on the part of the two great Syriac Christian jurist-bishops of the thirteenth century, Bar ʿEbroyo and his East Syrian contemporary ʿAbdishoʿ bar Brika (d. 1318). An examination of these developments demonstrates the historiographical utility of non-Muslim traditions in indexing the ebb and flow of the Islamization of intellectual culture (for which Bar ʿEbroyo is emblematic). It aptly brings to a close, moreover, our narrative of the transformations to Christian law, households, and communities engendered by Christian subjects' encounters with Islamic political and religious institutions. In many instances, the writings of the Middle East's jurist-bishops in the centuries after the breakup of centralized Abbasid power display the considerable degree to which Islamic law had come to define the parameters of their legal discourse and the social institutions they sought to regulate. At the same time, Syriac Christian legal works testify to the continued vibrancy of their autochthonous traditions amid the Islamic states and societies of the later medieval Middle East.

THE MEDIEVAL MIDDLE EAST AFTER ABBASID FRAGMENTATION

Our story thus far has revolved around the encounter between Christian elites and the early Abbasid Caliphate. Recalling al-Jahiz's caricature of Abbasid-era Christians captures nicely the dynamics of that encounter through the ninth century. From Egypt to the western foothills of the Iranian Plateau, Christians of one kind or another almost assuredly made up the majority of the caliphate's population; even if they were only a plurality, Muslims were certainly still in the minority outside of key cities and their immediate hinterlands. Demographics aside, however, the institutions of caliphal governance and the new Arabic disciplines of learning cultivated by Muslim elites were becoming ever more influential in structuring social relations and the parameters of intellectual culture for all the caliphate's subjects. Furthermore, the Abbasid Caliphate down to the mid-ninth century was a confident, powerful empire that stretched from Egypt to Khurasan and boasted a level of centralization impressive for any premodern state. It was in response to these contexts—a robust Christian demography, an emergent Islamic intellectual culture, a relatively centralized caliphate—that bishops like Timothy and Ishoʿbarnun laid the foundations of new Christian legal traditions and redefined the social constitution of Christian households and communities. From the later ninth century, however, the caliphate underwent considerable political, economic, and demographic changes, all of which impacted the West Syrian and East Syrian heartlands of northern Syria, the Jazira, and Iraq. These changes form the backdrop to the longer-term elaboration of Christian communal law and household forms, and the accommodation of both to Islamic norms, in the period from the fragmentation of Abbasid power through the Mongol khanate.

The prosperous cities of eighth- and ninth-century Iraq were the setting for the most innovative transformations in Christian traditions and communal institutions we have seen thus far, but the region's fortunes—and those of the Abbasids' empire as a whole—changed considerably from the later ninth century. It is a well-known story: after the civil war (809–13) between the Abbasid brothers al-Amin and al-Maʾmun had divided the dynasty's old base of military support, later caliphs began to rely on personal armies of slave soldiers and other dependents drawn from eastern Iran and Central Asia. With the assassination of al-Mutawakkil in 861, slave-soldier factions at the Abbasid court became kingmakers and often the true holders of power behind puppet caliphs. The instability this created at the empire's center meant that provincial governors became effectively independent rulers paying little more than nominal allegiance to the caliph; the Abbasids' continent-spanning centralized empire was no more. From the mid-tenth century, Iraq itself was ruled by Shiite Daylamis from the mountains of the Caspian Sea and then a succession of Turkish dynasties with roots in Central Asia until the Mongol conquest and sack of Baghdad in the mid-thirteenth century. As the Abbasids' empire fragmented, Iraq lost much of the material prosperity and population density it had earlier enjoyed. Intensive irrigation was the key to the region's agricultural wealth and to sustaining great cities like Baghdad and urban culture in general. Political instability meant neglect, and though we will never have absolute data, a host of indicators suggests that Iraq's population began to decline from its eighth- and ninth-century highs. Cities in Syria and especially Egypt increasingly became the region's economic, demographic, and political hubs.[2]

These circumstances affected the Christians as much as all the other communities of Iraq. As long as Baghdad remained the seat of the caliph and the location of his court (after its return from Samarra at the end of the ninth century), East Syrians and West Syrians continued to play significant roles in the city's intellectual life; the much-discussed salon culture of philosophical and theological inquiry of the later ninth and tenth centuries is a prominent example.[3] The central Iraqi city of Tikrit also remained an important West Syrian center. But to judge by the contraction of East Syrian dioceses from the end of the ninth century on, it appears that Christian numbers in central and southern Iraq were starting to diminish, likely a result of both conversion to Islam and the problems affecting the eastern caliphate as a whole.[4] The plains and hill country of the eastern Jazira around Mosul, which had always been the East Syrians' core territory, became more pronouncedly so with the decline of Abbasid power. The Mongol conquests of the thirteenth century devastated Baghdad and made Azerbaijan the new center of regional political power and courtly patronage; this largely finalized Christian retrenchment away from Iraq proper and into northern Mesopotamia.

The western Jazira and northern Syria, on the other hand, had a different experience after the decline of Abbasid power. Over the course of the tenth century the Byzantines conquered much of that frontier region and repopulated key parts of its highlands with West Syrian and Armenian Christians.[5] The subsequent incursions of Turkish pastoralists in the eleventh century marked the beginning of the long process of the Islamization of Anatolia as a whole. But between the Byzantine gains of the tenth century and the Mongol conquests of the thirteenth, the region's political map was a mishmash of competing Byzantine, Armenian, Crusader, and Turkish factions. One consequence of this was that Arabo-Islamic intellectual culture did not predominate to the degree that it did in the lowland towns of Syria and Iraq to the south. Syriac traditions of study remained strong in the highland region's monasteries and reached new peaks of literary productivity in the twelfth and thirteenth centuries, a period some scholars have taken to calling a "Syriac Renaissance."[6]

In contrast, the fourteenth century was marked by ongoing violence and disruptions for many Christians in the Jazira and eastern Anatolia, and our narrative will end then. Although much recent historiography has moved toward emphasizing constructive features of Mongol rule, it is important to recognize that the breakup of the Mongol Ilkhanate in the 1330s and its aftermath had destructive consequences for the settled populations in the region of our concern. Considerable violence attended the fall of the Ilkhanate as a variety of Mongol-Turkic confederations jockeyed for political supremacy;[7] outbreaks of plague and the conquests of Timur followed in later decades.[8] These ongoing disruptions resulted in a contraction of the geographic extent of Christian communities, particularly the East Syrians, and of the horizons of the intellectual life cultivated by their scholars compared to the preceding centuries.[9]

Though the Ottomans would eventually bring a degree of stability, the size and place of Syriac Christian communities in the Islamic Middle East changed significantly after the 1300s. Throughout the preceding centuries, however, Syriac Christians retained a significant, underappreciated presence in the region, and their traditions of family law offer glimpses into the fluctuations of the Islamization of the Middle East's intellectual culture and social institutions.

WEST SYRIANS, EAST SYRIANS, AND ISLAMIC INHERITANCE LAW

While the West Syrians have not featured as prominently as the East Syrians in our narrative so far, throughout the later medieval period their legal tradition stands out for the manner in which it incorporated Islamic legal norms and institutions. This is especially evident in West Syrian bishops' interest in Islamic inheritance law. The development of East Syrian inheritance law in the period after Abbasid fragmentation, on the other hand, exemplifies the greater independence from Islamic models of the Church of the East's more robust legal tradition.

The roots of the West Syrians' medieval civil law tradition went back to a series of ecclesiastical synods held in the eighth and ninth centuries that issued a body of foundational regulations in the area of family law, as we saw in Chapter 3. Though these testified to an interest in consolidating a body of communal civil norms in response to caliphal judicial reform and Islamic law, the West Syrian bishops involved in producing this legislation did not treat family law in the same depth as did their East Syrian contemporaries. In terms of genre, synodal legislation was traditional rather than innovative, and West Syrian bishops produced no extended legal treatises like those of contemporary East Syrian jurist-bishops in the ninth century. We attributed this difference generally to the fact that the centers of study where most West Syrian patriarchs received their intellectual formation—the monasteries of northern Syria and the western Jazira—were at a fair remove from the cities that were focal points for formative Islamic and East Syrian law. Although we know of a few further patriarchal synods and scattered legal writings after the ninth century, canon law would remain a more ancillary pursuit for West Syrian bishops until Bar ʿEbroyo.[10]

The main exception to this pattern in the medieval period is especially notable, however: a Syriac translation and redaction of the Islamic law of inheritance, extant in several recensions (plus one Arabic translation) and under several titles. The earliest manuscript witness is dated 1204; some recensions include attributions to ninth- or early tenth-century patriarchs, but these are almost certainly false, and the work's authorship and date of original composition remain unclear.[11] Its content, however, is not. On the whole it is Islamic inheritance law as elaborated in *fiqh* manuals and deriving ultimately from the Quran, with some of the Syriac recensions explicitly noting the source (e.g., by titling the text "calculation of inheritances according to the law of the Arabs [*nāmosā d-ṭayyāyē*]").[12] The multiple versions of this text demonstrate notably that Islamic law remained a significant resource on the occasions when West Syrian ecclesiastics sought to flesh out their communal legal tradition. This continued a trend visible in the sources of the ninth century, when West Syrian synodal legislation absorbed the Islamic contractual norms for marriage, requiring a guardian for the bride, two witnesses, and a marriage payment. While West Syrian bishops were distant enough intellectually from the centers of Islamic legal study that they did not cultivate confessional law especially assiduously, their tradition paradoxically came closely into line with Islamic law in these respects—in all likelihood, those basic procedural norms of the Muslim judiciary had become customary among Christians in northern Syria, and the bishops had no problem adopting them as ecclesiastical law since they had no doctrinal implications. The same pattern is evident in the West Syrians' incorporation of Islamic inheritance law into their canon of legal texts. Though we have no real evidence for the practical judicial use to which these tracts were put, it stands to reason that ecclesiastics would only adopt their norms (and actively identify their non-Christian provenance) if they were unobjectionable and familiar to some degree among contemporary Christians. It is thus probable that Islamic inheritance law had become more or less common practice for many West Syrian communities, whether they encountered it in Muslim courts, ecclesiastical ones, or both.

The West Syrian reception of Islamic inheritance law is further significant in that it shows West Syrian ecclesiastics continuing to gravitate toward Islamic models even after they had come into contact with and under the rule of other peoples, including Byzantine, Armenian, and Latin Christians. There are a mere two points in medieval West Syrian legal texts at which the recent influence of Byzantine or possibly Armenian family law and custom is apparent. One is the ritual of crowning the bride and groom at the wedding ceremony, mentioned in the canons of Yuhanon of Mardin of 1153 and described by Bar ʿEbroyo in the thirteenth century.[13] This ritual is attested in Constantinople, Anatolia, and Armenia in late antiquity,[14] but West Syrian canons from the eighth and ninth centuries that address betrothal make no mention of it; it appears in West Syrian texts only after the period of Byzantine expansion. A comparable case is a canon of the twelfth-century bishop Dionysios bar Salibi that decrees any marriage between first cousins null and void and prescribes the penance of adultery for transgressors.[15] West Syrian bishops had never prohibited cousin marriage before Dionysios, but Byzantine canon law had done so since the Council of Trullo in 692.[16] It is thus likely that the closer contacts between Byzantines and West Syrians occasioned by Byzantium's tenth-century Syrian and Anatolian conquests were behind the West Syrian adoption of the crowning ceremony and Dionysios's canon. Otherwise, however, there are no signs of the West Syrians overhauling their legal tradition even when new Christian resources were close at hand. As far as we know, West Syrian scribes never translated or even paid much attention to any texts from the rich tradition of post-Justinianic Byzantine law; instead, they copied the rules of Islamic inheritance in Syriac.

Overall, West Syrian family law after the ninth century indexes tellingly the hegemony of Islamic legal norms in dhimmi social life even in a frontier region like the western Jazira. West Syrian bishops never developed a communal law as robust as that of the East Syrians and more readily filled in its blanks with whatever materials were at hand. That usually meant Islamic law. West Syrian law, despite its goal of defining Christian social distinctiveness, propagated basic ideas of property rights and kinship that accorded with or simply reproduced Islamic models.

The later medieval history of East Syrian law is a strongly contrastive case. East Syrian bishops continued to cultivate confessional law as a learned discipline after the foundational activities of Ishoʿbokt, Timothy, and Ishoʿbarnun, as evidenced by their regular production of new Syriac legal treatises down to the fourteenth century. Inheritance became arguably the single most developed area of the East Syrian legal tradition, and it evolved mostly independently of Islamic law. Around the mid-ninth century ʿAbdishoʿ bar Bahriz composed a comprehensive treatise on inheritance law, possibly in multiple recensions,[17] that eschewed the varied and sometimes contradictory rulings found in his predecessors' law books for an entirely new system. A succession of jurist-bishops in the following centuries—Gabriel of Basra (d. 893), George of Arbela (fl. second half of the tenth century), Patriarch Elias I (r. 1028–49), and Elias bar Shennaya of Nisibis (d. 1056)—compiled their own treatments or collections of inheritance law; and they appear always to have used ʿAbdishoʿ's treatise and the earlier East Syrian law books, not Islamic law, as their source materials.[18] Unlike the West Syrian case, East Syrian inheritance law in the later medieval period developed through ecclesiastics analyzing, rearranging, and reinterpreting the norms of a corpus of Christian texts.

Islamic law might have influenced this tradition in a few small ways. Although we know the aforementioned Syriac tract of Islamic inheritance law mostly from West Syrian manuscripts, an Arabic translation of the text appears in one East Syrian manuscript and so must have circulated to some degree among East Syrian ecclesiastics.[19] It is also possible that ʿAbdishoʿ bar Bahriz based certain elements of his system of inheritance law on the Islamic example. ʿAbdishoʿ's treatise rejects the perspective of Ishoʿbokt, Timothy, and Ishoʿbarnun, examined in Chapter 4, that a daughter's dowry constitutes her only claim on her father's estate; instead, it makes her an heir alongside her father's male descendants, giving her half the share of a son (a ratio ʿAbdishoʿ applies to other classes of male and female heirs as well). ʿAbdishoʿ also guarantees a widow or widower a share in the deceased's estate. These norms parallel the Islamic law of inheritance, and may have been inspired by it, especially given that ʿAbdishoʿ's treatment departs from earlier East Syrian legal writings. But other than women's half shares and widows' rights, ʿAbdishoʿ's system is largely original,[20] and in any case the Church of the East's later jurist-bishops remained content to excerpt and comment upon East Syrian jurisprudential works more or less exclusively. East Syrian inheritance law is thus an example of a Christian legal tradition that was able to develop on the basis of its own received resources even as Islamic law became ever more predominant in the public life of the later medieval Middle East. This stands in contrast to West Syrian family law; West Syrian bishops had neither an extensive set of received norms nor a strongly developed tradition of dedicated jurisprudential study, and they readily turned to Islamic models to fill in lacunae in their confessional legal tradition.

ARABICIZING CHRISTIAN LAW

Inheritance law was not the only concern of jurist-bishops in the later medieval Middle East. The East Syrians, alongside Melkites, Copts, and some West Syrians, also took an interest in translating significant portions of the Christian legal heritage into Arabic, continuing a trend that had begun in the early centuries of the caliphate during Arabic's gradual rise to the status of a regional lingua franca. Importantly, Arabicization was not a neutral transfer of texts from one language to another; it frequently entailed the importation into Christian traditions of Islamic idioms, although not necessarily of Islamic legal norms.

Christian religious elites undertook the Arabicization of their legal traditions over the course of centuries and in centers of intellectual activity stretching from Iraq to Egypt. Melkite bishops had begun to translate into Arabic the chief Greek works of canon law in the early Abbasid period. They continued these efforts in later centuries with translations of the *Syro-Roman Law Book* and the Byzantine *Procheiros Nomos*.[21] These were received into the Coptic Church's legal tradition as well, and Copts produced a significant body of both Arabic translations of legal literature and original writings in the later medieval period.[22] Equally notable and somewhat earlier were the East Syrians' new Arabic translations of their substantial Syriac legal heritage. The principal works in this vein are Elias of Damascus's (fl. late ninth century) *al-Sunhawdus*, a translation of the collected canons of East Syrian synods, and Abu l-Faraj ʿAbdallah ibn al-Tayyib (d. 1043) of Baghdad's *Fiqh al-nasraniyya* (*The Jurisprudence of Christianity*).[23] The *Fiqh* is an extensive text; it includes translations of the full corpus of canonical East Syrian legal works as well as a systematic legal compendium modeled on Gabriel of Basra's. Also worth mentioning in this vein is the West Syrian Abu Nasr Yahya ibn Jarir (fl. eleventh century) of Tikrit's *Kitab al-Murshid*, an Arabic theological compendium with significant chapters on ecclesiastical order and lay marriage.[24] Combined with the Melkite materials, these East Syrian and West Syrian works constitute a substantial body of Arabic Christian law produced especially in centers of Arabic literary culture in the southern tier of the Fertile Crescent.

The main point of interest for our purposes is that translation into Arabic frequently entailed the reorganization of Christian law according to Islamic idioms and categories. Ibn al-Tayyib's writings offer some instructive examples. Active in eleventh-century Baghdad where he worked as a physician and a secretary to the East Syrian patriarch, Ibn al-Tayyib was well versed in a range of disciplines—philosophy, medicine, theology—that were by his time central to Arabic intellectual culture.[25] The very title of his Arabic compendium of East Syrian law, *Fiqh al-nasraniyya*, conveys the strong Islamic associations of that culture's idioms—it suggests that Christian law is not merely a diffuse array of canons and rulings but a *fiqh*, a scholarly tradition of jurisprudence like that of Islam. Islamic legal usages and the reformulation of Christian law they produce are on fullest display in another work of Ibn al-Tayyib's, a short treatise in which he gives his insider's view of the historical development of East Syrian law.

> Are the contracts of marriage, divorce, debts, and inheritance inscribed in the religion of Christianity [*dīn al-naṣrāniyya*] and stipulated in the Book of the Divine Law [*kitāb al-sharīʿa al-ilāhiyya*], meaning the pure Gospels, or are they delegated [*mufawwaḍa*] to the leaders and chiefs [*al-aʾimma wa-l-mudabbirīn*] by the holy power of God?
>
> . . . Until a bit before the time of Mar Timothy, the departed catholicos, the precepts [of Christian law, *al-farāʾiḍ*] did not pertain to worldly matters [*al-umūr al-ʿālamiyya*], but rather to the priesthood and its chiefs, because they had [the power of] *loosing and binding* [*al-ḥall wa-l-ʿaqd*, cf. Matthew 16:19]. Whatever they collectively accepted accorded with the root of Revelation [*aṣl al-sharʿ*] in the way of belief in the unity [of God], the Trinity, the resurrection, baptism, and the commandments of the Gospels [*al-awāmir al-injīliyya*]. . . . The departed Mar Timothy began to decide canons [*qawānīn*] concerning inheritance, debts, marriage, and things like these, having stated in the beginning of his writing, "I record with my hands these canons, bemoaning how I might establish a tradition [*asunn sunna*] for worldly matters when the Christian Law [*al-sharīʿa*

> *al-masīḥiyya*] does away with worldly commandments." This impelled him to invent a law [*ḥudūth sharīʿa*] that had these things [rules for worldly matters], for he feared that believers might follow a deviant path [*madhhab gharīb*]. After him came one who disputed with him [*khālafa ʿalayhi*] and established a tradition different from what he had [*sanna bi-khilāf mā sannahu*]. Had that [dispute] turned on a question of revelation [*bi-mūjib sharʿ*],[26] disagreement over it [*al-ikhtilāf fīhi*] would not have been permissible. But rather, it turned on a question of general welfare [*bi-mūjib maṣlaḥa*] arising from the Fathers' concern for the children of Christ [so disagreement was permissible].[27]

Ibn al-Tayyib's account is striking for the degree to which it mediates between Christian and Islamic notions of law while making use of Islamic legal concepts. On the one hand, Ibn al-Tayyib maintains a traditional Christian distinction between true Law and "worldly matters." In a narrative that should be quite familiar, he locates the beginnings of ecclesiastical concern for civil affairs in the time of Timothy, who notably had to "invent a law" (*ḥudūth sharīʿa*) rather than discern the rules embedded in God's revelation, which is what Muslim jurisprudents do. On the other hand, Ibn al-Tayyib's language is suffused with some of the basic terminology and categories of Islamic legal thought. Law arises from *uṣūl*, its roots, which include Christian doctrine but also the dictates of revealed scripture. Authoritative figures like Timothy and Ishoʿbarnun establish *sunna*, exemplary traditions of normative practice. *Ikhtilāf*, difference of opinion between jurist-bishops, is permissible over those prescriptive traditions not enjoined by the divine revelation itself.[28] In Ibn al-Tayyib's presentation, East Syrian bishops, by seeking to regulate social and marital practices in terms of Christian teaching, have rendered Christian law a true "Path"—a *sharīʿa*—in something approaching its Islamic sense.

These terminological usages exemplify well how Christian participation in Arabophone intellectual culture throughout the medieval period meant more than just linguistic change; doing jurisprudence in Arabic entailed constructing the law through Islamic categories and idioms. It did not, however, entail necessarily the adoption of Islamic legal norms into Christian family law. Even as Ibn al-Tayyib's writings suggest a close familiarity with Islamic legal thought, his treatment of marriage, divorce, and inheritance indicates how robust was his received tradition of confessional law. The *Fiqh al-nasraniyya* consists almost entirely of material drawn from the East Syrian law books, older works of canon law, and discussions thereof. There is one exceptional case in which Ibn al-Tayyib appears to have adopted a norm of Islamic provenance. In discussing the role of male guardians in contracting betrothals for their female charges, he states, "As long as the father lives, he has the authority to contract [his daughter's] betrothal [*mā dāma al-ab yaḥyā fal-ʿaqd lahu*]. If he dies, [that authority] belongs to [her] brothers after asking the permission of their sister [*baʿda stiʾdhān ukhtihim*]; if the brothers die, [her] paternal uncles [possess it]."[29] Here, Ibn al-Tayyib indicates that fathers have a special power of guardianship over their daughters; by stating explicitly that a woman's brothers must seek her permission to enact a betrothal contract with a prospective husband, he implies that her father operates under no such constraints and may marry her to whom he wishes. This position accords notably with the majority Islamic legal opinion, which maintains that a father can compel his virgin daughter to marry without her consent and regardless of her wishes (the Hanafis and some Shiites adding the caveat that he may not do so once she has reached legal majority). If any other agnate acts as a guardian, however, the bride's consent is required.[30] By contrast, the East Syrian law books of the early Abbasid period offer differing opinions on this issue, with at least Timothy stressing that the bride's consent to a marriage was essential.[31]

In this case, then, an Islamic norm looks to have entered East Syrian family law as an alternative to the inconsistent opinions of earlier Christian authorities. It is only one ruling, however, amid a considerable body of family law. The Arabicization of the East Syrians' jurisprudential tradition thus entailed significant reformulations of the nature of confessional law according to Islamic models; but its positive content remained largely distinct from Muslim *fiqh* even as the medieval Middle East and its intellectual culture became more and more Islamic.

ISLAM AND CHRISTIAN FAMILY LAW AT THE TWILIGHT OF THE "SYRIAC RENAISSANCE"

In the centuries following the breakup of the Abbasid Caliphate, the legal traditions of the Syriac churches absorbed a variety of influences from Islamic thought that affected either their content or structure. This development reached an apex with the works of two jurist-bishops in the thirteenth and early fourteenth centuries: the West Syrian Bar ʿEbroyo (often Latinized as Barhebraeus) and the East Syrian

ʿAbdishoʿ bar Brika. The two make for a meaningful end point to our narrative. Both composed extensive, comprehensive, summary works of Christian confessional law in Syriac that their respective churches soon acclaimed as singularly authoritative.[32] They happened to do so, moreover, not long before the major disruptions of the mid-1300s. Strikingly, we know of no major jurisprudential works by other Syriac bishops in the centuries after Bar ʿEbroyo and ʿAbdishoʿ.

Just as significantly, their works cap the respective trajectories of West Syrian and East Syrian family law as they intersected with Islamic law. If the West Syrian tradition readily absorbed a variety of Islamic norms at various stages of its historical development, Bar ʿEbroyo pushed this tendency to an even more systematic end. In his effort to present a comprehensive statement of confessional law, his *Nomocanon* (*Ktābā d-Huddāyē*) borrowed from and extensively mirrored the family law of the Shafiʿi *madhhab*. ʿAbdishoʿ, on the other hand, was able to draw on the more extensive resources of the East Syrian tradition for his two systematic treatises, the *Collection of Synodal Canons* (*Kunnāshā d-qānonē sunhādiqāyē*) and the *Order of Ecclesiastical Decisions* (*Ṭukkās dinē ʿēdtānāyē*). He thus largely eschewed direct appropriation from the now hegemonic and highly developed traditions of Islamic family law. Islamic norms and categories, however, remained touchstones against which ʿAbdishoʿ defined his Christian tradition.

Islamic Family Law in Bar ʿEbroyo's Nomocanon

Bar ʿEbroyo is a towering figure in Syriac Christianity and more prominent than most Syriac Christians in the historiography of the premodern Middle East. His renown rests principally on the sheer breadth of his writings, which ranged into almost every discipline of his contemporary intellectual culture, and on his engagement with Islamic texts and traditions. Born in Malatya in the northwest Jazira, Gregorios Bar ʿEbroyo (known in Arabic as Abu l-Faraj Ibn al-ʿIbri) spent his life traversing the thirteenth-century Middle East's shifting political boundaries among the Seljuqs of Rum, Crusaders, Ayyubids, and finally the Mongols. From 1264 until his death in 1286 he served as the chief bishop of the West Syrians' eastern dioceses.[33] Two features distinguished his exceptional intellectual career.[34] One was an encyclopedic interest in bringing all the sciences of his intellectual world into

Syriac literature in a comprehensive and systematic fashion. So, for example, his *Cream of Wisdom* is a compendium of Aristotelian philosophy; his chronicles are universal ones covering both political and ecclesiastical history. The second notable feature of Bar ʿEbroyo's body of work is the degree to which it drew both inspiration and substantive content from major Arabic and Persian Islamic texts. The *Cream of Wisdom*, for example, is based on the writings of Ibn Sina and Nasir al-Din al-Tusi.[35] More striking is Bar ʿEbroyo's reliance on material much more categorically Islamic than *falsafa*, perhaps most famously Abu Hamid al-Ghazali's *Ihyaʾ ʿulum al-din*, on which Bar ʿEbroyo modeled his *Ethicon*.[36]

Bar ʿEbroyo's compendium of confessional law, commonly called the *Nomocanon*, is marked by the same two features. The *Nomocanon* aims for encyclopedic comprehensiveness by presenting the sum total of all "ecclesiastical canons and worldly rulings" (*qānonē ʿēdtānāyē w-dinē ʿālmānāyē*); in this it is far and away the West Syrian tradition's most extensive legal work.[37] In its sections on civil law, for which the West Syrians could not boast of a wide range of authoritative texts and source materials, Bar ʿEbroyo drew heavily from the legal handbooks of al-Ghazali, written in the tradition of the Shafiʿi school of Islamic law.[38] This dependence is evident throughout the *Nomocanon*'s eighth chapter, "On Betrothal" (*meṭṭol mkirutā*), which despite its narrow title contains all of the work's marriage and divorce law. The chapter illustrates well Bar ʿEbroyo's method in combining Ghazalian and received Christian materials in order to elaborate a comprehensive West Syrian family law. More importantly, several of Bar ʿEbroyo's specific doctrines demonstrate how his compositional practice entailed not only the incorporation of Islamic norms into a Christian tradition but also the refracting of its theology of marriage through Islamic conceptions of sexuality and gender relations.

The simplest way to get a sense of how deeply Bar ʿEbroyo's *Nomocanon* is informed by Islamic law is to compare a few brief passages with corresponding ones from al-Ghazali's *al-Wasit*, the treatise that Bar ʿEbroyo appears mostly to have been working off of.[39] Take, for example, this simple statement concerning the household implements that a husband must provide to his wife upon marriage.

Al-Ghazali

He owes her household implements [*māʿūn al-dār*] . . . of clay, wood, or stone [*khazaf*, *khashab*, or *ḥajar*]. As for bronze [*nuḥāsiyya*], asking for it is a luxury; but it may be appropriate for a noblewoman [*sharīfa*].

Bar ʿEbroyo

He owes her a house with household vessels [*krāpātā*] of clay, wood, or stone [*paḥḥārā*, *qaysā*, or *kēpā*]; and if she is a noblewoman [*mṭahhamtā*], of bronze [*nḥāshā*].

No jurist-bishop prior to Bar ʿEbroyo had bothered to legislate details such as these; he has quite obviously translated them directly from al-Ghazali's work.[40] A more illuminating example of Bar ʿEbroyo's redactional method is the following doctrine, according to which a man should see his prospective bride's face before contracting the marriage.

Al-Ghazali

Concerning [the man] seeing [the prospective bride] after expressing the desire to marry her, this is preferable [*mustaḥabb*], the proof being [the Prophet's] statement, "Whoever wishes to marry a woman, let him look at her, for that facilitates affection between them." He must restrict himself to looking at her face, and [only] after having decided upon marriage as long as he approves of her. Asking for her consent to this viewing is not a necessary condition [*lā yushtaraṭ*]; rather, the permission of the Messenger of God suffices.

Bar ʿEbroyo

If the groom sees his bride before the betrothal, this is very good [*ṭāb paqḥā*], because of the severity of the separation should she not [turn out to] be in accordance with his desire. The canons allow seeing her face only, even if without her consent [*w-āpen d-lā b-ṣebyānāh*]. Without this reason, it is never appropriate to look at an unrelated woman . . . lest one fall into mental adultery. *Everyone who sees a woman such that he desires her, has already committed adultery with her in his heart* (Matthew 5:28).

Again, Bar ʿEbroyo's close textual reliance on al-Ghazali is evident in his reproduction of a cluster of specific doctrines: it is preferable that the groom see the bride, "preferable" being a technical Islamic legal category between "required" and "prohibited"; he may see no more than her face; her consent to the viewing is not required.[41] However, Bar ʿEbroyo has shorn these doctrines of the authoritative textual source—a prophetic Hadith—from which they derive in al-Ghazali's Islamic context. Instead, he attributes them vaguely to "the canons" and dresses them up with a teaching from the Gospels.

These examples are representative of Bar ʿEbroyo's method throughout the *Nomocanon*'s treatment of marriage: over and over again, he takes legal opinions, clusters of doctrines, and entire sections from al-Ghazali and translates or paraphrases them into Syriac. He makes no mention of their provenance; by adding references to a variety of biblical and other Christian texts, he effectively naturalizes them as part of his Christian legal tradition. If the *Nomocanon*'s chapter on Christian marriage law is deeply indebted to Shafiʿi jurisprudence as expounded in the writings of al-Ghazali, however, it is not simply a Syriac translation of Islamic family law. For one thing, Bar ʿEbroyo draws on a range of Christian sources, such as the Bible, West Syrian synodal legislation, the *Syro-Roman Law Book*, and East Syrian legal compendia, in addition to al-Ghazali.[42] For another, the *Nomocanon* is rooted in Christian teachings in the most potentially contentious areas. It does not allow polygamy; it allows divorce only in limited circumstances, and that section of the *Nomocanon*'s treatment of marriage is the least dependent on al-Ghazali.[43] This should give us pause over how we interpret the significance of the Islamic provenance of much of the *Nomocanon*'s law. In view of most key doctrines, it remains characteristically Christian. Furthermore, many a Christian thinker would hold that the material composition of the salad fork a husband brings home to his wife has no bearing on faith. If Bar ʿEbroyo reproduced a host of similarly mundane norms and framed them in terms of Christian authorities, he effectively rendered them Christian; their provenance is inconsequential.

Despite the casuistic specificity of most of the norms that Bar ʿEbroyo adopts from al-Ghazali, however, they add up in several ways to a significant reordering of Christian law and Christian marriage according to distinctly Islamic categories. This is especially evident in Bar ʿEbroyo's treatments of the guardianship of brides and the obligations attendant to the marriage contract. Each produces conceptions of gender hierarchy and the nature of the marriage bond itself that diverge from Christian tradition and align notably with Islamic thought. Regarding guardianship, the *Nomocanon* reproduces closely a set of key elements of Shafiʿi *fiqh*, similar to what we encountered earlier in Ibn al-Tayyib: a woman must have a male guardian to marry her off; her father has the primary claim to guardianship, followed by other male agnates; a father acting as guardian may compel his virgin daughter (Syriac *btultā*/Arabic *bikr*) to marry whomever he chooses regardless of her wishes, though the consent of a daughter who has been married previously (*mzawwagtā*/*thayyib*) is required.[44] By adopting these Shafiʿi perspectives on the father's powers of compulsion and the role of male agnates as guardians, Bar ʿEbroyo formalizes in West Syrian tradition the particular hierarchies of social power, stratified by gender and age, that they underwrite. Furthermore, those Shafiʿi opinions contradict earlier West Syrian sources. That a bride's consent is always necessary to make a marriage valid is emphasized frequently in West Syrian synodal legislation, which recognizes none of the powers of compulsion that the *Nomocanon* allows to fathers over their virgin daughters.[45] For example, one late ninth-century canon specifies that "no father, mother, brother, sister, person from among the householders, or boy or girl has the authority [*shulṭānā*] to betroth a boy or make a betrothal agreement for [*namkar*] a girl before they reach the age of fifteen, and then [only] with the consent [*shalmutā*] of the boy and the girl."[46] Not only does this canon recognize the necessity of a girl's (or any minor's) consent to a marriage; it also imagines an assortment of relatives, women as well as men, who might be involved in arranging marriages for their younger householders wider than the group of strictly agnatic males of al-Ghazali and the *Nomocanon*.

Thus, strands of Bar ʿEbroyo's own West Syrian legal tradition suggested conceptions of social hierarchy and male power different from those of Shafiʿi Islamic law. Yet when Bar ʿEbroyo sought to compile a systematic treatise of West Syrian marriage law, he privileged the intellectual resources offered by al-Ghazali and thus introduced those Islamic norms into his own tradition. An even more striking departure from Christian precedents results from Bar ʿEbroyo's reliance on al-Ghazali in his description of the purposes of marriage and sex. While Islamic traditions encompass many views on this subject, the common legal viewpoint posits marriage as a contractual relationship that brings into effect particular rights and duties for each party. Chief among the wife's duties, and the husband's rights, is that she be sexually available exclusively to him and at any time he may wish (with a few exceptions, such as when she is ill or menstruating). Many medieval jurists conceived the husband's furnishing of a marriage gift and maintenance as compensation for sexual access to his wife's body.[47] Provisions deriving from this conception of the marriage bond figure prominently in the *Nomocanon*. At one point, Bar ʿEbroyo reproduces a Ghazalian assertion that if a wife refuses her husband sex (*tetklē*/*imtināʿ al-istimtāʿ*), he does not have to provide maintenance.[48] Elsewhere, Bar ʿEbroyo gives the converse: if a husband does not deliver his wife's marriage gifts she does not owe him sexual availability (*shalliṭā d-teklē napshāh men shawtāputēh*). Otherwise, she may not restrict her husband's access to her body without one of the recognized reasons. Those reasons include preparing to receive communion as well as the couple's collective observation of days dedicated to prayer and fasting (with reference to 1 Corinthians 7:5), eminently Christian concerns, as well as others like pregnancy drawn from al-Ghazali. If a woman refuses her husband sex outside of those circumstances, however, Bar ʿEbroyo goes so far as to say that "she may be forced [into sex]" (*ba-qṭirā tetdbar*, although it is possible to interpret this phrase more vaguely as "she may be disciplined forcefully").[49]

Modern reactions to marital rape aside, these passages are notable for implying a sharply different conception of sexuality and the purposes of the marriage bond than Bar ʿEbroyo's received Christian tradition. That tradition put a primary value on virginity and continence and depicted lay marriage chiefly as a means to facilitate the reproduction of the species in an orderly manner.[50] While Middle Eastern Christians in Bar ʿEbroyo's day were doubtless fully familiar with the notion that marriage was also a contractual exchange entailing reciprocal obligations for the man and woman who were party to it, earlier West Syrian tradition exhibited no notion that that contract gave a husband such expansive rights to enjoy his and his wife's sexuality. Rather, the texts of Bar ʿEbroyo's received tradition maintained a more conservative conception of human sexuality as primarily geared to and appropriate for procreation. Marriage as contract providing a husband with the right to sex and to his wife's body was a characteristically Islamic legal conception; however familiar it already may have been to contemporary laypeople in practice, the fact that Bar ʿEbroyo actively inscribed it into a Christian legal tradition is striking.

The rights and duties pertaining to the marriage contract and the powers of male guardianship represent the most prominent ways in which Bar ʿEbroyo's reliance on al-Ghazali brought West Syrian marriage law—and its organizing principles of social power, family, and sexuality—closely in line with Islamic traditions. We know so little of social life in Bar ʿEbroyo's milieu and the following centuries that it is impossible to say whether his innovations had any effect on practice once the *Nomocanon* was recognized as the West Syrians' authoritative legal guide. As we have seen, the West Syrians had long been open to adopting Islamic norms into their tradition, including the betrothal contract in the ninth-century synodal legislation and then inheritance law, likely because those norms had become common practice among Christians living under Muslim rule. It is similarly possible that the Islamicized conceptions of social hierarchy and the marriage bond that Bar ʿEbroyo adopted from al-Ghazali had already been part of a more or less shared social framework among Middle Eastern communities, Muslim, Christian, or other, for a considerable time. But the novelty of their expression in a Christian law remains notable. In effect, even as Bar ʿEbroyo elaborated a comprehensive, definitively Christian tradition of communal and family law, he brought to an apex its long-term trajectory toward alignment with the norms of its Islamic milieu.

ʿAbdishoʿ bar Brika and the Autonomous Trajectory of East Syrian Law

By contrast, ʿAbdishoʿ bar Brika's two summary works of East Syrian law exhibit little engagement with Islamic marriage law, other than as an opposing standard against which to define Christian norms. This was largely a function of the much more established, substantial character that the East Syrian legal tradition had developed by the thirteenth century. Indeed, where Bar ʿEbroyo was the first West Syrian bishop to compose a comprehensive treatment of confessional law, several of ʿAbdishoʿ's East Syrian predecessors of earlier centuries had already done so. Gabriel of Basra in the ninth century, for example, had fashioned the first systematic East Syrian legal compendium by compiling and arranging excerpts of pseudo-apostolic works, East Syrian synodal canons, and rulings from bishops' law books. Gabriel's compendium encompassed ecclesiastical as well as civil affairs and drew from Ishoʿbokt and the *Syro-Roman Law Book* to cover civil areas beyond marriage and inheritance.[51] In the eleventh century, Ibn al-Tayyib included a paraphrased Arabic translation of Gabriel's work as the second part of his *Fiqh al-nasraniyya*.[52] The extensive tradition of East Syrian confessional law—embodied in these comprehensive collections as well as the varied corpus of legal texts on which they were based—was available to ʿAbdishoʿ when he began to compose his own systematic jurisprudential treatises, and contrasts with the much narrower range of West Syrian legal sources available to Bar ʿEbroyo.

ʿAbdishoʿ was active in the late thirteenth-century Jazira, where he served as the metropolitan bishop of Nisibis and Armenia until his death in 1318, a decade and a half before the final fragmentation of the Mongol Ilkhanate.[53] Because of his prolific output in a variety of theological and literary disciplines and the fact that he was a younger contemporary of Bar ʿEbroyo, he is commonly portrayed as Bar ʿEbroyo's East Syrian counterpart.[54] In the area of law, at least, the comparison is apt. Already in his own lifetime, ʿAbdishoʿ's Syriac legal compendia were acknowledged by the East Syrian hierarchy as the authoritative textual repositories of the community's law, much as Bar ʿEbroyo's *Nomocanon* was for the West Syrians. The two part ways, however, in that the marriage law sections of ʿAbdishoʿ's *Collection of Synodal Canons* and *Order of Ecclesiastical Decisions* are based almost wholly on the received Christian materials found in earlier compendia.[55] Much of the *Collection*, which appears to have been the more popular of ʿAbdishoʿ's legal works in view of its many more extant manuscript copies, is a reworking of Gabriel of Basra's compendium, although ʿAbdishoʿ tends to leave this and other sources unnamed.[56] The *Order* consists of large numbers of passages taken directly from earlier East Syrian legal works with attributions to the original sources. It also includes unattributed reworkings of sections of *al-Majmuʿ al-safawi*, a systematic legal compendium composed in Arabic by the Copt Abu l-Fadaʾil al-Safi Ibn al-ʿAssal (fl. mid-thirteenth century).[57]

The thoroughly Christian source material of the two works means that Islamic norms are almost nowhere in evidence in their respective tracts on marriage law, in marked contrast to Bar ʿEbroyo's *Nomocanon*.[58] Minor, partial exceptions prove the rule. In the *Order of Ecclesiastical Decisions*' discussion of guardianship, ʿAbdishoʿ lists the relatives eligible to serve as a bride's guardian in the order of their right to do so: father, grandfather, brother, paternal uncle, paternal uncle's son, maternal grandfather, maternal uncle, maternal uncle's son, and priest.[59] The list is unattributed and is not found in any other East Syrian source. The fact that it includes only male relatives is suggestive of Islamic law; in fact, it is almost identical to Bar ʿEbroyo's al-Ghazali-derived list in the *Nomocanon*, which in this instance looks to be ʿAbdishoʿ's source.[60] In this lone case, a norm of Islamic provenance has crept into ʿAbdishoʿ's *Order of Ecclesiastical Decisions*. Whatever minor significance that might have, however, is undercut by the fact that ʿAbdishoʿ gives a different, non-Islamic list of guardians (father, brother, paternal uncle, mother) in the *Collection of Synodal Canons*.[61]

For its part, the *Collection* includes two rulings that suggest Islamic influence. One is that a woman's silence indicates her consent to an offer of betrothal, which resembles the standard Islamic doctrine (applicable only to virgins; in Islamic law, previously married women's consent must be vocal).[62] In the second case, ʿAbdishoʿ appears to give fathers special powers of compulsion over their marriageable daughters, much like Ibn al-Tayyib's ruling discussed above. "As long as the father is alive, authority [to conclude a marriage for his daughter] is his [*dilēh [h]u shulṭānā*]"; for other prospective guardians, ʿAbdishoʿ's text specifies that they must "receive authority" to do so (*nessbun shulṭānā*) from the woman herself.[63] Notably, however, ʿAbdishoʿ actually rejects an Islamic-style interpretation of this norm. Immediately prior to the passage in question, the *Collection* specifies that "[a bride] may not be given to a man by her parents or by others without her will and consent [*belʿād ṣebyānāh w-puqdānāh*], contrary to that opinion of the outsiders [*tarʿitā hāy d-barrāyē*]."[64] ʿAbdishoʿ thus interprets the condition that a guardian must seek a female charge's consent to marriage as universally applicable, including to paternal guardians. He is well aware, furthermore, that this contradicts the standard Islamic doctrine, as evidenced by his rejection of the opinion of the "outsiders"—that is, Muslim jurists. Here, ʿAbdishoʿ appears at first to reproduce one of the few norms of Islamic marriage law that previous generations of East Syrian jurist-bishops had adopted; in fact, he reinterprets it with the specific purpose of distinguishing Christian from Islamic law.

Overall, ʿAbdishoʿ stands in contrast to Bar ʿEbroyo as an authoritative systematizer of his communal legal tradition, at least insofar as their activities related to Islamic family law. The compositional method of Bar ʿEbroyo's *Nomocanon* entailed the appropriation, redaction, and rearrangement of a considerable body of Islamic legal doctrines and institutions into West Syrian law. ʿAbdishoʿ, on the other hand, relied mainly on the textual resources of his own East Syrian tradition in composing the marriage law sections of both his *Collection* and *Order*. Islamic norms still hovered on the margins of ʿAbdishoʿ's intellectual world, evident in their intrusion into his discussions of gendered household hierarchies. But unlike Bar ʿEbroyo, ʿAbdishoʿ grappled with Islamic law mostly as a counterpoint against which to define his Christian tradition.

If demographic balances were beginning to shift and Arabo-Islamic intellectual culture was becoming increasingly predominant in tenth- and eleventh-century Syria, Iraq, and the Jazira, Christian (and other non-Muslim) traditions can provide a gauge of those transformations vital to the historiography of the region as a whole. The interactions between Islamic family law and Syriac and Arabic Christian legal traditions from the tenth century to the early fourteenth are exemplary in this respect. In northern Syria and the western Jazira, West Syrian bishops' interest in Islamic inheritance law highlights the continued influence of Islamic judicial practice and legal models among non-Muslim populations, even after a period of Byzantine conquest and partial Christian resurgence. In lowland urban centers including Damascus and Baghdad, East Syrian bishops translated the Church of the East's legal heritage into Arabic for the first time. Doing so entailed theorizing East Syrian law partially in terms of Islamic legal concepts. The positive content of East Syrian family law, however, remained largely distinct from Islamic norms, a characteristic evident as well in the new Syriac treatises on inheritance composed by East Syrian bishops in the same period.

In the thirteenth and early fourteenth centuries, the works of Bar ʿEbroyo and ʿAbdishoʿ capped the longer-term trajectories of West Syrian and East Syrian family law, respectively, as they took shape in relation to Islamic traditions and institutions. Since the early Abbasid period, East Syrian bishops had been actively engaged in producing legal texts and developing a communal legal tradition. When ʿAbdishoʿ sought to issue a comprehensive statement of communal family law, the East Syrian heritage could provide much of the material he needed.[65] For Bar ʿEbroyo, the situation was different. West Syrian canonical legislation was not sufficient for the kind of comprehensiveness that Bar ʿEbroyo typically sought in his writings, so he turned to the textual resources of Islamic law as an alternative. Significantly, Islamic law was not the only or most obvious resource available. Bar ʿEbroyo might easily have adapted more, for example, from East Syrian sources or the *Syro-Roman Law Book*. From this perspective, the accommodation of West Syrian family law to Islamic models had quite a lot to do with the singular figure of Bar ʿEbroyo; it is largely because a learned individual so open to drawing on the resources of other religions composed the *Nomocanon* that West Syrian law came to incorporate so many norms of Islamic provenance. On the other hand, the fact that Bar ʿEbroyo's *Nomocanon* was acclaimed as authoritative was possible only insofar as those norms were intelligible and acceptable to his Christian audience and its dominant conceptions of the workings of social life. In this connection, Bar ʿEbroyo offers an intensive and extensive example of a pattern we have seen before: West Syrian bishops tacitly adopted Islamic procedures and norms, such as the betrothal contract and the division of inheritances, that had presumably become common practice among the Christians of northern Syria and the Jazira.

East Syrian and West Syrian conceptions of law, the religious community, and the family were thus transformed markedly by their encounter with Islamic traditions and institutions over the course of the medieval period, but in different ways. In the early Abbasid period the East Syrian hierarchy found itself in the caliphate's heartlands and responded more readily to its institutional and intellectual developments. It was largely in reaction to caliphal judicial reform and the emergence of Islamic law that East Syrian bishops began the ongoing process of developing a specifically Christian family law, with the broader goal of promoting their vision of communal integrity in lands under Muslim rule. Islamic institutions and intellectual trends thus constituted the context for the early formation of a robust East Syrian civil law. While translation into Arabic entailed rethinking Christian law according to Islamic categories, the robustness of the early tradition meant that the substantive content of that law developed largely independently of Islamic norms. The West Syrians' distance from developments in the urban centers of early Abbasid Iraq, by contrast, meant that they were not compelled to develop an expansive civil and family law to the extent that the East Syrians did. Paradoxically, their lesser concern with law as a discipline of ecclesiastical study made them more open to the ad hoc adoption of Islamic norms that had effectively become customary, regional practice. If West Syrian bishops did not respond as actively to the imperatives of caliphal rule in the early period, the later result was a heavy reliance on Islamic intellectual resources for the very law that defined their community as Christian in an ever more Islamic Middle East.

CONCLUSION

Christians and Christian Law in the Making of the Medieval Islamic Empire

This book began from the premise that a historiography of the medieval Middle East focused solely on the formation of Islamic society, institutions, and traditions leaves a significant swath of the region's history obscure. From the mid-seventh century to the end of the ninth, the Islamic caliphate was an empire par excellence: a hierarchical polity ruling an enormous territory of great religious and cultural diversity, in which the Muslim ruling elite can have been only a sliver of the population. In the following years, political fragmentation was accompanied by the rising prominence of Arabo-Islamic intellectual culture and increasing Muslim numbers; yet non-Muslims remained integral to the region's landscape, from the Christian villages and monasteries of Egypt and the Fertile Crescent to the Zoroastrian mountaineers of Iran. While the historiography of many a world empire focuses precisely on the encounters between a ruling elite and its subjects, that of the medieval Middle East tends to leave non-Muslims entirely aside; once Muslims settle outside of Arabia, nascent Islamic society has arrived, and Muslims' activities define its unfolding and deserve the historiographical spotlight. Without diminishing the importance of those developments, this book has argued that we might arrive at a clearer image of the caliphate as a heterogeneous imperial society by shifting that spotlight to the empire's points of encounter with its extensive non-Muslim subject populations. The transformations to non-Muslim communities, institutions, and traditions engendered by those encounters are just as much the story of the formation of the medieval Middle East as is conversion to Islam or the emergence of Sufism, and deserve the same historiographical attention.

In this connection, the interactions between the Christian communities living in the early medieval caliphate's Fertile Crescent heartland and the institutions of caliphal governance and Islamic law prove exemplary. The establishment of the caliphate simultaneously undermined the judicial institutions of the Roman and Sasanian empires it replaced and allowed wide latitude to subject religious elites—bishops, rabbis, Zoroastrian priests—to claim expanded judicial prerogatives over their communities. Beginning in the seventh century and peaking in the ninth and tenth, West Syrian and especially East Syrian Christian bishops steadily expanded their communal legal traditions to cover civil affairs, an area into which ecclesiastical law had not previously ventured. Above all else, the bishops focused on the household and the practices by which it is formed and reproduced: the obligations between husband, wife, and other family members established by the legal relationship of marriage, and the paths by which property is transferred both intergenerationally and between related lineages. While Christian tradition had long put great emphasis on household piety and chaste sexuality, the bishops' claim to direct the material and social shape of Christian household relations was new. Their law effectively asserted that, in addition to ritual and festival participation, the connection between ecclesiastical justice and the household defined West Syrian and East Syrian Christians as subject socioreligious groups within the caliphate. Ultimately, the twin reformulations of Syriac Christian confessional law and the Christian household were the trickle-down effects of the establishment of Islamic imperial rule; caliphal governance and Islamic law motivated these transformations of subject communities' traditions and institutions. They thus represent the new formations of caliphal society as shaped and experienced by the numerous subjects who remained outside the ruling religion. By the very fact that those subjects were transformed by the Islamic empire, they must be integral to its social and intellectual history.

The particular forms of community that Syriac Christian family law articulated, however, could not be realized in practice so simply. The bishops' law revolved around several key prescriptions for laypeople, many of which specifically demarcated Christian marital practices from those of Muslims, Jews, and others. These prescriptions included participating in a priestly ritual that constituted the marriage bond as a legal relationship; prohibitions of divorce, polygamy, concubinage, and a variety of forms of close-kin marriage; heavy restrictions on marriage to non-Christians; and recognition of the general authority of ecclesiastics to oversee the division of inheritances. However, there were avenues of participation in Islamic institutions open to laypeople as well, and these created structural tensions in the bishops' vision of a confessional community constituted through the laity's exclusive patronage of ecclesiastical ones. Laypeople might have marriage contracts drawn up in Muslim courts; lay elites might seek favors from the caliph to circumvent ecclesiastical regulation of their households; men and women hemmed in by the strictures of Christian monogamy might seek divorces or, in some circumstances, apostatize before Muslim judges. These factors point again to the significant role of the Islamic empire and its institutions in shaping the new modes of association its subject non-Muslims fashioned for themselves. West Syrian and East Syrian Christians were not fully formed, autonomous religious communities that simply carried on from late antiquity to Muslim rule; they were reconfigured through laypeople's negotiation of the new claims that confessional law placed on the practices of family life with the often contradictory opportunities to organize the household offered by Islamic law and institutions.

The stark differences between Christian and Islamic law, combined with the greater institutional strength of the latter, created structural pressures that could always threaten to drain Christian numbers. Put simply, if the bishops strictly enforced the principles of Christian monogamy—no divorce, no polygamy—conversion to Islam became an option for laypeople in untenable conjugal situations or who simply wanted to arrange their household relations differently. Similarly, the fact that the legal order of the caliphate allowed non-Muslim women to marry Muslim men, but not Muslim women to marry Christians or Jews, gave Muslim communities a reproductive advantage as time and generations went by. We lack the data to measure whether and when these structural pressures actually had significant demographic effects, however, and they raise a converse question as well. Might the ecclesiastical claims to greater involvement in lay households have served to buttress Christian communal integrity? Although Muslim rule undoubtedly posed challenges, did it simultaneously facilitate the consolidation and strengthening of subject communal institutions?[1]

The answer is probably a qualified "yes," insofar as caliphal governance allowed for the expanded scope of ecclesiastical justice and the propagation, at least, of new notions of the Christian household. In this respect, our examination illustrates a particular mode of premodern empire-subject relations: subject communities and elites who, in conditions of relatively little physical coercion, accommodate to and partially internalize an imperial program without fully adopting the high culture—here, Islam—that would allow them entrance into the ruling stratum. This characterization of non-Muslims under Muslim rule is implicit in much scholarship on the subject, but it deserves to be highlighted, as it draws our attention to some distinctive features of medieval Islamic polities. In any imperial setting, a range of responses—varying forms of collaboration, accommodation, and opposition—are imaginable on the part of subject populations. As one indispensable study has emphasized, however, the early caliphate is distinctive in the history of empires in that it not only sought collaboration but made full membership in the community of the conquerors ostensibly no more difficult than conversion to Islam: "rarely have imperial powers set the bar to membership of their own favoured ranks so low."[2] From this perspective, it is even more striking that the Christian (and Jewish) populations of the Fertile Crescent and Egypt remained as integral to the caliphate's social, cultural, and religious landscape as they did, and for as long as they did; and it is perhaps a testament to the robustness of their communal institutions and to their effectiveness in reorganizing those institutions in their accommodation to Muslim rule.

A comparison to the experience of the Islamic empire in Iran, which appears to have Islamized earlier and more thoroughly than territories to the west, is useful here. If many Iranian elites collaborated with the Islamic empire, other rural highlanders frequently opposed Umayyad efforts to incorporate their territories into the caliphate. But crucially, they did so by "opting into" the imperial religious culture and participating in, or styling themselves as, Muslim opposition movements against Umayyad and then Abbasid perfidy. A significant result of this interaction with the Islamic empire—conversion and opposition from within—was the incorporation of various Khurrami or highland Iranian religious concepts into the Islamic tradition.[3] Unlike Khurrami mountaineers, the Christians of Syria, the Jazira, and Iraq were largely settled agriculturalists and townspeople with little in the way of martial traditions or attachment to local political autonomy (the landed aristocrats of the eastern Jaziran hill country are the exception that proves the rule).[4] Accommodation rather than opposition was a suitable response to the Islamic empire for them; but rather than shooting for full participation through conversion, a significant number of their elites kept to their ancestral religions and managed, in the context of laissez-faire caliphal rule, to actually consolidate certain of their confessional institutions and traditions. Iran is again an interesting contrast: the distinctive marital institutions, especially polyandry, of the Iranian east died out as those regions were incorporated into the caliphate and their populations converted to Islam more thoroughly.[5] Many Christians of the caliphate's Fertile Crescent heartland, by contrast, adapted to the Islamic empire through submission but not conversion, and this facilitated a certain consolidation of the distinctive forms of Christian marriage as defined by Syriac confessional law. For all the structural incentives to conversion and the often-capricious violence non-Muslims might face, this proved to be a fairly durable mode of interaction with Islamic polities.

While early Islam took shape amid and drew many of its characteristic elements from the established, intermingled monotheisms of late antiquity, Christian strategies of accommodation to Muslim rule in the medieval period demonstrate that Islamic traditions and institutions soon greatly influenced Christian ones. This dynamic becomes ever more conspicuous the later we move chronologically; East Syrian bishops adopted the idioms of Islamic law in their Arabic writings and West Syrians appropriated much of the very substance of Islamic family law, a trend best exemplified by Bar ʿEbroyo. By contrast, Christian legal traditions appear to have had little direct influence on those of Islam in our period. They remain, however, crucially important in historiographical terms in enriching and broadening our conceptions of Islamic society and intellectual culture. East Syrian family law rearranged and consolidated pre-Islamic Mesopotamian and Iranian practices, which reminds us that the Middle East's ancient heritage endured even as Islamic law came to structure much of the region's legal culture. Our examination of Christian disputes over the authority of reason and tradition in confessional lawmaking recast the standard narrative of the formation of Islamic law as a region-wide, cross-religious development.

Incorporating these non-Muslim perspectives and materials into our narratives brings into historiographical focus the diversity—religious, linguistic, ethnic, and otherwise—that fundamentally characterized the societies of the medieval Islamic world. The narrowed, exclusivist horizons of modern political communities have erased much of that heterogeneity over the last two hundred years; the indigenous Christians of the Middle East, heirs to the traditions studied in this book, have suffered the consequences only too acutely. To al-Jahiz, however, an Iraq nearly free of Christians—not to mention of Jews, Zoroastrians, Mandaeans, and others—would have been simply unrecognizable, no matter how much he bemoaned their presence. The inegalitarian hierarchies and, at times, violence of medieval Middle Eastern societies should not blind us to the mechanisms that they yet developed for dealing with and accommodating high degrees of religious diversity. The region's history was made only through the encounters, however fraught, of its myriad traditions.

NOTES

INTRODUCTION

Note to epigraph: Jāḥiẓ, *Thalāth rasāʾil*, 17, 21.

1. Jāḥiẓ, *Thalāth rasāʾil*, 18.

2. I draw inspiration for this formulation from Burbank and Cooper, *Empires in World History*, 1–22, especially the comments on "imperial repertoires" and "imperial intermediaries," as well as those on "colonial hegemony" in Yannakakis, *Art of Being In-Between*, xiii–xv, 1–30.

3. Excellent and influential examples include Lapidus, *Islamic Societies*, 5–340; Bennison, *Great Caliphs*; Berkey, *Formation of Islam*.

4. See Hoyland, *In God's Path*, 157–69, 207–30; Crone, *Nativist Prophets*.

5. Absolute demographics are unknowable. The classic attempt at modeling demographic Islamization is Bulliet, *Conversion to Islam*. Critiques of Bulliet suggest demographic balances in the Fertile Crescent and Egypt tipping decisively toward Islam much later than he suggested, often after 1000. See Carlson, "Contours of Conversion"; Tannous, "Syria Between Byzantium and Islam," 482–83, note 1143; el-Leithy, "Coptic Culture," 20–23.

6. E.g., Lapidus, *Islamic Societies*, 193–210; Bennison, *Great Caliphs*, 122–33; Berkey, *Formation of Islam*, 91–101, 159–75.

7. El-Leithy, "Coptic Culture," 27.

8. Burbank and Cooper, *Empires in World History*, 13–14.

9. Postcolonial and subaltern studies, in seeking to understand agency among oppressed and colonized peoples, have been especially attuned to "collusion between the dominator and the dominated." Webber, "Middle East Studies and Subaltern Studies," 11.

10. Roman imperial history provides instructive examples. See Burbank and Cooper, *Empires in World History*, 23–59; Wickham, *Inheritance of Rome*, 76–108.

11. The literature is extensive. See Villella, *Indigenous Elites and Creole Identity*; Ramos and Yannakakis, *Indigenous Intellectuals*; Yannakakis, *Art of Being In-Between*.

12. Crone, *Slaves on Horses*, 27–57; Robinson, *Empire and Elites*.

13. Crone, *Slaves on Horses*, 59–91; Gordon, *Breaking of a Thousand Swords*; de la Vaissière, *Samarcande et Samarra*.

14. E.g., Lapidus, *Islamic Societies*, 197.

15. An important exception framed in subaltern studies terms is Choksy, *Conflict and Cooperation*. Cairo Genizah scholarship has also been closely attentive to interactions with state figures and institutions in the shaping of medieval Jewish communities, but its findings are less often incorporated into mainstream Middle Eastern historiography. See, e.g., Cohen, *Jewish Self-Government in Medieval Egypt*; Rustow, *Heresy*, especially 67–108.

16. For an important argument along these lines, see Griffith, *Church in the Shadow*, 129–55.

17. E.g., Griffith, *Church in the Shadow*, 45–128.

18. Important exceptions are Morony, *Iraq*, 364–72; Simonsohn, *Common Justice*; Payne, "East Syrian Bishops."

19. Foundational studies of this material by legal historians include Kaufhold, "Sources"; idem, *Rechtssammlung*, 1–130; Selb, *Orientalisches Kirchenrecht*, vols. 1–2; Vööbus, *Kanonessammlungen*, vols. 1–2.

20. The first quotation is Harper, "Marriage and Family," 669; the second, Maynes and Waltner, *The Family*, x.

21. Brown, *Body and Society*; Harper, *Shame to Sin*. The Islamic response is treated in Sahner, "'The Monasticism of My Community Is *Jihād*.'"

22. Crone, *Nativist Prophets*, especially 391–450; Azad, "Living Happily Ever After."

23. See Brock, "The 'Nestorian' Church." For historical surveys, see Baum and Winkler, *Church of the East*; Baumer, *Church of the East*; Wilmshurst, *Martyred Church*.

24. See generally Hage, *Die syrisch-jakobitische Kirche*; Gillman and Klimkeit, *Christians in Asia*, 21–74.

25. See Griffith, "'Melkites,' 'Jacobites' and the Christological Controversies." See more generally Gillman and Klimkeit, *Christians*

in Asia, 21–74; Nasrallah, *Histoire du mouvement littéraire dans l'Eglise melchite*.

CHAPTER 1

Note to epigraph: Budge, *Histories of Rabban Hôrmîzd* 1:178–79/ 2.1:271–72.

1. On the text, see Budge, *Histories of Rabban Hôrmîzd* 2.1:xxxii–xxxiii; Van Rompay, "Bar ʿEdta, Rabban."

2. On social institutions, see the lucid discussion in Hofer, *Popularisation of Sufism*, 14–23 ("ways of doing things" is on p. 16). See also Scott, *Institutions and Organizations*, especially 55–85 (second quotation from p. 56); Martin, *Social Structures*, 1–25. For our purposes, the family, the household, and judicial institutions should also be included under the heuristic definition of social institutions given here.

3. Stone, *Kinship and Gender*, 175.

4. In Aristotle's famous formulation, male and female unite to create families and households, which then amalgamate to form their natural endpoint, the state (*Politics*, 12–14). Similar to the case of marriage, there are no universally valid definitions of the family and the household as social institutions. One concern of the following chapters is to identify the forms thereof particular to the societies under study. In my general usage, a household denotes a set of cohabiting individuals and the biological-reproductive, social-reproductive, and productive labors they undertake toward collective ends of some kind. Premodern households often included slaves and other dependents who were tied by labor, law, and sometimes affect to the household's core, biologically related family members but did not have the same rights to the family's social identity and property.

5. I draw here on the "working definition" of the family in Harper, "Marriage and Family," 669. See also an anthropologist's general definition of marriage: "everywhere it entails intimate, if not emotionally charged, relationships between spouses, and everywhere it creates in-laws" (Stone, *Kinship and Gender*, 175).

6. See Treggiari, *Roman Marriage*, 60–80, especially 60–61 for the legislation's motives.

7. Skjærvø, *Spirit of Zoroastrianism*, 33–34.

8. Satlow, *Jewish Marriage*, 76.

9. Brown, *Body and Society*; Harper, *Shame to Sin*.

10. Harper, *Shame to Sin*, 81. See also Brown, *Body and Society*, 33–57; Deming, *Paul on Marriage*.

11. On "encratism," see Harper, *Shame to Sin*, 105–7; Brown, *Body and Society*, 92–101. On ascetic trends in Syria, see Griffith, "Asceticism in the Church of Syria"; Brock, "Early Syrian Asceticism"; Koltun-Fromm, *Hermeneutics of Holiness*, 97–209. On monasticism, see Rousseau, "Monasticism"; Caner, "'Not of This World.'"

12. Rousseau, "Monasticism," 746; Rapp, *Holy Bishops in Late Antiquity*, 147–48. Though celibacy became a canonical requirement of the Byzantine episcopacy only in 692, it had been customarily so much earlier.

13. Harper, "Marriage and Family," 679–84, highlighting the first two elements.

14. Harper, *Shame to Sin*, 86–93; Koltun-Fromm, *Hermeneutics of Holiness*, 82–89; Brown, *Body and Society*, 55–56.

15. A singularly influential formulation of this principle is Clement of Alexandria's in *The Pedagogue*. See Harper, *Shame to Sin*, 103–17; Deming, *Paul on Marriage*, 97–101; Brown, *Body and Society*, 122–39; Miller, *Women in Early Christianity*, 257–67. Harper disputes the Stoic genealogy.

16. See generally Harper, *Shame to Sin*, 52–61; idem, "Marriage and Family," 668–84.

17. See Murray, *Symbols of Church*, 154–57; Edakalathur, *Theology of Marriage*; Griffith, "Asceticism in the Church of Syria"; Brock, "Early Syrian Asceticism"; Koltun-Fromm, *Hermeneutics of Holiness*, 97–209.

18. Murray, *Symbols of Church*, 131–42; Koltun-Fromm, *Hermeneutics of Holiness*, 108; Brock, "Bridal Chamber of Light." See also Minov, "Marriage and Sexuality in the Book of Steps."

19. Compare the following to the excerpts from Clement in Miller, *Women in Early Christianity*, 257–67.

20. Overbeck, *Opera selecta*, 387.

21. Mār Abā, *Letter* 3, Chabot, *Synodicon*, 82/335.

22. Bagnall, *Egypt in Late Antiquity*, 198–99; Harper, "Marriage and Family," 679–84.

23. In my general usage, "civil law" denotes bodies of prescriptions that govern relationships between persons. I draw this from comparable notions in contemporary European continental law: "the law of persons (natural and legal), the family, inheritance, property, and obligations" (Merryman and Pérez-Perdomo, *Civil Law Tradition*,

68). Where modern legal systems in the continental civil law tradition distinguish civil law proper from commercial and more broadly from public law, my usage is intended to distinguish heuristically prescriptions related to civil affairs from those pertaining to ritual practice or ecclesiastical organization in premodern settings.

24. The literature is vast. See Harries, "Roman Law and Legal Culture."

25. See Treggiari, *Roman Marriage*; Grubbs, *Women and the Law*; Arjava, *Women and Law*.

26. Harper, "Marriage and Family," 679.

27. See Harper, "Marriage and Family," 672–79; Grubbs, *Law and Family in Late Antiquity*; Arjava, *Women and Law*. Each of these maintains that many novel aspects of late antique Roman family law are better explained as adjustments to long-term transformations in the economic structures of the Roman family than as products of Christianization (Justinian's avowedly Christianizing legislation is the exception). Compare Giardina, "The Family," 392–99, which argues for stronger Christian influence in imperial legislation beginning with Constantine. Giardina readily acknowledges, however, that there was no "'perfect identity' between Christian doctrine and Roman law" (p. 393), which is the point I am emphasizing here. On the explicitly Christian framing of the Justinianic *Corpus iuris civilis*, see Humfress, "Law and Legal Practice," 167–68.

28. See Grubbs, *Women and the Law*, 187–210; Harper, "Marriage and Family," 678–79; Arjava, *Women and Law*, 177–89; Bagnall, "Church, State and Divorce"; Giardina, "The Family," 396–97. Giardina emphasizes Christian doctrine rather than managing conjugal property as the motivation for restrictions on divorce before Justinian.

29. Harper, "Marriage and Family," 682.

30. Harper, *Shame to Sin*, 161–67; Brown, *Body and Society*, 305–22.

31. See Wessel, "Formation of Ecclesiastical Law"; Ohme, "Sources of the Greek Canon Law"; Wagschal, *Law and Legality*, 32–42.

32. Basil of Caesarea, §59, *Letters* 2:109–10.

33. Wagschal, *Law and Legality*, 38–44; Troianos, "Byzantine Canon Law to 1100," 115–43.

34. Basil of Caesarea, §50, *Letters* 2:62; see Arjava, *Women and Law*, 167–77.

35. See Harper, "Marriage and Family," 681–82; Dauphin, "Brothels, Baths and Babes," 51–60.

36. Grubbs, *Women and the Law*, 122.

37. On the limited influence of Justinian's legislation on practices related to the family in late Roman Egyptian documents, see Beaucamp, "Byzantine Egypt and Imperial Law," 276–81.

38. For documents, see Urbanik, "Priestly Divorce," 214, note 33; Arnaoutoglou, "Marital Disputes," 16. On continuities between the Greek and Coptic divorce agreements, see Rowlandson, *Women and Society*, 212–13; between Greek and Coptic legal documents generally, see Richter, "Law of Coptic Legal Documents." There is a fifth-century gap in the documentary record of divorce agreements, but later ones show strong continuities with those of the fourth century and earlier (Bagnall, *Egypt in Late Antiquity*, 193–94).

39. Rowlandson, *Women and Society*, 211–12.

40. *P.Ness.* 33, Kraemer, *Excavations at Nessana* 3:104–6.

41. Rowlandson, *Women and Society*, 216–17.

42. *P.Ness.* 18 and 20, Kraemer, *Excavations at Nessana* 3:54–59, 63–65. For discussion, see Stroumsa, "People and Identities," 101–10; Cotton, "Change and Continuity," 213–15 (from whose translation I quote).

43. Stroumsa, "People and Identities," 36.

44. See Stroumsa, "People and Identities," 62–66.

45. Harper, "Marriage and Family," 684.

46. Simonsohn, *Common Justice*, 30; Cameron, *Mediterranean World*, 61–64.

47. Rowlandson, *Women and Society*, 213–14.

48. *P.Ness.* 57, Kraemer, *Excavations at Nessana* 3:161–67. The divorce procedure in this document resembles Islamic *khulʿ*; Crone argued (against Kraemer) that the two represent distinct iterations of the same regional practice (*Roman, Provincial and Islamic Law*, 97). The use of seven witnesses and the formula of mutual consent appear to be inspired by Roman law, or what the parties understood to be Roman law (Urbanik, "Priestly Divorce," 208–9, 217–18).

49. Urbanik, "Priestly Divorce," 211–16.

50. In heuristic terms, I understand a judicial institution to denote a regularized set of practices by which certain individuals of recognized authority issue regulations to others intended to govern their actions, and when those others seek such regulations from recognized authorities. Both judges and litigants participate in judicial institutions, moreover, with the shared moral-conceptual understanding that justice is the ultimate aim, even if they disagree on what that may mean concretely.

51. See Macuch, "Jewish Jurisdiction"; Simonsohn, *Common Justice*, 43–48; Payne, *State of Mixture*, 103–8; idem, "East Syrian Bishops," 22.

52. Morony, *Iraq*, 364–67; Simonsohn, *Common Justice*, 44–50.

53. See especially Payne, *State of Mixture*, 93–126; also Simonsohn, *Common Justice*, 47–50. Compare Morony, *Iraq*, 364–72, which argues for much stronger institutional boundaries between religious communities.

54. Per the synod of Bet Lapat of 484, Chabot, *Synodicon*, 623–24. Discussed in Payne, *State of Mixture*, 107; idem, "East Syrian Bishops," 7, 11–13.

55. Payne, *State of Mixture*, 103–8, 124–26. Simonsohn allows for a greater degree of systematization; see *Common Justice*, 49–50.

56. See Kaufhold, "Sources," 297–303; idem, *Rechtssammlung*, 4–24; Selb, *Orientalisches Kirchenrecht* 1:97–115.

57. Payne, *State of Mixture*, 93–126.

58. An ecclesiastical synod of 676 was the first to do so, on which see Chapter 2. Some scholars have argued otherwise on the basis of a homiletical passage attributed to the fifth-century theologian Narsay that states that a betrothal may not be enacted without a priest. See, e.g., Muraviev, "Les rites du mariage," 179; de Vries, *Sakramententheologie*, 253; Ritzer, *Le mariage dans les Églises chrétiennes*, 149–55; Feghali, "Origin et formation du mariage," 416. Kaufhold, however, has shown that this verse is almost certainly a later interpolation (*Rechtssammlung*, 75–76). Even if the verse is genuine, there is no trace of the position it endorses in the Church of the East's legal sources, and it is unwarranted to extrapolate a canonically enforced norm from one line of an admonitory homily.

59. Satlow, *Jewish Marriage*, 75; Biale, *Women and Jewish Law*, 46–48.

60. Macuch, "Zoroastrian Principles," 243.

61. Macuch, "Pahlavi Model Marriage Contract," 190–92, 196. Parentheses in the original.

62. See Payne, *State of Mixture*, 108–17; Hutter, "Mār Abā and the Impact of Zoroastrianism"; Bruns, "Christliche Ehe," 206–9; Chapter 6.

63. In addition to Chapter 4, see Weitz, "Shaping East Syrian Law," 96–109; Partsch, "Neue Rechtsquellen," 367–76; Payne's reference to "invisible local traditions," *State of Mixture*, 107.

64. Macuch, "Use of Seals"; Ritter, "On the Development of Sasanian Seals," 101–8; Khan, "Newly Discovered Arabic Documents," 211.

65. Payne, *State of Mixture*, 134–36; Gyselen, *Sasanian Seals and Sealings*, 40–41, 78–79; idem, "Les témoignages sigillographiques"; McDonough, "Bishops or Bureaucrats."

66. See Brock, "Baptismal Anointings"; idem, "Gewargis of Arbela, Psuedo-."

67. See Kaufhold, "Sources," 301, 305; idem, *Rechtssammlung*, 17–20; Selb, *Orientalisches Kirchenrecht* 1:148–53.

68. E.g., seals 1a, 21, 22, 41, and 45, Gyselen, "Les témoignages sigillographiques," 42, 46, 50–51.

69. Ḥnānishoʿ, §XI and §XIV, *Judicial Decisions*, 20–21, 26–27. The traveling priest (Greek *periodeutēs*, Syriac *sāʿorā*) had no fixed diocese and presumably served mainly rural areas. See Madey, "Chorepiscopi and Periodeutes."

70. Brown, "Late Antiquity," 304.

71. The literature is large. For an orientation, see Noegel, Walker, and Wheeler, introduction; Smith, "Here, There, and Anywhere."

72. Lesses, "Exe(o)rcising Power," 349.

73. "Sorcery" in the form of incantations, auguries, amulets, and the like receives routine condemnation in late antique canon law. E.g., synod of Ancyra, §24; synod of Laodicea, §36. Percival, *Seven Ecumenical Councils*, 74, 151. Among East Syrian synodal canons, see the synod of Isḥāq, §5; of Yosep, §19; of Ḥazqiyel, §3; of Ishoʿyahb I, §14; of Mār Abā, §23. Chabot, *Synodicon*, 24/264, 106/363–64, 116/375–76, 150–51/411, 548–49/559. Late antique Jewish discourses on sorcery often revolve less around particular practices than the individuals administering them—rabbis might employ apotropaic incantations that they label "sorcery" only when stereotypically ill-willed women are the practitioners. See Murray, "Female Corporeality," 209–19.

74. See generally Smith, "Here, There, and Anywhere," 24–27.

75. See Stratton, "Interrogating the Magic-Gender Connection," as well as the other essays in Stratton and Kalleres, *Daughters of Hecate*; Gager, *Curse Tablets*, 78–85; Murray, "Female Corporeality," 209–19; Lesses, "Exe(o)rcising Power." One East Syrian synodal canon mentions "dissolute women" (*neshē rapyātā*) as being particularly receptive to unlawful magic: synod of Ishoʿyahb I, §14, Chabot, *Synodicon*, 150/411.

76. See Shaked, Ford, and Bhayro, *Aramaic Bowl Spells*; Levene, "Incantation bowls, Babylonian." On magic bowls and household life, see Morony, "Magic and Society."

77. Morony, "Religion and the Aramaic Incantation Bowls"; Shaked, "Jews, Christians and Pagans"; idem, "Manichaean Incantation Bowls in Syriac"; idem, "Popular Religion."

78. On the prevalence of matronymics among bowl client names, see Morony, "Religion and the Aramaic Incantation Bowls," 418. See in a similar vein Golinkin, "Use of the Matronymic." Scholars tend to think that the magical practitioners themselves were men, given the scribal knowledge necessary to produce the incantations, although arguments have been made for the involvement of women in the bowls' production as well. Compare Becker, "Comparative Study of 'Scholasticism,'" 110–12, and Lesses, "Exe(o)rcising Power," 361–62.

79. Bowl JBA 27 (MS 1927/16); other bowls commissioned by this client include JBA 31, 32, and 42. See Shaked, Ford, and Bhayro, *Aramaic Bowl Spells*, 158, 160–61, 169–73, 197–99; on Bar-Sāhdē as a Christian name, see p. 100. On Elisur Bagdana, see Shaked, "Bagdāna, King of the Demons."

80. Shaked, "Popular Religion," 104; Morony, "Magic and Society," 95.

81. Compare Lesses, "Exe(o)rcising Power," 357–59.

82. E.g., bowls 2, 6, 27, 49, Moriggi, *Corpus of Syriac Incantation Bowls*, 27–31, 47–51, 134–37, 208–11. See further Geller, "Jesus' Theurgic Powers," 149–55; Shaked, "Jesus in the Magic Bowls." The relevant East Syrian canons are the synod of Yosep, §19; of Ḥazqiyel, §3. Chabot, *Synodicon*, 106/363–64, 116/375–76.

CHAPTER 2

Note to epigraph: Synod of George, Chabot, *Synodicon*, 215–16/480–82.

1. See Fiey, "Diocèses syriens orientaux du golf Persique," 209–19; Healey, "Christians of Qatar," 225–27.

2. Synod of George, Chabot, *Synodicon*, 216/482.

3. Synod of George, §13, Chabot, *Synodicon*, 224/487–88.

4. Hoyland, *In God's Path*, 128–33; Brock, "North Mesopotamia in the Late Seventh Century," 53, 61.

5. Hoyland, "New Documentary Texts," 398–403; Foss, "A Syrian Coinage of Muʿawiya?" Compare Johns, "Archaeology and the History of Early Islam."

6. On administrative continuity, see Hoyland, *In God's Path*, 98–102, 128–33, 139–41, with references. On administrative transformation beginning under ʿAbd al-Malik, see Hawting, *First Dynasty of Islam*, 61–66; Robinson, *ʿAbd al-Malik*, 59–80. On Egypt, where the most detailed evidence is available, see Sijpesteijn, *Shaping a Muslim State*, 49–216.

7. Edelby, "Legislative Autonomy of Christians in the Islamic World," 43–53.

8. The following discussion is particularly indebted to Payne, "East Syrian Bishops."

9. Payne, "East Syrian Bishops," 7, 11–13, discussing synod of George, §6, Chabot, *Synodicon*, 219–20/484–85. See also Morony, *Iraq*, 366–67.

10. On the texts and their authors, see Van Rompay, "Ḥenanishoʿ I"; idem, "Shemʿon of Rev Ardashir"; Kaufhold, "Sources," 305, 306; Selb, *Orientalisches Kirchenrecht* 1:176–77.

11. Shemʿon, §§1, 17, *Law of Inheritance*, 234–37, 248–49.

12. Ḥnānishoʿ, §XII, *Judicial Decisions*, 22–25, discussed in Payne, "East Syrian Bishops," 29.

13. Synod of Ishoʿyahb I, §7, Chabot, *Synodicon*, 144/405–6.

14. Selb, *Orientalisches Kirchenrecht* 1:176–77.

15. Shemʿon, §I, *Law of Inheritance*, 217.

16. Payne, "East Syrian Bishops"; also Simonsohn, *Common Justice*, 147–73.

17. E.g., Ishoʿyahb I's letter to Yaʿqob of Dayrin, §14, Chabot, *Synodicon*, 181–82/440–41, mentioned also in Payne, "East Syrian Bishops," 11.

18. Shemʿon, §I, *Law of Inheritance*, 212–13.

19. The later East Syrian legal tradition remembers no earlier works comparable to that of Shemʿon or Ḥnānishoʿ; the tradition's first systematic compendium, composed by Gabriel of Basra in the late ninth century, brings together extracts from Shemʿon and later law books but no otherwise earlier, unpreserved texts. See, e.g., Kaufhold, *Rechtssammlung*, 142–43, 154–55, 162–63.

20. See Troianos, "Byzantine Canon Law to 1100," 137–41; Wagschal, *Law and Legality*, 41–44.

21. See Salvesen, "Jacob of Edessa's Life and Work."

22. Menze, *Justinian and the Making of the Syrian Orthodox Church*; Griffith, *Church in the Shadow*, 134–35.

23. Jacob's collection survives in several eighth- and ninth-century manuscripts. See Kaufhold, "Sources," 247–48; Selb, *Orientalisches Kirchenrecht* 2:92–132; Vööbus, *Kanonessammlungen* 2:440–58; Teule, "Jacob of Edessa and Canon Law," 84–86.

24. See Hoyland, *Seeing Islam*, 601–10; Teule, "Jacob of Edessa and Canon Law," 86–99.

25. This is a clear trend in recent studies of the social history of late antiquity and early Islam. See, e.g., Papaconstantinou, "Between *Umma* and *Dhimma*"; Tannous, "Syria Between Byzantium and Islam," 213–575; idem, "You Are What You Read"; Penn, *Envisioning Islam*; Simonsohn, *Common Justice*, 1–21; Hoyland, "New Documentary Texts," 409–10; Donner, "From Believers to Muslims"; idem, *Muhammad and the Believers*. Compare Hoyland, review of Donner, *Muhammad and the Believers*.

26. See Chapter 1; Tannous, "You Are What You Read," 84–85; Griffith, "Arabic Account of ʿAbd al-Masīḥ," 362, 370.

27. Simonsohn, *Common Justice*, 7.

28. Generally Tannous, "Syria Between Byzantium and Islam"; idem, "You Are What You Read," 84–91.

29. Hoyland, *Seeing Islam*, 148–49, 180, 547–48; Crone, "First-Century Concept of '*Hiǧra*.'" Griffith emphasizes that *magaritai* and *mhaggrāyē* connoted the Arabs' purported descent from Hagar as well; see "Free Will in Christian *Kalām*," 151–54. That the connection to *muhājirūn*/"militant emigrants" is these terms' primary sense remains compelling.

30. Carlson, "Contours of Conversion," 798–99; also Penn, *Envisioning Islam*, 144–45.

31. See, e.g., Sizgorich, *Violence and Belief*, 144–230.

32. Jacob of Edessa, §104, *Responsa and Canons*, MS Mardin Church of the Forty Martyrs 310, fols. 213v–214r. Thanks are due to the Hill Museum and Manuscript Library, Collegeville, Minnesota, for providing access to a digital reproduction.

33. Jacob of Edessa, §69, *Canonical Resolutions*, 166–69.

34. For the former, see Nau, "Littérature canonique syriaque inédite," 128–30; for the latter, Anastasios, §74, *Questions and Answers*, 190. On Athanasios, see Penn, "Athanasios II of Balad." On Anastasios, see Munitiz's introduction to Anastasios, *Questions and Answers*, and Haldon, "Works of Anastasius of Sinai."

35. Anastasios, §76, *Questions and Answers*, 191.

36. On the Islamic legal perspective, see Fattal, *Statut légal*, 129–37; Friedmann, *Tolerance and Coercion in Islam*, 160–93.

37. Yawnon, *Letter to the Periodeutes Theodore*, MS Cambridge Additional 2023, fols. 254v–259r; Anastasios, §37, *Questions and Answers*, 141–42; Jacob of Edessa, §97, *Responsa and Canons*, MS Mardin Church of the Forty Martyrs 310, fol. 211v.

38. Payne, "East Syrian Bishops," 12. The novelty of George's canon is an original insight of Payne's to which the following discussion is much indebted.

39. Literally "lacking the trial of marriage" (*d-lā nsāy zuwwāgā*).

40. Literally "through things set down concerning litigation" (*men aylēn d-simin ʿal dinē*).

41. Synod of George, §13, Chabot, *Synodicon*, 223/487–88.

42. Perhaps only their fathers; the Syriac *abāhayhēn* is ambiguous.

43. In precise terms this canon concerns the betrothal contract, not the final consummation of marriage, but for the purposes of this chapter I use the two interchangeably. Chapter 4 draws out the distinctions.

44. See Brundage, *Law, Sex, and Christian Society in Medieval Europe*, 140; Duby, *The Knight, the Lady, and the Priest*, 177–85. Among the East Syrians, the early fourteenth-century patriarch Timothy II included betrothal in his list of the seven "mysteries" (*rāzē*), roughly analogous to western sacraments; this is the earliest attestation of an explicitly sacramental understanding of marriage among the East Syrians. See Kaufhold, *Rechtssammlung*, 79; compare de Vries, *Sakramententheologie*, 253–54.

45. It is possible that the Church of the East had done so before but that a record of the relevant canon has been lost. Even if this were the case, the fact that George saw fit to restate that claim in the terms and at the time that he did indicates that it had gone largely unobserved.

46. Healey, "Christians of Qatar," 227–33.

47. On Fars and apostolic foundation, see Fiey, "Diocèses syriens orientaux du golf Persique," 177–78.

48. Archaeological studies indicate that eastern Arabia was not densely settled in the sixth century, but considerable church and monastery construction from the late seventh into the ninth points to the rising prominence and wealth of local Christians (or at least the disposal of their wealth in a new pattern focused on Christian institutions). See Kennet, "Decline of Eastern Arabia"; idem, "Sasanian

Coins from ʿUmān and Baḥrain." Because this shift began around the time of George's career, it is difficult to have a sense of whether he would have seen Bet Qatraye as struggling or thriving (or indeed whether his activities had anything to do with the changes in the material record). Either way, the region's Christian communities had close connections to George's Mesopotamia, as indicated by the distinctive architectural styles characteristic of Christian remains in eastern Arabia and southern Iraq. Toral-Niehoff, "The ʿIbād of al-Ḥīra," 334–36.

49. Omar, "Islamization of the Gulf," 248–55.

50. Ishoʿyahb III, *Letters* 1:251; read *mazunāyē* for the text's *mrwny*ʾ, on which see Healey, "Christians of Qatar," 230, note 31. For a recent translation, see Penn, *When Christians First Met Muslims*, 36.

51. Carter, "Christianity in the Gulf," 101.

52. Ishoʿyahb III, *Letters* 1:265. For a recent edition with accompanying translation, see idem, "Letters to the Qataris," 50, 73.

53. Synod of George, §§6, 17, 18, Chabot, *Synodicon*, 219–20/484–85, 225/489.

54. Synod of George, §16, Chabot, *Synodicon*, 224/489.

55. Synod of George, §14, Chabot, *Synodicon*, 223–24/488.

56. E.g., the Islamic case in Friedmann, *Tolerance and Coercion in Islam*, 160–93.

57. Satlow, *Jewish Marriage*, 73–82; Biale, *Women and Jewish Law*, 44–69.

58. Satlow, *Jewish Marriage*, 76.

59. Satlow, *Jewish Marriage*, 83–87; Cotton, "Rabbis and the Documents"; idem, "Change and Continuity," 209–13.

60. Macuch, "Zoroastrian Principles"; Payne, *State of Mixture*, 108–17.

61. Important scholarship posits a discontinuity between Quranic law and later Islamic jurisprudence, most famously Schacht, *Origins of Muhammadan Jurisprudence*, especially 190–213. Quranic family law, however, is relatively extensive and remains the basis of the later tradition. Powers, *Studies in Qurʾan and Ḥadīth*, 209.

62. See Spectorsky, *Women in Classical Islamic Law*, 24–33.

CHAPTER 3

Note to epigraph: Timothy, *Law Book*, 57–60.

1. See Kennedy, *Prophet and the Age of the Caliphates*, 112–57; Crone, *Nativist Prophets*, 1–27.

2. Kennedy, "Feeding of the Five Hundred Thousand."

3. But compare Borrut, *Entre mémoire et pouvoir*, especially 321–81.

4. Crone, *Nativist Prophets*, 1–27; Van Bladel, "Bactrian Background of the Barmakids."

5. Hoyland, *In God's Path*, 207–30.

6. See, e.g., Cabrol, *Secrétaires nestoriens*.

7. El Shamsy, *Canonization*, 2; Berkey, *Formation of Islam*, 111–75; Bennison, *Great Caliphs*, 158–202; Bloom, *Paper Before Print*, 42–89.

8. Schacht, *Introduction*, 49–56; Hallaq, *Origins and Evolution*, 102–77; El Shamsy, *Canonization*.

9. See Zaman, *Religion and Politics Under the Early ʿAbbāsids*, 106–18.

10. Khan, "Newly Discovered Arabic Documents," 204–6.

11. Tillier, *Cadis d'Iraq*, 63–86; Simonsohn, *Common Justice*, 63–89.

12. El Shamsy, *Canonization*, 31–34.

13. Tillier, *Cadis d'Iraq*, 96–136, 426–33; Simonsohn, *Common Justice*, 67.

14. As documented in Tillier, *Cadis d'Iraq*.

15. Tillier, *Cadis d'Iraq*, 151–57; idem, "Judicial Authority and Qāḍīs' Autonomy," 127, citing Tsafrir, *History of an Islamic School of Law*, 116–19.

16. Ayoub, "Dhimmah in Qurʾan and Hadith"; Hoyland, "Earliest Attestation of the *Dhimma*."

17. Major studies include Fattal, *Statut légal*; Levy-Rubin, *Non-Muslims*.

18. On these texts, as well as a comparable tract by al-Shāfiʿī and the *Pact of ʿUmar*, which takes the form of a petition from Christians in Syria to the second Medinan caliph ʿUmar ibn al-Khattab (r. 634–44) but was actually a later invention, see variously Levy-Rubin, *Non-Muslims*, 52–87, 103–12, 171–76; Miller, "From Catalogue to Codes to Canon," 120–62; Cabrol, *Secrétaires nestoriens*, 153–60, 315–17.

19. Levy-Rubin construes al-Mutawakkil's edicts and the *Pact of ʿUmar* as effectively normative throughout the medieval period. Other studies suggest, however, that they became so only later and in specific regions, or that they served more as models to be invoked by rulers and activist Muslim jurists in particular political circumstances. See Miller, "From Catalogue to Codes to Canon," 203–35; Fattal, *Statut légal*, 96–110.

20. The following is especially dependent on Simonsohn, *Common Justice*, 91–204.

21. Simonsohn, *Common Justice*, 174–204.

22. Brody, *Geonim*, 54–66.

23. Timothy, *Law Book*, 56–57.

24. Ishoʿbokt, §I.i, *Jurisprudential Corpus*, 8–9.

25. For Basra and Rayy (Syriac Prāt d-Mayshān and Bēt Rāziqāyē), see Timothy, *Law Book*, 56–57; for Fars, Ishoʿbokt, §I.i, *Jurisprudential Corpus*, 9–10; for the Jazira (the East Syrian eparchy of Ātor around Mosul), ʿAbdishoʿ, *Order of Marriage*, 24–25.

26. Ishoʿbarnun, *Letter to Makarios*, addressed to a deacon in the town of Hira on the Euphrates; idem, *Letter to Isaac*, addressed to a traveling priest of Bet Qatraye; Yoḥannān IV, *Kitāb ilā rajul min ahl al-Yaman.*

27. Treated in Simonsohn, *Common Justice*, 109–14; Rose, "Islam and the Development of Personal Status Laws Among Christian Dhimmis."

28. Selb, *Orientalisches Kirchenrecht* 1:176–79; Kaufhold, "Sources," 304–7.

29. He was ordained by a patriarch Ḥnānishoʿ, which means either the first of that name in the 690s or the second in the 770s; most scholars lean toward the latter. See the notes in Sachau, *Syrische Rechtsbücher* 3:xi–x, 289; Van Rompay, "Ishoʿbokht"; Hoyland, *Seeing Islam*, 205–6. For general comments on the *Jurisprudential Corpus*, see Kaufhold, "Sources," 305–6; Selb, *Orientalisches Kirchenrecht* 1:177–78.

30. Ishoʿbokt, §I.i, *Jurisprudential Corpus*, 9–10.

31. For custom as a source of Ishoʿbokt's *Jurisprudential Corpus*, see, e.g., §IV.i.1 and §IV.v, pp. 94–95 and 120–23. On *dinē*, "judgments," as collectively constituting a civil law tradition, see §I.viii and §I.xiv, pp. 14–15 and 20–21, as well as the comments in Sachau, *Syrische Rechtsbücher* 3:xii–xiii.

32. Pigulevskaja, *Villes de l'État iranien*, 106–11; idem, "Die Sammlung der syrischen Rechtsurkunden des Ischobocht," 219–21;

Sachau, *Syrische Rechtsbücher* 3:xii–xiii; Macuch, "Ein mittelpersischer *terminus techincus*"; Payne, "East Syrian Bishops," 5–7.

33. Ishoʿbokt, §§III.i.1, V.vii–ix, VI.ix, *Jurisprudential Corpus*, 74–75, 154–69, 182–83.

34. See Griffith, *Church in the Shadow*, 45–48; Heimgartner, "Timothy I"; Berti, *Vita e studi.*

35. Ishoʿbokt, *Jurisprudential Corpus*, 2–3; Selb, *Orientalisches Kirchenrecht* 1:176–77.

36. Berti, *Vita e studi*, 280–83; Chabot, *Synodicon*, 12–15; Sachau, *Syrische Rechtsbücher* 2:xx; Kaufhold, "Römisch-byzantinisches Recht," 155. Compare Selb, *Orientalisches Kirchenrecht* 1:165–70. See also Thazhath, *Juridical Sources*, 75–76.

37. Kaufhold, "Römisch-byzantinisches Recht," 155.

38. Timothy, *To the ʿElamites*, *To Rabban Petyon*, and *To the ʿElamites* (letters 4, 9, and 12), in *Letters 1–39* 1:78–82, 91–100, 102–6. For numbering, titles, and content summaries of Timothy's epistolary corpus, see Bidawid, *Lettres du patriarche nestorien Timothée I*, 18–43.

39. Weitz, "Shaping East Syrian Law," 79–86. On the text generally, see Kaufhold, "Sources," 306; Selb, *Orientalisches Kirchenrecht* 1:178.

40. Ishoʿbarnun, *Law Book*; lacunae in the main published edition are filled in by Sauget, "Décisions canoniques." On the text, see Kaufhold, "Sources," 306; Selb, *Orientalisches Kirchenrecht* 1:178–79. On Ishoʿbarnun generally, see Van Rompay, "Ishoʿ bar Nun"; Mārī, ʿAmr, and Ṣalībā, *Akhbār* 1:74–75; Weitz, "Shaping East Syrian Law," 87–92.

41. Kaufhold, "Sources," 306–7; Selb, *Orientalisches Kirchenrecht* 1:179; Roggema, "ʿAbdishoʿ bar Bahrīz."

42. Published in Kaufhold, *Rechtssammlung*, 131–317. See as well Kaufhold, "Sources," 308–9; Selb, *Orientalisches Kirchenrecht* 1:73–75.

43. Other than the *Syro-Roman Law Book*, which had no substantive influence on the Persian and Iraqi bishops' law books. For ʿAbdishoʿ's citations of earlier authorities, see, e.g., *Order of Marriage*, 36–37, 50–51; for Gabriel's, Kaufhold, *Rechtssammlung*, 134–63.

44. Simonsohn, *Common Justice*, 173.

45. Three of six treatises in Ishoʿbokt, *Jurisprudential Corpus*; roughly 73 of 99 rulings in Timothy, *Law Book*; 86 of 130 rulings in Ishoʿbarnun, *Law Book*; all of ʿAbdishoʿ, *Order of Marriage.*

46. Timothy, §§18–28, *Law Book*, 72–75, lacking most of §§20–28 due to a lacuna in the manuscript from which Sachau worked. For the Syriac text of those rulings, see MS Mount Sinai St. Catherine's Monastery Syriac 82, fols. 67r–68v; MS Cambridge Additional 2023, fols. 27v–29v. For an Arabic translation, see Ibn al-Ṭayyib, *Fiqh al-naṣrāniyya* 1:185–86/176–77. I accessed a microfilm of the Mount Sinai manuscript in the holdings of the Library of Congress, Washington, D.C.

47. Timothy, §§29–45, *Law Book*, 74–91.

48. Timothy, §§46–99, *Law Book*, 90–117. §§76–80 treat miscellaneous subjects not related to inheritance.

49. E.g., Ishoʿbarnun, §§29, 45, 84, *Law Book*, 128–29, 134–37, 154–55.

50. E.g., Timothy, §§29–30, *Law Book*, 74–79.

51. Ishoʿbokt, §IV.i.3, *Jurisprudential Corpus*, 94–95.

52. Timothy, §49, *Law Book*, 92–93; Ishoʿbokt, §IV.i.4, *Jurisprudential Corpus*, 94–97.

53. Ishoʿbarnun, §47, *Law Book*, 136–37.

54. E.g., Ishoʿbarnun, §64, *Law Book*, 146–47.

55. Compare, for example, the *bayt* as described in Goitein, *Mediterranean Society* 3:1–2, notes 1–3.

56. See Brown, *Body and Society*, 122–39; Harper, *Shame to Sin*, 80–133.

57. On this imagery, see Murray, *Symbols of Church*, 131–42; Edakalathur, *Theology of Marriage*, 176–82; Brock, "Bridal Chamber of Light."

58. See Murray, *Symbols of Church*, 132. A noteworthy exception is when Timothy uses Eve's creation from Adam's rib (Genesis 2:21–23) to explain why he gives lesser inheritance shares to women than to men; see §§56, 58, *Law Book*, 94–99. Despite the typological significance of this comparison, however, Syriac legal works rarely mention it and never treat it as an organizing principle.

59. See Van Overstraeten, "Liturgies nuptiales des églises de langue syriaque."

60. E.g., Bennison, *Great Caliphs*, 123.

61. See Griffith, *Church in the Shadow*, 129–40 (quote on p. 129); idem, "'Melkites,' 'Jacobites' and the Christological Controversies"; Tannous, "You Are What You Read"; Morony, *Iraq*, 354–64; Becker, *Fear of God*.

62. Tannous, "You Are What You Read."

63. Berti, *Vita e studi*, 84–122.

64. E.g., Ephrem of ʿElam, *Letter to Gabriel bar Boktishoʿ*, on whether an East Syrian may receive communion from the "Romans and Jacobites" (he may not); Timothy, *To Bishop Solomon* (letter 1), *Letters* 1–39 1:3–29, on rebaptism of miaphysites who return to East Syrian orthodoxy; Ishoʿbarnun, §47, *Letter to Makarios*, MS Birmingham Mingana Syriac 586, fol. 439r, on receiving communion from West Syrians or Melkites. See also Ishoʿbarnun, §§126, 128, *Law Book*, 174–75. I accessed microfiches of the Mingana manuscript in the holdings of Princeton University's Firestone Library.

65. Jāḥiẓ, *Thalāth rasāʾil*, 21.

66. That subaltern women's bodies and the cultural values ascribed to them have become a frequent arena of contestation among colonial power, modern states, and subaltern resistance is a common theme in postcolonial studies. For a theoretical orientation, see Kalisa, *Violence*, 19–41. In a Middle East context, a classic account of competing colonial and indigenous discourses of the veil and female sexual modesty is Ahmed, *Women and Gender in Islam*, 144–68.

67. Timothy, §§26–27, *Law Book*, MS Mount Sinai St. Catherine's Monastery Syriac 82, fol. 68v; Ibn al-Ṭayyib, *Fiqh al-naṣrāniyya* 1:186/177; Ishoʿbarnun, §§10–11, 119, *Law Book*, 122–23, 170–71; ʿAbdishoʿ, §43, *Order of Marriage*, 36–37.

68. See, e.g., Halevi, *Muhammad's Grave*. Timothy, for example, has merely one ruling on testimony, one on oaths (forbidding Christians from taking them), one on property rights related to slaveholding, and two on ecclesiastical property (§§76–80, *Law Book*, 106–9).

69. Sizgorich, *Violence and Belief*, 244, and pp. 231–71 generally.

70. Timothy, §§12–13, 26–27, 74–76, *Law Book*, 66–69, 106–8, and MS Mount Sinai St. Catherine's Monastery Syriac 82, fol. 68v; Ibn al-Ṭayyib, *Fiqh al-naṣrāniyya* 1:186/177.

71. While some of the jurist-bishops acknowledge theoretically the diversity of inheritance practices among Christians, each prescribes a single, preferred model. Compare, e.g., Ishoʿbarnun, §51 and §62, *Law Book*, 138–41, 144–47. See Weitz, "Shaping East Syrian Law," 100–101.

72. E.g., Ishoʿbokt, §§II.iv, IV.i.5, IV.i.14, *Jurisprudential Corpus*, 38–41, 96–101, 106–8; Ishoʿbarnun, §25, *Law Book*, 126–27.

73. Ishoʿbarnun, §27, *Law Book*, 128–29.

74. Rustow, "Jews and Muslims," 79, in reference to the geonim and their academies.

75. Jurist-patriarchs Timothy and Ishoʿbarnun sat at Baghdad; jurist-bishop ʿAbdishoʿ bar Bahriz was responsible for the Mosul region; Timothy received requests for legislation from the bishops of Basra and Rayy, on which see his *Law Book*, 56–57.

76. Young, *Patriarch, Shah and Caliph*, 133–39; Fiey, *Chrétiens syriaques*, 36–60.

77. Becker, *Fear of God*, 120. See also idem, "Dynamic Reception of Theodore of Mopsuestia," 41.

78. See Kaufhold, "Sources," 245–46; Vööbus, *Kanonessammlungen* 1:5–71; Selb, *Orientalisches Kirechenrecht* 2:119–29. A single early thirteenth-century manuscript preserves in chronological order these synods; no others follow, indicating that they represent a discrete body of legislation. The manuscript has been published as Vööbus, *Synodicon*; for the synods, see 2:1–64/1–68.

79. The former by Patriarch Yuḥanon III (r. 846–73), the latter anonymous. Vööbus, *Synodicon* 2:46–50/49–53, 167–80/173–85.

80. Twenty-six of the roughly forty-one synodal canons treating civil law. The other civil subjects include funerary customs, non-ecclesiastical courts, and loans and debts.

81. E.g., synod of Kyriakos, §§31, 33, 35–37, Vööbus, *Synodicon* 2:13–15/15–17.

82. Simonsohn, *Common Justice*, 147–73.

83. The definitive edition and study is Kaufhold and Selb, *Syrisch-römische Rechtsbuch*; on dating the translation, see 1:51–52. Compare the comments in Brock, review of Kaufhold and Selb.

84. See Witakowski, "Dionysios"; idem, "Giwargis"; idem, "Quryaqos." On Yuḥanon III, Ignatius II, and Dionysios II, see Michael the Syrian, *Chronique* 3:116, 119–20.

85. See Brody, *Geonim*, 1–232.

86. Rustow, *Heresy*, 5.

87. See Brody, *Geonim*, 235–332; Rustow, *Heresy*, 36–66 ("book culture" is on p. 36).

88. I am indebted here to the lucid synthesis in chapter 2 of Krakowski, *Coming of Age in Medieval Egypt*, and thankful to the author for sharing a pre-publication copy. See further Brody, *Geonim*, 249–82; Rustow, *Heresy*, 3–12; idem, "Jews and the Islamic World," 95–96.

89. Rustow, *Heresy*, 4.

90. See Brody, *Geonim*, 85–95; Olszowy-Schlanger, "Karaite Legal Documents"; idem, "Early Karaite Family Law."

91. Brody, *Geonim*, 67–82; Rustow, "Jews and the Islamic World," 96.

92. See Brody's comments that "the cultural elite associated with the Geonic academies remained largely unaffected" by Islamic trends until the time of Seʿadyah, Gaon of Sura, 928–42; *Geonim*, 235, and pp. 35–66 generally.

93. Simonsohn, *Common Justice*, 197.

94. Rustow, "Jews and the Islamic World," 95–96; Brody, *Geonim*, 216–32.

95. Rustow, *Heresy*, xvii, and pp. 3–35 and 67–108 generally.

96. See Brody, *Geonim*, 249–66.

97. See Nemoy, "Two Controversial Points"; Olszowy-Schlanger, "Early Karaite Family Law," 279–84; Brody, *Geonim*, 95.

98. See generally Brody, *Geonim*, 249–82.

99. On impoverishment and decline, see Kreyenbroek, "Zoroastrian Priesthood"; Daryaee, "Zoroastrianism Under Islamic Rule," 105–9. On conversion, see Shaked, "Islam," 491, with references; Choksy, *Conflict and Cooperation*, 69–109; Bulliet, *Conversion to Islam*, 16–32. Compare Bulliet's findings on Iran to Carlson, "Contours of Conversion," on Syria.

100. See Daryaee, "Zoroastrianism Under Islamic Rule," 110.

101. See Daryaee, "Zoroastrianism Under Islamic Rule," 109–10; Andrés-Toledo, "Primary Sources," 524–27; Macuch, "Pahlavi Literature."

102. Stausberg, "Invention of a Canon," 268. See also Choksy, *Conflict and Cooperation*, 116–17.

103. See Macuch, "Law in Pre-Modern Zoroastrianism," 292–93, with references.

104. E.g., the *Rivāyat of Ādurfarrbay and Farrbay-srōsh*, *Rivāyat accompanying the Dādestān ī dēnīg*, and *Rivāyat of Ēmēd ī Ashawahishtān*, on which see Macuch, "Pahlavi Literature," 136–37, 143–46, and Andrés-Toledo, "Primary Sources," 526–27.

105. Griffith, "'Melkites,' 'Jacobites' and the Christological Controversies," 11–13.

106. Griffith, *Church in the Shadow*, 48–53.

107. See Kaufhold, "Sources," 225–36.

108. *Al-Jāmiʿ wujūh al-īmān*, MS British Library Oriental 4950, fols. 185r–197v. On the text, see Griffith, *Church in the Shadow*, 57–60; Swanson, "*Al-Jāmiʿ wujūh al-īmān*." Thanks are due to Fr. Sidney Griffith for sharing his microfilm of the manuscript.

109. See the theological treatises discussed in Griffith, *Church in the Shadow*, 57–60.

110. Sahner, "Christian Martyrs and the Making of an Islamic Society," 279. On the martyrologies generally, see, in addition to Sahner, Hoyland, *Seeing Islam*, 336–86; Griffith, "Christians, Muslims, and Neo-Martyrs"; idem, *Church in the Shadow*, 147–55.

111. E.g., Anthony Rawḥ al-Qurashī in the former case; Bacchus Ḍaḥḥāk and Elias of Damascus in the latter. Griffith, "Christians, Muslims, and Neo-Martyrs," 196–200; Hoyland, *Seeing Islam*, 363–65.

112. See el-Leithy, "Coptic Culture," 1–33, compared to the findings in Carlson, "Contours of Conversion"; Swanson, *Coptic Papacy in Islamic Egypt*, 65, 189, note 47.

113. Papaconstantinou, "Historiography, Hagiography, and the Making of the Coptic 'Church of the Martyrs.'"

114. See Kaufhold, "Sources," 263–87.

115. I borrow "coproduction" from Nirenberg, *Neighboring Faiths*, 5.

116. Shemʿon, §I, *Law of Inheritance*, 214–17.

117. Johnson, "Law in Early Christianity."

118. Ishoʿbokt, §I.x, *Jurisprudential Corpus*, 16–17. See further Shemʿon, §I, *Law of Inheritance*, 212–19.

119. Ishoʿbokt, §I.i, *Jurisprudential Corpus*, 8–9.

120. Timothy, *Law Book*, 57–58.

121. E.g., Cook, "Origins of *Kalām*"; Berkey, *Formation of Islam*, 95–96; Hoyland, "Early Islam," 1062–69.

122. Timothy, *Law Book*, 57–60.

123. Timothy, *Law Book*, 54–55. See similarly Ishoʿbokt, §I.xii, *Jurisprudential Corpus*, 18–21.

124. Morony, "Religious Communities," 113.

CHAPTER 4

Note to epigraph: Timothy, §30, *Law Book*, 76–77.

1. Synod of George, §13, Chabot, *Synodicon*, 223/487–88.

2. E.g., Ishoʿbokt, §§III.i.1, III.i.7, III.i.9, III.ii.1, IV.i.5.a, IV.i.15, *Jurisprudential Corpus*, 74–79, 100–101, 108–9; Timothy, §29, *Law Book*, 74–75.

3. Ishoʿbokt, §III.i.1, *Jurisprudential Corpus*, 74–75; Timothy, §28, *Law Book*, 74–75, MS Mount Sinai St. Catherine's Monastery

Syriac 82, fol. 68v; Ibn al-Ṭayyib, *Fiqh al-naṣrāniyya* 1:186/177; Ishoʿbarnun, §29, *Law Book*, 128–29; ʿAbdishoʿ, *Order of Marriage*, 38–39. See also Kaufhold, *Rechtssammlung*, 71–74.

4. Synod of Kyriakos, §31; also synod of Yuḥanon III, §15; synod of Ignatius II, §11; synod of Dionysios II, §7. Vööbus, *Synodicon* 2:13–14/15, 41–42/45, 56–57/60, 60/64. See Selb, "Zur Christianisierung."

5. Ishoʿbarnun, §29, *Law Book*, 128–29.

6. Timothy, §30, *Law Book*, 78–79. For the West Syrians, who emphasize the consent of both fathers and spouses, see the canons cited in note 4 above.

7. E.g., Ishoʿbokt, §§III.i.1, III.ii.1, III.ix, *Jurisprudential Corpus*, 74–75, 78–79, 84–85; Timothy, §§29–35, *Law Book*, 74–85; Ishoʿbarnun, §§19–24, *Law Book*, 124–27. See Kaufhold, *Rechtssammlung*, 71; Selb, "Zur Christianisierung," 4–6.

8. Timothy, §§30, 41, *Law Book*, 76–79, 88–89.

9. For an overview, see Satlow, *Jewish Marriage*, 69.

10. Timothy, §30, *Law Book*, 76–77; Ishoʿbarnun, §§21, 46, 59, 102, *Law Book*, 124–25, 136–37, 142–43, 162–63. Among the West Syrians, see synod of Kyriakos, §32; synod of Yuḥanon III, §13. Vööbus, *Synodicon* 2:14/15–16, 41/44. By the eleventh century the East Syrians' hierarchy required a wedding ritual involving priestly blessings and the crowning of the spouses, perhaps adopted from Byzantine practice. See Kaufhold, *Rechtssammlung*, 76–78.

11. Timothy, §73, *Law Book*, 106–7.

12. Synod of George, §§9–10; synod of Kyriakos, §§31, 34; synod of Dionysios I, §6. Vööbus, *Synodicon* 2:3–4/5, 13–14/15–16, 30–31/33.

13. Arjava, *Women and Law*, 202–5.

14. E.g., Rabbulā of Edessa, *Commandments and Admonitions*, in Overbeck, *Opera selecta*, 221; Bagnall, "Church, State and Divorce," 49.

15. E.g., Gregory Nazianzen, *Oration* 37, in *Discours* 32–37, 283–85.

16. Ishoʿbokt, §II.xi, *Jurisprudential Corpus*, 56–59.

17. Timothy, §36, *Law Book*, 86–87.

18. Ishoʿbokt, §§II.xii–xiv, *Jurisprudential Corpus*, 58–65.

19. Timothy, §§36, 42, *Law Book*, 84–89; Ishoʿbarnun, §§5–6, 16–17, 35, 101, 114, *Law Book*, 120–25, 130–31, 160–63, 168–69. The published edition of Timothy's text has "death" (*mawtā*) instead of Ishoʿbokt's "murder" (*qeṭlā*); a later East Syrian work that cites Timothy's ruling restores the latter, which looks to be the correct

reading. See ʿAbdishoʿ, §17, *Collection*, 215. Ishoʿbarnun never mentions murder as grounds for divorce.

20. E.g., Ishoʿbokt, §IV.i.4, *Jurisprudential Corpus*, 94–97; Timothy, §§49–50, *Law Book*, 90–93; Ishoʿbarnun, §51, *Law Book*, 138–41.

21. E.g., Timothy, §§53–54, *Law Book*, 94–95; Ishoʿbarnun, §54, *Law Book*, 140–41.

22. E.g., Ishoʿbokt, §III.i.7, *Jurisprudential Corpus*, 76–77; Timothy, §§62, 73, *Law Book*, 100–101, 106–7; Ishoʿbarnun, §43, *Law Book*, 134–35; synod of Kyriakos, §33, Vööbus, *Synodicon* 2:14/16.

23. Compare Timothy, §73, *Law Book*, 106–7, and Ishoʿbarnun, §§19, 20, 30, *Law Book*, 124–25, 128–31.

24. E.g., Ishoʿbokt, §§II.xii, III.vi, *Jurisprudential Corpus*, 58–61, 82–83; Timothy, §§29–31, *Law Book*, 74–81.

25. Shemʿon, §1, *Law of Inheritance*, 236–37. See also Ishoʿbokt's invocation of the specter of the "insolent, disobedient wife" (*anttā paknitā wa-mṣaʿʿrānitā*), whom he allows a husband to divorce: §II.xi, *Jurisprudential Corpus*, 58–59.

26. Ishoʿbokt, §IV.3, *Jurisprudential Corpus*, 94–95.

27. See, e.g., Timothy, §§49, 50, 51, 66, 67, 81, 83, *Law Book*, 90–93, 102–5, 108–11; Ishoʿbarnun, §62, *Law Book*, 146–47.

28. Ishoʿbokt, §IV.i.14, *Jurisprudential Corpus*, 106–7.

29. E.g., Ishoʿbokt, §§IV.i.13–14, *Jurisprudential Corpus*, 106–8; Timothy, §§49, 53, *Law Book*, 90–95. Ishoʿbarnun acknowledges that customs in this area differ; in some regions sons may inherit more from their mothers, in others daughters will have an equal claim: §113, *Law Book*, 168–69.

30. Compare Macuch, "Inheritance"; Shilo, "Succession"; Hallaq, *Sharīʿa*, 289–95.

31. The research and conclusions detailed in this section have been published in a different form in Weitz, "Shaping East Syrian Law," 98–105.

32. Greengus, "Old Babylonian Marriage Contract."

33. See, e.g., Rapoport, "Matrimonial Gifts"; Friedman, *Jewish Marriage in Palestine*.

34. See, e.g., Driver and Miles, *Assyrian Laws*, 166–68, 173–86; idem, *Babylonian Laws* 1:249–50; Satlow, *Jewish Marriage*, 69.

35. Satlow, *Jewish Marriage*, 69–83; Tucker, *Women, Family, and Gender*, 41–50.

36. See, e.g., Driver and Miles, *Babylonian Laws* 1:272; idem, *Assyrian Laws*, 238–39; Macuch, "Inheritance," 129; Payne, *State of Mixture*, 114; idem, "East Syrian Bishops," 19–20; Satlow, *Jewish Marriage*, 207–8. For the similar example of ancient Greek law, see Just, *Women in Athenian Law*, 89–90.

37. See Arjava, *Women and Law*, 63.

38. See the overview in Hallaq, *Sharīʿa*, 291–95.

39. This pattern changes with ʿAbdishoʿ bar Bahriz, who presents a reorganized system of inheritance, and later East Syrian jurist-bishops. See Yaron, "New Nestorian Source," 273; Chapter 9.

40. Ishoʿbokt, §§IV.i.1–4, *Jurisprudential Corpus*, 94–97. See Payne, "East Syrian Bishops," 20.

41. Timothy, §§49, 50, 81, 99, *Law Book*, 90–93, 108–9, 114–17; Ishoʿbarnun, §§51, 62, *Law Book*, 138–41, 146–47.

42. Timothy, §§66, 67, 83, *Law Book*, 102–5, 110–11. See Aptowitzer, *Syrischen Rechtsbücher*, 71–74; Yaron, "New Nestorian Source," 272, note 52; Weitz, "Shaping East Syrian Law," 104–6.

43. Shaki, "Divorce."

44. E.g., Shaki, "Divorce," 444; Williams, §§34d, 41, *Pahlavi Rivāyat* 2:61, 69. On crimes in Zoroastrian thought, see Jany, "Criminal Justice in Sasanian Persia"; Kiel, "Systematization of Penitence in Zoroastrianism," 122.

45. Thaʿālibī, *Ghurar akhbār mulūk al-furs*, 260.

46. Timothy, §75, *Law Book*, 106–7.

47. Rapoport, "Matrimonial Gifts," 1.

48. Synod of Kyriakos, §33, Vööbus, *Synodicon* 2:14/16.

49. E.g., the entries in Kaufhold and Selb, *Syrisch-römische Rechtsbuch* 1:227.

50. See synod of Kyriakos, §31; of Yuḥanon III, §15; of Ignatius II, §11; of Dionysios II, §7. Vööbus, *Synodicon* 2:13–14/15, 41–42/45, 56–57/60, 60/64.

51. Synod of Kyriakos, §31, Vööbus, *Synodicon* 2:13–14/15.

52. See Tucker, *Women, Family, and Gender*, 41–50; Ibn Qudāma, *Mughnī* 9:344–51.

53. Tucker, *Women, Family, and Gender*, 42–43; Ibn Qudāma, *Mughnī* 9:398–407.

54. E.g., the entries in Kaufhold and Selb, *Syrisch-römische Rechtsbuch* 1:222, 252, 255.

CHAPTER 5

Note to epigraph: Ishoʿbokt, §III.i.9, *Jurisprudential Corpus*, 78–79.

1. Morony, "Religious Communities," 113. See, e.g., Bennison, *Great Caliphs*, 123–24; Lapidus, *Islamic Societies*, 194.

2. Morony, "Religious Communities," 113; idem, *Iraq*, 367 and 332–83 generally.

3. E.g., Simonsohn, *Common Justice*; Tannous, "You Are What You Read"; Papaconstantinou, "Between *Umma* and *Dhimma*."

4. Excellent examples include Safran, *Defining Boundaries in al-Andalus*; Rustow, *Heresy*.

5. E.g., Timothy, §§40, 71, 77, *Law Book*, 86–87, 104–5, 108–9. See generally Tannous, "Syria Between Byzantium and Islam," 287–315; otherwise, there is exceedingly little social-historical scholarship on the Eucharist and the anathema in the medieval Middle East. For an overview of the subject in medieval Christian Europe, see Vodola, *Excommunication*.

6. Timothy, §13, *Law Book*, 66–69; Ishoʿbarnun, §115, *Law Book*, 168–71. Synod of Kyriakos, §25; synod of Dionysios I, §4; synod of Dionysios II, §§19, 24. Vööbus, *Synodicon* 2:12/14, 29–30/32–33, 63–64/67–68. See Simonsohn, *Common Justice*, 154–56.

7. Simonsohn, *Common Justice*, 147–48.

8. Timothy, §§12–13, *Law Book*, 66–69.

9. Simonsohn, *Common Justice*, 150–53. On George's canon, see Chapter 2. The one West Syrian canon on the subject appears to prescribe the anathema for those who contract non-ecclesiastical, "worldly marriages" (*zuwwāgē ʿālmānāyē*), in contrast to the East Syrian position. Synod of Dionysios I, §6, Vööbus, *Synodicon* 2:30–31/33. For lack of further evidence the following discussion leaves the West Syrians aside.

10. Ishoʿbokt, §III.i.9, *Jurisprudential Corpus*, 78–79.

11. Ishoʿbarnun, §29, *Law Book*, 128–29.

12. Simonsohn, *Common Justice*, 152.

13. See also Timothy, §28, which prescribes a Christian betrothal ceremony but no penalty for other practices: *Law Book*, MS Mount Sinai St. Catherine's Monastery Syriac 82, fol. 68v; Ibn al-Ṭayyib, *Fiqh al-naṣrāniyya* 1:186/177.

14. Ishoʿbokt, §§III.i.2–5, *Jurisprudential Corpus*, 74–77.

15. Marriage contract 40, Grohmann, *Arabic Papyri* 1:82–85. See Simonsohn, *Common Justice*, 151. Another example of 918,

concluded between individuals with the Christian names Marqūrah (*mrqwrh*, Merkorios) and the daughter of Pantelis (*bnṭls*), is marriage contract 43, Grohmann, *Arabic Papyri* 1:94–96. See another example of 948 between a deacon named Theodore (*t͟hydr . . . al-shammās*) and one Dbēlī Adāy, granddaughter of a priest (*dbly ʾdʾy ibnat Yuḥannis Buqṭur bin Yuḥannis al-qissīs*), as well as a receipt of 989 for the payment of a deferred marriage portion issued by Theodore's son Qīriqah (Kerykos or Kyriakos, *qyrqh bin t͟hydr . . . al-Naṣrānī*) to his wife, perhaps named Elenah (*ʾlynh . . . al-Naṣrānī* [*sic*]). Abbott, "Arabic Marriage Contracts"; documents 10 and 15, Khoury, *Chrestomathie*, 26–28, 38–40. Abbott points out that Grohmann's contracts 40 and 43 do not identify explicitly the parties as Christian; therefore, we cannot rule out the possibility that they were recent converts to Islam ("Arabic Marriage Contracts," 59). It is reasonable to presume, however, that by the late ninth century a convert would have been unlikely to give a markedly Christian name, rather than an adopted Arabic Muslim one, to a Muslim scribe to record in a legal document.

16. E.g., synod of George, §§9–10, Vööbus, *Synodicon* 2:3–4/5; Timothy, §33, *Law Book*, 80–83.

17. See, e.g., Spectorsky, *Women in Classical Islamic Law*, 105–41.

18. See Tucker, *Women, Family, and Gender*, 86–92, 100–104.

19. E.g., the list in Rapoport, "Matrimonial Gifts," 34–35.

20. Document 17, Khoury, *Chrestomathie*, 42–43. For early modern examples of Christians registering divorces in state courts, see Tucker, *In the House of the Law*, 86–87; Al-Qattan, "*Dhimmī*s in the Muslim Court," 434–35.

21. See Biale, *Women and Jewish Law*, 72–84; Friedman, *Jewish Marriage in Palestine* 1:312–13.

22. Timothy, §35, *Law Book*, 84–85; MS Mount Sinai St. Catherine's Monastery Syriac 82, fol. 69v, filling in lacunae in the published edition.

23. Ishoʿbokt, §§II.x, III.xi, *Jurisprudential Corpus*, 54–57, 86–88; Timothy, §§34–35, *Law Book*, 82–85; Ishoʿbarnun, §80, *Law Book*, 152–53.

24. Ishoʿbarnun, §127, *Law Book*, 174–75.

25. Ishoʿbarnun, §28, *Law Book*, 128–29; Ishoʿbokt, §II.xi, *Jurisprudential Corpus*, 56–59.

26. Jāḥiẓ, *Thalāth rasāʾil*, 21.

27. Tucker, *Women, Family, and Gender*, 95–100, 109–11. An Egyptian documentary example of 1069 is number 18, Khoury, *Chrestomathie*, 43–46.

28. Tucker, *Women, Family, and Gender*, 92. See, e.g., Mālik, *Muwaṭṭa'*, 342; Shaybānī, *Aṣl* 10:253–56; Shāfiʿī, *Umm* 6:110–12; ʿAbd al-Razzāq, §§10720–726, *Muṣannaf* 6:253–54; Ibn Abī Shayba, §§16749–766, *Muṣannaf* 9:165–67 (with a few minority opinions suggesting ten months instead of one year); Ibn Qudāma, *Mughnī* 10:82–83, compiling the views of early jurists and mentioning the very few dissenting opinions. We have no real records of court decisions from this period; I therefore cite in this chapter the major Islamic legal authorities and collections of legal traditions contemporary with the Syriac jurist-bishops, as these offer the best picture of the conceivable differences between Christian and Muslim judicial practice in their milieu.

29. Shāfiʿī, *Umm* 6:215–20; Saḥnūn, *Mudawwana* 2:142, 145.

30. Shaybānī (and Ibn Ḥajar), §401, *Kitāb al-Āthār*, 85, although al-Shaybānī argues against the Mālikīs on precisely this point in *Ḥujja* 3:443–53. For various early legal opinions on this issue, see ʿAbd al-Razzāq §§10700–702 and §§10707–711, *Muṣannaf* 6:249–51; Ibn Abī Shayba, §§16561–563, *Muṣannaf* 9:113–14; Ibn Qudāma, *Mughnī* 10:55. Opposition to allowing the wife of a chronically ill man to choose marital dissolution is most commonly associated with Kufan scholars, including Ibrāhīm al-Nakhaʿī and Sufyān al-Thawrī, and their earlier authorities, like ʿAlī and Ibn Masʿūd.

31. Timothy, §72, *Law Book*, 104–7. See similarly Ishoʿbarnun, §11, *Letter to Isaac*, MS Birmingham Mingana Syriac 587, fols. 366v–367r. I accessed microfiches of the manuscript in the holdings of Princeton University's Firestone Library.

32. Ishoʿbokt, §§III.vi.1–5, *Jurisprudential Corpus*, 82–83.

33. Ishoʿbokt, §§III.i.7, ii.1–2, *Jurisprudential Corpus*, 76–80. The language of "hating" one's spouse, using the root *s-n-y*, is found in formulas for wife-initiated divorce proceedings in a range of Aramaic literary and documentary legal texts from ancient to medieval times; see Friedman, *Jewish Marriage in Palestine* 1:313–20. One wonders whether Ishoʿbokt's translator was drawing on knowledge of an Aramaic "common law" institution of this kind in rendering this passage with the same terminology.

34. On the jurisprudence, see Friedmann, *Tolerance and Coercion in Islam*, 163–70. For examples from late medieval Egypt, see

el-Leithy, "Coptic Culture," 62–64. See also Shatzmiller, "Marriage, Family, and the Faith."

35. See Zinger, "Women, Gender and Law," 49 (note 102), 96, 115, 123, 309 (note 13).

36. The ruling is preserved in ʿAbdishoʿ, §17, *Order of Ecclesiastical Decisions*, MS Vatican Syriac 520, fol. 167v; in Latin translation, *Ordo iudiciorum ecclesiasticorum*, 170. On Yoḥannān bar Abgārē's extant legal writings, see Kaufhold, "Sources," 303, 311.

37. See Friedman, *Jewish Marriage in Palestine* 1:312–46; idem, "Ransom-Divorce."

38. Zinger, "Women, Gender and Law," 132–41.

39. See Rapoport, *Marriage, Money and Divorce*, 72–73.

40. See Goitein, *Mediterranean Society* 3:189–205 (quotation on p. 189); also Kraemer, "Women Speak for Themselves," 192–98.

41. See generally Bentley, "Hemispheric Integration"; Gellens, "Search for Knowledge in Medieval Muslim Societies."

42. Goitein, *Mediterranean Society* 3:189.

43. ʿAbd al-Razzāq, §§12320–322, *Muṣannaf* 7:86–88. The last version adds an interesting note on the typical *jinn* diet, which is said to consist of "That over which God's name has not been uttered. And fool" (*mā lam yudhkar ism Allāh ʿalayhi wa-l-fūl*).

44. Although this opinion is primarily associated with the Mālikīs, its attestation in traditions with Iraqi *isnāds* (usually attributed to ʿUmar) and among the non-Sunni schools indicates its early, wide spread. See, e.g., Mālik, *Muwaṭṭaʾ* 3:280–81; for Iraqi traditions, Bayhaqī, §§15568–569, *Sunan* 7:732; for the Ibadis, Abū Ghānim, *Mudawwana* 2:285; for the Twelvers, Kulaynī, §§106.1–4, *Kāfī*, 976–77; for the Ismailis, Qāḍī al-Nuʿmān, *Daʿāʾim al-islām* 2:238–39.

45. E.g., Shaybānī, *Ḥujja* 4:49–60.

46. See Shāfiʿī, *Umm* 6:235–38; similarly among the Mālikīs, Saḥnūn, *Mudawwana* 2:180–84. See generally Ibn Qudāma, *Mughnī* 11:360–64.

47. See Tucker, *In the House of the Law*, 82–84; Imber, review of Tucker.

48. See Biale, *Women and Jewish Law*, 102–10.

49. See Goitein, *Mediterranean Society* 3:189–90.

50. Timothy, §§29, 31–33, 71, *Law Book*, 74–83, 104–5.

51. Timothy, §31, *Law Book*, 78–79.

52. Timothy, §§31–32, *Law Book*, 78–81. Ishoʿbokt permits the dissolution of a marriage in which the wife is left without maintenance

for seven years, an exception but still less flexible than the Islamic doctrine. §III.ix, *Jurisprudential Corpus*, 84–85.

53. Timothy, §33, *Law Book*, 80–81.

54. See similarly Ishoʿbarnun, §78, *Law Book*, 152–53.

55. Timothy, §33, *Law Book*, 80–83.

56. Timothy, §31, *Law Book*, 78–81.

57. Timothy, §33, *Law Book*, 80–83.

58. On Timothy's correspondence with Central Asia, see Dickens, "Patriarch Timothy I and the Metropolitan of the Turks," 117–21; for mention of his letters to India, see Ibn al-Ṭayyib, *Fiqh al-naṣrāniyya* 2:119/121, 149/152.

CHAPTER 6

Note to epigraphs: Balādhurī, *Ansāb* 1:99; Ishoʿbarnun, §4, *Letter to Makarios*, MS Birmingham Mingana Syriac 586, fol. 433v.

1. Ishoʿbarnun, §4, *Letter to Makarios*, MS Birmingham Mingana Syriac 586, fol. 433v.

2. Timothy, §§18–27, of which only §§18–19 are found in the published edition of his Syriac *Law Book* on pp. 72–73. For the original Syriac of §§19–27, see MS Mount Sinai St. Catherine's Monastery Syriac 82, fols. 67r–68v. For §§18–27 in Arabic translation, see Ibn al-Ṭayyib, *Fiqh al-naṣrāniyya* 1:185–86/176–77 (quotation from §23).

3. The literature is vast. See, e.g., Stone, *Kinship and Gender*, 61–206; Fox, *Kinship and Marriage*; Lévi-Strauss, *Elementary Structures of Kinship*.

4. Timothy, §19, *Law Book*, the quotation here taken from the Arabic translation in Ibn al-Ṭayyib, *Fiqh al-naṣrāniyya* 1:185/176.

5. Shaw and Saller, "Close-Kin Marriage in Roman Society?"

6. Grubbs, *Women and the Law*, 136–38.

7. Grubbs, *Women and the Law*, 140.

8. *Canons of the Apostles*, §19, Percival, *Seven Ecumenical Councils*, 595; Grubbs, *Women and the Law*, 163–65; Rabbulā of Edessa, *Commandments and Admonitions*, in Overbeck, *Opera selecta*, 221; Doran, *Stewards of the Poor*, 77, 89. See Pitsakis, "Législation et stratégies matrimoniales," 677–80.

9. Grubbs, *Women and the Law*, 137–38, 140–43, 161–63.

10. Theodoret, *Correspondance* 1:79–80.

11. Satlow, *Jewish Marriage*, 157.

12. *Canons of the Apostles*, §19, Percival, *Seven Ecumenical Councils*, 595.

13. Grubbs, *Women and the Law*, 140–43, 161–65.

14. See Satlow, *Jewish Marriage*, 186–89.

15. Grubbs, *Women and the Law*, 165. See further condemnations of men who marry their sisters-in-law or the former wives of their brothers, sons, fathers, or uncles: council of Neocaesarea, §2, Percival, *Seven Ecumenical Councils*, 79–80; Basil of Caesarea, *Letters* 1:314–19 (*To Diodorus*) and 2:52 (§23), 114 (§§76–79); *Letter of a Bishop to His Friend*, §4, Vööbus, *Synodicon* 1:181/172. See also Lee, "Close-Kin Marriage in Late Antique Mesopotamia"; the sixth-century Roman legislation against "unlawful marriages," which Lee takes to indicate consanguineous unions, could just as well have targeted affine ones.

16. Synod of George, §8; synod of Kyriakos, §§35–37; synod of Yuḥanon III, §12. Vööbus, *Synodicon* 2:3/5, 14–15/16–17, 41/44.

17. Synod of George, §6; Yuḥanon III, *On Unlawful Marriages*, §§1–2; synod of Dionysios II, §14. Vööbus, *Synodicon* 2:3/5, 46/49, 61–62/66.

18. Jacob of Edessa, §71, *Canonical Resolutions*, 168–71.

19. See Frandsen, *Incestuous and Close-Kin Marriage*, 60–118; de Jong, *Traditions of the Magi*, 424–32.

20. Cited in Frandsen, *Incestuous and Close-Kin Marriage*, 94.

21. Skjærvø, *Spirit of Zoroastrianism*, 33; Macuch, "Incestuous Marriage."

22. See Macuch, "Inheritance," 130–34; idem, "Zoroastrian Principles," 235–40; Payne, *State of Mixture*, 108–17.

23. I am dependent here on Payne, *State of Mixture*, especially 103–17. See also Hutter, "Mār Abā and the Impact of Zoroastrianism."

24. Mār Abā, *Letter* 3, Chabot, *Synodicon*, 82–83/335.

25. See again Payne, *State of Mixture*, 103–17.

26. See in this connection an undated document in which an association of Christian artisans pledges to follow the prescriptions of Mār Abā: Brock, "Regulations for an Association of Artisans," discussed in Payne, *State of Mixture*, 123–24.

27. Timothy, *To the ʿElamites* (letter 4) and *To the ʿElamites* (letter 12), *Letters* 1–39 1:78–82, 102–6 (quotations on p. 79). Timothy's Roman sources include the *Canons of the Apostles*, synod of Neocaesarea, and *Syro-Roman Law Book*. For details, see Kaufhold,

"Sources," 300; Kaufhold and Selb, *Syrisch-römische Rechtsbuch* 2:336–37.

28. Putman, *L'église et l'islam*, 34–35; Berti, *Vita e studi*, 243–64.

29. Timothy, *Letters 1–39* 1:105.

30. Synod of Bet Lapat, Chabot, *Synodicon*, 623–24.

31. Timothy, §23, Ibn al-Ṭayyib, *Fiqh al-naṣrāniyya* 1:185/176–77.

32. The literature is extensive. See, e.g., Altuntek, "Bone and Flesh, Seed and Soil"; Holy, *Kinship, Honour and Solidarity*; Kasdan and Murphy, "Structure of Parallel Cousin Marriage." In anthropological jargon parallel cousins are the children of two brothers or two sisters; cross cousins are the children of a brother and sister.

33. Ṭabarānī, §7964, *Muʿjam* 8:246.

34. See Goitein, *Mediterranean Society* 3:27–33; el-Leithy, "Coptic Culture," 364–67.

35. ʿAbdishoʿ, *Order of Marriage*, 36–37.

36. E.g., Budge, *Coptic Martyrdoms* 1:398 (cited in Brown, *Body and Society*, 250); Theodoret, *Correspondance* 1:79–80; van Gelder, *Close Relationships*, 13, 18, 23–28, 43–45, 77.

37. Compare the classic reformulation of cousin marriage as practical strategy rather than structural rule in Bourdieu, *Outline of a Theory of Practice*, 30–71.

38. Timothy, §23, *Law Book*, MS Mount Sinai St. Catherine's Monastery Syriac 82, fols. 67v–68r. The text is unpublished; suggested amendments are noted in parentheses.

39. See also Ishoʿbokt, §§II.i.1–2, *Jurisprudential Corpus*, 28–29; Timothy, §22, *Law Book*, MS Mount Sinai St. Catherine's Monastery Syriac 82, fol. 67v, and Ibn al-Ṭayyib, *Fiqh al-naṣrāniyya* 1:185/176.

40. It is worth noting that Byzantine canon law had prohibited cousin marriage at the Council of Trullo in 692, on which see Pitsakis, "Législation et stratégies matrimoniales," 680–81. There is no evidence that Timothy knew anything of this council or took inspiration from it, however, and in any case his ruling presents only the analogy as its rationale.

41. Vööbus, *Synodicon* 2:46–50/49–53 (examples on p. 46/49–50).

42. ʿAbdishoʿ, *Order of Marriage*, 26–27.

43. See ʿAbdishoʿ, *Order of Marriage*, 26–35; the example is §15, pp. 32–33.

44. I borrow "jurists' law" from Layish, "Transformation of the *Sharīʿa*."

45. The literature is vast. See Gutas, *Greek Thought, Arabic Culture*; Nagel, *History of Islamic Theology*, 93–170.

46. Schacht, *Introduction*, 37–56; Hallaq, *Origins and Evolution*, 74–76, 113–21; El Shamsy, *Canonization*, 17–43.

47. Brody, *Geonim*, 85–95; Nemoy, *Karaite Anthology*, 3–11.

48. See Rustow, *Heresy*, 23–34 (quote on p. 23); Gil, "Origins of the Karaites."

49. Nemoy, *Karaite Anthology*, 125–26; idem, "Two Controversial Points"; Olszowy-Schlanger, "Early Karaite Family Law," 279–84.

50. Griffith, *Church in the Shadow*, 45–48.

51. See Chapter 3.

52. Ishoʿbarnun, §4, *Letter to Makarios*, MS Birmingham Mingana Syriac 586, fol. 433v.

53. Ishoʿbarnun, §26, *Law Book*, 126–27.

54. Ishoʿbarnun, §23, *Selected Questions*, 30/facsimile fols. 12v–13r.

55. See Young, *Biblical Exegesis*, 161–85; Becker, *Fear of God*, 118–19.

56. In fact, Antiochene exegetical traditions account for why Abraham and Sarah became cousins in East Syrian biblical interpretation in the first place. The background is a rabbinic tradition that identified Sarah with Yiskah, daughter of Abraham's brother Haran in the genealogical passage Genesis 11:26–30, making Abraham and Sarah uncle and niece. The identification of Sarah with Yiskah made its way into late antique Christian exegesis as well (e.g., Ephrem, *Selected Prose Works*, 148, treating Genesis 11:29; Ishoʿbarnun, *Selected Questions*, 130–35). For Christian exegetes, however, the resultant kin relationship between Abraham and Sarah, which was unproblematic for the rabbis, clashed with the Christian-Roman aversion to uncle-niece marriage. To solve this issue, Theodore of Mopsuestia's exegesis as reproduced by Ishoʿbarnun moved Haran and Sarah back a generation: it created a second Haran, "the elder" (*rabbā*), said to be Abraham's uncle, and identified him as Sarah's father (Ishoʿbarnun, §23, *Selected Questions*, 30; idem, §26, *Law Book*, 126–27). Antiochene exegesis thus creatively rescued Abraham and Sarah from an un-Christian uncle-niece marriage by making them first cousins. From that perspective, Timothy's prohibition of cousin marriage did no more than plunge them into a second unlawful union. On the rabbinic exegetical background to this issue, see Firestone, "Prophethood, Marriageable Consanguinity, and Text," 331–40. Thanks are

due to Joseph Witztum for pointing me to this problem in Jewish exegesis and its relationship to the East Syrian case.

57. Further evidence from Timothy's epistolary corpus suggests that he was somewhat less versed in disciplines of biblical learning than Ishoʿbarnun: Berti, *Vita e studi*, 139, 284–85.

58. Hallaq, *Origins and Evolution*, 5.

59. Schacht, *Introduction*, 37–68; Hallaq, *Origins and Evolution*, 102–49; El Shamsy, *Canonization*. An argument against the central importance of al-Shāfiʿī as put forward by Schacht is Hallaq, "Was al-Shafiʿi the Master Architect?" El Shamsy reemphasizes al-Shāfiʿī's thought as pivotal.

60. Payne, *State of Mixture*, 109.

61. E.g., Ishoʿbokt, §§II.vi–x, *Jurisprudential Corpus*, 42–57.

62. Polliack, "Rethinking Karaism." See similarly Astren, "Islamic Contexts of Medieval Karaism."

63. Cook, "Origins of *Kalām*"; Schacht, *Origins of Muhammadan Jurisprudence*, 99–100; Wegner, "Islamic and Talmudic Jurisprudence," 44–49.

64. See Rustow, *Heresy*.

CHAPTER 7

Note to epigraph: Ḥnānishoʿ, §XV, *Judicial Decisions*, 26–29. The passage quoted calls the deacon only "so-and-so" (*pulān*); his proper name, Daniel, is given two lines later. Karka d-Bet Slok is Karka d-Bet "somewhere" (*pulān*) in the text; but the only known Karka is Karka d-Bet Slok (see Payne, "East Syrian Bishops," 17n57). Kufa in the text is Syriac ʿĀqulā.

1. Some of the research and conclusions of this chapter have been published in a different form in Weitz, "Polygyny and East Syrian Law."

2. Hallaq, *Sharīʿa*, 277–78.

3. Shaki, "Family Law," 185; El Cheikh, *Women, Islam, and Abbasid Identity*, 81–83; Imber, *Ottoman Empire*, 75–84.

4. Goody, *Development of the Family*, 41–43; Herlihy, *Medieval Households*, 38–49.

5. See Kennedy, *When Baghdad Ruled the Muslim World*, 167–68.

6. See Macuch, "Incestuous Marriage," 144; idem, "Zoroastrian Principles," 235–36.

7. Thanks are due to Robert Hoyland for pointing me in this direction.

8. Harper, *Slavery in the Late Roman World*, 285–91; Arjava, *Women and Law*, 210–17.

9. See Harper, *Slavery in the Late Roman World*, 281–85 and 281–325 generally.

10. See Chapter 1.

11. §33, Vööbus, *Canons Ascribed to Mārūtā* 1:80–81/2:69 (whence the quotation). Mār Abā, *Letter* 3; synod of Ishoʿyahb I, §13; synod of Bet Lapat. Chabot, *Synodicon*, 82–83/335–38, 148–50/409–11, 623–24.

12. See the accounts in Guidi, *Chronicle of Khuzistan*, 17–19, and Scher, *Chronicle of Seert*, *Patrologia Orientalis* 13:509–10. Only the latter mentions polygamy as a point of contention.

13. Guidi, *Chronicle of Khuzistan*, 19; Scher, *Chronicle of Seert*, *Patrologia Orientalis* 13:498.

14. See Fiey, *Pour un Oriens Christianus novus*, 134; Yāqūt, *Muʿjam al-buldān* 3:262.

15. Guidi, *Chronicle of Khuzistan*, 21–22; Scher, *Chronicle of Seert*, *Patrologia Orientalis* 13:521–25.

16. See Morony, *Iraq*, 350–51. On lay-ecclesiastical factional strife generally, see pp. 346–54.

17. See Payne, *State of Mixture*, 123–24.

18. Brock, "Regulations for an Association of Artisans," 58. For the Syriac text, see Kaufhold, *Rechtssammlung*, 176–77.

19. Payne, *State of Mixture*, 124.

20. Hoyland, *In God's Path*, 157–58.

21. See Chapter 2, and more specifically Anastasios, §§37, 100, *Questions and Answers*, 141–42, 228–30; Yawnon, *Letter to the Periodeutes Theodore*, MS Cambridge Additional 2023, fols. 254v–259r; Jacob of Edessa, §97, *Responsa and Canons*, MS Mardin Church of the Forty Martyrs 310, fol. 211v; synod of George, §16, Chabot, *Synodicon*, 224/489. On a contemporary East Syrian saint's life in which a merchant in Bet Qatraye is excoriated for keeping a concubine (*druktā*), see Payne, "Monks, Dinars and Date Palms," 99–106.

22. Ḥnānishoʿ, §XV, *Judicial Decisions*, 26–29.

23. See, e.g., the reference to men keeping multiple wives "far" (*b-ruḥqā*) from one another in the synod of George, §16, Chabot, *Synodicon*, 224/489. See similarly Timothy, §71, *Law Book*, 104–5, and an episode from a Melkite hagiography recounted in Wood,

"Christian Authority Under the Early Abbasids," 264–65. On the Genizah, see Friedman, "Polygyny in Jewish Tradition and Practice," 37–38, 49.

24. Ḥnānishoʿ, §XV, *Judicial Decisions*, 28, lines 2–4.

25. Ishoʿbokt, §II.xi, *Jurisprudential Corpus*, 56–59; Ishoʿbarnun, §3, *Law Book*, in Sauget, "Décisions canoniques," facsimile fol. 1. Synod of Kyriakos, §34; synod of Dionysios I, §6. Vööbus, *Synodicon* 2:14/16, 30/33.

26. Synod of Dionysios I, §6, Vööbus, *Synodicon* 2:30/33; ʿAbdishoʿ, *Order of Marriage*, 40–41. See similarly Ishoʿbokt, §IV.iv.6, *Jurisprudential Corpus*, 116–17; Timothy, §70, *Law Book*, 104–5; Ishoʿbarnun, §§100–101, *Law Book*, 160–63; Yoḥannān IV, *Kitāb ilā rajul min ahl al-Yaman*, §16, MS Vatican Arabic 157, fols. 88v–89r and MS Mardin Chaldean Cathedral 333, fols. 183v–184r. Thanks are due to the Hill Museum and Manuscript Library, Collegeville, Minnesota, for providing access to a digital reproduction of the latter manuscript. It was catalogued previously as Diyarbakır 157, for which see Scher, *Notice sur les manuscrits syriaques*, 78.

27. See Spectorsky, *Women in Classical Islamic Law*, 30, 95–97.

28. See, e.g., the comments on the different qualities of slaves from different lands in Ibn Buṭlān, *Risāla jāmiʿa*, 352. See also Richardson, "Singing Slave Girls," 105–8.

29. See el-Leithy, "Coptic Culture," 382–433.

30. See al-Heitty, "Contrasting Spheres of Free Women and *jawārī*" (on the Barmakid wife, p. 34); Caswell, *Slave Girls of Baghdad*.

31. See Ibn Abī Uṣaybiʿa, *ʿUyūn*, 183–278; Ullmann, *Medizin*, 108–28; Ghanīma, "Bukhtīshūʿ al-ṭabīb al-nasṭūrī wa-usratuhu"; Dols, "Origins of the Islamic Hospital."

32. Qifṭī, *Ikhbār*, 110; Ibn Abī Uṣaybiʿa, *ʿUyūn*, 184–85.

33. Mārī, ʿAmr, and Ṣalībā, *Akhbār* 1:74.

34. Mārī, ʿAmr, and Ṣalībā, *Akhbār* 1:79.

35. Bar ʿEbroyo, *Chronicle*, 158.

36. Qifṭī, *Ikhbār*, 253; Ibn Abī Uṣaybiʿa, *ʿUyūn*, 248.

37. See Rowson, "Categorization of Gender and Sexual Irregularity," 76, note 27.

38. Mārī, ʿAmr, and Ṣalībā, *Akhbār* 1:78.

39. Ishoʿbokt, §IV.iv.6, *Jurisprudential Corpus*, 116–17.

40. Timothy, §70, *Law Book*, 104–5.

41. Ishoʿbarnun, §101, *Law Book*, 160–63.

42. See Wertheimer, "Children of Disorder"; Ross, "Concubinage in Anglo-Saxon England."

43. See Brockopp, *Early Mālikī Law*, 192–203.

44. E.g., Powers, *Law, Society, and Culture in the Maghrib*, 23–52.

45. Ibn Ḥabīb, *Kitāb al-Muḥbir*, 45–46.

46. Examples from the early Abbasid period of sub-royal Muslim elites who had children by slave concubines include one al-Nāṭifī, with the slave poet ʿInān (c. 800); Ibn Rāʾiq (tenth century), with Sarīra; Aḥmad Ibn Ḥanbal (d. 855), with Ḥusn; Jaʿfar al-Ṣādiq (d. 765), the sixth Imam of the Twelver Shiites, who had the seventh, Mūsā al-Kāẓim, by a Berber slave. See Ibn al-Sāʿī, *Consorts of the Caliphs*, 10–11, 138–39; Suyūṭī, *Mustaẓraf*, 20–21; Anthony, "Mahdī and the Treasures of Ṭālaqān," 482, note 76. See in general Gordon, "Khāqānid Families," 241; Bray, "Men, Women and Slaves," 136.

47. Qifṭī, *Ikhbār*, 72–73; Ibn Abī Uṣaybiʿa, *ʿUyūn*, 201–9. On Bukhtīshūʿ's children, see pp. 73 and 209, respectively.

48. Ibn Abī Uṣaybiʿa, *ʿUyūn*, 210; Ullmann, *Medizin*, 110–11 (§§5–7).

49. Mārī, ʿAmr, and Ṣalībā, *Akhbār* 1:79; Bar ʿEbroyo, *Chronicle*, 158, giving the sons' names.

50. I give a likely reading of the fragments and note complications in the endnotes. See also Graf, *Geschichte* 2:111; Ullmann, *Medizin*, 111 (§5a).

51. Bar ʿEbroyo, *Chronicle*, 158.

52. Mārī, ʿAmr, and Ṣalībā, *Akhbār* 1:85–89 (quote on p. 87). See also Fiey, *Chrétiens syriaques*, 121–23. Mārī's chronicle specifies that Yūḥannā ibn Bukhtīshūʿ was bishop of Mosul and born of a concubine but not that his father was Bukhtīshūʿ ibn Jibrīl. Bar ʿEbroyo's chronicle makes that identification explicit.

53. Ibn Abī Uṣaybiʿa, *ʿUyūn*, 276–77. Ibn Abī Uṣaybiʿa groups entries of family members together; Yūḥannā's comes many pages after Bukhtīshūʿ's distinguished line and mentions no connections to that family.

54. A daughter objected to renovations that effaced Yūḥannā's burial marker in the church in which he had been interred. Mārī, ʿAmr, and Ṣalībā, *Akhbār* 1:90, lines 19–22.

55. See Yoḥannān IV, *Kitāb ilā rajul min ahl al-Yaman*, MS Vatican Arabic 157, fols. 85v–86r and MS Mardin Chaldean Cathedral 333, fols. 177v–178v.

56. Yoḥannān IV, *Kitāb ilā rajul min ahl al-Yaman*, §16, MS Vatican Arabic 157, fol. 88v and MS Mardin Chaldean Cathedral 333, fol. 183v.

57. Yoḥannān IV, *Kitāb ilā rajul min ahl al-Yaman*, §16, MS Vatican Arabic 157, fols. 88v–89r and MS Mardin Chaldean Cathedral 333, fols. 183v–184r.

CHAPTER 8

Note to epigraph: Jacob of Edessa, §104, *Responsa and Canons*, MS Mardin Church of the Forty Martyrs 310, fols. 213v–214r. On Jacob's dates and correspondents, see Teule, "Jacob of Edessa and Canon Law," 83, 92.

1. Brubaker, *Grounds for Difference*, 105.

2. Koltun-Fromm, *Hermeneutics of Holiness*, 89–94; Hayes, *Gentile Impurities*, 92–98.

3. Hayes, *Gentile Impurities*, 98–102.

4. Council of Laodicea, §§10, 31; council of Chalcedon, §14. Percival, *Seven Ecumenical Councils*, 129, 149, 278–79.

5. Sivan, "Why Not Marry a Jew?"

6. §20, Vööbus, *Canons Ascribed to Mārūtā* 1:71–72/2:62. On the set of canons in question, pseudepigraphically ascribed to the Fathers of the Council of Nicaea, see Kaufhold, "Sources," 299; Selb, *Orientalisches Kirchenrecht* 1:97–102.

7. §34, Vööbus, *Canons Ascribed to Mārūtā* 1:81/2:69.

8. §20, Vööbus, *Canons Ascribed to Mārūtā* 1:72/2:62.

9. See generally Payne, *State of Mixture*.

10. Morony, *Iraq*, 349–50; Brock and Harvey, *Holy Women of the Syrian Orient*, 64–65; synod of Yosep, §§10–11, Chabot, *Synodicon*, 102/359–60.

11. Synod of Yosep, §11, Chabot, *Synodicon*, 102/360.

12. One East Syrian synod emphasizes the traditional, blanket prohibition: synod of Ishoʿyahb I, §27, Chabot, *Synodicon*, 158–59/418.

13. Fattal, *Statut légal*, 129–37; Friedmann, *Tolerance and Coercion in Islam*, 160–66.

14. See Ibn Isḥāq, *Life of Muhammad*, 653; Friedmann, *Tolerance and Coercion in Islam*, 181; Tannous, "Syria Between Byzantium and Islam," 525.

15. See Hoyland, *In God's Path*, 158; Tannous, "Syria Between Byzantium and Islam," 524–28.

16. Marinides, "Anastasius of Sinai," 301–2; Anastasios, §76, *Questions and Answers*, 191; Ṭabarī, *Ta'rīkh* 5:2375.

17. See Chapter 2.

18. E.g., Tannous, "Syria Between Byzantium and Islam," 213–575; Donner, "From Believers to Muslims."

19. See, e.g., Fisher, *Between Empires*, 40–46, 108–16; Hoyland, *In God's Path*, 14–27; al-Qāḍī, "Non-Muslims in the Muslim Conquest Army," 88–93.

20. Synod of George, §14, Chabot, *Synodicon*, 223–24/488. See also Chapter 2.

21. Anastasios, §74, *Questions and Answers*, 190.

22. Nau, "Littérature canonique syriaque inédite," 128–30. Penn contends that Athanasios's *ḥanpē* are actual pagans (*Envisioning Islam*, 165–66). But *ḥanpē* soon became a standard Syriac term for Muslims, the setting is northern Syria in the late seventh century, and the "food of pagan sacrifices" (*mēkultā d-debḥē ḥanpāyē*) that Athanasios's letter condemns, which Penn takes to mean pagan feasts, is better understood as *ḥalāl* meat slaughtered with the requisite pronunciation of the *basmala*, or perhaps as an *ʿīd* feast. Hoyland also suggests that "Muslims were uppermost in Athanasius' mind" in this passage (*Seeing Islam*, 149).

23. Jacob of Edessa, §104, *Responsa and Canons*, MS Mardin Church of the Forty Martyrs 310, fols. 213v–214r.

24. See Friedmann, *Tolerance and Coercion in Islam*, 172–75.

25. Bayhaqī, §13986, *Sunan* 7:280, cited in Friedmann, *Tolerance and Coercion in Islam*, 173.

26. Synod of George, §§12–13; synod of Kyriakos, §§14, 37; synod of Yuḥanon III, §23. Vööbus, *Synodicon* 2:4/5, 10/12, 15/17, 44/47. Timothy, §27, *Law Book*, MS Mount Sinai St. Catherine's Monastery Syriac 82, fol. 68v, and Ibn al-Ṭayyib, *Fiqh al-naṣrāniyya* 1:186/177; Ishoʿbarnun, §§10, 119, *Law Book*, 122–23, 170–71.

27. Timothy, §26, *Law Book*, MS Mount Sinai St. Catherine's Monastery Syriac 82, fol. 68v, and Ibn al-Ṭayyib, *Fiqh al-naṣrāniyya* 1:186/177; Ishoʿbarnun, §11, *Law Book*, 122–23; ʿAbdishoʿ, §43, *Order of Marriage*, 36–37.

28. Synod of George, §12; synod of Kyriakos, §14. Vööbus, *Synodicon* 2:4/5, 10/12.

29. Friedmann, *Tolerance and Coercion in Islam*, 187–90.

30. See Friedmann, *Tolerance and Coercion in Islam*, 160–66.

31. §29, Anklesaria, *Pahlavi Rivāyat of Āturfarnbag* 2:61–62.

32. El-Leithy, "Coptic Culture," 62–100, on which the following is dependent. "Single-generation conversion" is el-Leithy's coinage.

33. See Yarbrough, "Did ʿUmar b. ʿAbd al-ʿAzīz Issue an Edict Concerning Non-Muslim Officials?" If such an edict did predate al-Mutawakkil's, regarding which Yarbrough expresses skepticism, "it is not possible to say with confidence what it was" (p. 200).

34. See Cabrol, *Secrétaires nestoriens*, 153–60; Fiey, *Chrétiens syriaques*, 87–94.

35. See the inheritance strategies detailed in el-Leithy, "Coptic Culture," 91–97.

36. See entries §§7, 15, 24, Cabrol, *Secrétaires nestoriens*, 271–75.

37. Qurṭubī, *Ṣilat taʾrīkh al-Ṭabarī*, 164. Compare the interpretation in Cabrol, *Secrétaires nestoriens*, 159, and Fiey, *Chrétiens syriaques*, 120.

38. E.g., the chronological division between "The Consolidation of Islam, 750–1000" and "Medieval Islam, 1000–1500" in Berkey, *Formation of Islam*, or the demographic tipping points suggested in Bulliet, *Conversion to Islam*.

39. E.g., the Arabic theological idioms adopted by Christians and Jews. See Griffith, *Church in the Shadow*, 45–105; Brody, *Geonim*, 235–48, 283–99.

40. See Carlson, "Contours of Conversion," 805.

41. Although this was more often a result of the little interest the Mongols showed in religious divisions among their subjects than a specific policy toward Christianity. See Gillman and Klimkeit, *Christians in Asia*, 139–42; Jackson, "Mongols and the Faith of the Conquered," 262, 273; idem, *Mongols and the Islamic World*, 312–18.

CHAPTER 9

Note to epigraph: Bar ʿEbroyo, *Nomocanon*, 118.

1. Compare Ghazālī, *Wasīṭ* 5:26–27; idem, *Wajīz* 2:6.

2. See el-Hibri, "Empire in Iraq"; Bonner, "Waning of Empire"; Kennedy, "Late ʿAbbasid Pattern."

3. Griffith, *Church in the Shadow*, 45–128.

4. Wilmshurst, *Ecclesiastical Organisation*, 17.

5. See MacEvitt, *Crusades and the Christian World of the East*, 35–43; Dagron, "Minorités ethniques et religieuses dans l'Orient byzantin."

6. See Teule, "Syriac Renaissance."

7. See Wing, *Jalayirids*, 74–100.

8. On the spread of the plague in the fourteenth century, see Dols, *Black Death*, 35–67.

9. See Wilmshurst, *Ecclesiastical Organisation*, 16–19; Gillman and Klimkeit, *Christians in Asia*, 142–43; Baumer, *Church of the East*, 223–33.

10. The canons of synods held in 1064, 1166, 1169, and 1174 do not survive. Extant sources include the canons of a local synod convened in Mardin in 1153 and the *Penitential Canons* of Dionysios bar Ṣalibi (d. 1171). See Kaufhold, "Sources," 246, 250; Vööbus, *Kanonessammlungen* 1:104–21, 2:405–39.

11. The most detailed examination of the textual history is Kaufhold, "Über die Entstehung" (see p. 67 for a chart of the manuscripts), building on the text editions and studies in idem, *Syrische Texte zum islamischen Recht*; idem, "Islamisches Erbrecht." See also idem, "Sources," 253–54.

12. Vööbus, *Synodicon* 2:64/68, 86/92, 89/95.

13. Synod of Yuḥanon of Mardin, §28, Vööbus, *Synodicon* 2:248–49/261–62; Bar ʿEbroyo, *Nomocanon*, 121.

14. Kaufhold, *Rechtssammlung*, 78. See pp. 76–78 on the crowning ritual making its way into East Syrian tradition, the reasons for which are less evident than in the West Syrian case.

15. Dionysios bar Ṣalibi, §12, *Penitential Canons*, MS British Library Oriental 4403, fols. 162v–163r. See similarly Bar ʿEbroyo, *Nomocanon*, 126.

16. As had Byzantine civil law since the Isaurian emperors' *Ecloga* of the mid-eighth century. Pitsakis, "Législation et stratégies matrimoniales," 680–83.

17. Kaufhold, "Ein weiteres Rechtsbuch," especially 115–16.

18. On the texts, see Kaufhold, "Sources," 307–10; Selb, *Orientalisches Kirchenrecht* 1:180–86. Only Gabriel's has been published. For his treatment of inheritance, made up of excerpts of earlier East Syrian sources as well as of the *Syro-Roman Law Book*, see Kaufhold, *Rechtssammlung*, 134–63. For a sense of Elias I's East Syrian sources, see Kaufhold, "Ein weiteres Rechtsbuch." Elias of Nisibis's tract is based on that of Elias I; idem, "Sources," 310. The manuscript incipit of George's treatise describes the text as based on the opinions (*reʿyānē*) of Timothy, Ishoʿbarnun, and other East Syrian figures; George of Arbela, *Collection of Mar George*, MS Birmingham Mingana Syriac 587, fol. 403r.

19. Kaufhold, "Über die Entstehung," 59–60. It is worth noting that a marginal note in the manuscript attributes this text to the East Syrian patriarch Yoḥannān bar Abgārē, and that a medieval East Syrian chronicle asserts that the same individual issued inheritance regulations that accorded with Islamic law. Kaufhold has shown, however, that these ascriptions likely result from misunderstandings of a very confused manuscript history; the possibility that Yoḥannān composed a *fiqh*-inspired treatment of inheritance remains possible but is unsubstantiated by the textual evidence. See "Über die Entstehung"; "Ein weiteres Rechtsbuch."

20. On ʿAbdishoʿ's relationship to Islamic law overall, see the analysis and evaluation in Yaron, "New Nestorian Source," 269–76.

21. Kaufhold, "Sources," 235–36.

22. See Kaufhold, "Sources," 263–87.

23. See Graf, *Geschichte* 2:133–34, 173–76; Selb, *Orientalisches Kirchenrecht* 1:72–76; Kaufhold, "Sources," 309–11. Elias's work remains unpublished.

24. See Graf, *Geschichte* 2:259–62; Kaufhold, "Sources," 254. The *Murshid*'s section treating lay marriage is published in Aydin, *Die Ehe bei den Syrisch-Orthodoxen*, 191–230.

25. Butts, "Ibn al-Ṭayyib."

26. Reading *sh-r-ʿ*, the sense of which is much more appropriate to the context, for the manuscript's *sh-r-ḥ*. Arabic *ʿayn* and *ḥāʾ* are orthographically similar in their final-position forms and phonemically related, and thus easily confused by a scribe.

27. Ibn al-Ṭayyib, *Masʾala fī al-tazwīj wa-l-ṭalāq*, MS Vatican Arabic 157, fols. 91r (introductory question) and 91v (passages from the response); MS Mardin Chaldean Cathedral 333, fols. 187v–188r, 189r–189v. Thanks are due to Luke Yarbrough for advice on the interpretation and translation of this passage.

28. See generally Hallaq, *Sharīʿa*, 39–43, 72–82. Muslim jurists would soon theorize *maṣlaḥa* as a principle of legal reasoning, but Ibn al-Ṭayyib was probably writing too early to be using this term in a technical *fiqh* sense. See Hallaq, "Considerations," 686.

29. Ibn al-Ṭayyib, §2, *Fiqh al-naṣrāniyya* 2:3/3–4.

30. For the Sunni schools, see Ibn Qudāma, *Mughnī* 9:398–407; for Ḥanafī opinions, see Marghīnānī, *Hidāya* 2:476–77, 480–81; for the Twelver Shiites, see Ṭūsī, *Mabsūṭ* 4:162–63 and Ḥillī, *Mukhtalaf al-shīʿa* 7:114–15. I leave aside the Zaydis, Ibadis, and Ismailis as they did not have significant presences in Ibn al-Ṭayyib's Iraq.

31. Timothy, §30, *Law Book*, 78–79. See also Chapter 4.

32. See Kaufhold, "Sources," 252–53, 311–13; Takahashi, *Barhebraeus*, 227–43; Selb, *Orientalisches Kirchenrecht* 1:223–26, 2:154–57; Vööbus, *Kanonessammlungen* 2:499–552.

33. See Takahashi, *Barhebraeus*, 1–57.

34. Takahashi, *Barhebraeus*, 96–104.

35. Teule, "Transmission of Islamic Culture."

36. See Weitz, "Al-Ghazālī, Bar Hebraeus, and the 'Good Wife,'" and the works of Teule cited on p. 203, note 2.

37. Bar ʿEbroyo, *Nomocanon*, 2.

38. Nallino, "Il diritto musulmano nel Nomocanone." Khadra, "Nomocanon de Bar Hebraeus," returns to the subject of the Bar ʿEbroyo-Ghazālī relationship but unfortunately gives few specific textual comparisons to support its claims.

39. *Al-Wasīṭ* is a rearranged abridgment of al-Ghazālī's *al-Basīṭ*, a much longer commentary on a work of al-Juwaynī. Al-Ghazālī subsequently composed *al-Wajīz*, a further abridgment of the *Wasīṭ*. See ʿAbd al-ʿAẓīm Maḥmūd al-Dīb's introduction to Juwaynī, *Nihāyat al-maṭlab* 1:*b-j*. It is clear that Bar ʿEbroyo had to have worked off of the *Wasīṭ*, although it is possible that he had the shorter *Wajīz* at hand as well (see the following note); whether he had access to the *Basīṭ*, which remains unpublished, requires further study.

40. Ghazālī, *Wasīṭ* 6:209; Bar ʿEbroyo, *Nomocanon*, 156. The corresponding section in al-Ghazālī's *Wajīz* includes the "clay, wood, or stone" list but makes no mention of the noblewoman's bronze, one of many indications that Bar ʿEbroyo had one of al-Ghazālī's longer treatises at hand. See *Wajīz* 2:115.

41. Ghazālī, *Wasīṭ* 5:28–29; Bar ʿEbroyo, *Nomocanon*, 118.

42. E.g., Bar ʿEbroyo, *Nomocanon*, 118 (Proverbs and Ben Sira), 125 ("laws of the Greek kings," i.e., the *Syro-Roman Law Book*), 128 (East Syrians Timothy and Ishoʿbarnun), 129 (canons of Dionysios I Telmaḥroyo and Jacob of Edessa). On Gabriel of Basra as Bar ʿEbroyo's East Syrian source, see Kaufhold, *Rechtssammlung*, 51–55.

43. Bar ʿEbroyo, *Nomocanon*, 142–53.

44. Bar ʿEbroyo, *Nomocanon*, 123–24, relying on Ghazālī, *Wasīṭ* 5:63–70 and/or *Wajīz* 2:11.

45. See the synods of Kyriakos, §31; of Yuḥanon III, §15; of Ignatius II, §11; of Dionysios II, §7. Vööbus, *Synodicon* 2:13/15, 42/45, 56–57/60, 60/64.

46. Synod of Ignatius II, §11, Vööbus, *Synodicon* 2:56/60.

47. See Tucker, *Women, Family, and Gender*, 52–53.

48. Bar ʿEbroyo, *Nomocanon*, 157, relying on Ghazālī, *Wasīṭ* 6:214 and/or *Wajīz* 2:116.

49. Bar ʿEbroyo, *Nomocanon*, 139, relying on Ghazālī, *Wasīṭ* 5:223–25 and/or *Wajīz* 2:30–31.

50. See Chapter 1. Closer to Bar ʿEbroyo's time, see the discussion in Yaḥyā ibn Jarīr's *Kitāb al-Murshid*, published in Aydin, *Die Ehe bei den Syrisch-Orthodoxen*, 192–97.

51. For an edition of the extant fragments and a definitive study, see Kaufhold, *Rechtssammlung*. See also idem, "Sources," 308–9; Selb, *Orientalisches Kirchenrecht* 1:73–75.

52. Kaufhold, "Sources," 310.

53. Kaufhold, introduction, xvii–xviii.

54. E.g., Wright, *Short History of Syriac Literature*, 265–90.

55. Note, however, that ʿAbdishoʿ interacts with Islamic literatures in his Arabic theological writings. See Rassi, "'What Does the Clapper Say?'"

56. See Kaufhold, introduction, xvi–xvii; idem, *Rechtssammlung*, 57–64, 324–33 (a chart of ʿAbdishoʿ's original sources).

57. See Kaufhold, "Der Richter in den syrischen Rechtsquellen," especially 111–13. On *al-Majmūʿ al-ṣafawī*, see idem, "Sources," 285–86.

58. Ibn al-ʿAssāl had in fact incorporated much Islamic law in the *Majmūʿ* (see Kaufhold, "Der Richter in den syrischen Rechtsquellen") but not in its treatment of marriage; ʿAbdishoʿ's source base remained thoroughly Christian in this respect.

59. ʿAbdishoʿ, *Order of Ecclesiastical Decisions*, §9.8, MS Vatican Syriac 520, fol. 157v; *Ordo iudiciorum ecclesiasticorum*, 185.

60. Bar ʿEbroyo, *Nomocanon*, 123, relying on Ghazālī, *Wasīṭ* 5:68 and/or *Wajīz* 2:11. Bar ʿEbroyo's list differs from ʿAbdishoʿ's only in adding the bride's brother's son between her brother and paternal uncle.

61. ʿAbdishoʿ, §5, *Collection*, 211–12.

62. ʿAbdishoʿ, §2, *Collection*, 210. See Tucker, *Women, Family, and Gender*, 42.

63. ʿAbdishoʿ, §5, *Collection*, 211–12.

64. ʿAbdishoʿ, §4, *Collection*, 211.

65. With the caveat that ʿAbdishoʿ's texts are shorter and are not full of very specific rulings like those that Bar ʿEbroyo adopted from Ghazālī.

CONCLUSION

1. Thanks are due to Marina Rustow for pointing me in this direction.

2. Crone, *Nativist Prophets*, 16.

3. Crone, *Nativist Prophets*, especially 160–88, 453–93.

4. See Robinson, *Empire and Elites*, 90–108.

5. See Azad, "Living Happily Ever After"; Crone, *Nativist Prophets*, 391–450.

BIBLIOGRAPHY

Primary Sources

ʿAbd al-Razzāq ibn Hammām al-Ṣanʿānī. *Al-Muṣannaf.* Edited by Ḥabīb al-Raḥmān al-Aʿẓamī. 12 vols. Johannesburg: al-Majlis al-ʿIlmī, n.d.

ʿAbdishoʿ bar Bahriz. *Order of Marriage and Inheritance.* Published as *Ordnung der Ehe und der Erbschaften sowie Entscheidung von Rechtsfällen.* Edited and translated by Walter Selb. Vienna: Hermann Böhlaus Nachf., 1970.

ʿAbdishoʿ bar Brikā. *Collection of Synodal Canons.* Published as *Collectio canonum synodicorum.* Edited by A. Mai. *Scriptorum Veterum Nova Collectio* 10. Rome: Typis Collegii Urbani, 1838.

———. *Order of Ecclesiastical Decisions.* MS Vatican Syriac 520, folios 3v–214r. Published in Latin translation as *Ordo iudiciorum ecclesiasticorum.* Translated by J.-M. Vosté. *Codificazione Canonica Orientale, Fonti* 2.25. Vatican City: Typis Polyglottis Vaticanis, 1940.

Abū Ghānim Bishr al-Khurāsānī. *Al-Mudawwana al-kubrā.* Edited by Muṣṭafā ibn Ṣāliḥ Bājū. 3 vols. Muscat: Wizārat al-Turāth al-Qawmī wa-l-Thaqāfa, 2007.

Anastasios of Sinai. *Questions and Answers.* Edited and translated by Joseph A. Munitiz. Turnhout: Brepols, 2011.

Anklesaria, Behramgore Tahmuras, ed. and trans. *The Pahlavi Rivāyat of Āturfarnbag and Farnbag-Srōš.* 2 vols. Bombay: Peshotan K. Anklesaria, 1969.

ʿArīb ibn Saʿd al-Qurṭubī. *Ṣilat taʾrīkh al-Ṭabarī.* Edited by M. J. de Goeje. Leiden: Brill, 1897.

Aristotle. *The Politics and the Constitution of Athens.* Edited by Stephen Everson. Revised edition. Cambridge: Cambridge University Press, 1996.

Balādhurī, Aḥmad ibn Yaḥyā al-. *Ansāb al-ashrāf.* Edited by Maḥmūd al-Fardūs al-ʿAẓm. 26 vols. Damascus: Dār al-Yaqẓa al-ʿArabiyya, 1996.

Bar ʿEbroyo. *Chronicle*. Published as *Chronicon syriacum/Ktābā d-Maktbānut zabnē*. Edited by Paul Bedjan. Paris: Maisonneuve, 1890.

———. *Nomocanon/Ktābā d-Huddāyē*. Edited by Paul Bedjan. Leipzig: Otto Harrassowitz, 1898.

Basil of Caesarea. *Letters*. Translated by Sister Agnes Clare Way. 2 vols. Washington, D.C.: Catholic University of America Press. 1951–55.

Bayhaqī, Aḥmad ibn al-Ḥusayn al-. *Al-Sunan al-kubrā*. Edited by Muḥammad ʿAbd al-Qādir ʿAṭā. 11 vols. Beirut: Dār al-Kutub al-ʿIlmiyya, 2003.

Budge, E. A. W., ed. and trans. *Coptic Martyrdoms in the Dialect of Upper Egypt*. 2 vols. London: British Museum, 1914.

———. *The Histories of Rabban Hôrmîzd the Persian and Rabban Bar-ʿIdtâ*. 2 vols. London: Luzac and Co., 1902.

Chabot, J.-B., ed. and trans. *Synodicon orientale ou recueil de synodes nestoriens*. Paris: Imprimerie nationale, 1902.

Dionysios bar Ṣalibi. *Penitential Canons*. MS British Library Oriental 4403, folios 147r–181v.

Doran, Robert, trans. *Stewards of the Poor: The Man of God, Rabbula, and Hiba in Fifth-Century Edessa*. Kalamazoo: Cistercian Publications, 2006.

Driver, G. R., and John C. Miles, trans. *The Assyrian Laws*. Oxford: Clarendon Press, 1935.

———. *The Babylonian Laws*. 2 vols. Oxford: Clarendon Press, 1952.

Ephrem of ʿElam. *Letter to Gabriel bar Boktishoʿ*. MS Birmingham Mingana Syriac 587, folios 357v–360r.

Ephrem the Syrian. *Selected Prose Works*. Translated by Edward G. Mathews Jr. and Joseph P. Amar. Edited by Kathleen McVey. Washington, D.C.: Catholic University of America Press, 1994.

George of Arbela. *Collection of Mar George*. MS Birmingham Mingana Syriac 587, folios 401r–403r.

Ghazālī, Abū Ḥāmid al-. *Al-Wajīz fī fiqh al-imām al-Shāfiʿī*. Edited by ʿAlī Muʿawwaḍ and ʿĀdil ʿAbd al-Mawjūd. 2 vols. Beirut: Dār al-Arqam, 1997.

———. *Al-Wasīṭ fī al-madhhab*. Edited by Aḥmad Maḥmūd Ibrāhīm. 7 vols. Al-Ghūriyya, Egypt: Dār al-Salām, 1997.

Gregory Nazianzen. *Discours 32–37*. Edited by Claudio Moreschini and translated by Paul Gallay. Paris: Éditions du CERF, 1985.

Grohmann, Adolf, ed. and trans. *Arabic Papyri in the Egyptian Library*. 6 vols. Cairo: Egyptian Library Press, 1934.

Guidi, Ignatius, ed. and trans. *Chronicle of Khuzistan*. In *Chronica minora*, vol. 1, 15–39. Leipzig: Otto Harrassowitz, 1903.

Ḥillī, al-ʿAllāma al-Ḥasan ibn Yūsuf al-. *Mukhtalaf al-shīʿa fī aḥkām al-sharīʿa*. 10 vols. Qum: Markaz al-Abḥāth wa-l-Dirāsāt al-Islāmiyya, 1991/92.

Ḥnānishoʿ I. *Judicial Decisions*. Published as *Richterliche Urteile des Patriarchen Chenânîschô*. In *Syrische Rechtsbücher*, edited and translated by Eduard Sachau, vol. 2, 1–51.

Ibn Abī Shayba, ʿAbd Allāh ibn Muḥammad. *Al-Muṣannaf*. Edited by Muḥammad al-ʿAwwāma. 26 vols. Beirut: Dār Qurṭuba, 2006.

Ibn Abī Uṣaybiʿa. *ʿUyūn al-anbāʾ fī ṭabaqāt al-aṭibbāʾ*. Edited by Nizār Riḍā. Beirut: Dār Maktabat al-Ḥayāt, 1965.

Ibn Buṭlān, al-Mukhtār ibn al-Ḥasan. *Risāla jāmiʿa li-funūn nāfiʿa fī shirā al-raqīq wa-taqlīb al-ʿabīd*. In *Nawādir al-makhṭūṭāt*, vol. 4, edited by ʿAbd al-Salām Hārūn, 351–89. Cairo: Muṣṭafā al-Bābī al-Ḥalabī, 1973.

Ibn Ḥabīb, Abū Jaʿfar Muḥammad. *Kitāb al-Muḥbir*. Edited by Ilse Lichtenstadter. Beirut: Dār al-Āfāq al-Jadīda, n.d.

Ibn Isḥāq. *The Life of Muhammad*. Translated by A. Guillaume. Oxford: Oxford University Press, 1955.

Ibn Qudāma, Muwaffaq al-Dīn ʿAbdallāh ibn Aḥmad. *Al-Mughnī*. Edited by ʿAbdallāh ibn ʿAbd al-Muḥsin al-Turkī and ʿAbd al-Fattāḥ Muḥammad al-Ḥulw. 15 vols. Cairo: Hajr, 1986.

Ibn al-Sāʿī. *Consorts of the Caliphs*. Edited and translated by Shawkat M. Toorawa et al. New York: New York University Press, 2015.

Ibn al-Ṭayyib, Abū al-Faraj ʿAbdallāh. *Fiqh al-naṣrāniyya*. Published as *Fiqh an-naṣrānīya: "Das Recht der Christenheit."* Edited and translated by W. Hoenerbach and O. Spies. 2 vols. in 4. Louvain: Imprimerie orientaliste, 1956.

———. *Masʾala fī al-tazwīj wa-l-ṭalāq*. MS Vatican Arabic 157, folios 91r–92v. MS Mardin Chaldean Cathedral 333, folios 187v–191v.

Ishoʿbarnun. *Law Book*. Published as *Gesetzbuch des Patriarchen Jesubarnun*. In *Syrische Rechtsbücher*, edited and translated by Eduard Sachau, vol. 2, 119–77.

———. *Letter to Isaac, Periodeutes of Bet Qatraye*. MS Birmingham Mingana Syriac 587, folios 360r–367v.

———. *Letter to Makarios, Deacon of Hira*. MS Birmingham Mingana Syriac 586, folios 431v–441v.

———. *The Selected Questions of Ishō bar Nūn on the Pentateuch*. Introduced, edited, translated, and with commentary by Ernest G. Clarke. Leiden: Brill, 1962.

Ishoʿbokt. *Jurisprudential Corpus*. Published as *Corpus juris des persischen Erzbischofs Jesubocht*. In *Syrische Rechtsbücher*, edited and translated by Eduard Sachau, vol. 3, 1–201.

Ishoʿyahb III of Adiabene. "Ishoʿyahb III of Adiabene's Letters to the

Qataris." Edited and translated by Mario Kozah. In *An Anthology of Syriac Writers from Qatar in the Seventh Century*, edited by Kozah et al., 43–88. Piscataway, N.J.: Gorgias Press, 2015.

———. *Letters*. Published as *Liber epistularum*. Edited and translated by Rubens Duval. 2 vols. Leipzig: Otto Harrassowitz, 1904–5.

Jacob of Edessa. *Canonical Resolutions*. Published as *Jacobi Edesseni resolutiones canonicæ*. In *Dissertatio de Syrorum fide et disciplina in re Eucharistica*, edited and translated by Thomas Joseph Lamy, 98–171. Louvain: Vanlinthout, 1859.

———. *Responsa and Canons*. MS Mardin Church of the Forty Martyrs 310, folios 195r–216v.

Jāḥiẓ, Abū ʿUthmān al-. *Thalāth rasāʾil*. Edited by J. Finkel. Cairo: al-Maṭbaʿa al-Salafiyya, 1926.

Al-Jāmiʿ wujūh al-īmān. MS British Library Oriental 4950, folios 1r–197v.

Juwaynī, Imām al-Ḥaramayn al-. *Nihāyat al-maṭlab fī dirāyat al-madhhab*. Edited by ʿAbd al-ʿAẓīm Maḥmūd al-Dīb. 21 vols. Jidda: Dār al-Minhāj lil-Nashr wa-l-Tawzīʿ, 2007.

Kaufhold, Hubert, and Walter Selb, eds. and trans. *Das syrisch-römische Rechtsbuch*. 3 vols. Vienna: Verlag der Österreichischen Akademie der Wissenschaften, 2002.

Khoury, Raif Georges, ed. *Chrestomathie de papyrologie arabe*. Leiden: Brill, 1993.

Kraemer, Casper J., Jr., ed. *Excavations at Nessana*. Vol. 3, *Non-Literary Papyri*. Princeton, N.J.: Princeton University Press, 1958.

Kulaynī, Muḥammad ibn Yaʿqūb al-. *Furūʿ al-kāfī*. Beirut: Muʾassasat al-Aʿlamī lil-Maṭbūʿāt, 2005.

Mālik ibn Anas. *Al-Muwaṭṭaʾ*. Edited by Abū Usāma Salīm ibn ʿĪd al-Hilālī al-Salafī. 5 vols. Dubai: Majmūʿat al-Furqān al-Tijāriyya, 2003.

Marghīnānī, ʿAlī ibn Abī Bakr al-. *Al-Hidāya sharḥ bidāyat al-mubtadī*. Edited by Muḥammad Muḥammad Tāmir and Ḥāfiẓ ʿĀshūr Ḥāfiẓ. 4 vols. Cairo: Dār al-Salām, 2000.

Mārī ibn Sulaymān, ʿAmr ibn Mattā, and Ṣalībā ibn Yūḥannā. *Akhbār faṭārikat kursī al-mashriq min kitāb al-majdal*. Edited by Enrico Gismondi. 2 vols. Rome: C. de Luigi, 1896–99.

Michael the Syrian. *Chronique de Michel le Syrien, patriarche jacobite d'Antioche (1166–1199)*. Edited and translated by J.-B. Chabot. 4 vols. Paris: Ernest Leroux, 1899–1910.

Miller, Patricia Cox, ed. and trans. *Women in Early Christianity: Translations from Greek Texts*. Washington, D.C.: Catholic University of America Press, 2005.

Moriggi, Marco. *A Corpus of Syriac Incantation Bowls: Syriac Magical Texts from Late-Antique Mesopotamia.* Leiden: Brill, 2014.

Nau, F. "Littérature canonique syriaque inédite." *Revue de l'Orient chrétien* 14 (1909): 1–49, 113–30.

Overbeck, J., ed. *S. Ephraemi Syri, Rabulae episcopi Edesseni, Balaei aliorumque: Opera selecta.* Oxford: E typographeo Clarendoniano, 1865.

Percival, Henry R., trans. *The Seven Ecumenical Councils of the Undivided Church.* New York: Charles Scribner's Sons, 1900.

Qāḍī al-Nuʿmān, al-. *Daʿāʾim al-islām.* Edited by Āṣif ibn ʿAlī Aṣghar Fayḍī. 2 vols. Beirut: Dār al-Aḍwāʾ, 1991.

Qifṭī, ʿAlī ibn Yūsuf al-. *Kitāb ikhbār al-ʿulamāʾ bi-akhbār al-ḥukamāʾ.* Edited by Muḥammad Amīn al-Khānjī. Muḥāfaẓat Miṣr: Maṭbaʿat al-Saʿāda, 1908.

Sachau, Eduard, ed. and trans. *Syrische Rechtsbücher.* 3 vols. Berlin: Georg Reimer, 1907–14.

Saḥnūn ibn Saʿīd al-Tanūkhī. *Al-Mudawwana al-kubrā.* 4 vols. Beirut: Dār al-Kutub al-ʿIlmiyya, 1994.

Sauget, Joseph-Marie. "Décisions canoniques du Patriarche Išoʿbarnūn encore inédites." *Apollinaris* 35 (1962): 259–65.

Scher, Addai, ed. and trans. *Chronicle of Seert.* Published as *Histoire nestorienne inédite (Chronique de Séert).* In *Patrologia Orientalis* 4 (1908): 213–313; 5 (1910): 217–344; 7 (1911): 97–203; and 13 (1919): 437–639.

Shāfiʿī, Muḥammad ibn Idrīs al-. *Al-Umm.* Edited by Rifʿat Fawzī ʿAbd al-Muṭṭalib. 11 vols. Al-Manṣūra, Egypt: Dār al-Wafāʾ, 2008.

Shaked, Shaul, James Nathan Ford, and Siam Bhayro, eds. *Aramaic Bowl Spells: Jewish Babylonian Aramaic Bowls.* Vol. 1, *Manuscripts in the Schøyen Collection.* Leiden: Brill, 2013.

Shaybānī, Muḥammad ibn al-Ḥasan al-. *Al-Aṣl.* Edited by Mehmet Boynukalın. 13 vols. Qatar: Wizārat al-Awqāf, 2012.

———. *Al-Ḥujja ʿalā ahl al-Madīna.* Edited by Mahdī Ḥasan al-Kaylānī. 4 vols. Beirut: ʿĀlam al-Kutub, n.d.

Shaybānī, Muḥammad ibn al-Ḥasan al-, and Ibn Ḥajar al-ʿAsqalānī. *Kitāb al-Āthār wa-yalīhi al-Īthār bi-maʿrifat ruwāt al-Āthār.* Karachi: Idārat al-Qurʾān wa-l-ʿUlūm al-Islāmiyya, 1998/99.

Shemʿon of Revardashir. *Law of Inheritance.* Published as *Erbrecht oder Canones des persischen Erzbischofs Simeon.* In *Syrische Rechtsbücher,* edited and translated by Eduard Sachau, vol. 3, 203–53.

Suyūṭī, Jalāl al-Dīn al-. *Al-Mustaẓraf min akhbār al-jawārī.* Edited by Ṣalāḥ al-Dīn al-Munajjid. Beirut: Dār al-Kitāb al-Jadīd, 1967.

Ṭabarānī, Sulaymān ibn Aḥmad al-. *Al-Muʿjam al-kabīr.* Edited by Ḥamdī

ʿAbd al-Majīd al-Salafī. 13 vols. Baghdad: al-Dār al-ʿArabiyya lil-Ṭibāʿa, 1978.

Ṭabarī, Muḥammad ibn Jarīr al-. *Taʾrīkh al-rusul wa-l-mulūk*. Edited by M. J. de Goeje et al. 15 vols. Leiden: Brill, 1879–1901.

Thaʿālibī, Abū Manṣūr ʿAbd al-Malik ibn Muḥammad al-. *Ghurar akhbār mulūk al-furs wa-siyarihim/Histoire des rois des perses*. Edited by H. Zotenberg. Paris: Imprimerie nationale, 1900.

Theodoret of Cyrrhus. *Correspondance*. Edited and translated by Yvan Azéma. 4 vols. Paris: Éditions du Cerf, 1955.

Timothy I. *Law Book*. Published as *Gesetzbuch des Patriarchen Timotheos*. In *Syrische Rechtsbücher*, edited and translated by Eduard Sachau, vol. 2, 53–117. Excerpts in MS Mount Sinai St. Catherine's Monastery Syriac 82, folios 65v–73r. MS Cambridge Additional 2023, folios 25v–34r.

———. *Letters 1–39*. Published as *Epistulae I*. Edited and translated by Oscar Braun. 2 vols. Paris and Leipzig: Peeters, 1914–15.

Ṭūsī, Shaykh al-Ṭāʾifa Muḥammad ibn al-Ḥasan al-. *Al-Mabsūṭ fī fiqh al-imāmiyya*. Edited by Muḥammad al-Bāqir al-Bihbūdī. 8 vols. Tehran: al-Maṭbaʿa al-Murtaḍawiyya li-Iḥyāʾ al-Āthār al-Jaʿfariyya, 1967/68.

Vööbus, Arthur, ed. and trans. *The Canons Ascribed to Mārūtā of Maipherqaṭ and Related Sources*. 2 vols. Louvain: Peeters, 1982.

———. *The Synodicon in the West Syrian Tradition*. 2 vols. in 4. Louvain: Secrétariat du CorpusSCO, 1975–76.

Williams, A. V., ed. and trans. *The Pahlavi Rivāyat Accompanying the Dādestān ī Dēnīg*. 2 vols. Copenhagen: Royal Danish Academy of Sciences and Letters, 1990.

Yāqūt ibn ʿAbdallāh al-Ḥamawī. *Muʿjam al-buldān*. 5 vols. Beirut: Dār Ṣādir, 1977.

Yawnon the Bishop. *Letter to the Periodeutes Theodore*. MS Cambridge Additional 2023, folios 254v–259r.

Yoḥannān IV bar Abgārē (Yūḥannā ibn ʿĪsā al-Jāthalīq). *Kitāb ilā rajul min ahl al-Yaman*. MS Vatican Arabic 157, folios 85v–90v. MS Mardin Chaldean Cathedral 333, folios 177v–187v.

Secondary Literature

Abbott, Nabia. "Arabic Marriage Contracts Among Copts." *Zeitschrift der Deutschen Morgenländischen Gesellschaft* 95 (1941): 59–81.

Ahmed, Leila. *Women and Gender in Islam: Historical Roots of a Modern Debate*. New Haven, Conn.: Yale University Press, 1993.

Altuntek, N. Serpil. "Bone and Flesh, Seed and Soil: Patriliny by Father's Brother's Daughter Marriage." *Ethnology* 45.1 (2006): 59–70.

Andrés-Toledo, Miguel Ángel. "Primary Sources: Avestan and Pahlavi." In Stausberg, Vevaina, and Tessmann, *Wiley Blackwell Companion to Zoroastrianism*, 519–28.

Anthony, Sean W. "The Mahdī and the Treasures of Ṭālaqān." *Arabica* 59 (2012): 459–83.

Aptowitzer, Victor. *Die syrischen Rechtsbücher und das mosaisch-talmudische Recht*. Vienna: A. Hölder, 1909.

Arnaoutoglou, Ilias. "Marital Disputes in Greco-Roman Egypt." *Journal of Juristic Papyrology* 25 (1995): 11–28.

Arjava, Antti. *Women and Law in Late Antiquity*. Oxford: Clarendon Press, 1996.

Astren, Fred. "Islamic Contexts of Medieval Karaism." In *Karaite Judaism: A Guide to Its History and Literary Sources*, edited by Meira Polliack, 145–77. Leiden: Brill, 2003.

Aydin, Emanuel. *Die Ehe bei den Syrisch-Orthodoxen (die Suryoye)*. Vienna: Stiftung St. Ephrem zur Förderung der syrisch-orthodoxen Kultur, 1995.

Ayoub, Mahmoud. "Dhimmah in Qur'an and Hadith." *Arab Studies Quarterly* 5.2 (1983): 172–82.

Azad, Arezou. "Living Happily Ever After: Fraternal Polyandry, Taxes and 'the House' in Early Islamic Bactria." *Bulletin of the School of Oriental and African Studies* 79.1 (2016): 33–56.

Bagnall, Roger S. "Church, State and Divorce in Late Roman Egypt." In *Florilegium Columbianum: Essays in Honor of Paul Oskar Kristeller*, edited by Karl-Ludwig Selig and Robert Somerville, 41–61. New York: Italica Press, 1987.

———. *Egypt in Late Antiquity*. Princeton, N.J.: Princeton University Press, 1993.

Baum, Wilhelm, and Dietmar W. Winkler. *The Church of the East: A Concise History*. London: Routledge, 2003.

Baumer, Christoph. *The Church of the East: An Illustrated History of Assyrian Christianity*. London: I. B. Tauris, 2006.

Beaucamp, Joëlle. "Byzantine Egypt and Imperial Law." In *Egypt in the Byzantine World*, edited by Roger S. Bagnall, 271–87. Cambridge: Cambridge University Press, 2007.

Becker, Adam H. "The Comparative Study of 'Scholasticism' in Late Antique Mesopotamia: Rabbis and East Syrians." *Association for Jewish Studies Review* 34.1 (2010): 91–113.

———. "The Dynamic Reception of Theodore of Mopsuestia in the Sixth Century: Greek, Syriac, and Latin." In *Greek Literature in Late Antiquity: Dynamism, Didacticism, Classicism*, edited by Scott Fitzgerald Johnson, 29–47. Aldershot, UK: Ashgate, 2006.

——. *Fear of God and the Beginning of Wisdom: The School of Nisibis and Christian Scholastic Culture in Late Antique Mesopotamia*. Philadelphia: University of Pennsylvania Press, 2006.

Bennison, Amira K. *The Great Caliphs: The Golden Age of the ʿAbbasid Empire*. New Haven, Conn.: Yale University Press, 2010.

Berkey, Jonathan P. *The Formation of Islam: Religion and Society in the Near East, 600–1800*. Cambridge: Cambridge University Press, 2003.

Berti, Vittorio. *Vita e studi di Timoteo I, patriarca christiano di Baghdad*. Paris: Association pour l'avancement des études iraniennes, 2009.

Bentley, Jerry H. "Hemispheric Integration, 500–1500 C.E." *Journal of World History* 9.2 (1998): 237–54.

Biale, Rachel. *Women and Jewish Law*. New York: Schocken Books, 1984.

Bidawid, Raphaël J. *Les lettres du patriarche nestorien Timothée I*. Vatican City: Biblioteca Apostolica Vaticana, 1956.

Bloom, Jonathan M. *Paper Before Print: The History and Impact of Paper in the Islamic World*. New Haven, Conn.: Yale University Press, 2001.

Bonner, Michael. "The Waning of Empire, 861–945." In *The New Cambridge History of Islam*. Vol. 1, *The Formation of the Islamic World: Sixth to Eleventh Centuries*, edited by Chase Robinson, 305–59. Cambridge: Cambridge University Press, 2010.

Borrut, Antoine. *Entre mémoire et pouvoir: L'espace syrien sous les derniers Omeyyades et les premiers Abbassides*. Leiden: Brill, 2011.

Bourdieu, Pierre. *Outline of a Theory of Practice*. Translated by Richard Nice. Cambridge: Cambridge University Press, 1977.

Bray, Julia. "Men, Women and Slaves in Abbasid Society." In *Gender in the Early Medieval World: East and West, 300–900*, edited by Leslie Brubaker and Julia M. H. Smith, 121–46. Cambridge: Cambridge University Press, 2004.

Brock, Sebastian P. "The Baptismal Anointings According to the Anonymous *Expositio officiorum*." *Hugoye* 1.1 (1998): 5–17.

——. "The Bridal Chamber of Light: A Distinctive Feature of the Syriac Liturgical Tradition." *The Harp* 18 (2005): 179–91.

——. "Early Syrian Asceticism." *Numen* 20.1 (1973): 1–19.

——. "Gewargis of Arbela, Psuedo-." In Brock et al., *Gorgias Encyclopedia of the Syriac Heritage*, 176.

——. "The 'Nestorian' Church: A Lamentable Misnomer." *Bulletin of the John Rylands Library* 78.3 (1996): 23–35.

——. "North Mesopotamia in the Late Seventh Century: Book XV of John Bar Penkāyē's *Rīš Mellē*." *Jerusalem Studies in Arabic and Islam* 9 (1987): 51–75.

———. "Regulations for an Association of Artisans from the Late Sasanian or Early Arab Period." In *Transformations of Late Antiquity: Essays for Peter Brown*, edited by Philip Rousseau and Manolis Papoutsakis, 51–62. Farnham, UK: Ashgate, 2009.

———. Review of Kaufhold and Selb, *Das syrisch-römische Rechtsbuch. Journal of Semitic Studies* 52 (2007): 161–64.

Brock, Sebastian P., and Susan Ashbrook Harvey. *Holy Women of the Syrian Orient.* Updated edition. Berkeley: University of California Press, 1987.

Brock, Sebastian P., et al., eds. *Gorgias Encyclopedic Dictionary of the Syriac Heritage.* Piscataway, N.J.: Gorgias Press, 2011.

Brockopp, Jonathan E. *Early Mālikī Law: Ibn ʿAbd al-Ḥakam and His Major Compendium of Jurisprudence.* Leiden: Brill, 2000.

Brody, Robert. *The Geonim of Babylonia and the Shaping of Medieval Jewish Culture.* New Haven, Conn.: Yale University Press, 1998.

Brown, Peter. *The Body and Society: Men, Women, and Sexual Renunciation in Early Christianity.* New York: Columbia University Press, 1988.

———. "Late Antiquity." In *A History of Private Life.* Vol. 1, *From Pagan Rome to Byzantium*, edited by Paul Veyne, 235–312. Cambridge, Mass.: Harvard University Press, 1987.

Brubaker, Rogers. *Grounds for Difference.* Cambridge, Mass.: Harvard University Press, 2015.

Brundage, James A. *Law, Sex, and Christian Society in Medieval Europe.* Chicago: University of Chicago Press, 1987.

Bruns, Peter. "Die christliche Ehe im Synodalrecht der Kirche des Ostens." In *Il matrimonio dei cristiani: Esegesi biblica e diritto romano*, 197–209. Rome: Institutum patristicum Augustinianum, 2009.

Bulliet, Richard W. *Conversion to Islam in the Medieval Period: An Essay in Quantitative History.* Cambridge, Mass.: Harvard University Press, 1979.

Burbank, Jane, and Frederick Cooper. *Empires in World History: Power and the Politics of Difference.* Princeton, N.J.: Princeton University Press, 2011.

Butts, Aaron M. "Ibn al-Ṭayyib." In Brock et al., *Gorgias Encyclopedic Dictionary of the Syriac Heritage*, 206–7.

Cabrol, Cécile. *Les secrétaires nestoriens à Bagdad, 762–1258 AD.* Beirut: Université Saint-Joseph, 2012.

Cameron, Averil. *The Mediterranean World in Late Antiquity: AD 395–600.* London: Routledge, 1993.

Caner, Daniel F. "'Not of This World': The Invention of Monasticism." In *A Companion to Late Antiquity*, edited by Philip Rousseau, 588–600. Chichester: Wiley-Blackwell, 2009.

Carlson, Thomas A. "Contours of Conversion: The Geography of Islamization in Syria, 600–1500." *Journal of the American Oriental Society* 135.4 (2015): 791–816.

Carter, R. A. "Christianity in the Gulf During the First Centuries of Islam." *Arabian Archaeology and Epigraphy* 19 (2008): 71–108.

Caswell, F. Matthew. *The Slave Girls of Baghdad: The Qiyān in the Early Abbasid Era*. London: I. B. Tauris, 2011.

El Cheikh, Nadia Maria. *Women, Islam, and Abbasid Identity*. Cambridge, Mass.: Harvard University Press, 2015.

Choksy, Jamsheed K. *Conflict and Cooperation: Zoroastrian Subalterns and Muslim Elites in Medieval Iranian Society*. New York: Columbia University Press, 1997.

Cohen, Mark R. *Jewish Self-Government in Medieval Egypt: The Origins of the Office of Head of the Jews, ca. 1065–1126*. Princeton, N.J.: Princeton University Press, 1980.

Contadini, Anna. *A World of Beasts: A Thirteenth-Century Illustrated Arabic Book on Animals (the "Kitāb Naʿt al-Ḥayawān") in the Ibn Bakhtīshūʿ Tradition*. Leiden: Brill, 2012.

Cook, Michael A. "The Origins of *Kalām*." *Bulletin of the School of Oriental and African Studies* 43.1 (1980): 32–43.

Cotton, Hannah M. "Change and Continuity in Late Legal Papyri from Palaestina Tertia: *Nomos Hellênikos* and *Ethos Rômaikon*." In *Jews, Christians, and the Roman Empire: The Poetics of Power in Late Antiquity*, edited by Natalie B. Dohrmann and Annette Yoshiko Reed, 209–21. Philadelphia: University of Pennsylvania Press, 2013.

———. "The Rabbis and the Documents." In *Jews in a Graeco-Roman World*, edited by Martin Goodman, 167–79. Oxford: Clarendon Press, 1998.

Crone, Patricia. "The First-Century Concept of '*Hiǧra*.'" *Arabica* 41.3 (1994): 352–87.

———. *The Nativist Prophets of Early Islamic Iran: Rural Revolt and Local Zoroastrianism*. Cambridge: Cambridge University Press, 2012.

———. *Roman, Provincial and Islamic Law: The Origins of the Islamic Patronate*. Cambridge: Cambridge University Press, 1987.

———. *Slaves on Horses*. Cambridge: Cambridge University Press, 1980.

Dagron, Gilbert. "Minorités ethniques et religieuses dans l'Orient byzantin à la fin du Xe et au XIe siècle: L'immigration syrienne." *Travaux et mémoires* 6 (1976): 177–216.

Daryaee, Touraj. "Zoroastrianism Under Islamic Rule." In Stausberg, Vevaina, and Tessmann, *Wiley Blackwell Companion to Zoroastrianism*, 103–18.

Dauphin, Claudine. "Brothels, Baths and Babes: Prostitution in the Byzantine Holy Land." *Classics Ireland* 3 (1996): 47–72.

De Jong, Albert. *Traditions of the Magi: Zoroastrianism in Greek and Latin Literature.* Leiden: Brill, 1997.

Deming, Will. *Paul on Marriage and Celibacy: The Hellenistic Background of 1 Corinthians 7.* 2nd edition. Grand Rapids, Mich.: Eerdmans, 2004.

De Vries, Wilhelm. *Sakramententheologie bei den Nestorianern.* Rome: Pont. Institutum Orientalium Studiorum, 1947.

Dickens, Mark. "Patriarch Timothy I and the Metropolitan of the Turks." *Journal of the Royal Asiatic Society*, 3rd series 20.2 (2010): 117–39.

Dols, Michael W. *The Black Death in the Middle East.* Princeton, N.J.: Princeton University Press, 1977.

———. "The Origins of the Islamic Hospital: Myth and Reality." *Bulletin of the History of Medicine* 61.3 (1987): 367–90.

Donner, Fred M. "From Believers to Muslims: Confessional Self-Identity in the Early Islamic Community." *Al-Abhath* 50–51 (2002–3): 9–53.

———. *Muhammad and the Believers at the Origins of Islam.* Cambridge, Mass.: Belknap Press, 2010.

Duby, Georges. *The Knight, the Lady, and the Priest: The Making of Modern Marriage in Medieval France.* Translated by Barbara Bray. New York: Pantheon Books, 1983.

Edakalathur, Louis. *The Theology of Marriage in the East Syrian Tradition.* Rome: Mar Thoma Yogam, 1994.

Edelby, Néophyte. "The Legislative Autonomy of Christians in the Islamic World." Translated by Bruce Inksetter. In *Muslims and Others in Early Islamic Society*, edited by Robert Hoyland, 37–82. Aldershot, UK: Ashgate, 2004.

Fattal, Antoine. *Le statut légal des non-musulmans en pays d'Islam.* Beirut: Impr. Catholique, 1958.

Feghali, J. "Origin et formation du mariage dans le droit des eglises de langue syriaque." *L'année canonique* 17 (1973): 413–31.

Fiey, Jean Maurice. *Chrétiens syriaques sous les Abbassides surtout à Bagdad (749–1258).* Louvain: Secrétariat du CorpusSCO, 1980.

———. "Diocèses syriens orientaux du golf Persique." In *Mémorial Mgr Gabriel Khouri-Sarkis*, 177–219. Louvain: Impr. orientaliste, 1969.

———. *Pour un Oriens Christianus novus: Répertoire des diocèses Syriaques orientaux et occidentaux.* Stuttgart: Franz Steiner Verlag, 1991.

Firestone, Reuven. "Prophethood, Marriageable Consanguinity, and Text: The Problem of Abraham and Sarah's Kinship Relationship and the

Response of Jewish and Islamic Exegetes." *Jewish Quarterly Review* 83 (1993): 331–47.

Fisher, Greg. *Between Empires: Arabs, Romans, and Sasanians in Late Antiquity*. Oxford: Oxford University Press, 2011.

Foss, Clive. "A Syrian Coinage of Muʿawiya?" *Revue Numismatique* 158 (2002): 353–65.

Fox, Robin. *Kinship and Marriage: An Anthropological Perspective*. New edition. Cambridge: Cambridge University Press, 1983.

Frandsen, Paul John. *Incestuous and Close-Kin Marriage in Ancient Egypt and Persia: An Examination of the Evidence*. Copenhagen: Museum Tusculanum Press, 2009.

Friedman, Mordechai A. "Divorce upon the Wife's Demand as Reflected in Manuscripts from the Cairo Geniza." *Jewish Law Annual* 4 (1981): 103–27.

———. *Jewish Marriage in Palestine: A Cairo Geniza Study*. 2 vols. Tel Aviv: Tel-Aviv University, the Chaim Rosenberg School of Jewish Studies, 1980–81.

———. "Polygyny in Jewish Tradition and Practice: New Sources from the Cairo Geniza." *Proceedings of the American Academy for Jewish Research* 49 (1982): 33–68.

———. "The Ransom-Divorce: Divorce Proceedings Initiated by the Wife in Medieval Jewish Practice." *Israel Oriental Studies* 6 (1976): 288–307.

Friedmann, Yohanan. *Tolerance and Coercion in Islam: Interfaith Relations in the Muslim Tradition*. Cambridge: Cambridge University Press, 2003.

Gager, John G. *Curse Tablets and Binding Spells from the Ancient World*. Oxford: Oxford University Press, 1992.

Gellens, Sam I. "The Search for Knowledge in Medieval Muslim Societies: A Comparative Approach." In *Muslim Travellers: Pilgrimage, Migration, and the Religious Imagination*, edited by Dale Eickelman and James Piscatori, 50–65. Berkeley: University of California Press, 1990.

Geller, Markham J. "Jesus' Theurgic Powers: Parallels in the Talmud and Incantation Bowls." *Journal of Jewish Studies* 28.2 (1977): 141–55.

Ghanīma, Yūsuf. "Bukhtīshūʿ al-ṭabīb al-nasṭūrī wa-usratuhu." *Al-Mashriq* 8 (1905): 1097–1105.

Giardina, Andrea. "The Family in the Late Roman World." In *The Cambridge Ancient History*. Vol 14, *Late Antiquity: Empire and Successors A.D. 425–600*, edited by Averil Cameron and Bryan Ward-Perkins, 392–415. Cambridge: Cambridge University Press, 2001.

Gil, Moshe. "The Origins of the Karaites." In *Karaite Judaism: A Guide to Its History and Literary Sources*, edited by Meira Polliack, 73–118. Leiden: Brill, 2003.

Gillman, Ian, and Hans-Joachim Klimkeit. *Christians in Asia Before 1500*. New York: Routledge, 1999.

Goitein, S. D. *A Mediterranean Society*. Vol. 3, *The Family*. Berkeley: University of California Press, 1978.

Golinkin, David. "The Use of the Matronymic in Prayers for the Sick." *These Are the Names: Studies in Jewish Onomastics*. Vol. 3, edited by Aaron Demsky, 59–72. Ramat Gan: Bar-Ilan University Press, 2002.

Goody, Jack. *The Development of the Family and Marriage in Europe*. Cambridge: Cambridge University Press, 1983.

Gordon, Matthew S. *The Breaking of a Thousand Swords: A History of the Turkish Military of Samarra (A.H. 200–275/815–889 C.E.)*. Albany: SUNY Press, 2000.

———. "The Khāqānid Families of the Early ʿAbbasid Period." *Journal of the American Oriental Society* 121.2 (2001): 236–55.

Graf, Georg. *Geschichte der christlichen arabischen Literatur*. 5 vols. Vatican City: Biblioteca Apostolica Vaticana, 1944–53.

Greengus, Samuel. "The Old Babylonian Marriage Contract." *Journal of the American Oriental Society* 89.3 (1969): 505–32.

Griffith, Sidney H. "The Arabic Account of ʿAbd al-Masīḥ an-Nağrānī al-Ghassānī." *Le Muséon* 98 (1985): 331–74.

———. "Asceticism in the Church of Syria: The Hermeneutics of Early Syrian Monasticism." In *Asceticism*, edited by Vincent L. Wimbush and Richard Valantasis, 220–45. New York: Oxford University Press, 1995.

———. "Christians, Muslims, and Neo-Martyrs: Saints' Lives and Holy Land History." In *Sharing the Sacred: Religious Contacts and Conflicts in the Holy Land, First–Fifteenth Centuries CE*, edited by Arieh Kofsky and Guy G. Stroumsa, 163–207. Jerusalem: Yad Izhak Ben Zvi, 1998.

———. *The Church in the Shadow of the Mosque: Christians and Muslims in the World of Islam*. Princeton, N.J.: Princeton University Press, 2008.

———. "Free Will in Christian *Kalām*: Moshe bar Kepha Against the Teachings of the Muslims." *Le Muséon* 100 (1987): 143–59.

———. "'Melkites,' 'Jacobites' and the Christological Controversies in Arabic in Third/Ninth-Century Syria." In *Syrian Christians Under Islam: The First Thousand Years*, edited by David Thomas, 9–55. Leiden: Brill, 2001.

Grubbs, Judith Evans. *Law and Family in Late Antiquity: The Emperor Constantine's Marriage Legislation*. Oxford: Clarendon Press, 1995.

———. *Women and the Law in the Roman Empire: A Sourcebook on Marriage, Divorce and Widowhood*. London: Routledge, 2002.

Gutas, Dimitri. *Greek Thought, Arabic Culture: The Graeco-Arabic Trans-*

lation Movement in Baghdad and Early ʿAbbāsid Society (2nd–4th/8th–10th centuries). London: Routledge, 1998.

Gyselen, Rika. *Sasanian Seals and Sealings in the A. Saeedi Collection*. Louvain: Peeters, 2007.

———. "Les témoignages sigillographiques sur la présence chrétienne dans l'empire sassanide." In *Chrétiens en terre d'Iran: Implantation et acculturation*, edited by Rika Gyselen, 17–78. Paris: Association pour l'avancement des études iraniennes, 2006.

Hage, Wolfgang. *Die syrisch-jakobitische Kirche in frühislamischer Zeit*. Wiesbaden: Otto Harrassowitz, 1966.

Haldon, John. "The Works of Anastasius of Sinai: A Key Source for the History of Seventh-Century Mediterranean Society and Belief." In *The Byzantine and Early Islamic Near East*. Vol. 1, *Problems in the Literary Source Material*, edited by Averil Cameron and Lawrence I. Conrad, 107–47. Princeton, N.J.: Darwin Press, 1992.

Halevi, Leor. *Muhammad's Grave: Death Rites and the Making of Islamic Society*. New York: Columbia University Press, 2011.

Hallaq, Wael B. "Considerations on the Function and Character of Sunnī Legal Theory." *Journal of the American Oriental Society* 104.4 (1984): 679–89.

———. *The Origins and Evolution of Islamic Law*. Cambridge: Cambridge University Press, 2005.

———. *Sharīʿa: Theory, Practice, Transformations*. Cambridge: Cambridge University Press, 2009.

———. "Was al-Shafiʿi the Master Architect of Islamic Jurisprudence?" *International Journal of Middle East Studies* 25.4 (1993): 587–605.

Harper, Kyle. *From Shame to Sin: The Christian Transformation of Sexual Morality in Late Antiquity*. Cambridge, Mass.: Harvard University Press, 2013.

———. "Marriage and Family." In *The Oxford Handbook of Late Antiquity*, edited by Scott Fitzgerald Johnson, 667–714. Oxford: Oxford University Press, 2012.

———. *Slavery in the Late Roman World, AD 275–425*. Cambridge: Cambridge University Press, 2011.

Harries, Jill. "Roman Law and Legal Culture." In *The Oxford Handbook of Late Antiquity*, edited by Scott Fitzgerald Johnson, 789–814. Oxford: Oxford University Press, 2012.

Hawting, G. R. *The First Dynasty of Islam*. 2nd edition. London: Routledge, 2000.

Hayes, Christine E. *Gentile Impurities and Jewish Identities: Intermarriage and Conversion from the Bible to the Talmud*. Oxford: Oxford University Press, 2002.

Healey, John F. "The Christians of Qatar in the 7th Century A.D." In *Studies in Honour of Clifford Edmund Bosworth*, vol. 1, edited by Ian Richard Netton, 222–37. Leiden: Brill, 2000.

Heimgartner, Martin. "Timothy I." In *Christian-Muslim Relations: A Bibliographical History*. Vol. 1, *(600–900)*, edited by David Thomas and Barbara Roggema, 515–19. Leiden: Brill, 2009.

Heitty, Abd al-Kareem al-. "The Contrasting Spheres of Free Women and *jawārī* in the Literary Life of the Early ʿAbbāsid Caliphate." *Al-Masāq* 3 (1990): 31–51.

Herlihy, David. *Medieval Households*. Cambridge, Mass.: Harvard University Press, 1985.

El-Hibri, Tayeb. "The Empire in Iraq, 763–861." In *The New Cambridge History of Islam*. Vol. 1, *The Formation of the Islamic World: Sixth to Eleventh Centuries*, edited by Chase Robinson, 269–304. Cambridge: Cambridge University Press, 2010.

Hofer, Nathan. *The Popularisation of Sufism in Ayyubid and Mamluk Egypt*, 1173–1325. Edinburgh: Edinburgh University Press, 2015.

Holy, Ladislav. *Kinship, Honour and Solidarity: Cousin Marriage in the Middle East*. Manchester: Manchester University Press, 1989.

Hoyland, Robert G. "The Earliest Attestation of the *Dhimma* of God and His Messenger and the Rediscovery of P. Nessana 77 (60s AH/680 CE)." In *Islamic Cultures, Islamic Contexts: Essays in Honor of Professor Patricia Crone*, edited by Behnam Sadeghi et al., 51–71. Leiden: Brill, 2015.

———. "Early Islam as a Late Antique Religion." In *The Oxford Handbook of Late Antiquity*, edited by Scott Fitzgerald Johnson, 1053–77. Oxford: Oxford University Press, 2012.

———. *In God's Path: The Arab Conquests and the Creation of an Islamic Empire*. Oxford: Oxford University Press, 2014.

———. "New Documentary Texts and the Early Islamic State." *Bulletin of the School of Oriental and African Studies* 69.3 (2006): 395–416.

———. Review of Donner, *Muhammad and the Believers at the Origins of Islam*. *International Journal of Middle East Studies* 44.3 (2012): 573–76.

———. *Seeing Islam as Others Saw It: A Survey and Evaluation of Christian, Jewish and Zoroastrian Writings on Early Islam*. Princeton, N.J.: Darwin Press, 1997.

Humfress, Caroline. "Law and Legal Practice in the Age of Justinian." In *The Cambridge Companion to the Age of Justinian*, edited by Michael Maas, 161–84. Cambridge: Cambridge University Press, 2005.

Hutter, Manfred. "Mār Abā and the Impact of Zoroastrianism on Christianity in the 6th Century." In *Religious Themes and Texts of Pre-Islamic Iran*, edited by Carlo G. Cereti, Mauro Maggi, and Elio Provasi, 167–73. Wiesbaden: Dr. Ludwig Reichert Verlag, 2003.

Imber, Colin. *The Ottoman Empire, 1300–1650: The Structure of Power.* New York: Palgrave Macmillan, 2002.

———. Review of Tucker, *In the House of the Law: Gender and Islamic Law in Ottoman Syria and Palestine. British Journal of Middle Eastern Studies* 26.2 (1999): 310–11.

Jackson, Peter. "The Mongols and the Faith of the Conquered." In *Mongols, Turks and Others: Eurasian Nomads and the Sedentary World*, edited by Reuven Amitai and Michal Biran, 235–90. Leiden: Brill, 2005.

———. *The Mongols and the Islamic World: From Conquest to Conversion.* New Haven, Conn.: Yale University Press, 2017.

Jany, János. "Criminal Justice in Sasanian Persia." *Iranica Antiqua* 42 (2007): 347–86.

Johns, Jeremy. "Archaeology and the History of Early Islam: The First Seventy Years." *Journal of the Economic and Social History of the Orient* 46 (2003): 411–36.

Johnson, Luke Timothy. "Law in Early Christianity." In *Christianity and Law: An Introduction*, edited by John Witte Jr. and Frank S. Alexander, 53–69. Cambridge: Cambridge University Press, 2003.

Just, Roger. *Women in Athenian Law and Life.* London: Routledge, 1989.

Kalisa, Chantal. *Violence in Francophone African and Caribbean Women's Literature.* Lincoln: University of Nebraska Press, 2009.

Kasdan, Leonard, and Robert F. Murphy. "The Structure of Parallel Cousin Marriage." *American Anthropologist*, new series 61.1 (1959): 17–29.

Kaufhold, Hubert. Introduction to ʿAbdishoʿ bar Brikā, *The Nomocanon of Abdisho of Nisibis: A Facsimile Edition of MS 64 from the Collection of the Church of the East in Trissur*, edited by István Perczel. 2nd edition, xi–xxiii. Piscataway, N.J: Gorgias Press, 2009.

———. "Islamisches Erbrecht in christlich-syrischer Überlieferung." *Oriens Christianus* 59 (1975): 19–35.

———. *Die Rechtssammlung des Gabriel von Baṣra und ihr Verhältnis zu den anderen juristischen Sammelwerken der Nestorianer.* Berlin: J. Schweitzer Verlag, 1976.

———. "Der Richter in den syrischen Rechtsquellen: Zum Einfluß islamischen Rechts auf die christlich-orientalische Rechtsliteratur." *Oriens Christianus* 68 (1984): 91–113.

———. "Römisch-byzantinisches Recht in den kirchen syrischer Tradition." In *The Meeting of Eastern and Western Canons: Proceedings of the International Congress*, edited by Raffaele Coppola, 133–64. Bari: Cacucci, 1994.

———. "Sources of Canon Law in the Eastern Churches." In *The History of Byzantine and Eastern Canon Law to 1500*, edited by Wilfried Hartmann and Kenneth Pennington, 215–342. Washington, D.C.: Catholic University of America Press, 2012.

———. *Syrische Texte zum islamischen Recht: Das dem nestorianischen Katholikos Johannes V. bar Abgārē zugeschriebene Rechtsbuch*. Munich: Verlag der bayerischen Akademie der Wissenschaften, 1971.

———. "Über die Entstehung der syrischen Texte zum islamischen Recht." *Oriens Christianus* 69 (1985): 54–72.

———. "Ein weiteres Rechtsbuch der Nestorianer—das Erbrecht des Johannes?" In *Gedächtnisschrift für Wolfgang Kunkel*, edited by Dieter Nörr and Dieter Simon, 103–16. Frankfurt: Vittorio Klostermann, 1984.

Kennedy, Hugh. "The Feeding of the Five Hundred Thousand: Cities and Agriculture in Early Islamic Mesopotamia." *Iraq* 73 (2011): 177–99.

———. "The Late ʿAbbasid Pattern, 945–1050." In *The New Cambridge History of Islam*. Vol. 1, *The Formation of the Islamic World: Sixth to Eleventh Centuries*, edited by Chase Robinson, 360–93. Cambridge: Cambridge University Press, 2010.

———. *The Prophet and the Age of the Caliphates: The Islamic Near East from the Sixth to the Eleventh Century*. Harlow, UK: Longman, 1986.

———. *When Baghdad Ruled the Muslim World: The Rise and Fall of Islam's Greatest Dynasty*. Cambridge, Mass.: Da Capo Press, 2009.

Kennet, Derek. "The Decline of Eastern Arabia in the Sasanian Period." *Arabian Archaeology and Epigraphy* 18 (2007): 86–122.

———. "Sasanian Coins from ʿUmān and Baḥrain." In *Current Research in Sasanian Archaeology, Art and History*, edited by Derek Kennet and Paul Luft, 55–64. Oxford: Archaeopress, 2008.

Khadra, Hanna. "Le Nomocanon de Bar Hebraeus: Son importance juridique entre les sources chrétiennes et les sources musulmanes." PhD diss., Pontifical Lateran University, 2005.

Khan, Geoffrey. "Newly Discovered Arabic Documents from Early Abbasid Khurasan." In *From al-Andalus to Khurasan: Documents from the Medieval Muslim World*, edited by Petra M. Sijpesteijn et al., 201–15. Leiden: Brill, 2007.

Kiel, Yishai. "The Systematization of Penitence in Zoroastrianism in Light of Rabbinic and Islamic Literature." *Bulletin of the Asia Institute*, new series 22 (2008): 119–35.

Koltun-Fromm, Naomi. *Hermeneutics of Holiness: Ancient Jewish and*

Christian Notions of Sexuality and Religious Community. Oxford: Oxford University Press, 2010.

Kraemer, Joel L. "Women Speak for Themselves." In *The Cambridge Genizah Collections: Their Contents and Significance*, edited by Stefan C. Reif, 178–216. Cambridge: Cambridge University Press, 2002.

Krakowski, Eve. *Coming of Age in Medieval Egypt: Female Adolescence, Jewish Law, and Ordinary Culture*. Princeton, N.J.: Princeton University Press, 2017.

Kreyenbroek, Philip G. "The Zoroastrian Priesthood After the Fall of the Sasanian Empire." In *Transition Periods in Iranian History*, 151–66. Louvain: Association pour l'avancement des Études Iraniennes, 1987.

Lapidus, Ira M. *Islamic Societies to the Nineteenth Century: A Global History*. Cambridge: Cambridge University Press, 2012.

Layish, Aharon. "Transformation of the *Sharīʿa* from Jurists' Law to Statutory Law in the Contemporary Muslim World." *Die Welt des Islams*, new series 44.1 (2004): 85–113.

Lee, A. D. "Close-Kin Marriage in Late Antique Mesopotamia." *Greek, Roman and Byzantine Studies* 29.4 (1988): 403–22.

El-Leithy, Tamer. "Coptic Culture and Conversion in Medieval Cairo, 1293–1524 A.D." PhD diss., Princeton University, 2005.

Lesses, Rebecca. "Exe(o)rcising Power: Women as Sorceresses, Exorcists, and Demonesses in Babylonian Jewish Society of Late Antiquity." *Journal of the American Academy of Religion* 69.2 (2001): 343–75.

Levene, Dan. "Incantation bowls, Babylonian." In *The Encyclopedia of Ancient History*, edited by Roger S. Bagnall et al., 3437–40. Chichester: Wiley-Blackwell, 2013.

Lévi-Strauss, Claude. *The Elementary Structures of Kinship*. Translated by James H. Bell, Rodney Needham, and John R. von Sturmer. Revised edition. Boston: Beacon Press, 1969.

Levy-Rubin, Milka. *Non-Muslims in the Early Islamic Empire: From Surrender to Coexistence*. New York: Cambridge University Press, 2011.

MacEvitt, Christopher. *The Crusades and the Christian World of the East: Rough Tolerance*. Philadelphia: University of Pennsylvania Press, 2007.

Macuch, Maria. "Incestuous Marriage in the Context of Sasanian Family Law." In *Ancient and Middle Iranian Studies*, edited by Macuch, Dieter Weber, and Desmond Durkin-Meisterernst, 133–48. Wiesbaden: Harrassowitz Verlag, 2010.

———. "Inheritance i. Sasanian Period." In Yarshater, *Encyclopædia Iranica* 13:129–34.

———. "Jewish Jurisdiction Within the Framework of the Sasanian Legal System." In *Encounters by the Rivers of Babylon: Conversations Between*

Jews, Christians and Babylonians in Antiquity, edited by Uri Gabbay and Shai Secunda, 147–60. Tübingen: Mohr Siebeck, 2014.

———. "Law in Pre-Modern Zoroastrianism." In Stausberg, Vevaina, and Tessmann, *Wiley Blackwell Companion to Zoroastrianism*, 289–98.

———. "Ein mittelpersischer *terminus techincus* im syrischen Rechtskodex des Īšōʿbōḫt und im sasanidischen Rechtsbuch." In *Studia Semitica necnon Iranica*, edited by Maria Macuch, Christa Müller-Kessler, and Bert G. Fragner, 149–60. Wiesbaden: Harrassowitz, 1989.

———. "Pahlavi Literature." In *The Literature of Pre-Islamic Iran*, edited by Ronald E. Emmerick and Maria Macuch, 116–96. New York: I. B. Tauris, 2009.

———. "The Pahlavi Model Marriage Contract in the Light of Sasanian Family Law." In *Iranian Languages and Texts from Iran and Turan: Ronald E. Emmerick Memorial Volume*, edited by Maria Macuch, Mauro Maggi, and Werner Sundermann, 183–204. Wiesbaden: Harrassowitz Verlag, 2007.

———. "The Use of Seals in Sasanian Jurisprudence." In *Sceaux d'Orient et leur emploi*, edited by Rika Gyselen, 79–87. Bures-sur-Yvette: Groupe pour l'étude de la civilisation du Moyen-Orient, 1997.

———. "Zoroastrian Principles and the Structure of Kinship in Sasanian Iran." In *Religious Themes and Texts of Pre-Islamic Iran*, edited by Carlo G. Cereti, Mauro Maggi, and Elio Provasi, 231–45. Wiesbaden: Dr. Ludwig Reichert Verlag, 2003.

Madey, John. "Chorepiscopi and Periodeutes in the Light of the Canonical Sources of the Syro-Antiochene Church." *Christian Orient* 5 (1984): 167–83.

Marinides, Nicholas. "Anastasius of Sinai and Chalcedonian Christian Lay Piety in the Early Islamic Near East." In *The Late Antique World of Early Islam: Muslims Among Christians and Jews in the East Mediterranean*, edited by Robert G. Hoyland, 293–311. Princeton, N.J.: Darwin Press, 2015.

Martin, John Levi. *Social Structures*. Princeton, N.J.: Princeton University Press, 2009.

Maynes, Mary Jo, and Ann Waltner. *The Family: A World History*. Oxford: Oxford University Press, 2012.

McDonough, Scott. "Bishops or Bureaucrats? Christian Clergy and the State in the Middle Sasanian Period." In *Current Research in Sasanian Archaeology, Art and History*, edited by Derek Kennet and Paul Luft, 87–92. Oxford: Archaeopress, 2008.

Menze, Volker L. *Justinian and the Making of the Syrian Orthodox Church*. Oxford: Oxford University Press, 2008.

Merryman, John Henry, and Rogelio Pérez-Perdomo. *The Civil Law Tradition.* 3rd edition. Stanford, Calif.: Stanford University Press, 2007.

Miller, Daniel Earl. "From Catalogue to Codes to Canon: The Rise of the Petition to ʿUmar Among Legal Traditions Governing Non-Muslims in Medieval Islamicate Societies." PhD diss., University of Missouri-Kansas City, 2000.

Minov, Sergey. "Marriage and Sexuality in the Book of Steps: From Encratism to Orthodoxy." In *Breaking the Mind: New Studies in the Syriac Book of Steps*, edited by Kristian S. Heal and Robert A. Kitchen, 221–61. Washington, D.C.: Catholic University of America Press, 2014.

Morony, Michael G. *Iraq After the Muslim Conquest.* Princeton, N.J.: Princeton University Press, 1984.

———. "Magic and Society in Late Sasanian Iraq." In *Prayer, Magic, and the Stars in the Ancient and Late Antique World*, edited by Scott Noegel, Joel Walker, and Brannon Wheeler, 83–107. University Park: Pennsylvania State University Press, 2003.

———. "Religion and the Aramaic Incantation Bowls." *Religion Compass* 1.4 (2007): 414–29.

———. "Religious Communities in Late Sasanian and Early Islamic Iraq." *Journal of the Economic and Social History of the Orient* 17.2 (1974): 113–35.

Muraviev, Alexei. "Les rites du mariage dans les églises de langue syriaque." In *Les liturgies syriaques*, edited by F. Cassingena-Trévedy and I. Jurasz, 173–82. Paris: Geuthner, 2006.

Murray, Michele. "Female Corporeality, Magic, and Gender in the Babylonian Talmud." *Religion and Theology* 15 (2008): 199–224.

Murray, Robert. *Symbols of Church and Kingdom.* Revised edition. Piscataway, N.J.: Gorgias Press, 2004.

Nagel, Tilman. *The History of Islamic Theology.* Princeton, N.J.: Markus Wiener, 2000.

Nallino, Carlo Alfonso. "Il diritto musulmano nel Nomocanone siriaco cristiano di Barhebreo." *Rivista degli studi orientali* 9 (1921–23): 512–80. Republished in *Raccolta di scritti editi e inediti*, edited by Maria Nallino, 4:214–300. Rome: Istituto per l'Oriente, 1939–48.

Nasrallah, Joseph. *Histoire du mouvement littéraire dans l'Eglise melchite du Ve au XXe siècle.* 4 vols. Louvain: Peeters, 1979–89.

Nemoy, Leon. *Karaite Anthology: Excerpts from the Early Literature.* New Haven, Conn.: Yale University Press, 1952.

———. "Two Controversial Points in the Karaite Law of Incest." *Hebrew Union College Annual* 49 (1978): 247–65.

Nirenberg, David. *Neighboring Faiths: Christianity, Islam, and Judaism in the Middle Ages and Today.* Chicago: University of Chicago Press, 2014.

Noegel, Scott, Joel Walker, and Brannon Wheeler. Introduction to *Prayer, Magic, and the Stars in the Ancient and Late Antique World*, edited by Noegel, Walker, and Wheeler, 1–17. University Park: Pennsylvania State University Press, 2003.

Ohme, Heinz. "Sources of the Greek Canon Law to the Quinisext Council (691/2): Councils and Church Fathers." In *The History of Byzantine and Eastern Canon Law to 1500*, edited by Wilfried Hartmann and Kenneth Pennington, 24–114. Washington, D.C.: Catholic University of America Press, 2012.

Olszowy-Schlanger, Judith. "Early Karaite Family Law." In *Karaite Judaism: A Guide to its History and Literary Sources*, edited by Meira Polliack, 275–90. Leiden: Brill, 2003.

———. "Karaite Legal Documents." In *Karaite Judaism: A Guide to its History and Literary Sources*, edited by Meira Polliack, 255–74. Leiden: Brill, 2003.

Omar, F. "The Islamization of the Gulf." In *The Islamic World from Classical to Modern Times: Essays in Honor of Bernard Lewis*, edited by C. E. Bosworth et al., 247–57. Princeton, N.J.: Darwin Press, 1989.

Papaconstantinou, Arietta. "Between *Umma* and *Dhimma*: The Christians of the Near East Under the Umayyads." *Annales islamologiques* 42 (2008): 127–56.

———. "Historiography, Hagiography, and the Making of the Coptic 'Church of the Martyrs' in Early Islamic Egypt." *Dumbarton Oaks Papers* 60 (2006): 65–86.

Partsch, Josef. "Neue Rechtsquellen der nestorianischen Kirche." *Zeitschrift der Savigny-Stiftung für Rechtsgeschichte*, Romanistische Abteilung 30 (1909): 355–98.

Payne, Richard E. "East Syrian Bishops, Elite Households, and Iranian Law After the Muslim Conquest." *Iranian Studies* 48.1 (2015): 5–32.

———. "Monks, Dinars and Date Palms: Hagiographical Production and the Expansion of Monastic Institutions in the Early Islamic Persian Gulf." *Arabian Archaeology and Epigraphy* 22 (2011): 97–111.

———. *A State of Mixture: Christians, Zoroastrians, and Iranian Political Culture in Late Antiquity.* Berkeley: University of California Press, 2015.

Penn, Michael Philip. "Athanasios II of Balad." In Brock et al., *Gorgias Encyclopedic Dictionary of the Syriac Heritage*, 46.

———. *Envisioning Islam: Syriac Christians and the Early Muslim World.* Philadelphia: University of Pennsylvania Press, 2015.

———. *When Christians First Met Muslims: A Sourcebook of the Earliest Syriac Writings on Islam*. Berkeley: University of California Press, 2015.

Pigulevskaja, Nina V. "Die Sammlung der syrischen Rechtsurkunden des Ischobocht und des Matikan." In *Akten des vierundzwanzigsten Internationalen Orientalisten-Kongresses*, edited by Herbert Franke, 219–21. Wiesbaden: Deutsche Morgenländische Gesellschaft, 1959.

———. *Les villes de l'État iranien aux époques parthe et sassanide: Contribution à l'histoire sociale de la Basse Antiquité*. Paris: Mouton, 1963.

Pitsakis, Constantin G. "Législation et stratégies matrimoniales: Parenté et empêchements de mariage dans le droit byzantine." *L'Homme* 154/55 (2000): 677–96.

Polliack, Meira. "Rethinking Karaism: Between Judaism and Islam." *Association for Jewish Studies Review* 30.1 (2006): 67–93.

Powers, David S. *Law, Society, and Culture in the Maghrib*, 1300–1500. Cambridge: Cambridge University Press, 2009.

———. *Studies in Qur'an and Ḥadīth: The Formation of the Islamic Law of Inheritance*. Berkeley: University of California Press, 1986.

Putman, Hans. *L'église et l'islam sous Timothée I (*780–823*)*. Beirut: Dar el-Machreq Éditeurs, 1975.

Al-Qāḍī, Wadād. "Non-Muslims in the Muslim Conquest Army in Early Islam." In *Christians and Others in the Umayyad State*, edited by Antoine Borrut and Fred M. Donner, 83–127. Chicago: Oriental Institute of the University of Chicago, 2016.

Al-Qattan, Najwa. "*Dhimmī*s in the Muslim Court: Legal Autonomy and Religious Discrimination." *International Journal of Middle East Studies* 31.3 (1999): 429–44.

Ramos, Gabriela, and Yanna Yannakakis, eds. *Indigenous Intellectuals: Knowledge, Power, and Colonial Culture in Mexico and the Andes*. Durham, N.C.: Duke University Press, 2014.

Rapoport, Yossef. *Marriage, Money and Divorce in Medieval Islamic Society*. Cambridge: Cambridge University Press, 2005.

———. "Matrimonial Gifts in Early Islamic Egypt." *Islamic Law and Society* 7.1 (2000): 1–36.

Rapp, Claudia. *Holy Bishops in Late Antiquity: The Nature of Christian Leadership in an Age of Transition*. Berkeley: University of California Press, 2005.

Rassi, Salam. "'What Does the Clapper Say?' An Interfaith Discourse on the Christian Call to Prayer by ʿAbdīshōʿ bar Brīkhā." In *Islam and Christianity in Medieval Anatolia*, edited by A. C. S. Peacock, Bruno De Nicola, and Sara Nur Yıldız, 263–84. Farnham, UK: Ashgate, 2015.

Richardson, Kristina. "Singing Slave Girls (*Qiyan*) of the ʿAbbasid Court in the Ninth and Tenth Centuries." In *Children in Slavery through the Ages*, edited by Gwyn Campbell, Suzanne Miers, and Joseph C. Miller, 105–18. Athens: Ohio University Press, 2009.

Richter, Sebastian. "Law of Coptic Legal Documents." In *Law and Legal Practice in Egypt from Alexander to the Arab Conquest*, edited by James G. Keenan, J. G. Manning, and Uri Yiftach-Firanko, 28–30. Cambridge: Cambridge University Press, 2014.

Ritter, Nils C. "On the Development of Sasanian Seals and Sealing Practice: A Mesopotamian Approach." In *Seals and Sealing Practices in the Near East: Developments in Administration and Magic from Prehistory to the Islamic Period*, edited by Ilona Regulski, Kim Duistermaat, and Peter Verkinderen, 99–114. Leuven: Peeters, 2012.

Ritzer, Korbinian. *Le mariage dans les Églises chrétiennes du Ier au XIe siècle*. Paris: Les Éditions du Cerf, 1970.

Robinson, Chase F. *ʿAbd al-Malik*. Oxford: Oneworld, 2005.

———. *Empire and Elites After the Muslim Conquest: The Transformation of Northern Mesopotamia*. Cambridge: Cambridge University Press, 2000.

Roggema, Barbara H. "ʿAbdishoʿ bar Bahrīz." In Brock et al., *Gorgias Encyclopedic Dictionary of the Syriac Heritage*, 3.

Rose, Richard B. "Islam and the Development of Personal Status Laws Among Christian Dhimmis: Motives, Sources, Consequences." *Muslim World* 72 (1982): 159–79.

Ross, Margaret Clunies. "Concubinage in Anglo-Saxon England." *Past & Present* 108 (1985): 3–34.

Rousseau, Philip. "Monasticism." In *The Cambridge Ancient History*. Vol. 14, *Late Antiquity: Empire and Successors A.D. 425–600*, edited by Averil Cameron and Bryan Ward-Perkins, 745–80. Cambridge: Cambridge University Press, 2001.

Rowlandson, Jane. *Women and Society in Greek and Roman Egypt*. Cambridge: Cambridge University Press, 1998.

Rowson, Everett K. "The Categorization of Gender and Sexual Irregularity in Medieval Arabic Vice Lists." In *Body Guards: The Cultural Politics of Gender Ambiguity*, edited by Julia Epstein and Kristina Straub, 50–79. New York: Routledge, 1991.

Rustow, Marina. *Heresy and the Politics of Community: The Jews of the Fatimid Caliphate*. Ithaca, N.Y.: Cornell University Press, 2008.

———. "Jews and the Islamic World: Transitions from Rabbinic to Medieval Contexts." In *The Bloomsbury Companion to Jewish Studies*, edited by Dean Phillip Bell, 90–120. London: Bloomsbury, 2015.

———. "Jews and Muslims in the Eastern Islamic World." In *A History of*

Jewish-Muslim Relations: From the Origins to the Present Day, edited by Abdelwahab Meddeb and Benjamin Stora, 75–98. Princeton, N.J.: Princeton University Press, 2013.

Safran, Janina M. *Defining Boundaries in al-Andalus: Muslims, Christians, and Jews in Islamic Iberia.* Ithaca, N.Y.: Cornell University Press, 2015.

Sahner, Christian C. "Christian Martyrs and the Making of an Islamic Society in the Post-Conquest Period." PhD diss., Princeton University, 2015.

———. "'The Monasticism of My Community Is Jihad': A Debate on Asceticism, Sex, and Warfare in Early Islam." *Arabica* 64 (2017): 149–83.

Salvesen, Alison. "Jacob of Edessa's Life and Work: A Biographical Sketch." In *Jacob of Edessa and the Syriac Culture of His Day*, edited by Bas ter Haar Romeny, 1–10. Leiden: Brill, 2008.

Satlow, Michael L. *Jewish Marriage in Antiquity.* Princeton, N.J.: Princeton University Press, 2001.

Schacht, Joseph. *An Introduction to Islamic Law.* Oxford: Clarendon Press, 1982.

———. *The Origins of Muhammadan Jurisprudence.* Oxford: Clarendon Press, 1950.

Scher, Addai. *Notice sur les manuscrits syriaques et arabes conservés à l'archevèché chaldéen de Diarbékir.* Paris: Imprimerie nationale, 1907.

Scott, W. Richard. *Institutions and Organizations: Ideas, Interests, and Identities.* 4th edition. Los Angeles: SAGE, 2014.

Selb, Walter. *Orientalisches Kirchenrecht.* Vol. 1, *Die Geschichte des Kirchenrechts der Nestorianer (von den Anfängen bis zur Mongolenzeit).* Vienna: Österreichische Akademie der Wissenschaften, 1981.

———. *Orientalisches Kirchenrecht.* Vol. 2, *Die Geschichte des Kirchenrechts der Westsyrer (von den Anfängen bis zur Mongolenzeit).* Vienna: Österreichische Akademie der Wissenschaften, 1989.

———. "Zur Christianisierung des Eherechts." In *Eherecht und Familiengut in Antike und Mittelalter*, edited by Dieter Simon, 1–14. Munich: R. Oldenbourg Verlag, 1992.

Shaked, Shaul. "Bagdāna, King of the Demons, and Other Iranian Terms in Babylonian Aramaic Magic." In *Papers in Honour of Professor Mary Boyce*, edited by H. W. Bailey et al., 2:511–25. Leiden: Brill, 1985.

———. "Islam." In Stausberg, Vevaina, and Tessmann, *Wiley Blackwell Companion to Zoroastrianism*, 491–98.

———. "Jesus in the Magic Bowls. Apropos Dan Levene's '. . . and by the name of Jesus . . .'" *Jewish Studies Quarterly* 6.4 (1999): 309–19.

———. "Jews, Christians and Pagans in the Aramaic Incantation Bowls of the Sasanian Period." In *Religions and Cultures: First International Con-*

ference of "Mediterraneum," edited by Adriana Destro and Mauro Pesce, 61–89. Binghamton: SUNY Binghamton, 2001.

———. "Manichaean Incantation Bowls in Syriac." *Jerusalem Studies in Arabic and Islam* 24 (2000): 58–92.

———. "Popular Religion in Sasanian Babylonia." *Jerusalem Studies in Arabic and Islam* 21 (1997): 103–17.

Shaki, Mansour. "Divorce ii. In the Parthian and Sasanian Periods." In Yarshater, *Encyclopædia Iranica* 7:444–45.

———. "Family Law i. In Zoroastrianism." In Yarshater, *Encyclopædia Iranica* 9:184–89.

El Shamsy, Ahmed. *The Canonization of Islamic Law.* New York: Cambridge University Press, 2013.

Shatzmiller, Maya. "Marriage, Family, and the Faith: Women's Conversion to Islam." *Journal of Family History* 21 (1996): 235–66.

Shaw, Brent D., and Richard P. Saller. "Close-Kin Marriage in Roman Society?" *Man*, new series 19.3 (1984): 432–44.

Shilo, Shmuel. "Succession." In *The Principles of Jewish Law*, edited by Menachem Elon, 445–53. Jerusalem: Keter, 1975.

Sijpesteijn, Petra M. *Shaping a Muslim State: The World of a Mid-Eighth-Century Egyptian Official.* Oxford: Oxford University Press, 2013.

Simonsohn, Uriel I. *A Common Justice: The Legal Allegiances of Christians and Jews Under Early Islam.* Philadelphia: University of Pennsylvania Press, 2011.

Sivan, Hagith S. "Why Not Marry a Jew? Jewish—Christian Marital Frontiers in Late Antiquity." In *Law, Society, and Authority in Late Antiquity*, edited by Ralph W. Mathisen, 208–19. Oxford: Oxford University Press, 2001.

Sizgorich, Thomas. *Violence and Belief in Late Antiquity: Militant Devotion in Christianity and Islam.* Philadelphia: University of Pennsylvania Press, 2008.

Skjærvø, Prods Oktor. *The Spirit of Zoroastrianism.* New Haven, Conn.: Yale University Press, 2012.

Smith, Jonathan Z. "Here, There, and Anywhere." In *Prayer, Magic, and the Stars in the Ancient and Late Antique World*, edited by Scott Noegel, Joel Walker, and Brannon Wheeler, 21–36. University Park: Pennsylvania State University Press, 2003.

Spectorsky, Susan A. *Women in Classical Islamic Law: A Survey of the Sources.* Leiden: Brill, 2010.

Stausberg, Michael. "The Invention of a Canon: The Case of Zoroastrianism." In *Canonization and Decanonization*, edited by Arie van der Kooij and Karel van der Toorn, 257–77. Leiden: Brill, 1998.

Stausberg, Michael, Yuhan Sohrab-Dinshaw Vevaina, and Anna Tessmann, eds. *The Wiley Blackwell Companion to Zoroastrianism*. Chichester: Wiley-Blackwell, 2015.

Stone, Linda. *Kinship and Gender: An Introduction*. 5th edition. Boulder, Colo.: Westview Press, 2014.

Stratton, Kimberly B. "Interrogating the Magic-Gender Connection." In *Daughters of Hecate: Women and Magic in the Ancient World*, edited by Stratton and Dayna S. Kalleres, 1–37. Oxford: Oxford University Press, 2014.

Stratton, Kimberly B., and Dayna S. Kalleres, eds. *Daughters of Hecate: Women and Magic in the Ancient World*. Oxford: Oxford University Press, 2014.

Stroumsa, Rachel. "People and Identities in Nessana." PhD diss., Duke University, 2008.

Swanson, Mark N. "*Al-Jāmiʿ wujūh al-īmān*." In *Christian-Muslim Relations: A Bibliographical History*. Vol. 1, *(600–900)*, edited by David Thomas and Barbara Roggema, 791–98. Leiden: Brill, 2009.

———. *The Coptic Papacy in Islamic Egypt (641–1517)*. Cairo: American University in Cairo Press, 2010.

Takahashi, Hidemi. *Barhebraeus: A Bio-Bibliography*. Piscataway, N.J.: Gorgias Press, 2005.

Tannous, Jack. "Syria Between Byzantium and Islam: Making Incommensurables Speak." PhD diss., Princeton University, 2010.

———. "You Are What You Read: Qenneshre and the Miaphysite Church in the Seventh Century." In *History and Identity in the Late Antique Near East*, edited by Philip Wood, 83–102. Oxford: Oxford University Press, 2013.

Teule, Herman G. B. "Jacob of Edessa and Canon Law." In *Jacob of Edessa and the Syriac Culture of His Day*, edited by Bas ter Haar Romeny, 83–100. Leiden: Brill, 2008.

———. "The Syriac Renaissance." In *The Syriac Renaissance*, edited by Herman G. B. Teule et al., 1–30. Leuven: Peeters, 2010.

———. "The Transmission of Islamic Culture to the World of Syriac Christianity: Barhebraeus' Translation of Avicenna's *Kitāb al-Išārāt wa-l-tanbīhāt*. First Soundings." In *Redefining Christian Identity: Cultural Interaction in the Middle East since the Rise of Islam*, edited by J. J. van Ginkel, H. L. Murre-van den Berg, and T. M. van Lint, 167–84. Louvain: Peeters, 2005.

Thazhath, Andrews. *The Juridical Sources of the Syro-Malabar Church*. Kottayam, India: Pontifical Oriental Institute of Religious Studies, 1987.

Tillier, Mathieu. *Les cadis d'Iraq et l'état Abbasside (132/750–334/945)*. Damascus: IFPO, 2009.

———. "Judicial Authority and *Qāḍīs*' Autonomy Under the ʿAbbāsids." *Al-Masāq* 26.2 (2014): 119–31.

Toral-Niehoff, Isabel. "The ʿIbād of al-Ḥīra: An Arab Christian Community in Late Antique Iraq." In *The Qur'ān in Context: Historical and Literary Investigations into the Qur'ānic Milieu*, edited by Angelika Neuwirth, Nicolai Sinai, and Michael Marx, 323–47. Leiden: Brill, 2010.

Treggiari, Susan. *Roman Marriage: Iusti Coniuges from the Time of Cicero to the Time of Ulpian*. Oxford: Clarendon Press, 1991.

Troianos, Spyros. "Byzantine Canon Law to 1100." In *The History of Byzantine and Eastern Canon Law to 1500*, edited by Wilfried Hartmann and Kenneth Pennington, 115–69. Washington, D.C.: Catholic University of America Press, 2012.

Tsafrir, Nurit. *The History of an Islamic School of Law: The Early Spread of Hanafism*. Cambridge, Mass.: Islamic Legal Studies Program, Harvard Law School, 2004.

Tucker, Judith E. *In the House of the Law: Gender and Islamic Law in Ottoman Syria and Palestine*. Berkeley: University of California Press, 1998.

———. *Women, Family, and Gender in Islamic Law*. New York: Cambridge University Press, 2008.

Ullmann, Manfred. *Die Medizin im Islam*. Leiden: Brill, 1970.

Urbanik, Jakub. "A Priestly Divorce in the Seventh Century Palestine: Various Legal Orders at Work (The Case of *P. Ness*. III 57, A. 689)." In *Marriage: Ideal—Law—Practice*, edited by Zuzanna Służewska and Urbanik, 199–218. Warsaw: Warsaw University, 2005.

Vaissière, Étienne, de la. *Samarcande et Samarra: Élites d'Asie centrale dans l'empire abbaside*. Paris: Association pour l'avancement des études iraniennes, 2007.

Van Bladel, Kevin. "The Bactrian Background of the Barmakids." In *Islam and Tibet—Interactions Along the Musk Routes*, edited by Anna Akasoy, Charles Burnett, and Ronit Yoeli-Tlalim, 43–88. Farnham, UK: Ashgate, 2011.

Van Gelder, G. J. H. *Close Relationships: Incest and Inbreeding in Classical Arabic Literature*. London: I. B. Tauris, 2005.

Van Overstraeten, Jeanne-Ghislaine. "Les liturgies nuptiales des églises de langue syriaque et le mystère de l'église-épouse." *Parole de l'Orient* 8 (1977–78): 235–310.

Van Rompay, Lucas. "Bar ʿEdta, Rabban." In Brock et al., *Gorgias Encyclopedic Dictionary of the Syriac Heritage*, 56.

———. "Ḥenanishoʿ I." In Brock et al., *Gorgias Encyclopedic Dictionary of the Syriac Heritage*, 194–95.

———. "Ishoʿ bar Nun." In Brock et al., *Gorgias Encyclopedic Dictionary of the Syriac Heritage*, 215.

———. "Ishoʿbokht of Rev Ardashir." In Brock et al., *Gorgias Encyclopedic Dictionary of the Syriac Heritage*, 216.

———. "Shemʿon of Rev Ardashir." In Brock et al., *Gorgias Encyclopedic Dictionary of the Syriac Heritage*, 374.

Villella, Peter B. *Indigenous Elites and Creole Identity in Colonial Mexico, 1500–1800*. New York: Cambridge University Press, 2016.

Vodola, Elisabeth. *Excommunication in the Middle Ages*. Berkeley: University of California Press, 1986.

Vööbus, Arthur. *Syrische Kanonessammlungen: Ein Beitrag zur Quellenkunde*. 2 vols. Louvain: Secrétariat du CorpusSCO, 1970.

Wagschal, David. *Law and Legality in the Greek East: The Byzantine Canonical Tradition, 381–883*. Oxford: Oxford University Press, 2015.

Webber, Sabra J. "Middle East Studies and Subaltern Studies." *Middle East Studies Association Bulletin* 31.1 (1997): 11–16.

Wegner, Judith Romney. "Islamic and Talmudic Jurisprudence: The Four Roots of Islamic Law and Their Talmudic Counterparts." *American Journal of Legal History* 26.1 (1992): 25–71.

Weitz, Lev. "Al-Ghazālī, Bar Hebraeus, and the 'Good Wife.'" *Journal of the American Oriental Society* 134.2 (2014): 203–23.

———. "Polygyny and East Syrian Law: Local Practices and Ecclesiastical Tradition." In *The Late Antique World of Early Islam: Muslims Among Christians and Jews in the East Mediterranean*, edited by Robert Hoyland, 157–91. Princeton, N.J.: Darwin Press, 2015.

———. "Shaping East Syrian Law in ʿAbbāsid Iraq: The Law Books of Patriarchs Timothy I and Išōʿ Bar Nūn." *Le Muséon* 129 (2016): 71–116.

Wertheimer, Laura. "Children of Disorder: Clerical Parentage, Illegitimacy, and Reform in the Middle Ages." *Journal of the History of Sexuality* 15.3 (2006): 382–407.

Wessel, Susan. "The Formation of Ecclesiastical Law in the Early Church." In *The History of Byzantine and Eastern Canon Law to 1500*, edited by Wilfried Hartmann and Kenneth Pennington, 1–23. Washington, D.C.: Catholic University of America Press, 2012.

Wickham, Chris. *The Inheritance of Rome: Illuminating the Dark Ages 400–1000*. New York: Viking Penguin, 2009.

Wilmshurst, David. *The Ecclesiastical Organisation of the Church of the East, 1318–1923*. Louvain: Peeters, 2000.

———. *The Martyred Church: A History of the Church of the East.* Bishop's Stortford, UK: East & West Publishing, 2011.

Wing, Patrick. *The Jalayirids: Dynastic State Formation in the Mongol Middle East.* Edinburgh: Edinburgh University Press, 2016.

Witakowski, Witold. "Dionysios of Tel Maḥre." In Brock et al., *Gorgias Encyclopedic Dictionary of the Syriac Heritage,* 127–28.

———. "Giwargis of Bʿeltan." In Brock et al., *Gorgias Encyclopedic Dictionary of the Syriac Heritage,* 178.

———. "Quryaqos." In Brock et al., *Gorgias Encyclopedic Dictionary of the Syriac Heritage,* 347–48.

Wood, Philip. "Christian Authority Under the Early Abbasids: The *Life of Timothy of Kakushta.*" *Proche-Orient chrétien* 61 (2011): 258–74.

Wright, William. *A Short History of Syriac Literature.* London: Adam and Charles Black, 1894.

Yannakakis, Yanna. *The Art of Being In-Between: Native Intermediaries, Indian Identity, and Local Rule in Colonial Oaxaca.* Durham, N.C.: Duke University Press, 2008.

Yarbrough, Luke. "Did ʿUmar b. ʿAbd al-ʿAzīz Issue an Edict Concerning Non-Muslim Officials?" In *Christians and Others in the Umayyad State,* edited by Anoine Borrut and Fred M. Donner, 173–206. Chicago: Oriental Institute of the University of Chicago, 2016.

Yaron, Reuven. "A New Nestorian Source." *Tijdschrift voor Rechtsgeschiedenis* 40 (1972): 263–76.

Yarshater, Ehsan, ed. *Encyclopædia Iranica.* London: Routledge and Kegan Paul, 1985–present.

Young, Frances M. *Biblical Exegesis and the Formation of Christian Culture.* Cambridge: Cambridge University Press, 1997.

Young, William G. *Patriarch, Shah and Caliph.* Rawalpindi, Pakistan: Christian Study Centre, 1974.

Zaman, Muhammad Qasim. *Religion and Politics Under the Early ʿAbbāsids: The Emergence of the Proto-Sunnī Elite.* Leiden: Brill, 1997.

Zinger, Oded. "Women, Gender and Law: Marital Disputes According to Documents from the Cairo Geniza." PhD diss., Princeton University, 2014.

INDEX

Italic page numbers indicate illustrations.

Abbasid Caliphate, 6, 63–105; analogical reasoning and law in intellectual culture of, 67, 160–65, 251; civil war (809–13), 225; coming to power, 64–66; conflict with provincial Muslim elites in, 6; development of key institutions of governance and society, 64–65, 67–69, 225; distorted historiography of, 3–5, 217–18, 247; interreligious marriage between Christians and Muslims in, 210–12; Iranian Muslims in administrative posts of, 66–67; Islamic identity in, 69; Islamic jurisprudence's formation during, 67–68, 71, 211; Jews in early Abbasid Caliphate, 92–94; long-standing cultural effect of, 3–4; move of imperial city to Iraq, 65; as multireligious, multiethnic empire, 1–3, 63–64, 67, 70, 82, 88–98, 101, 103, 122, 224; non-Muslims' effect on social order of, 67, 99; non-Muslims' religiosity, regulation of, 87; polygamy in upper echelons of caliphal society, 173; slaves and concubinage in, 184–88, 288n46; social order of early Abbasid period, 82, 87, 99, 102; Zoroastrians in early Abbasid Caliphate, 94–95. *See also* family life of Christians in early Abbasid Caliphate; marriage

ʿAbdishoʿ bar Bahriz, 111, 157, 162, 184, 268n43, 271n75, 276n39; *Order of Marriage and Inheritance,* 76, 162, 230, 268n45

ʿAbdishoʿ bar Brika, 224, 235, 241–43, 295n55; *Collection of Synodal Canons,* 235, 242–43; compared to Bar ʿEbroyo's *Nomocanon,* 242–45; *Order of Ecclesiastical Decisions,* 235, 242–43

ʿAbd al-Malik (caliph), 43

Abraham and Sarah, as cousin marriage, 165–66, 284n56

Abu Hanifa, 68, 69, 164

Abu Nasr Yahya ibn Jarir: *Kitab al-Murshid,* 232

Abu Yusuf, 68; *Kitab al-Kharaj,* 70

adultery. *See* extramarital sex; polygamy

affine marriages, 150–51, 162

ʿAnan ben David, 163, 168

Anastasios of Sinai, 52–53, 208–9

anathema (excommunication from receiving Eucharist), 133, 198, 277n5, 277n9; used to prohibit interreligious marriage, 212; used to prohibit litigation in Muslim courts, 126–29; used to prohibit polygamy, 173, 177–78, 186, 190, 198

anthropological definition of marriage, 255n5; close-kin marriage and, 147–48, 283n32

apostasy, 11, 56, 57, 59, 113, 133, 136–37, 205, 214, 249

Arabicization, 219, 224, 231–34

Arabic language: Melkites' use of, 10, 96–97; Qaraites' use of, 168; translating ancient scientific and philosophical texts into, 163; translating Christian literature into, 7–8, 231–34, 244

Arabo-Islamic intellectual culture: Abbasid Caliphate's analogical reasoning and law, 160–65, 171, 251; broad effect across all caliphate's subjects, 224–25; in Christian writings, 8, 83; in Coptic thought, 97; in intellectual transformation of Middle East in

Shiites, 168, 234
slaves: *bayta* including, 81; polygamy and, 193–95; in premodern households, 255n4; sexual exploitation of, 23, 35, 52, 176, 184–86; spiritual status of Christian concubines of Muslim masters, 52. *See also* concubinage
sorcery. *See* magical practices
Stoic philosophy, 22, 23
Synodicon (Church of the East), 75
Syria: as center of Umayyad Caliphate, 65; importance in later medieval period, 226; Melkites in, 10, 95–97. *See also* East Syrian Christians; West Syrian Christians
Syriac writings: Christian literature in, 7–8, 17; East Syrian ecclesiastical identity tied to, 10, 30; on incantation bowls, 37–39; Isho'bokt's *Corpus* translated from Middle Persian into, 75; Islamic law of inheritance (dated 1204) illustrative of West Syrian tradition, 228–29; post-Abbasid fragmentation and, 226; Syriac Renaissance, designation of twelfth and thirteenth centuries as, 226
Syro-Roman Law Book, 75, 90, 120–21, 231, 238, 241, 268n43

Talaq, 132–33, 135, 137. *See also* divorce: Islamic law's doctrine of
Talmud, 31, 60, 92, 94, 118, 168. *See also* Babylonian Talmud
Theodore of Mopsuestia, 10, 52, 89, 165–66, 169, 284n56
Theodoret of Cyrrhus, 150
Theodosios (patriarch), 186, 190, 204
Timothy I (patriarch), 268n45, 270n68; on children born in slave-master relationship, 191–92; on Christians in world to come, 102; on close-kin marriage, 145–48, 155–58, 160–61, 165, 170, 283n40, 284n56; compared to George I, 63; compared to Ibn al-Tayyib, 233; compared to Isho'barnun, 285n57; on diversity among humans, 63, 100, 101; on divorce, grounds for, 114, 119, 134, 136, 140–43, 274–75n19; on dowry, 118–19; East Syrian law building upon, 230; on family law and marriage, 79, 109, 111, 234; on inheritance rights, 115, 196, 269n58; on interreligious marriage, 211; Isho'bokt's work and, 74–75; legal analogy, use of, 164–65, 168; life and times of, 74, 88, 164, 219, 225, 271n75; Middle Persian jurisprudence's influence on, 90, 164–65; on Muslim courts, Christians taking legal matters to, 72, 85, 86, 120, 128; on patriarchal social order, 81; on slave concubines, 186, 189; writing and compiling legal canon, 75–76, 78
traveling priests, 260n69

'Ubaydallah ibn Sulayman ibn Wahb, 215
Umayyad Caliphate: conflict with provincial Muslim elites in, 6; diversity of peoples in, 4, 43–47, 50; Greek divorce documents from Nessana and, 29; interreligious marriage with conquerors in, 201–2, 208–9; Jacob of Edessa's ecclesiastical legal canon under, 48–49; judicial institutions under, 64, 68, 72; map of medieval Islamic caliphate, 45; overthrown by Abbasids, 64–66. *See also* marriage under Umayyad Caliphate

virginity, 9, 21–22, 23–24, 39, 240

West Syrian Christians (Syriac Orthodox): in Abbasid Caliphate, 69, 73, 84; anathema, use of, 126–27; civil law in early Abbasid Caliphate, 89, 91, 121, 236; close-kin marriage and, 155, 229; compared to Copts, 98; compared to East Syrians, 10, 48–49, 89–92, 103, 121, 155–56, 227–28, 231; creation of ecclesiastical legal canon for, 48–49, 52–53; distance from Iraqi centers of legal study, effect of, 90–91, 245; financial obligations of marriage, 114; inheritance practices of, 89, 116, 224, 227–31; interreligious marriage and, 209–12, 213; Islamic law's influence on, 91, 117, 120–22, 227–30, 248; marriage and betrothal ritual of, 89, 111, 121, 223; monasteries of, 91; slaves and concubinage, 184; synods, 89, 127, 151, 211, 271n78; *Syro-Roman Law Book* and, 90. *See also* Bar 'Ebroyo, Gregorios
women: divorcing men, 113, 135–38, 279n30, 279n33; feminine gendering of incantations, 37–38,

ACKNOWLEDGMENTS

I have been fortunate to receive during the research, writing, and production of this book support from Princeton University, the Mellon Foundation and the American Council of Learned Societies, and the Catholic University of America. Many thanks are due to the staff of the British Library, Cambridge University Library, Princeton's Firestone Library, the Library of Congress, CUA's Mullen and ICOR Libraries, and the Vatican Library for providing access to manuscripts and welcoming places to work. The Hill Museum and Manuscript Library deserves special thanks for providing access to reproductions of two important manuscripts and for its ongoing work of preserving the material heritage of the Middle East's Christian communities.

Parts of Chapter 4 were published previously in different form in "Shaping East Syrian Law in ʿAbbāsid Iraq: The Law Books of Patriarchs Timothy I and Išōʿ Bar Nūn," *Le Muséon* 129 (2016): 71–116, as was a different version of Chapter 7 in "Polygyny and East Syrian Law: Local Practices and Ecclesiastical Tradition," in Robert Hoyland, ed., *The Late Antique World of Early Islam: Muslims Among Christians and Jews in the East Mediterranean* (Princeton, N.J.: Darwin Press, 2015), 157–91. I thank Peeters and Darwin Press for accommodating the publication of those materials in the present book.

The individual debts I have incurred researching and writing this book are many. Adam Becker, Mark R. Cohen, Michael Cook, and Marina Rustow were exemplary mentors throughout the process in their standards for scholarship, the acuity of their criticisms, and the many offhand comments that shaped the direction of the project in ways they may not even realize. Derek Krueger and two anonymous reviewers read the entire manuscript; their invaluable feedback went a long way toward turning a draft into a book, as did the thoughtful comments of Cam Grey, Christian Sahner, Eric Weitz, and Luke Yarbrough on several individual chapters. I am grateful to the editors and staff at the University of Pennsylvania Press for shepherding the book from proposal to publication. Amal Marogy, Michael Reynolds, Christian Sahner, and Jack Tannous gave me the opportunity to present pieces of this book at a stimulating 2016 workshop where much of its framing (finally) fell into place. Kutlu Akalın, Ayhan Aktar, Reyhan Aktar, and Hanna Kerkinni very kindly helped me and hosted me on a trip to Diyarbakır and the Tur ʿAbdin in 2013 that laid important seeds for the book's development. Manu Radhakrishnan was a welcome traveling partner. Conversations over the years with Joel Blecher (who brainstormed the title, among other contributions), Aaron Butts, Thomas Carlson, Florian Jäckel, Eve Krakowski, Nick Marinides, Brigitta van Rheinberg, Jack Tannous, Oded Zinger, and assuredly others whom I've neglected to mention shaped the book further. Carol Hunt Weitz used her considerable digital photography skills to render and refine my unprofessional photographs. Monica Blanchard and Fr. Columba Stewart helped secure images and rights. William L. Nelson created the maps. Whatever appreciation I have for Arabic and Syriac literature would not be half of what it is without Abdallah Siraj and Manolis Papoutsakis. Benjamin Weitz is a constant source of inspiration even when he doesn't have much sense of what I may be working on. I am grateful for both the welcoming collegiality and the dedication to scholarship of my colleagues at CUA's Department of History.

I owe a special debt to teachers and friends in Egypt and Syria. My time in the region whose history I study fell amid American occupation and grassroots demands for justice and change, and at the end of the day I was only a visitor who would live with the muted implications of those events on the other side of the Atlantic, not their immediate, palpable consequences. I never felt anything less than privileged to be there while I was. Whether or not those teachers and friends see themselves as heirs to the traditions, Muslim and Christian, studied in this book, I hope they would feel that it does the history it recounts justice.

I dedicate this book to my parents, Carol Hunt Weitz and Eric Weitz. Without their love, support, and guidance, I would not be who I am or where I am today.